Preserving

Preserving

The Canning and Freezing
Guide for All Seasons

PAT CROCKER

HarperCollins*Publishers*Ltd

Published by HarperCollins Publishers Ltd

First Edition

Photo on page 13 courtesy of Lee Valley Tools Ltd.

Photo on page 137 courtesy of Dave Schaeffer.

Photo on page 497 courtesy of L. Dearie-Bruce.

HarperCollins books may be purchased for educational, business, or sales promotional use through our Special Markets Department.

HarperCollins Publishers Ltd

2 Bloor Street East, 20th Floor

Toronto, Ontario, Canada

M4W 1A8

www.harpercollins.ca

Library and Archives Canada Cataloguing in Publication

Crocker, Pat

Preserving : The Canning and Freezing Guide for All Seasons / Pat Crocker.

ISBN 978-1-55468-610-0

1. Canning and preserving. 2. Frozen foods. I. Title.

TX603.C76 2011   641.4'2   C2010-907007-0

Printed and bound in China

9 8 7 6 5 4 3 2 1

www.foodwedsherbs.blogspot.com

www.riversongherbals.com

"Winter is an etching, spring a watercolor,
summer an oil painting and autumn
a mosaic of them all."

STANLEY HOROWITZ

To the true heroes of the food system, the people who grow the produce, nurture the livestock, feed and milk the goats, and make the cheese—the people who carry around the very earth at the tips of their fingers.

IN MEMORY OF DARLA MARIE GRAHAM (DUNN)

1953-2010

Contents

Introduction

THE "EAT LOCAL, BUY SEASONAL" food movement is changing the way we think and act—taking us right back to how our forebears thought and acted. If locally raised and produced food is the "new organic," then preserving the harvest is the "new food technique."

But while we may be returning to some of the old ways, there are a few significant differences between our great-grandparents' need to survive and our desire to eat well and be part of a slow food revolution. First, our ancestors in this harsh land tilled the soil themselves, whereas we have access to local produce from a wide array of venues, including community gardens, CSA co-operatives, farmer's markets, greengrocers and supermarkets.

Secondly, the preserving pioneers were content to put plain beans on the table in January. For us, perhaps that jar of organic green and wax beans we pickled will be the star of a winter Niçoise Salad (page 201) with grilled whitefish or perch. Preserving has moved beyond survival. Our jars of brilliant Pomegranate Pepper Jelly (page 488) and Peaches and Cream Relish (page 381) are reminders that we can take back an important part of the food chain and dine as though we were at a fine restaurant.

Why another book on preserving?

Because along with the why and the how to make the most of local bounty, today's young homemakers, parents, working mothers, singles or first-time cooks want to be creative when using those precious jewels that shimmer so brightly on pantry shelves. They want to eat well every day, and they want to use their own preserves rather than contribute to the food factory conglomerates. *Preserving* is different from almost all other books on the subject because it offers stunningly easy recipes using the exceptional preserves found in these pages.

It is comforting to know that a pantry full of flavourful food sits ready to be used. With the twist of a lid and the recipes in this book, you can serve restaurant-style dishes with home-style quality and economy.

Preserving is a practical book with simple concepts. It follows the seasons and the diverse foods they bring to our market basket and kitchen pantry. And it offers great ideas for what to do with the homemade sauces, chutneys, pickles, jams and jellies. This book is the key to the modern-day preserving puzzle. Our time spent preserving is an enjoyable part of our busy life—a relaxing end in and of itself—but *Preserving* also saves us time by providing quick, homemade everyday recipes for using up our homemade bounty.

Why bother with seasonal foods?

Eating seasonally—that is, buying and cooking food at the peak of ripeness grown close to where we live—ensures that we pay attention to the natural rhythms of the earth. It forces us out into the countryside or the garden or the weekly market to see, literally, "what's up"— which plant has poked a pale green blade of life through the soil toward our grateful plate.

Local, seasonal foods tend to be more economical because there is a glut of the same plant at the same time. They taste better, store longer and may even be healthier because they have not travelled an average of 2,400 kilometres to get to your kitchen. Besides being eco-nomical, developing local and seasonal food habits is healthy for individuals, communities and the global environment.

Why all the fuss about local food?

Good farmers know their business. They grow varieties of fruits and vegetables for the right reasons—nutrition, taste and cooking properties—not because they fit a mechanical picker or transport well. Their varieties are naturally suited to the soil and weather conditions of their area. These farmers might be preserving heritage varieties; they might even be follow-ing organic principles; and they know the food they produce, from seed to table. Moreover, they are certainly in touch with their customers and listen to their concerns. We all benefit when good farmers can stay in business.

Of course, there are other, measurable reasons for buying locally produced food. Docu-mented facts about the number of kilometres produce travels, its ripeness at time of har-vesting, the methods employed to keep it "edible," the barrels of fossil fuels used and the wasteful packaging involved are all cause for concern. The conventional food system's reli-ance on factory farming, irradiation, genetic engineering and pesticides—and their lacklus-tre record vis-à-vis food safety and animal welfare—is less than desirable, not to mention the accumulated effects these factors are having on the health of both the environment and the individuals consuming factory food.

But for me, it is simple: get to know the guy who raises the turnips and you will eat better and probably be healthier.

An apple is an apple, right?

In a word: no. You don't have to know the genealogy of plants to eat well, but you do need to know that every fruit and every vegetable you eat is one of perhaps dozens, hundreds or even thousands of varieties that we have to choose from. For example, some estimates put the number of apple varieties worldwide at a whopping 7,500; there is a unique variety of Greek fava bean that clings to life nowhere else in the world but on the island of Santorini; and Prince Louis Albert de Broglie grows more than 600 kinds of heritage tomatoes at his château in the Loire Valley. We definitely need to know that there is more out there than Granny Smith and Delicious.

So why is our choice in apples limited to four or five varieties? Factory farms, distributors and large chain supermarkets are interested only in narrowing the choice to what is easy: easy to grow, harvest, transport, purchase, display and sell. Their concerns run counter to our concerns. By becoming more aware of the plants we might enjoy, we can start asking for a wider variety of plant food and, perhaps more importantly, we will become engaged in the issues surrounding the preservation of diversity and with heritage varieties.

In my view, genetically altered or copyrighted seeds or plants bred to produce sterile seeds are not in our best interest—in fact, they reward only the chemical companies that invent them.

There is one more reason to search out local, seasonal varieties: it forces us to experiment with plants and varieties we may not have tasted. The first time I bit into a wedge of Green Zebra tomato, I was instantly transported back 40 years to the front porch of my parents' home on a sweltering late-September evening. The true tomato essence of that one bite communicated the smell of slightly burnt toast spread with old nippy cheddar cheese (from a foil-lined wooden box, not a plastic tub), the sound of a World Series game on the radio and the aromatic flavour of my father's purple-red beefsteak, carved into thick slabs and sprinkled with salt and pepper. Up until that moment, I had forgotten the fragrance and taste of real tomatoes and the sound of baseball on a transistor radio.

—Pat Crocker

Conserve

6 cups (1 L)

lated suga

nly s   ded
ns, co   opped   *golden seedle*
eber
co   arsely chopped

mL) jars in boiling water (see page xx) and
(see page xx).

kettle, combine the sugar and water. Bring
Add orange slices and raisins. Reduc
increase heat to high and re
xture thickens. Remove

About the Photographs

Like the recipes in this book, all of the food photographs are of real food in real recipes. They were shot in my kitchen either prior to, during or just after a recipe was tested. If a spoon is askew, it is because I dropped it to grab the camera. If the raspberry curd in the tiramisù is starting to ooze out of the layers, it is because I didn't thicken it and pipe it into the layers using a pastry bag in order to get a perfectly straight line. You wouldn't resort to the things that food stylists do in order to capture the one perfect slice, scoop or slab, so I have not employed artificial styling techniques in the photographs on these pages. Instead, what I hope has been transferred through both the recipes and their photographs is a love for the integrity of the food and a desire to preserve its essence.

Preserving Basics

FOOD SPOILS BECAUSE OF BACTERIA, yeasts or moulds in the soil, in the food, in the air or on kitchen tools and equipment surfaces. This is a natural process that happens even if fresh fruit and vegetables are stored in the refrigerator. The goal of preserving is to control moisture, acid, nutrients and warm temperatures so that deteriorating agents are deprived of what they need to work their destruction.

Preserving methods such as salting or immersing in vinegar or heavy sugar syrups have been used for centuries, but the canning process was discovered as a result of the Napoleonic Wars in the early 19th century. Canning does two things: it sterilizes both the container and the food by using heat, and it hermetically seals the container so that micro-organisms do not contaminate the food after it has been sterilized.

Essential: It is important to wash produce (even organic produce) because that is the first step in reducing bacteria, yeasts and moulds, as well as in keeping food fresh. Washing removes contaminants, including dust, soil, large numbers of micro-organisms and organic matter, and it is a critical first step in the sterilization process.

Preserving the Harvest

Produce does not improve with preserving, so use only fresh, just-ripe, blemish-free fruit and vegetables. I try to clear my kitchen and my work schedule before going to market so that I have the rest of the day (perhaps even the next day as well) to enjoy the preserving ritual that comes with seasonal produce.

Essential: Harvest or purchase fruit and vegetables at the peak of ripeness, and eat or preserve immediately or, at the most, within one or two days.

If you can't preserve immediately, chill produce right away and keep it in the refrigerator at 32°F (0°C). Bring a cooler or insulated bags and a block of ice for transporting ingredients home from the market or pick-your-own farm. All produce is heat sensitive, but berries, asparagus, greens and other tender fruit and vegetables are particularly vulnerable.

Fruit and vegetables (zucchini in particular) all produce a glut—they ripen all at once—and flood the garden and markets, begging to be dealt with immediately. Knowing what is "in season" each month is the key to being able to drop everything in order to preserve at the peak of harvest.

Acidity of Foods

Fruit and vegetables are considered to be either high or low in acid, and it is the acid content that determines the method used to process them for long-term storage.

High-acid foods can be safely heat processed in boiling water. High-acid foods are foods with a pH of 4.6 or lower. Most fruits, jams, jellies and fruit spreads are high-acid. Some fruits, such as figs, and some vegetables, notably tomatoes, are not quite acid, but when vinegar or lemon juice is added, they may be safely processed in a boiling water canner for a specified length of time.

Low-acid foods must be heat processed in a pressure canner because the bacteria that thrive on them are resistant to the temperature of boiling water processing (212°F/100°C). Vegetables, meats, poultry and seafood soups, stews, sauces, dips and vegetable spreads, or any foods with a pH higher than 4.6 are low-acid foods.

Pectin

All land plants contain pectin in their cell walls. Pectin is made up of a complex set of polysaccharides (carbohydrate) essential to binding cells together. Due to the gel-like nature of some forms of pectin, they are considered to be a soluble fibre that has been shown to reduce blood cholesterol levels in humans.

Apples and crabapples, quinces, plums, currants, gooseberries, cranberries, oranges and other citrus fruits (rind and pips) contain high levels of the type of pectin perfect for jelly making. Soft fruits, like cherries, raspberries and strawberries, have relatively low pectin levels.

Pectin in the high-yielding plants is the substance that makes preserves jell, or firm up. In the past, the first step in making a fruit preserve was to extract the pectin from one or a combination of the high-pectin fruits. This extraction process involved boiling high-pectin fruits to a mash and then straining the juice in a couple of stages. Pectin in the juice was then added to low-pectin fruit like strawberries to make jam, jelly, spreads and other fruit preserves.

Commercially made pectin is available in powder and liquid form, and now "low sugar" pectin is sold, which allows for a reduced amount of sugar to be used in jams and other traditionally sweet preserves. Made from apples or citrus fruits, commercial pectin (there are several brands available) is similar to homemade pectin, except that it always works if package directions are followed; homemade pectin requires guesswork and may not always produce a reliable result. See page 29, "Homemade Pectin".

Testing for the Jelly Stage
You only need to test for the jelly stage when you are not using commercial pectin. When commercial pectin is used following the package directions or the recipes in this book, the mixture will always set, or jell. Some of the recipes in this book do not use commercial pectin, but rely on the natural pectin in the fruit. So it's important to know how to test for the jelly stage.

When a mixture of fruit or fruit juice, sugar and acid (usually in the form of lemon juice) is boiled rapidly, or "hard" boiled, eventually it will reach the "jelly stage." Depending on the natural pectin in the fruit, this could take anywhere from 30 minutes to 2 hours. Testing is important to see if the mixture has reached the jelly stage, so the highly concentrated fruit-sugar mixture does not go past it and on to the soft or even hard candy stage. Anyone who has ever forgotten a pan of strawberry jam on the burner and come back to find soft strawberry toffee can attest to the importance of this test. There are three ways to test for the jelly stage.

Three Ways to Test for the Jelly Stage

1. The Thermometer Test: The jelling point for jelly is 220°F (104°C). Using a candy thermometer is the most accurate way to measure the temperature of a preserve. Once the mixture has reached 220°F (104°C), remove it from the heat to keep it from progressing to the soft and hard ball candy stages.

2. The Sheet Test: Using a cold metal spoon, scoop out some boiling jelly. Before the mixture has reached the jelly stage, it will drip off the spoon in two separate drops. When the mixture comes off the spoon in a sheet or when two drops come together before dripping off the spoon, the jelly is done.

3. The Plate Test (top right): Drop a tablespoon (15 mL) of the mixture onto a cold plate and freeze for 5 minutes. Remove the plate from the freezer. The mixture is done if it wrinkles when pushed with a fork (bottom right).

Essential: Remove the kettle from the heat while you are doing sheet or plate tests, because if heated past the jelly stage, the mixture will go to the soft ball candy stage.

Home Canning Equipment and Methods

There may be some lingering habits from the past that are confusing the whole issue of sterilization and food safety for you. Years ago it was thought that high concentrations of sugar, salt and vinegar were enough to preserve high-acid foods (without processing after the food was canned) as long as they were packed into sterilized jars and sealed properly. That was called the Open Kettle Method of canning, and you may still find recipes for jams made with high-acid fruits that use it. I must say that, for the most part, the technique worked, and I used it myself. But I wouldn't want to be the individual who, in February, discovered her favourite strawberry jam warming itself in the cold cellar with little green angora-like sweaters—or worse, the person who poisoned someone with home preserves!

The Open Kettle Method relies on four things for a safe product. First, it can only be used with high-acid foods (fruit). Second, it hard boils the mixture, meaning the fruit and sugar mixture is brought to a rolling boil that cannot be stirred down, and it is held there for 20 minutes or longer. Third, the jars and lids must be able to seal hermetically—there can be no nicks in the jar rims, and you must use new lids every time—or you must seal the top of the food with a thin layer of food-grade wax. Last (and this is the most difficult to achieve), the jars, lids, kitchen utensils and anything else that will come into contact with the preserve must be sterile.

Today, we want quick results and have come to rely on commercial pectin to thicken our fruit condiments, sometimes even if they are already high in natural fruit pectin. This is convenient, but in doing so, we eliminate the need for the hard boil, which kills spore-forming bacteria. Bernardin, the preserving experts, recommend that the only way to ensure complete safety of canned foods is to use a boiling water bath or pressure-canning technique in clean, hot preserving jars that are capped with new flat tops and screw bands. When food is processed for the specified length of time, the food, as well as the jar and lid, are sterilized, so unlike with the Open Kettle Method, the jars only need to be hot, not sterilized, before packing them with food.

Essential: Always process canned food using either the Boiling Water Method or the Pressure Canner Method.

When I first started this book, I was not clear about using the oven for heating preserving jars. I had never used that method, but I knew people did. Again, I went to the experts, the people who manufacture preserving jars. Their answer: Do not heat canning jars in the oven because hot and cold spots can occur, causing the jars to explode when filled with boiling food.

Equipment

If you are only preserving fruit and making jams, jellies and fruit spreads, some small tools, a jam kettle and a large pot will be all you need. If you plan to include vegetables (other than pickles, which can be processed using the Boiling Water Canner Method), you will need a pressure canner.

Jars and Lids

I have heard of people using all sorts of recycled jars and lids (even antique, glass-top types) to preserve, and some say they have never had a problem. I recommend that only Mason jars be trusted with your precious condiment gems, because these jars are specifically designed to withstand the high temperatures of heat processing, as well as the subsequent cooling.

Essential: For preserving, never use recycled jars that previously held commercial food products. The lids will not seal properly, and the jars may not hold up to water boiling and subsequent cooling.

Mason jars are sealed with two-piece lids—flat tops and screw bands. Always use new

Choose the size of jar according to the recipe and how you will use it later in recipes. You can recycle Mason jars (if they have no nicks or cracks) and the screw band part of the lids, but use new flat tops each time you preserve. Basic jar sizes shown here are (clockwise from top): quart (4 cups/1 L), 1 cup (250 mL), pint (2 cups/500 mL).

flat tops because, once sealed, they must be pried off, leaving the rims raised (sometimes only slightly) enough that a perfect seal will not be possible next time. The gummy ring around the inside of the flat top allows for the airtight seal. The ring is softened when the lids are heated (see step 2 in the Boiling Water Method, page 18). The screw band holds the flat top in place while the food inside the jar is heating. Steam from the hot food escapes, causing a vacuum inside the jar that pulls the flat top down and creates a hermetic seal. Screw bands must only be tightened firmly by hand (see step 5 in the Boiling Water Method, page 19) in order to allow the steam to escape. Later, once a seal is obtained (see step 8 in the Boiling Water Method, page 19), the bands can be removed, cleaned and stored for the next batch of preserves.

Small Tools

I find that using tools designed for a specific task makes the job easier. My canning equipment includes a thermometer, magnetic lid lifter, non-metallic air releaser and headspace measure, stainless steel wide-mouth funnel and expandable jar lifter.

Kettles
Preserving Pans

Although any large, deep pot or saucepan can be used to boil fruit and sugar for jams, the heavier the pan, the less the risk of scorching, because the heat will be evenly distributed across the base. Be sure to use a pot deep enough to allow for the mixture to bubble up, which can happen rather quickly once the sugar melts into the juice.

This Maslin pan is an excellent choice for boiling.

Photo courtesy of Lee Valley Tools Ltd.

My favourite preserving pan is a stainless steel Maslin pan. Conical in shape, with a narrow, heavy base that fits modern burners, the pan flares slightly from bottom to top, which allows for maximum evaporation of liquid. Various brands have capacities from 6 to 12 quarts (6 to 12 L). A very long wooden spoon is essential for stirring the mixture as it boils.

Boiling Water Canner

Foods that are high in acid—most fruit and some vegetables with vinegar and lemon juice added—can be processed using a boiling water canner. I use a large pot measuring 12 inches (30 cm) in diameter and 10 inches (25cm) high as my boiling water canner. It's big enough to hold five 1-quart (1 L) jars and deep enough to allow for an inch (2.5 cm) of water to safely boil above the jars. Don't find out the hard way—with a scald or burn—that your pot or saucepan isn't deep enough to allow for 1 inch (2.5 cm) of rapidly boiling water above the tops of the jars. There must be a minimum of 3 inches (8 cm) of space in the pot above the jars. A lid helps bring the water to a boil faster. The rack keeps the jars from coming into direct contact with the heat at the bottom of the pan and allows the boiling water to heat the entire outside of the jars.

Pressure Canner

Using a pressure canner is essential for low-acid foods because the bacteria that thrive on these foods can only be destroyed at temperatures higher than that of boiling water. A wide variety of pressure canners are available. Pressure canners range from 6-quart (6 L) to 24-quart (24 L) capacity. Some are electric, while others are heated on the top of the stove.

Methods

Preparing and Canning Fruit

Fruit should be preserved at the peak of ripeness. If you must store fruit, keep it unwashed for a day and wash just before preserving. Directions for preparing the various fruits are included in the preparation notes for each. What follows are some general comments about preparing fruit for canning.

1. Wash

Rinse small fruit under running water, or wash in several changes of water, lifting the fruit out of the water so that the dirt does not settle back on it.

Use a sieve and gentle water spray for berries. Do not let them soak in water.

2. Keep Light Flesh from Browning

Many fruits and some vegetables with light-coloured flesh will darken rapidly after peeling exposes them to oxygen in the air. Ascorbic acid (vitamin C) prevents oxidative browning in most fruits. Use 1 tsp (5 mL) crystalline ascorbic acid or six 500 mg vitamin C tablets or 1/3 cup (75 mL) bottled lemon juice per 1 gallon (4 L) of cool water.

3. Make a Syrup or Use Juice or Water

Sugar helps canned fruit hold its shape, colour and flavour. For that reason, sugar syrups are often used for canning fruit. Use 1 to 1-1/2 cups (250 to 375 mL) syrup per quart (1 L) to cover the fruit. Syrups range from very light to very heavy. For the canned fruit recipes in this book, light syrup is included with canning directions, but the following chart gives sugar and liquid proportions for other types of syrups.

PROPORTIONS FOR SUGAR SYRUPS

Syrup	Water or juice	Sugar	Yield of syrup	Calories per cup
Very light	4 cups (1 L)	½ cup (125 mL)	4 cups (1 L)	77
Light	4 cups (1 L)	1 cup (250 mL)	4-½ cups (1.125 L)	154
Medium	4 cups (1 L)	2 cups (500 mL)	5 cups (1.25 L)	308
Heavy	4 cups (1 L)	3 cups (750 mL)	5-½ cups (1.375 L)	420
Very heavy	4 cups (1 L)	4 cups (1 L)	6-½ cups (1.625 L)	563

TO MAKE SYRUP: In a heavy-bottomed saucepan, combine granulated sugar with water; stir until dissolved. Bring to a gentle boil over high heat. Reduce heat and keep hot.

ALTERNATIVES TO SUGAR SYRUP: Unsweetened apple juice, white grape juice, pineapple juice or a combination of the three juices can be used in place of a sugar syrup. Water can be used but tends to dilute the taste of the fruit.

Note: Commercial non-sugar sweeteners are not recommended for canning since they tend to lose their sweetening effect upon heating, and some become bitter.

4. Pack Fruit into Jars

Fruit can be packed raw into jars or blanched and packed hot. I prefer to pack firm fruit hot because it is less likely to float in the syrup, but raw-packing tender fruit helps it keep some texture.

Raw Pack (above and middle): Spoon cold, raw fruit into clean, hot jars, shaking the jars to pack tightly (unless otherwise directed). A pair of long food tweezers or a chopstick helps to position the pieces.

Cover with boiling hot syrup, juice or water, leaving the correct amount of headspace. Run a thin non-metallic utensil around the inside of the jar to release air and recheck the headspace, adding more hot syrup if necessary.

Hot Pack: Heat fruit in syrup. Pack hot fruit and syrup loosely into clean, hot jars, leaving the correct headspace. Run a thin non-metallic utensil around the inside of the jar. Recheck the headspace, adding more hot syrup if necessary.

5. Cap with Lids and Bands

Wipe the jar rims and threads with a clean damp cloth or towel to remove any syrup or fruit bits that might prevent a proper seal (above left). Centre a flat lid on each jar. Screw on the metal band as firmly as you can (above right).

6. Process

Process according to times given for each fruit, using the Boiling Water Method (page 18).

Essential: If a recipe recommends only one method, follow those directions and do not attempt to use another pack method.

Storing Canned Foods

Storing Opened Canned Foods

Plan to use your homemade preserves within a year, or sooner. Once opened, pay attention to the jars in your refrigerator. Some things keep longer than others once the seal has been broken. Generally, high-acid fruits, jams, jellies, pickles and fruit spreads will keep in the refrigerator for up to a month after opening. Low-acid foods, such as vegetables, meats, soups, stews and dips, must be kept in the refrigerator and used within a week after opening.

Keep preserves in a cool, dark place. This pine jam cupboard was built for storing preserves in a cool basement.

Boiling Water Method, Step by Step

Use for processing high-acid fruit, jam, jelly, high-acid preserves, and tomatoes or pickles with vinegar or lemon juice added.

1. Wash jars and lids in hot soapy water or dishwasher. Arrange jars on a rack in the boiling water canner. Fill the jars and canner with hot water to at least 1 inch (2.5 cm) above the tops of the jars. Heat the water to just under a boil and keep it lightly simmering until ready to fill with hot preserve.

2. Set screw bands aside. Heat flat tops in simmering (not boiling) water (180°F/82°C). Also heat lifters, funnels, ladles and tongs. Keep tops hot until ready to use.

3. Prepare preserve as per recipe. Left: Ladle hot food into a hot jar, leaving a headspace as follows: 1/4 inch (5 mm) for jams and jellies; 1/2 inch (1 cm) or 1 inch (2.5 cm) for all other recipes, including fruit, pickles, tomatoes and other high-acid condiments. Right: Be accurate with measuring headspace because it is necessary for achieving a good seal.

4. Remove air bubbles by sliding a flat, non-metallic utensil around the inside of the filled jar. Adjust headspace if necessary. Wipe jar rim clean using a clean damp cloth.

Essential: Fill and cap one jar at a time.

5. Centre the flat disc of the lid on the jar. Apply the screw band, using only hand strength to tighten just until resistance is met.

6. Place filled jar back in canner with hot water and fill remaining jars following steps 3 to 5. When all the jars are filled, add more hot water if necessary to keep the water level 1 inch (2.5 cm) above jar tops. Cover the canner and bring water to a full rolling boil over high heat. Process the filled jars by boiling for the time specified in the recipe.

7. After boiling is done, turn off heat and remove canner lid. Let canner sit for about 5 minutes or until water becomes still. Using a jar lifter, lift jars straight out of canner onto a clean towel or cooling rack. Let jars cool upright, undisturbed for 24 hours. Do not tighten screw bands.

8. Check seals: jars are sealed safely if the lid tops curve downward and do not move when pressed with a fingertip. You can remove screw bands and clean and store them for next use or leave them on the jars. Wipe jars, label and store in a cool, dark place.

Preparing and Canning Vegetables (and low-acid fruit)

Choose firm, crisp vegetables at the peak of ripeness and try to use them the same day. If that is not possible, store for as short a time as possible—up to three days in a cool place or slightly longer in the refrigerator. Directions for preparing each vegetable are found in the preparation notes. What follows are some general comments about preparing produce for pressure canning.

1. Wash

Swish tender vegetables in water to which a drop of food-safe soap has been added. Scrub root vegetables using a vegetable brush. Trim vegetables according to the individual type and the recipe.

2. Keep Light Flesh from Browning

Light-fleshed fruit and vegetables (like artichokes and carrots) will darken when exposed to oxygen in the air. Ascorbic acid (vitamin C) prevents oxidative browning in most fruit and vegetables.

3. Make a Brine or use Broth or Water

Prepare brine according to the recipe. Vinegar helps to lower the pH and adds flavour to vegetables. When vinegar or lemon juice brine is added to vegetables, the food can be processed using the Boiling Water Method. When canning vegetables in water or broth, they must be processed using a pressure cooker.

4. Pack Vegetables into Jars

Vegetables can be packed raw into jars (Raw Pack) or preheated and packed hot (Hot Pack). Some recipes call for a specific method; in other recipes, the decision to hot- or raw-pack is left up to you. Not only do I use the Raw Pack Method with fruit, but also with tender vegetables like asparagus.

Raw Pack: Arrange cold, raw vegetables in clean, hot jars, shaking the jar to pack tightly. Cover with boiling brine, water or juice, leaving 1 inch (2.5 cm) of headspace. Run a thin non-metallic utensil around the inside of the jar to release air and recheck the headspace, adding more hot liquid if necessary.

Hot Pack: Precook vegetables in brine, juice or water. Pack hot vegetables and brine loosely into clean, hot jars, leaving 1 inch (2.5 cm) of headspace. Run a thin non-metallic utensil around the inside of the jar to release air and recheck the headspace, adding more hot liquid if necessary.

5. Cap with Lids and Bands

Wipe the jar rims and threads with a clean damp cloth or towel to remove any syrup or bits that might prevent a proper seal.

Centre a flat lid on each jar. Screw on the metal band as firmly as you can.

6. Process

Process in a pressure canner (page 22) according to directions in given recipe.

Pressure Canner Method, Step by Step

Use for processing low-acid vegetables, fruits, meats, poultry and seafood, as well as soups, stews, sauces, dips and vegetable spreads.

1. Wash jars and lids in hot soapy water or dishwasher. Arrange jars on a rack in the pressure canner. Add 2 to 3 inches (5 to 8 cm) water and heat to a simmer over medium-high heat.

2. Set screw bands aside. Heat flat lid tops in simmering (not boiling) water (180°F/82°C). Also heat lifters, funnels, ladles and tongs. Keep tops hot until ready to use.

3. Prepare and fill jars according to recipe. Leave a 1-inch (2.5 cm) headspace. Using a flat, non-metallic utensil, remove air bubbles by sliding utensil around the inside of the filled jar. Adjust headspace if necessary. Wipe jar rim clean using a clean, damp cloth.

4. Centre a flat lid on top of each jar. Apply the screw band, using only hand strength to tighten until resistance is met.

5. Place filled jars back in pressure canner and adjust water level as directed by canner manufacturer. Lock canner lid in place and turn heat to high. Follow manufacturer's directions to vent canner (allow steam to escape) for the specified time (usually 10 to 15 minutes of strong steam venting through vent port or petcock).

6. If using a weighted gauge, place the correct weight over the vent port. Follow recipe chart or manufacturer's chart and count processing time from the time the pressure for your elevation reaches the required level.

7. When processing time is complete, turn off the heat. Let canner stand undisturbed until pressure drops to zero. Allow 2 minutes longer before removing the canner lid (tilt lid away to avoid escaping steam).

8. Using a jar lifter, lift jars straight out of canner. Cool jars upright and undisturbed for 24 hours. Do not tighten screw bands.

9. Check seals: jars are sealed safely if the lids curve downward and do not move when pressed with fingertips. You can remove the screw bands, cleaning and storing them for the next use, or leave them on the jars. Wipe jars, label and store in a cool, dark place.

Freezing

Freezing fruit and vegetables in order to preserve them is convenient, easy, fast and generally suitable. Most frozen foods remain true to their original form with minimal loss of colour and flavour. Perhaps most importantly, nutrient loss is minimal. Having a separate upright or chest freezer is ideal for accommodating large quantities of produce, along with extra pies and baked goods, leftovers, supermarket meats purchased on special, and holiday cooking.

Essential: A freezer must maintain a minimum constant 0°F or -18°C. Look for a freezer that is adjustable to -20°F (-28.8°C) so that you can quick-freeze an initial batch to prevent large ice crystals from forming in the food.

Chest versus Upright Freezers

Chest freezers come in a wide variety of sizes, from 5 to 25 cubic feet (0.14 to 0.70 cubic metres) or more. They keep the cold in when the door is open because the cold air settles downward. Chest freezers are hard to organize, and it is hard to locate small packages in them. Furthermore, they take up more floor space. (However, I have a narrow model that I use as an extra counter in my pantry, so it is perfect for my needs.)

Upright freezers generally provide 16 to 21 cubic feet (0.45 to 0.59 cubic metres) of space, and because much of the food is at eye level, packages are easier to organize and find. Cold spills out every time the door is opened, so the unit requires more energy, making upright freezers slightly more costly to run.

Essential: Strive to keep the freezer at no less than three-quarters full at all times. That way it will operate efficiently, using less power than when fully stocked. Fill it with bags of ice in summer months when it may not be full.

Packaging for the Freezer

A wide array of containers—pliable and rigid plastic, heavily waxed cardboard, or glass containers—are available for freezing preserves safely, but the key to retaining the highest quality in your foods is a material that provides a moisture-vapour barrier. That means that drying frigid air must be sealed out and the liquids in your preserves sealed in.

Freezing Essentials

▶ If using bags, be sure to purchase heavy-duty plastic bags specifically labelled for use in the freezer.
▶ Make sure lids fit securely for an airtight seal.

▶ Use only Mason jars, leaving the headspace specified in the recipe, and allow the food to cool completely before freezing.

▶ Rigid containers with straight sides and stackable tops and bottoms save freezer space.

▶ Pack food in 1-cup (250 mL), 2-cup (500 mL) or 4-cup (1 L) portions, depending on recipe requirements or how you will use the preserves.

▶ Label packages with the food name or recipe title, as well as the date, and keep rotating older packages to the front/top for use before more recent additions.

▶ Although frozen fruit and vegetables can last longer, it is wise to use frozen fruit within eight months of freezing, and frozen vegetables and herbs within six months.

Glossary

Acidulate: A method of preventing the oxidation of white-fleshed fruits and vegetables (oxidation causes the cut flesh to turn brown). To acidulate, immerse the flesh in water with vitamin C, made by mixing 1 tsp (5 mL) crystalline ascorbic acid or six 500 mg vitamin C tablets in 1 gallon (4 L) cool water. Acidulate a small amount of fruit or vegetables by brushing or tossing them in lemon juice.

Aggregate fruit: Fruit that grows in clusters around a core. Raspberries, blackberries and strawberries are examples of aggregate fruit.

Blanching: A technique that slows down or halts the deteriorating action of enzymes. To blanch fruit, vegetables and nuts, small amounts are scalded by immersing them in boiling water for a short period of time. This process makes it very easy for the skins of some fruits and vegetables to be removed.

Brine: A salt and water solution used to soak foods.

Chutney: A sweet-sour condiment made from a mixture of fruit and/or vegetables that is cooked until soft or until it forms a cohesive pulp. Sugar, spices, salt and vinegar are key ingredients, along with the fruit/vegetables. Nuts, seeds, raisins, dates, figs and other ingredients may be added. Long, slow cooking thickens chutneys and softens the mixture.

Clingstone: A type of peach, nectarine or apricot whose flesh grows tightly around the stone, making it difficult to remove.

Compote: A stew-like product made by poaching one or several different fruits in a spiced liquid.

Cone colander: A cone-shaped sieve used for separating clear juice from fruit.

Conserve: A preserve of whole or chopped pieces of fruit suspended in thick syrup. Conserve is chunkier than jam and often includes more than just the fruit. The addition of nuts, raisins, liqueur or brandy, figs or currants, and herbs takes a mixture from a jam to a conserve.

Freestone: A type of peach, nectarine or apricot whose flesh does not grow tightly around the stone, making it easy to remove.

Freezer burn: Dry white patches on frozen food, caused by exposure to the dry air of the freezer; moisture is sucked out when the packaging is thin or torn. Prevent freezer burn by using freezer-quality bags and packages that provide a good seal, and only fill containers to the designated headspace so that air is not sealed in.

Fruit butter: Smooth and thick, butters are concentrated, soft, spreadable fruit and sugar mixtures that tend to be less sweet than jams and jellies.

Fruit cheese: A mixture similar to a fruit butter but thicker, fruit cheese is a semi-sweet concentrated fruit spread often served with a cheese tray. Use it like peanut butter.

Fruit curd: Usually made from citrus juice (lemon is the most popular, but berry juice can be used), curd is a softly thickened sauce-like mixture that is used as a tart filling, as a sauce for desserts and fresh fruit, and as a base for trifle or other cake desserts. Curd is thickened with eggs and butter. Keeps in sterilized jars in the refrigerator for up to 1-1/2 months.

Fruit syrup: A syrup made from sugar and juice, boiled until it is slightly thickened. Syrups are used to flavour and sweeten drinks and gelatin desserts, as dessert sauces for puddings and cakes, and to sweeten sliced berries or fruit.

Hard boil: During the making of jam and jelly, the fruit and sugar mixture is brought to a rolling boil that cannot be stirred down.

Headspace: The space between the top of the food or liquid and the underside of the canning lid. This is the space that allows for swelling of the food as it is processed. Pay attention to the space as directed in the recipe—it is essential for helping to create a vacuum seal.

Hermetic seal: The seal that results when the jar is completely airtight, protecting the sterilized food from recontamination by airborne mould, yeast or bacteria.

High-acid foods: Foods or recipes with a pH of 4.6 or lower. Most fruits, jams, jellies and fruit spreads are high-acid. Some fruits, such as figs, and some vegetables, notably tomatoes, are considered to be high-acid when vinegar or lemon is added.

Hull: (Noun) the crown or cap of a strawberry; (verb) to remove the crown or cap of a strawberry.

Jam: A dense preserve of mashed, sliced or whole fruit that has been sweetened and jellied. Jam has a soft, spreadable consistency. Often lemon juice and pectin are added to help jams set. Sugar is important to the jam-making process to help pectin set and to retard bacteria growth. With the introduction of no-sugar-needed pectin (see Resources, page 525), sugar is no longer essential to jam making as long as the manufacturer's instructions are followed for making and sterilizing the jam.

Jelly: A translucent, clear mixture made from fruit juice or strained fruit pulp. A jelly holds its shape when turned out of its container and can be set in a mould. High-pectin fruits, like apples and citrus, do not require added pectin to jell, whereas low-pectin fruits do. Crabapples, apples, damsons (wild plums), gooseberries and currants are old-time favourites for jelly.

Low-acid foods: Foods or recipes low in acid, including vegetables, meats, poultry and seafood, soups, stews, sauces, dips and vegetable spreads, and any foods with a pH higher than 4.6.

Marmalade: Traditionally made from thick or thin shreds of the rind of oranges (Seville or Temple oranges) or other citrus fruits. Sometimes berries, shredded vegetables or shredded ginger are suspended in a jelly and called "marmalade."

Melting flesh: A term applied to some varieties of freestone peaches or nectarines. The fruit bruises easily, and the flesh becomes soft quickly after picking or when canned. When sliced, the flesh is ragged at the pit side. Melting flesh peaches or nectarines can be clingstone or freestone.

Non-reactive pot: The large concentrations of salt and acid (vinegar or lemon juice) in preserves can interact with metal utensils. It is always best to use pottery, glass, stainless steel or enamelled equipment for mixing and cooking preserves.

Oxidation: The reaction that occurs when oxygen in the air meets the exposed flesh of some fruit and vegetables. When light-coloured produce is peeled or cut, the oxygen turns the exposed flesh brown. *See also* Acidulate.

Preserves: This term has two meanings: the first is a broad reference to sweet spreads, jams or jellies that are canned; the second refers to a mixture of small chunks of translucent fruit or whole berries suspended in syrup, which is often lightly jellied. Stem ginger in syrup is a classic preserve.

Relish: A pickled product made from chopped fruit or vegetables; may be sweet or savoury.

Stem ginger: The pink, tender stems growing directly out of the gingerroot. Stem ginger is not usually available fresh but rather preserved in syrup.

Sterilization: A process that removes or destroys all forms of microbial life, including bacterial spores.

Homemade Pectin
Extracting Pectin from Apples

Any variety of tart cooking apple, crabapple, quince, plum, gooseberry or citrus fruit may be boiled down to make a mash in the first step of pectin making. To boil apples: Wash and chop fine, including cores, pips and stems. Weigh and add 2 cups (500 mL) water and 1 tbsp (15 mL) lemon juice for every 1 lb (500 g) of apples. Cover and boil rapidly for 30 minutes, stirring occasionally.

The apple mash is strained in two stages. The first press is through a rough cone strainer with a cone-shaped wooden pusher. Specialty stores may still carry the cone strainer and its stand. You might also see them in thrift stores and at flea markets from time to time.

In the second press, the mash collected from the first strain is poured into the now cheesecloth-lined cone strainer, or a large fine sieve lined with cheesecloth, and allowed to drip overnight without squeezing or pressing. Use the strained liquid in jams and other preserves.

Spring

"Spring makes its own statement, so loud and clear that the gardener seems to be only one of the instruments, not the composer."

—GEOFFREY B. CHARLESWORTH

Apricots

ITS BOTANICAL NAME, *Prunus armeniaca*, notwithstanding, the apricot is actually not native to Armenia but originated in Manchuria and northern China. The name is derived from the Latin *praecocia*, meaning "precious" or "precocious." Either English word is very apt for this early-blooming, early-ripening gem. Although the apricot tree tolerates temperatures as cold as −22°F (−30°C) or lower, its early flowers are killed with spring frosts such as those typical in the northern United States and southern Canada. That means that the harvest is no sure thing from year to year. Most North American apricots are grown in British Columbia, California, Washington and Utah. Since the apricot's peak season is mid-May through June, I have placed it in the Spring Recipes chapter, but in your area, local apricots may not appear until early summer.

Essential: The leaves and seeds contain hydrogen cyanide, a poison. This is the same toxin that gives almonds their characteristic flavour. Even though it is usually present in too small a quantity to do any harm, and in very small amounts has been shown to stimulate respiration and improve digestion, like any other bitter seed, apricot seeds (and leaves) should not be eaten.

Good Preserving Varieties

Apricots can be small, medium, large, extra large, jumbo or extra jumbo in size, depending on the variety and growing conditions. **Aprium**, a trademarked hybrid fruit, is a three-quarter apricot/one-quarter plum cross. **Honey Rich**, **Flavor Delight** and **Tasty Rich** are popular Aprium varieties. If you find Apriums at your local market, use them as you would an extra-sweet apricot. Some other apricot hybrids, such as **Peachcotums** (a peach, apricot and plum hybrid), **Plumcots** and **Cherrycots**, have been adapted for cooler regions.

Blenheim (Royal): Thick yellow-orange flesh; very juicy fruit with sweet-tangy and aromatic flavour. This classic medium-to-large California apricot is a popular eat-out-of-hand variety that also holds its texture and shape well for canning. Available early to mid-season.

Earligold: Golden yellow with a rich and juicy flesh, this medium-size fruit is available early for canning.

Gold Kist: Well-balanced sweet-tart flavour and a red-blushed yellow skin. Medium to large fruit. Use for canning, freezing, drying and for eating fresh. Early harvest.

Moongold: Plum-size apricot with golden skin and flesh; sweet, tangy flavour. Use fresh, canned or for jam. Early to mid-season harvest.

Moorpark: Large, sweet, aromatic and juicy, with a full plum flavour. Use fresh, canned or for jam.

Purchasing/Storing
• 1 lb (500 g) yields 2 to 2-1/2 cups (500 to 625 mL) peeled pitted apricot halves.
• You will need about 1-1/4 lb (625 g) for each quart (1 L) jar.

Buy local whenever possible because apricots sold anywhere but in the location they were grown are picked at an underripe stage; while they will ripen in colour, texture and juiciness, their flavour and sweetness will remain at the point they were picked. Select firm golden-orange fruits with no touch of green, wrinkling or bruising. Ripe apricots yield to slight pressure. If absolutely necessary, ripen in a paper bag at room temperature, away from sunlight; check daily. Use immediately once ripened.

Good With
• Anise herbs such as chervil, tarragon and sweet cicely; spicy herbs like basil, bay, thyme.
• Sweet seasonings such as cinnamon, ginger, cardamom, nutmeg, vanilla, almond.
• Soft cheeses such as brie, Camembert, Boursault, feta, creamy blue.
• Other fruit, such as raspberries, blueberries, peaches, nectarines, cherries, oranges.
• Toasted almonds, pecans and walnuts, raisins, white chocolate.
• Chicken; mild fish, such as tilapia, haddock, halibut and flounder.
• Cherry brandy, orange liqueur, anisette.

Preparation
Wash apricots in a sink full of cool water to which a drop of food-safe soap has been added. Rinse well and pat dry. Blanch apricots in boiling water for 30 to 45 seconds. Immerse in cold water for 30 to 45 seconds. Drain and pat dry. Slip off the skins. Cut lengthwise in half and remove the stone.

To prevent discolouration, peeled, pitted apricot halves are immersed in water with 1 tsp (5 mL) crystalline ascorbic acid for every 2 cups (500 mL) water. You can use six 500 mg vitamin C tablets in 1 gallon (4 L) cool water.

Canning Apricots
See detailed canning information, page 14.

1. Prepare Equipment: Wash and heat pint (2-cup/500 mL) or quart (1 L) jars, and heat the lids, funnel, ladle and tongs (see page 18).

2. Make a Light Syrup: In a large saucepan, combine 1 cup (250 mL) granulated sugar with 4 cups (1 L) water; stir until dissolved. Bring to a gentle boil over high heat. Makes 4-1/2 cups (1.125 L) syrup, enough for three or four 1-quart (1 L) jars of apricots.

Note: You can use the same amount of apple juice or white grape juice in place of the light syrup.

3. Pack apricots into jars either hot or raw.

Make a Raw Pack: Fill hot jars with peeled fruit, cut side down and packed fairly tightly. Cover with hot syrup or juice, leaving a 1/2-inch (1 cm) headspace. Run a non-metallic utensil around the inside of the jar to allow air to escape. Add hot syrup, if necessary, to leave a 1/2-inch (1 cm) headspace. Wipe sealing edge of jars with a clean, damp, lint-free cloth. Position flat lids over the tops of jars and hand-tighten screw bands.

OR

Make a Hot Pack: Add apricot halves to gently boiling syrup or juice and boil for a minute. Fill hot jars with hot fruit and cooking liquid, leaving a 1/2-inch (1 cm) headspace. Run a non-metallic utensil around the inside of the jar to allow air to escape. Add more hot fruit or liquid, if necessary, to leave a 1/2-inch (1 cm) headspace. Wipe sealing edge of jars with a clean, damp, lint-free cloth. Position flat lids over the tops of jars and hand-tighten screw bands.

4. Process apricots in a canner: Use a Boiling Water Canner according to the chart below.

Processing Times at Different Altitudes for Apricots in a BOILING WATER Canner					
Pack Style	**Jar Size**	**0–1000 ft**	**1001–3000 ft**	**3001–6000 ft**	**6000+ ft**
HOT	Pints	20 min	25 min	30 min	35 min
	Quarts	25 min	30 min	35 min	40 min
RAW	Pints	25 min	30 min	35 min	40 min
	Quarts	30 min	35 min	40 min	45 min

OR

Process apricots in a Pressure Canner following manufacturer's directions for steam pressure and time at your altitude.

5. Cool, Label and Store: Lift jars from canner and place on a clean towel or rack. Do not re-tighten screw bands. Let the jars cool to room temperature. This may take from 12 to 24 hours. Remove and store screw bands. Check lid seals (see page 19). Wipe and label sealed jars. Store in a cool, dark place.

apricot compote

Like other spring foods—namely asparagus, wild leeks, rhubarb and fiddleheads—fresh apricots will not be available very long. I tend to eat a lot of them once the local crop is available, almost to the point of becoming temporarily tired of them, knowing it will be a full year until I can indulge again. This simple mélange of fleshy apricots and orange liqueur is a sophisticated way to extend the sweet tang and brilliant orange colour of fresh apricots.

MAKES ABOUT 5 CUPS (1.25 L)

5 cups (1.25 L) sliced peeled apricots (about 3 lb/1.5 kg)
2 tbsp (25 mL) grated orange rind
1-1/4 cups (300 mL) freshly squeezed orange juice
1/4 cup (50 mL) orange liqueur (Grand Marnier)

2 tbsp (25 mL) freshly squeezed lemon juice
1 tbsp (15 mL) crushed or ground coriander seeds
5 cups (1.25 L) granulated sugar

1. Heat six 1-cup (250 mL) jars in boiling water, and scald the lids, lifter, funnel and tongs (see page 18).

2. In a Maslin pan or canning kettle, combine apricots, orange rind, orange juice, orange liqueur, lemon juice and coriander seeds. Bring to a boil over high heat. Stir in the sugar, 1 cup (250 mL) at a time, stirring to dissolve before adding the next cup. Boil, stirring frequently, until the mixture becomes thick and coats the back of a wooden spoon, about 15 minutes. Test the gel.

Setting Point

Compote has reached the setting point when a candy thermometer reaches the jelly stage, 212°F (100°C). See page 9 for other jell tests.

3. Skim off and discard any foam. Fill hot jars, leaving a 1/4-inch (5 mm) headspace. Run a thin non-metallic utensil around the inside of the jar to allow air to escape. Add more hot compote, if necessary, to leave a 1/4-inch (5 mm) headspace. Wipe rims, top with flat lids and screw on metal rings. Return jars to the hot water bath, topping up with hot water if necessary. Bring to a full rolling boil and process jars for 10 minutes (see page 35).

4. Remove canner lid and wait 5 minutes before removing jars to a towel or rack to cool completely. Check seals, label and store in a cool place for up to 1 year.

Use: I like to decorate the jars with ribbon and give as hostess gifts, especially in December, when the days are short and these brilliant gems are so cheery. Spread on toast or spoon on top of hot cereal, cornmeal and baked puddings, especially rice puddings.

apricot beef

This dish is fast and richly flavoured, thanks to the tart-sweet apricot compote. Using a wok or cast iron grilling pan sears the beef and keeps the moisture inside, making it a "steakhouse special." If you start with a hot grill and pay attention to timing, you can cook the meat to the exact temperature you desire: 4 to 5 minutes for medium-rare, up to 10 minutes for well done. Serve with braised greens or a green salad and/or bistro-style garlic mashed potatoes. Pass the remaining compote from the jar with the beef.

MAKES 4 SERVINGS

1/4 cup (50 mL) Apricot Compote
　(recipe page 36)
1 tbsp (15 mL) rice vinegar
1/2 lb (250 g) beef filet or pork loin,
　trimmed

sea salt and cracked pepper
2 tbsp (25 mL) olive oil

1. In a bowl large enough to hold the beef filet, combine Apricot Compote and vinegar. Add beef filet to the bowl and brush with apricot mixture. Grind salt and pepper over top and let stand for 15 minutes.

2. In a wok or cast iron grilling pan, heat olive oil over high heat, to just under the smoking point. Use more oil if necessary. Add beef and cook for 4 to 5 minutes (medium-rare), turning often. Remove to a board, cover with a lid or foil and let stand for 5 to 10 minutes before slicing.

scarlet blush apricot freezer conserve

The beautiful pink-to-red blush on some varieties of apricot skin is reflected in this easy condiment. Don't be tempted to add more raspberries—the small amount is just enough to give a very rosy glow to the yellow-orange apricots. No matter when I use this conserve, I am instantly reminded of happy warm summer sunsets, my particular favourite sunset site being the beach at Southampton, Ontario, on Lake Huron. This conserve has everything going for it: it's easy, low-sugar and convenient for travelling. I use it as an ice block in my picnic cooler, and by the time we are ready to set up our alfresco lunch, it's ready to spoon over pound cake, scones or angel cake.

MAKES 5 CUPS (1.25 L)

1-1/2 cups (375 mL) granulated sugar
**1 pkg (1-1/2 oz/45 g) freezer jam
  pectin crystals**
**3-1/2 cups (875 mL) chopped peeled
  apricots**

1/2 cup (125 mL) fresh or frozen raspberries
1 tbsp (15 mL) freshly squeezed lemon juice

1. In a bowl, combine sugar and pectin and stir to blend well. Add apricots, raspberries and lemon juice. Stir for 3 minutes.

2. Ladle conserve into five 1-cup (250 mL) plastic or glass freezer containers, leaving 1/2-inch (1 cm) headspace. Squeeze out air and seal tightly. Let conserve stand at room temperature until thickened, about 30 minutes. Label and store in the refrigerator for up to 3 weeks or freeze for up to 1 year.

Use: Scarlet Blush Apricot Freezer Conserve is always ready to top pancakes, pound cake, ice cream, fresh fruit salads and waffles, or to accompany custard or muffins. It's just a great treat to have in the freezer.

Freezing Apricots

1. **Select Equipment:** Select suitable-size freezer containers, bags or Mason jars (see page 24).

2. **Pack in Syrup:** In a saucepan, combine 2-1/2 cups (625 mL) granulated sugar and 1/2 tsp (2 mL) crystalline ascorbic acid or three 500 mg vitamin C tablets. Stir in 4 cups (1 L) water. Bring to a gentle boil over high heat, stirring frequently. Reduce heat and gently boil for 3 minutes. Let cool. Fill pint (2-cup/500 mL) or quart (1 L) freezer containers with halved or sliced apricots to within 3 to 4 inches (7 to 10 cm) of the top. Pour syrup over top; use 1 cup (250 mL) syrup per quart (1 L) of prepared fruit. Squeeze out air; leave 1-inch (2.5 cm) headspace. Seal, label and freeze.

OR

Dry Pack: Fill pint (2-cup/500 mL) or quart (1 L) freezer containers with halved or sliced apricots to within 3 to 4 inches (7 to 10 cm) of the top. Pour dry granulated sugar over top; use 1/2 cup (125 mL) sugar per quart (1 L) of prepared fruit. Squeeze out air; leave 1-inch (2.5 cm) headspace. Seal, label and freeze.

Raspberries

THE PERENNIAL BUSH-TYPE RASPBERRY plant produces fruit on woody stems or canes. Like blackberries, raspberries are an aggregate fruit: each raspberry is actually a cluster of fruit with many bead-like fruits, called druplets, gathered around a core or receptacle. Each druplet contains one seed, and every raspberry has from 100 to 120 seeds. It is these tiny seeds that aggravate some people, so many recipes call for raspberry mixtures to be strained in order to remove them.

Good Preserving Varieties

American Red Raspberry (*Rubus strigosus*) plants can be divided into two categories: everbearing, which produce fruit in late spring or early summer to midsummer and again in the fall; and summer-bearing varieties, which produce only one harvest in summer. While red raspberries are the most common, you may find yellow/gold, purple and black raspberries at markets in your area. There are dozens of varieties to choose from, but generally look for a local variety with large, firm fruit that is bright red or black or purple in colour.

Canby: Large red berries; a midsummer variety; originated in Oregon.
Gatineau: From Ontario; red berries are medium in size and arrive very early in summer.
Heritage: Medium berries with good flavour; harvested in spring and fall.
Titan: Very large red berries; good for canning and freezing; mid- to late-summer harvest; originated in New York.

Purchasing/Storing

- You will need six to eight 1/2-pint (1-cup/250 mL) baskets (about 3 lb/1.5 kg) raspberries for each 1-quart (1 L) jar.
- Choose dry, ripe, plump, firm, sweet raspberries with uniform colour, shape and size.
- Raspberries are highly perishable and should be transported in a cooler; use immediately because they spoil easily, especially if allowed to stand at room temperature.

Good With

- Anise herbs such as sweet cicely, tarragon, chervil.
- Sweet seasonings such as ginger, vanilla, almond.
- Semi-soft cheeses such as Asadero, fontina and Monterey Jack.
- Other fruit, such as apricots, peaches, nectarines, bananas, cherries, plums.
- Other berries, such as blackberries, blueberries, currants, elderberries, gooseberries, huckleberries, loganberries, mulberries, strawberries.
- Toasted almonds and pecans, chocolate, lemon desserts.
- Chicken; mild fish such as tilapia, orange roughy and haddock.

Preparation

Keep perishable soft berries, such as raspberries, blueberries, blackberries and strawberries, unwashed and refrigerated until just before using. Wash a small amount at a time by holding under lightly flowing cool water for a few seconds.

Canning Raspberries

See detailed canning information, page 14.

1. Prepare Equipment: Wash and heat pint (2-cup/500 mL) or quart (1 L) jars, and scald the lids, funnel, ladle and tongs (see page 18).

2. Make a Light Syrup: In a large saucepan, combine 1 cup (250 mL) granulated sugar with 4 cups (1 L) water; stir until dissolved. Bring to a gentle boil over high heat. Makes 4-1/2 cups (1.125 L) syrup, enough for three or four 1-quart (1 L) jars of raspberries.
Note: You can use the same amount of apple juice or white grape juice in place of the light syrup.

3. Pack raspberries into jars raw (use Raw Pack Method because berries are soft).
Make a Raw Pack: Fill jars with fruit and shake the jar gently while filling to pack fairly tightly. Cover with hot syrup or juice, leaving a 1/2-inch (1 cm) headspace. Run a non-metallic utensil around the inside of the jar to allow air to escape. Add hot liquid, if necessary, to leave a 1/2-inch (1 cm) headspace. Wipe sealing edge of jars with a clean, damp, lint-free cloth. Position flat lids over the tops of jars and hand-tighten screw bands.

4. Process raspberries in a canner: Use a Boiling Water Canner according to the chart below.

Processing Times at Different Altitudes for Raspberries in a BOILING WATER Canner					
Pack Style	**Jar Size**	**0–1000 ft**	**1001–3000 ft**	**3001–6000 ft**	**6000+ ft**
HOT	Pints	15 min	20 min	25 min	30 min
	Quarts	20 min	25 min	30 min	35 min
RAW	Pints	20 min	25 min	30 min	35 min
	Quarts	25 min	30 min	35 min	40 min

OR

Process raspberries in a Pressure Canner following manufacturer's directions for steam pressure and time at your altitude.

5. Cool, Label and Store: Lift jars from canner and place on a clean towel or rack. Do not retighten screw bands. Let the jars cool to room temperature. This may take from 12 to 24 hours. Remove and store screw bands. Check lid seals (see page 19). Wipe and label sealed jars. Store in a cool, dark place.

raspberry coulis

Chefs use fruit or vegetable coulis to give desserts and main dishes a professional finish. This recipe is really a raspberry sauce that can be squeezed from a bottle for decorating plates and desserts, along with the other uses listed below. Bay adds a spicy dimension that acts as a foil for the sweetness of the coulis. I often bring this out for special birthday cake occasions and when I just need to add a homemade touch to frozen yogurt or ice cream. Even store-bought cheesecake is extra sophisticated when served on this gorgeous bright red sauce.

MAKES 6 CUPS (1.5 L)

12 cups (3 L) fresh or frozen raspberries
1 cup (250 mL) unsweetened apple juice
1 tbsp (15 mL) grated lemon rind
2 bay leaves

1-1/2 cups (375 mL) granulated sugar
3/4 cup (175 mL) corn syrup
1/2 cup (125 mL) freshly squeezed orange juice

1. Heat six 1-cup (250 mL) jars in boiling water, and scald the lids, lifter, funnel and tongs (see page 18).

2. In a Maslin pan or canning kettle, combine raspberries, apple juice, lemon rind and bay leaves. Bring to a gentle boil over medium heat, stirring frequently. Crush the berries using a potato masher. Gently boil for about 5 minutes or until berries have softened into a mush.

3. Press mixture through a fine-mesh strainer, using a spatula to extract as much liquid as possible. Discard seeds, rind and bay leaves. Return raspberry juice to the pan and bring to a boil over high heat. Gradually add sugar, stirring until dissolved. Continue boiling gently; gradually add corn syrup and orange juice, stirring constantly. Bring to a full rolling boil, stirring constantly. Boil hard for 15 minutes.

4. Fill hot jars, leaving a 1/4-inch (5 mm) headspace. Run a thin non-metallic utensil around the inside of the jar to allow air to escape. Add more hot coulis, if necessary, to leave a 1/4-inch (5 mm) headspace. Wipe rims, top with flat lids and screw on metal rings. Return jars to the hot water bath, topping up with hot water if necessary. Bring to a full rolling boil and process jars for 10 minutes (see page 19).

5. Remove canner lid and wait 5 minutes before removing jars to a cooling rack to cool completely. Check seals, label and store in a cool place for up to 1 year.

Use: Drizzle over lemon cakes and pound cakes, crêpes and pancakes, ice cream and custards. Pool a few spoonfuls of raspberry coulis on a dessert plate or in a bowl and pile fresh fruit, puddings or custards over top.

raspberry tiramisù

A heavenly light dessert (pictured on page 47), this half-frozen cake layered with raspberry and cheese is easily made a day or two in advance. If the vanilla cake base is frozen one or two days ahead, the cheese and raspberry layers can be added in stages; freeze after each step. By doing this, your tiramisù will have a polished, professional look. Bring the cake out of the freezer one hour before serving.

Using a springform pan makes the job of removing the layered cake so much easier because the sides of the pan unhinge and slip easily away, leaving the cake on the base of the pan.

MAKES 8 TO 10 SERVINGS

VANILLA CAKE BASE
9-inch (23 cm) springform pan, lightly oiled
Preheat oven to 350°F (180°C)

2 eggs
1 cup (250 mL) granulated sugar
1-1/4 cups (300 mL) all-purpose flour
1 tsp (5 mL) baking powder

1/2 cup (125 mL) milk
1/3 cup (75 mL) vegetable oil
1/2 tsp (2 mL) pure vanilla extract

1. In a mixing bowl, beat eggs until light in colour. Add sugar and beat with an electric mixer until slightly thickened, about 1 minute. Add flour, baking powder, milk, vegetable oil and vanilla. Beat for about 1 minute or just until the batter is smooth and creamy. Don't overbeat. Pour the batter into the prepared springform pan.

2. Bake in preheated oven for 20 to 30 minutes or until the top is golden and a toothpick inserted into the centre comes out clean. Loosen around the edge of the cake with a thin knife and let the cake cool completely on a wire rack. Leaving the cake on the pan base, remove the side rim; wash rim and set aside. Cake base can be wrapped and stored for up to 2 days or wrapped tightly, labelled and frozen for up to 1 month.

FILLING
Springform side rim, lightly oiled

1 lb (500 g) ricotta cheese
1/2 cup (125 mL) vanilla yogurt
1/2 cup (125 mL) mascarpone cheese
1/3 cup (75 mL) icing sugar

1 cup (250 mL) Raspberry Curd (page 46)
1 Vanilla Cake Base on a springform base
  (recipe left)
1/2 cup (125 mL) fresh or frozen raspberries

1. In a food processor or blender, combine ricotta cheese, yogurt, mascarpone cheese and icing sugar; blend until smooth.

2. Fit the prepared side rim of the springform pan back around the cake base. Spread about two-thirds of the raspberry curd over the cake.

3. Pour the ricotta mixture over the raspberry curd and spread evenly with a spatula. Some of the cheese mixture may flow down the sides of the cake.

4. Place the cake in the freezer, being careful to keep it level, for at least 30 minutes or overnight. Spread the remaining raspberry curd over the cheese layer and return to the freezer or refrigerator until ready to serve. Remove from the freezer at least 1 hour before serving. Remove the rim of the springform pan and arrange raspberries around the top of the tiramisù.

raspberry curd

I love having this buttery, rich curd in my pantry because of its versatility and also because it makes a welcome gift any time of the year. It is similar to Lemon Curd (or Lemon Butter) but not as tart, so you can use it with sweeter desserts than you would the lemon version. If you freeze fresh raspberries, you can make Raspberry Curd any time of the year. It should be used within three weeks (if you can keep family from dipping into it right out of the jar!). Using the apples in the curd lightens up the intense raspberry flavour and colour, and helps to thicken the curd.

MAKES 4 CUPS (1 L)

**2-1/2 cups (625 mL) fresh or frozen
raspberries (12 oz/375 g)**
**4 cups (1 L) chopped cooking apples
(unpeeled)**
grated rind and juice of 1 lemon

3/4 cup (175 mL) butter, cut into chunks
1-1/2 cups (375 mL) granulated sugar
4 eggs, lightly beaten

1. Heat four 1-cup (250 mL) jars in boiling water, and scald the lids, lifter, funnel and tongs (see page 18).

2. In a saucepan, combine raspberries, apples, lemon rind and juice. Bring to a boil over medium-high heat, stirring occasionally. Reduce the heat to medium and simmer for 15 minutes, stirring occasionally, or until fruit is soft.

3. Purée the mixture by rubbing it through a sieve into a non-reactive bowl. Discard seeds and pulp.

4. Add butter, sugar and eggs to the raspberry purée. Place the bowl over a pan of simmering water and stir until the sugar is dissolved and the butter is melted. Continue to cook, stirring constantly, until the curd thickens enough to coat the back of a wooden spoon.

5. Fill hot jars, leaving a 1/4-inch (5 mm) headspace. Wipe rims, top with flat lids and screw on metal rings. Return jars to the hot water bath, topping up with hot water if necessary. Bring to a full rolling boil and process jars for 10 minutes (see page 19).

6. Remove canner lid and wait 5 minutes before removing jars to a cooling rack to cool completely. Check seals, label and store in the refrigerator for up to 2 months.

Use: This is a rich, buttery, silky-smooth confection that stands in for custard as a base for fruit tarts and flans. Substitute it for whipped cream as a topping for desserts, or thin with 1 tbsp (15 mL) rice vinegar and drizzle over fruit salads. Use it as a spread on toast or scones and as a filling for layer cakes and crêpes.

sweet raspberry vinegar

Before refrigeration, a popular way to preserve the unique taste of raspberries was to make vinegar from the macerated fresh berries. Stored in stoneware crocks or green glass jars, the vinegar was mixed with cool spring water or carbonated water for a refreshing summer drink called a "shrub." You can make it in the winter using frozen raspberries.

MAKES 3 CUPS (750 ML)

6 cups (1.5 L) fresh or frozen raspberries, divided

1-3/4 cups (425 mL) red or white wine vinegar, divided

2-1/2 cups (625 mL) granulated sugar

1. In a large non-reactive bowl or crock, combine 3 cups (750 mL) of the raspberries with 1-1/4 cups (300 mL) of the vinegar. Cover and let stand at room temperature for 24 hours.

2. Using a potato masher, mash the raspberries to a pulp. Strain the pulp through a coarse sieve set over a large non-reactive bowl or crock.
Press on solids with the back of a wooden spoon to release as much juice as possible.

3. Add remaining raspberries and vinegar to the strained juice. Cover and let stand for 24 hours at room temperature. Mash with a potato masher and strain the mixture through a coarse sieve into a Maslin pan or saucepan, pressing on solids with the back of a wooden spoon to release as much juice as possible. Discard pulp and seeds.

4. Meanwhile, sterilize three 1-cup (250 mL) jars, and scald the lids, lifter, funnel and tongs (see page 18).

5. Bring the strained juice to a boil over high heat, stirring frequently. Add sugar, 1 cup (250 mL) at a time, stirring until the sugar has been dissolved before adding the next cup. Boil lightly, stirring occasionally, for 10 to 15 minutes or until the mixture is thickened and is reduced to about 3 cups (750 mL). Do not overboil.

6. Fill hot jars, leaving a 1/4-inch (5 mm) headspace. Wipe rims, top with flat lids and screw on metal rings. Let cool on a towel or wire rack. Label and store in the refrigerator for up to 3 months.

Use: Substitute Sweet Raspberry Vinegar for rice vinegar in stir-fry dishes and fruit salads.

sweet raspberry vinaigrette

Try one of the nut oils—hazelnut, almond or walnut—in place of virgin olive oil in this sweet and tangy dressing. It's lovely on fruit and in light spring salads with baby arugula and other spring greens. Drizzle it over avocado, asparagus and almonds or walnuts. It is a beautiful red, with just the right amount of tangy sweetness.

MAKES 1/2 CUP (125 ML)

1/3 cup (75 mL) nut oil (see above)
3 tbsp (45 mL) Sweet Raspberry Vinegar (page 48)

In a jar with a tight-fitting lid, combine nut oil and vinegar. Put the lid on and shake well.

Freezing Raspberries

1. Select Equipment: Select suitable-size freezer containers, bags or Mason jars (see page 24).

2. Dry Pack

a) If you want whole raspberries to decorate cakes or for use in fruit salads, the best way to ensure that they hold their shape during freezing is to fast-freeze them individually. Arrange washed, completely dry berries in a single layer, without touching each other, on a cookie sheet. Fast-freeze for 1 hour. Pack into freezer containers (no need to leave headspace). Squeeze out air; seal, label and return to freezer.

OR

b) Fill pint (2-cup/500 mL) or quart (1 L) freezer containers with raspberries to within 3 to 4 inches (7 to 10 cm) of the top. Pour dry granulated sugar over top; use 1/2 cup (125 mL) sugar per quart (1 L) of prepared fruit. Squeeze out air; leave 1-inch (2.5 cm) headspace. Seal, label and freeze.

OR

Pack in Syrup: In a saucepan, combine 2-1/2 cups (625 mL) granulated sugar and 4 cups (1 L) water. Bring to a gentle boil over high heat, stirring frequently. Reduce heat and gently boil for 3 minutes. Let cool. Fill pint (2-cup/500 mL) or quart (1 L) freezer containers with raspberries to within 3 to 4 inches (7 to 10 cm) of the top of the container. Pour syrup over top; use 1 cup (250 mL) syrup per quart (1 L) of prepared fruit. Squeeze out air; leave 1-inch (2.5 cm) headspace. Seal, label and freeze.

OR

Crush: Using a potato masher, crush raspberries in a non-reactive bowl (or for seedless purée, press through a fine sieve into a non-reactive bowl). For every quart (1 L) of crushed raspberries, add 1 cup (250 mL) granulated sugar. Stir until the sugar is dissolved. Pack into freezer containers, leaving a 1-inch (2.5 cm) headspace. Seal, label and freeze.

Rhubarb

I LIST RHUBARB (*RHEUM RHABARBARUM*) as a fruit because of the way we use it, but in fact it is a vegetable belonging to the buckwheat family of plants. This is a plant that I see in both rural and city gardens everywhere in southwestern Ontario, where I live, and all across North America (except for southern states) because it thrives in climates where the temperatures dip below 40°F (4°C).

In the early spring, when not much else is happening in the garden, plump, oval bubble-like growths are emerging from the rhubarb crowns in the barely thawed earth, sometimes even through snow. If you watch closely, you can see that the thin membrane of the rusty red bubble splits under the pressure of the growing sprout and a tightly curled red, purple or green leaf bursts forth. From that stage, it is usually less than a month before we can begin to harvest the tart stalks of rhubarb. Each variety has slightly varying degrees of tartness, but overall this is a crop that requires some degree of sugar coating.

Essential: Leaves are poisonous.

Good Preserving Varieties
Rhubarb varieties are classed as red, green or speckled (pink), with red being the most widely available. All rhubarb varieties stand up well to the rigours of canning and freezing. Some of my favourites are listed below.

Canada Red: Produces shorter, more slender stalks than other varieties, but is tender and very sweet, with good red colour.
Cherry Red (also known as Cherry or Early Cherry): Long, thick stalks that are a rich red inside and out; an excellent variety for preserving; juicy, tender and sweet.
Crimson Red (also called Crimson, Crimson Cherry or Crimson Wine): Grows tall; plump, brightly coloured red stalks.
Valentine: Good hearty variety for canning; has broad, deep red stalks that retain a good rosy colour when cooked; somewhat lower in acid than other red varieties.
Victoria: A speckled type that produces medium stalks that are sweet and not tough or stringy. Although there is some variation in stalk colour depending on the cultivar, in general the light green stalks develop pink speckling, especially at the bottom.

Purchasing/Storing
- 1 lb (500 g) trimmed rhubarb yields 2 cups (500 mL) coarsely cubed rhubarb.
- You will need 1-1/2 lb (750 g) for each quart (1 L) jar.

Select firm, crisp, thin stalks that are 8 to 15 inches (20 to 38 cm) long. Cut rhubarb should snap when bent. To harvest, twist off the leaf stalk at the soil line, cut off and safely dispose of the leaf. Rhubarb can be stored for up to 2 weeks if tightly covered and kept in the crisper drawer of the refrigerator.

Good With
- Herbs such as bay, chervil, tarragon, sweet cicely.
- Sweet seasonings such as cinnamon, ginger, cloves, nutmeg, vanilla.
- Savoury spices such as cardamom, cumin, coriander.
- Other fruit, such as strawberries, raspberries, peaches, nectarines, apricots, prunes, plums.
- Toasted almonds, pecans and walnuts, currants.
- Egg puddings and custards.
- Game birds such as goose, duck, pheasant, quail, grouse, partridge, guinea fowl.

Preparation
Even if grown organically, rhubarb is still a plant that contacts the soil while growing, so it should be washed before using. Swish rhubarb in a sink full of cool water to which a drop or two of food-safe liquid soap has been added. Rinse well, drain and pat dry. Cut stalks into 1/2- to 1-inch (1 to 2.5 cm) pieces.

Canning Rhubarb

See detailed canning information, page 14.

1. Prepare Equipment: Wash and heat pint (2-cup/500 mL) or quart (1 L) jars, and scald the lids, funnel, ladle and tongs (see page 18).

2. Stew with Sugar: In a Maslin pan or canning kettle, combine 1/2 cup (125 mL) granulated sugar for every 4 cups (1 L) of rhubarb chunks. Let the mixture stand at room temperature until the juice appears. This could take 30 minutes or longer, depending on the amount of rhubarb. Bring to a boil over medium-high heat; remove from heat and skim off any foam.

3. Pack rhubarb into jars hot (the tartness of rhubarb requires that it be stewed with sugar and not packed raw).

Hot Pack Method: Fill hot jars with stewed rhubarb, leaving a 1/2-inch (1 cm) headspace. Run a non-metallic utensil around the inside of the jar to allow air to escape. Add more hot rhubarb, if necessary, to leave a 1/2-inch (1 cm) headspace. Wipe sealing edge of jars with a clean, damp, lint-free cloth. Position flat lids over the tops of jars and hand-tighten screw bands.

4. Process rhubarb in a canner: Use a Boiling Water Canner according to the chart below.

Processing Times at Different Altitudes for Stewed Rhubarb in a BOILING WATER Canner					
Pack Style	**Jar Size**	**0–1000 ft**	**1001–3000 ft**	**3001–6000 ft**	**6000+ ft**
HOT	Pints	15 min	20 min	25 min	30 min
	Quarts	20 min	25 min	30 min	35 min
RAW	Pints	20 min	25 min	30 min	35 min
	Quarts	25 min	30 min	35 min	40 min

OR

Process rhubarb in a Pressure Canner following manufacturer's directions for steam pressure and time at your altitude.

5. Cool, Label and Store: Lift jars from canner and place on a clean towel or rack. Do not re-tighten screw bands. Let the jars cool to room temperature. This may take from 12 to 24 hours. Remove and store screw bands. Check lid seals (see page 19). Wipe and label sealed jars. Store in a cool, dark place.

rhubarb orange chutney

Being a cool-season perennial, rhubarb thrives in regions that have temperatures below 40°F (4°C), because this is essential for the plant to break dormancy. I think every Canadian has a rhubarb story. Mine involves a small bowl of sugar, a stalk of rhubarb and a quiet space between the garden and the orchard—a deliciously sweet-sour memory of simple times. A good rhubarb patch will produce for a decade or more.

MAKES 8 CUPS (2 L)

8 cups (2 L) chopped fresh rhubarb
3 cups (750 mL) coarsely chopped onions
2 cups (500 mL) golden raisins
1-1/2 cups (375 mL) cider vinegar
2 tbsp (25 mL) grated orange rind
3/4 cup (175 mL) freshly squeezed
   orange juice
1/4 cup (50 mL) freshly squeezed
   lemon juice
6 cloves garlic, finely chopped
2 tbsp (25 mL) finely chopped
   fresh gingerroot

3 cups (750 mL) granulated sugar
3 cups (750 mL) lightly packed brown sugar
1 tbsp (15 mL) pickling salt
1 tbsp (15 mL) mustard seeds
2 tsp (10 mL) ground allspice
2 tsp (10 mL) ground coriander
1 tsp (5 mL) hot red pepper flakes, or
   to taste
1/2 tsp (2 mL) ground cinnamon
1/4 tsp (1 mL) ground cloves

1. Heat four 1-pint (2-cup/500 mL) jars in boiling water, and scald the lids, lifter, funnel and tongs (see page 18).

2. In a Maslin pan or canning kettle, combine rhubarb, onions, raisins, vinegar, orange rind, orange juice, lemon juice, garlic and ginger. Bring to a boil over high heat, stirring constantly. Add granulated and brown sugars, 1 cup (250 mL) at a time, stirring to dissolve before adding the next cup. Reduce heat and boil gently, stirring occasionally, for 45 minutes. Add salt, mustard seeds, allspice, coriander, red pepper flakes, cinnamon and cloves. Boil gently, stirring frequently, for about 40 minutes or until mixture thickens enough to mound on a wooden spoon.

3. Skim off and discard any foam. Fill hot jars, leaving a 1/4-inch (5 mm) headspace. Run a thin non-metallic utensil around the inside of the jar to allow air to escape. Add more hot chutney, if necessary, to leave a 1/4-inch (5 mm) headspace. Wipe rims, top with flat lids and screw on metal rings. Return jars to the hot water bath, topping up with hot water if necessary. Bring to a full rolling boil and process jars for 10 minutes (see page 19).

4. Remove canner lid and wait 5 minutes before removing jars to a towel or rack to cool completely. Check seals, label and store in a cool place for up to 1 year.

Use: A very good condiment with game and wild meats; the tartness of the rhubarb cuts through the fat of duck and goose meats and mellows dark turkey meat.

grilled rhubarb orange chicken burgers

In the summer, grilled chicken breasts are an easy and healthy alternative to hamburgers. I keep boneless, skinless chicken breasts in a freezer bag, separated by waxed paper so that no matter how many people drop by, I always have an easy grilling dinner solution. The rhubarb lends a sweet-tart taste to chicken or game birds. Let the chicken thaw in the chutney overnight in the refrigerator or at room temperature for about 2 hours before grilling time. Sometimes I have rushed the thawing process and found that if chicken breasts are grilled when just slightly frozen, they stay moister during the dry cooking. Just be sure that they are cooked through. Chicken breasts are done when the juices run clear and there is no sign of pink or redness. Be sure to pass extra chutney for guests to add to their "burger."

MAKES 4 SERVINGS

2 boneless, skinless chicken breasts, halved lengthwise
1/4 cup (50 mL) Rhubarb Orange Chutney (page 56)
1 tbsp (15 mL) olive oil + extra for brushing

4 burger buns or 8 baguette slices
4 slices brie cheese, at room temperature
roasted red pepper or tomato slices, and mixed salad leaves, to serve

1. In a shallow dish, lay out the chicken breasts in single layer. Spoon Rhubarb Orange Chutney over top and let stand, covered, for 30 minutes at room temperature or overnight in the refrigerator.

2. Heat the olive oil in a cast iron grilling pan on high or heat barbecue to high. Char-grill the chicken for 2 minutes per side or until cooked through (see above).

3. Meanwhile, brush the bun halves with oil and grill for 1 minute or until lightly toasted. Cover lower bun halves with grilled chicken and top with softened brie. Let guests top their own sandwiches with roasted red pepper, tomato and greens.

rhubarb and raspberry jam

The combination of tart rhubarb and pure raspberry sweetness is balanced by the apple in this jam. It can be used to top brie in a sandwich or salad, and also steps into breakfast duty for topping pancakes, waffles, scones and muffins. The taste is very fruity.

MAKES 6 CUPS (1.5 L)

3 cups (750 mL) chopped fresh rhubarb
3 cups (750 mL) fresh raspberries
1 cup (250 mL) finely chopped cored
   peeled apple
4 cups (1 L) granulated sugar

3 tbsp (45 mL) freshly squeezed
   lemon juice
1 pouch (3 oz/85 mL) liquid pectin

1. In a Maslin pan or canning kettle, combine rhubarb, raspberries and apple. Add sugar and lemon juice. Stir well and let stand at room temperature until the juice appears, about 20 minutes.

2. Meanwhile, heat four 1-cup (250 mL) jars in boiling water, and scald the lids, lifter, funnel and tongs (see page 18).

3. Bring fruit mixture to a full rolling boil over high heat, stirring constantly. Stir in the pectin. Boil hard, stirring constantly, for 1 minute. Skim off and discard any foam. Fill hot jars, leaving a 1/4-inch (5 mm) headspace. Run a thin non-metallic utensil around the inside of the jar to allow air to escape. Add more hot jam, if necessary, to leave a 1/4-inch (5 mm) headspace. Wipe rims, top with flat lids and screw on metal rings. Return jars to the hot water bath, topping up with hot water if necessary. Bring to a full rolling boil and process jars for 10 minutes (see page 19).

4. Remove canner lid and wait 5 minutes before removing jars to a towel or rack to cool completely. Check seals, label and store in a cool place for up to 1 year.

Use: Rich red and sweet-tart in taste, this is a surprisingly delicious jam to spread on muffins and serve with scrambled eggs. It brightens everything you team it with.

Freezing Rhubarb

1. Blanch Rhubarb: Wash, trim and cut into 1-inch (2.5 cm) chunks or lengths to fit the freezer package you will be using. Blanch in boiling water for 1 minute, timing after the water returns to a boil. Immerse in cold water for 1 minute. Drain and pat dry.

2. Pack in Syrup: In a saucepan, combine 2-1/2 cups (625 mL) granulated sugar and 4 cups (1 L) water. Bring to a gentle boil over high heat, stirring frequently. Reduce heat and gently boil for 3 minutes. Let cool. Fill pint (2-cup/500 mL) or quart (1 L) freezer bags or jars with chunks or lengths to within 3 to 4 inches (7 to 10 cm) of the top of the bag. Pour syrup over top; use 1 cup (250 mL) syrup per quart (1 L) of prepared fruit. Squeeze out air; leave 1-inch (2.5 cm) headspace. Seal, label and freeze.

OR

Dry-Pack, Unsweetened: Fill pint (2-cup/500 mL) or quart (1 L) freezer bags with rhubarb chunks or rhubarb lengths to within 3 to 4 inches (7 to 10 cm) of the top of the bag. Squeeze out air; leave 1-inch (2.5 cm) headspace. Seal, label and freeze.

Strawberries

LIKE THE RASPBERRY, THE CONE-SHAPED STRAWBERRY is an aggregate fruit with about 100 tiny seeded fruits gathered around a central hub, called a "peduncle." Jams and preserves are often strained in order to remove the seeds. Anglo-Saxons had their *stréawbrerige*, the French still have their *fraises de bois* (wood strawberries from woodland meadows), and North Americans have *Fragaria vesca Americana*, a native wild strawberry still considered the tastiest of all varieties now in existence.

Good Preserving Varieties

The strawberry came into cultivation in Europe around the end of the 13th century. Explorers of the New World discovered a large variety, *Fragaria virginiana*, widely used and cultivated by Natives, and brought it back to Europe to be bred with the smaller varieties. New varieties of the succulent heart-shaped delicacy were developed only 200 years ago, with more than 1,000 types springing from two European and two New World berries.

Depending on the variety, strawberry plants bear fruit from early, to mid, to late in the season, so your local growers could have strawberries from June to July. The day-neutral strawberry plant is an everbearing type that produces fruit from June through October. Flavour, size and flesh quality of strawberries will vary with soil and weather conditions from year to year, as well as with the age of the plants. Most varieties are great for freezing and for making preserves.

Allstar: Large-size late variety; orange-red colour; firm flesh with very good flavour.
Annapolis: Medium- to large-size early variety; orange to red; plump and firm berries.
Evangeline: Medium-size early variety; beautiful fruit, firm skin, pleasing shape, with large green, easy-to-remove calyx; the berries are richly aromatic.
Glooscap: Medium- to large-size early variety; dark colour with pale raised seeds; decaps easily, making it good for freezing.
Seascape: Day-neutral variety with very large berry; peaks in August and early September; bright, light red fruit with excellent flavour; good for freezing.

Purchasing/Storing

1 lb (500 g) yields 2 cups (500 mL) sliced strawberries.

Strawberries should be dry, evenly shaped and firm (not hard), with even bright red colour. Berries with green spots or white around the crowns do not ripen well after they are picked. Strawberries are very perishable and should be transported from the market in a cooler. Store only if necessary, unwashed, for one or two days in the refrigerator; they deteriorate at room temperature.

Good With

- Anise herbs such as tarragon, chervil and sweet cicely.
- Peppery seasonings such as nasturtium, watercress, black pepper.
- Semi-hard cheeses such as Gouda, Jarlsberg.
- Other fruit, such as apricots, peaches, nectarines, rhubarb.
- Other berries, such as blackberries, blueberries, loganberries, mulberries, raspberries.
- Toasted walnuts, pine nuts and sunflower seeds; chocolate; lemon and citrus desserts.
- Balsamic vinegar.
- Chicken; mild fish such as haddock, tilapia, orange roughy, sole.

Preparation

Do not wash strawberries until just before preserving. Remove caps (hull). Using a sieve, hold 1 or 2 quarts (1 or 2 L) at a time under lightly flowing cool water for a few seconds. Do not soak. Drain and pat dry.

Canning Strawberries

Because of the high water content of strawberries, canning them produces a poor-quality product. The texture becomes mushy and the colour brownish, making them unappealing, so I recommend preserving them in jams, jellies, spreads, compotes and other forms.

Crushing Fruit for Jam and Sauce

When a smooth texture is desired (and the juice from soft fruit must be extracted when making jelly), the fruit is crushed or mashed. To crush soft fruit, wash and trim as directed for each fruit. Arrange fresh fruit in a single layer in a large flat dish (a glass pie plate works well) or in a large mixing bowl.

Using a potato masher, crush small whole berries or halved larger strawberries until soft and pulpy. Measure each lot as you crush it and transfer to a non-reactive bowl or the pan. Continue to crush fresh fruit until you have the amount needed for the recipe.

strawberry sauce

I have included directions for both freezing and canning this delicious sauce because I like the convenience of having an easy dessert solution with the twist of a lid. But I know that other people, much more organized than I, prefer to save preparation time by freezing it. Either way, having a strawberry sauce ready for any dessert, waffle or pancake I throw at it is very satisfying. You can halve the recipe by using half the amount of strawberries, lemon, sugar and brown sugar but keeping the amounts for the molasses and Sweet Raspberry Vinegar the same.

MAKES 8 CUPS (2 L)

8 cups (2 L) halved fresh strawberries
grated rind and juice of 1 lemon
1/2 cup (125 mL) granulated sugar
1/2 cup (125 mL) packed brown sugar
1 tbsp (15 mL) molasses

1 tbsp (15 mL) Sweet Raspberry Vinegar
(page 48 or store-bought) or balsamic
vinegar

In a Maslin pan or canning kettle, crush strawberries with a potato masher (see sidebar on page 62). Add lemon rind and lemon juice. Stir in granulated and brown sugar, molasses and raspberry vinegar. Bring to a full rolling boil over high heat, stirring until the sugar dissolves. Boil hard, stirring occasionally, for 15 minutes. Skim off and discard any foam.

If freezing:

Let cool and ladle into four 1-pint (2-cup/500 mL) freezer containers. Squeeze out air; leave 1-inch (2.5 cm) headspace. Seal, label and freeze.

If canning:

1. Heat eight 1-cup (250 mL) jars in boiling water, and scald the lids, lifter, funnel and tongs (see page 18).

2. Fill hot jars, leaving a 1/4-inch (5 mm) headspace. Run a thin non-metallic utensil around the inside of the jar to allow air to escape. Add more hot sauce, if necessary, to leave a 1/4-inch (5 mm) headspace. Wipe rims, top with flat lids and screw on metal rings. Return jars to the hot water bath, topping up with hot water if necessary. Bring to a full rolling boil and process jars for 10 minutes (see page 19).

3. Remove canner lid and wait 5 minutes before removing jars to a towel or rack to cool completely. Check seals, label and store in a cool place for up to 1 year.

Use: Once you have this in your freezer or pantry, you will find dozens of ways to serve it. At breakfast or brunch, top waffles, pancakes, crêpes, muffins, coffee cakes, scones and other baked products or eggy puddings. Piped out of a squeeze bottle or drizzled over warm cakes, it lends a professional finish to desserts. Mix it with oil and vinegar for a fruit dressing.

classic strawberry jam with pectin

Nature works in wondrous ways. Whether by accident or by design, the delicately lacy-leaved herb sweet cicely happens to be at its peak during strawberry season. Sweet cicely (Myrrhis odorata, see page 94), with its sweet anise flavour, is the perfect foil for the fresh, tart flavour of strawberries. For fresh eating, use sweet cicely generously—3 or 4 tbsp (45 or 50 mL) chopped fresh per cup (250 mL) of fresh strawberries. For preserving, use considerably less, as I have done here.

On the other hand, fresh French tarragon (Artemesia dracunculus sativa, adds a sophisti-cated, peppery zing to fresh and cooked strawberry dishes, but use it sparingly—about 1 tbsp (15 mL) chopped fresh tarragon for every 1 cup (250 mL) of fresh strawberries. In this recipe, I am judicious with the tarragon because it will have lots of time to infuse the jam as it sits in the jam cupboard.

In my view, there are three ways to make classic strawberry jam, a favourite of almost every-one. The traditional way was to add some tart cooking apples for their natural pectin and boil the fruit mixture long in order to make the jam set. That was the only way to get a thick, jammy texture, but it did alter the pure taste of the strawberries. Once powdered and liquid fruit pectin became available to home cooks, sometime in the first half of the 20th century, it was possible to use low-acid fruit such as strawberries without adding high-acid apples or citrus peel, and the result was a pure, more strawberry-tasting jam. Nowadays, again thanks to food science, we are able to reduce (or actually eliminate) the amount of sugar in jam by using no-sugar-needed pectin. Predictably, my preference falls in the middle of the road: pure fruit and sugar, using commercial pectin to help it set. But because there are people who, for health reasons (Type 2 diabetes for one), have not enjoyed the taste of homemade jam for a long time, I am including the method for making no-sugar strawberry jam (page 66).

MAKES 8 CUPS (2 L)

5 cups (1.25 L) crushed strawberries
2 tbsp (25 mL) freshly squeezed
  lemon juice
1 pkg (1–3/4 oz/49 to 57 g) fruit pectin
  crystals

7 cups (1.75 L) granulated sugar
3 tbsp (45 mL) finely chopped fresh sweet
  cicely or tarragon, optional

1. Heat eight 1-cup (250 mL) jars in boiling water, and scald the lids, lifter, funnel and tongs (see page 18).

2. In a Maslin pan or canning kettle, combine strawberries and lemon juice. Sprinkle pectin over fruit and stir until dissolved. Bring to a full rolling boil over high heat, stirring constantly. Add sugar in a steady stream, all at once and stirring constantly. Return to a full rolling boil that cannot be stirred

down. Boil, stirring constantly, for 1 minute. Remove the pan from the heat and stir in sweet cicely, if using. Stir for 5 minutes.

3. Skim off and discard any foam. Fill hot jars, leaving a 1/4-inch (5 mm) headspace. Run a thin non-metallic utensil around the inside of the jar to allow air to escape. Add more hot jam, if necessary, to leave a 1/4-inch (5 mm) headspace. Wipe rims, top with flat lids and screw on metal rings. Return jars to the hot water bath, topping up with hot water if necessary. Bring to a full rolling boil and process jars for 10 minutes (see page 19).

4. Remove canner lid and wait 5 minutes before removing jars to a towel or rack to cool completely. Check seals, label and store in a cool place for up to 1 year.

low- or no-sugar strawberry jam

If you use No Sugar Needed Fruit Pectin, you can choose to either lower the amount of sugar or eliminate the sugar altogether by substituting artificial granular sugar replacement. What follows is the recipe for using no sugar.

MAKES 4 CUPS (1 L)

4 cups (1 L) crushed strawberries
1 cup (250 mL) unsweetened apple or white grape juice
1 pkg (1.75 oz/49 to 57 g) No Sugar Needed Fruit Pectin

1 cup (250 mL) low-calorie granular sweetener

1. Heat five 1-cup (250 mL) jars in boiling water, and scald the lids, lifter, funnel and tongs (see page 18).

2. In a Maslin pan or canning kettle, combine strawberries and apple juice. Sprinkle pectin over fruit and stir until dissolved. Bring to a full rolling boil over high heat, stirring constantly. Boil, stirring frequently, for 5 minutes. Remove the pan from the heat and stir in sweetener.

3. Skim off and discard any foam. Fill hot jars, leaving a 1/4-inch (5 mm) headspace. Run a thin non-metallic utensil around the inside of the jar to allow air to escape. Add more hot jam, if necessary, to leave a 1/4-inch (5 mm) headspace. Wipe rims, top with flat lids and screw on metal rings. Return jars to the hot water bath, topping up with hot water if necessary. Bring to a full rolling boil and process jars for 10 minutes (see page 19).

4. Remove canner lid and wait 5 minutes before removing jars to a towel or rack to cool completely. Check seals, label and store in a cool place for up to 1 year.

strawberry cappuccino

If you have frozen strawberries, they actually work better than fresh in this smooth drink because blending in frozen fruit will make it thicker. This drink is quick, easy and so good for you. The strawberry jam intensifies the strawberry flavour but is not absolutely essential.

MAKES 2 SERVINGS

2 cups (500 mL) chopped fresh or frozen strawberries
1 cup (250 mL) vanilla yogurt

1/4 cup (50 mL) Classic Strawberry Jam (page 64) or Strawberry Sauce (page 63)

In a blender, combine strawberries, yogurt and strawberry jam. Blend until smooth.

scone wedges with strawberry jam

Still a spring ritual in church basements and community halls all over rural Canada, invitingly homey strawberry festivals launch buckets of local strawberries toward a delectable end. Once sliced and sugared, they virtually float atop homemade flaky biscuits or scones crowned with great dollops of real whipped cream.

2 baking sheets, lightly oiled
Preheat oven to 425°F (220°C)
MAKES 16 SCONE WEDGES

2 cups (500 mL) unbleached all-purpose flour
1/3 cup (75 mL) granulated sugar
2 tsp (10 mL) baking powder
1/2 tsp (2 mL) salt
6 tbsp (90 mL) cold butter
3/4 cup (175 mL) dried currants

1/2 cup (125 mL) heavy (whipping) cream or milk
2 large eggs, beaten
1 cup (250 mL) Classic Strawberry Jam (page 64 or store-bought)
3 cups (750 mL) whipped cream

1. In a mixing bowl, sift together flour, sugar, baking powder and salt. Using a pastry blender or 2 knives, cut in the butter until the mixture resembles coarse crumbs. Add currants and toss to combine.

2. Whisk cream and eggs. Make a well in the centre of the flour mixture and pour in the egg mixture all at once. Using a fork, mix the wet ingredients into the dry ingredients until the dough begins to clump together. Lightly knead the dough in the bowl with your fingertips for about 10 seconds. Do not overmix the dough or the scones will be tough.

3. Turn out the dough onto a lightly floured surface and divide into 2 pieces. Using your hands, form one piece into a ball and flatten it to form a circle measuring 5 inches (12 cm) in diameter and 3/4 inch (2 cm) thick. Transfer the flattened disc to a prepared baking sheet. Cut the circle of dough into 8 wedges. Using a metal spatula, move the wedges around the pan, to allow about 1 inch (2.5 cm) of space between each. Repeat with the second piece of dough.

4. Bake in preheated oven for 8 to 12 minutes or until puffed and lightly brown around the edges. Be careful not to overbake and burn the wedges on the bottom. Transfer to a cooling rack and let cool for 2 to 3 minutes.

5. To serve: Cut a scone wedge in half. Drop 3 tbsp (45 mL) strawberry jam over the bottom piece. Replace the other wedge and top with a dollop of whipped cream.

strawberry rhubarb freezer pie filling

For this sweet-tart pie filling, the rhubarb is stewed until it forms a sweetened, thick sauce in which the strawberries float. Do bring the strawberries to a boil, but as soon as they reach that point, remove the pan from the heat altogether to keep them somewhat intact. If the strawberries are small, leave them whole; otherwise cut large ones in half. Three cups (750 mL) of frozen filling will fill a standard 9-inch (23 cm) pie.

MAKES ENOUGH FOR TWO 9-INCH (23 cm) PIES

5 cups (1.25 L) chopped fresh or frozen rhubarb
2 cups (500 mL) chopped apple
juice of 1/2 orange
juice of 1/2 lemon

1/2 tsp (2 mL) salt
1-1/2 cups (375 mL) packed brown sugar
1 cup (250 mL) granulated sugar
8 cups (2 L) fresh strawberries, whole if small, halved if large

1. In a Maslin pan or canning kettle, combine rhubarb, apple, orange juice and lemon juice. Sprinkle salt over top and let stand at room temperature for 30 minutes. Stir in the brown and granulated sugars. Bring to a boil over medium-high, stirring constantly. Reduce heat and boil gently for 10 to 15 minutes or until rhubarb is tender and mixture is thick. Add strawberries and bring to a boil. Remove from heat and let cool.

2. Divide pie filling between two 1-quart (1 L) freezer bags. Press out air and seal. Shape into two empty pie plates, label and freeze. Remove pie plates when filling is frozen.

Use: As delightful as pies and galettes are (see page 72), you don't have to make them in order to use this sweet-tart filling. You can heat it and spoon it over custard, yogurt or ice cream; use it to top cheesecake or as a sauce for chocolate mousse, cakes and other desserts. Having it in the freezer has saved me from dessert-less dinners many times.

To Make Strawberry Rhubarb Pie: Thaw a 3-cup (750 mL) container of Strawberry Rhubarb Freezer Pie Filling and mix it with 2 tbsp (25 mL) quick-cooking tapioca. Preheat oven to 400°F (200°C). Line a 10-inch (25 cm) pie plate with pastry (see Strawberry Rhubarb Galette, page 72) or purchase a 9-inch (23 cm) pie shell. Fill the shell with the strawberry rhubarb filling. Dot the top with 2 tbsp (25 mL) butter, cut into small pieces. Make an open lattice pastry top for the pie or cut a round of foil about 8 inches (20 cm) in diameter and place in the centre of the pie. Bake in preheated oven for 20 minutes. Reduce heat to 350°F (180°C) and bake for 30 to 40 minutes or until pastry is golden and filling is bubbly.

Wait until the rhubarb has thickened before adding the strawberries because if you cook both at the same time, the strawberries will soften to a jam consistency.

I like to fill a freezer bag with 3 cups (750 mL) of filling and freeze it in a pie plate so that when the filling is frozen and the pie plate is removed, the filling is frozen roughly in the shape of the dish. I can then fill the pastry with partially thawed filling and bake for a bit longer than if the filling were completely thawed.

strawberry rhubarb galette

There are a few interpretations of what a galette actually is. In France it can mean a large buckwheat crepe that is filled with cooked meats or fish, cheese and vegetables or with sweet fruits like apples or berries. At other times, a galette describes any number of flat, rustic cakes or tarts. Puff pastry squares spread with mascarpone cheese or almond paste, topped with sliced apples and glazed with honey or simple syrup are an elegant type of galette. Here in North America, we use the term for a fruit-filled tart where the bottom pastry is folded up over the filling. I find that rolling one big bottom pastry disc is easier: less pastry to mess with and the result is delightfully whimsical and informal.

9-inch pie plate
Preheat oven to 400°F (200°C)
MAKES 1 GALETTE PLUS PASTRY FOR ONE MORE

2-1/2 cups (625 mL) all-purpose flour
2 tbsp (25 mL) granulated sugar
1/2 tsp (2 mL) salt
1/4 tsp (1 mL) ground cardamom
1/2 cup (125 mL) unsalted butter, cut into
  1/2-inch (1 cm) pieces, chilled

2/3 cup (150 mL) ice water
3 cups (750 mL) Strawberry Rhubarb
  Freezer Pie Filling (page 70), thawed
1/3 cup (50 mL) tapioca

1. In a large bowl, combine flour, sugar, salt and cardamom. Using a pastry blender or 2 knives, cut in the chilled butter until pieces are the size of peas. If using a food processor to blend in the butter, use the pulse button (or an on/off motion) and blend until the butter is evenly distributed but still in pieces about the size of sugar cubes.

2. Add ice water all at once to the flour and butter. Mix the ingredients until they begin to come together as dough. If you are using a food processor, add the water all at once through the opening in the lid with the motor running. Be careful not to overmix or the pastry will be tough. Gather the dough into a ball with your hands.

3. Cut the dough in half and shape it into 2 discs. Wrap the discs in plastic wrap and refrigerate for at least 1 hour. (This recipe makes enough dough for 2 tarts; you can freeze one of the discs for future use if you like, for up to 2 months. Thaw in the refrigerator 1 day before using.)

4. Unwrap one pastry disc. On a lightly floured surface, roll out disc until it is about 1/4 inch (5 mm) thick. Using 2 lifters, or rolling it around the rolling pin, transfer it to a 9-inch (23 cm) pie plate, allowing the excess to hang over the sides. Press the dough so that it lines the bottom and sides of the plate.

Combine pie filling and tapioca. Pour the mixture into the pie shell. Lift up the overhanging pastry edges and fold toward the centre of the pie, pleating the dough as needed to make it fit. This folded-over pastry will partially cover the filling, leaving an open central portion where the filling will show.

5. Bake in preheated oven for 20 minutes. Reduce heat to 350°F (180°C) and bake for 30 to 40 minutes or until pastry is golden and filling is bubbly.

Freezing Strawberries

1. Select Equipment: Select suitable-size freezer containers, bags or Mason jars (see page 24).

2. Pack in Syrup: In a saucepan, combine 2-1/2 cups (625 mL) granulated sugar and 4 cups (1 L) water. Bring to a gentle boil over high heat, stirring frequently. Reduce heat and gently boil for 3 minutes. Let cool. Fill pint (2-cup/500 mL) or quart (1 L) freezer containers with whole or halved strawberries to within 3 to 4 inches (7 to 10 cm) of the top. Pour syrup over top; use 1 cup (250 mL) syrup per quart (1 L) of prepared fruit. Squeeze out air; leave 1-inch (2.5 cm) headspace. Seal, label and freeze.

OR

Dry Pack:

a) If you want whole strawberries to decorate cakes or for use in fruit salads, the best way to ensure that they hold their shape during freezing is to fast-freeze them individually. Arrange completely dry berries in a single layer, without touching each other, on a cookie sheet. Fast-freeze for 1 hour. Pack into freezer containers (no need to leave headspace); squeeze out air. Seal, label and return to freezer.

b) Fill pint (2-cup/500 mL) or quart (1 L) freezer containers with whole or halved strawberries to within 3 to 4 inches (7 to 10 cm) of the top. Pour dry granulated sugar over top; use 1/2 cup (125 mL) sugar per quart (1 L) of prepared fruit. Squeeze out air; leave 1-inch (2.5 cm) headspace. Seal, label and freeze.

OR

Crush: Using a potato masher, crush strawberries in a non-reactive bowl (or for seedless purée, press through a fine sieve into a non-reactive bowl). For every quart (1 L) of crushed strawberries, add 1 cup (250 mL) granulated sugar and 1 tbsp (15 mL) lemon juice. Stir until the sugar is dissolved. Pack into freezer containers, leaving a 1-inch (2.5 cm) headspace. Seal, label and freeze.

Artichokes

YOU MIGHT THINK THAT ARTICHOKES RESEMBLE THISTLES, and you would be right. These perennial plants belong to the sunflower family, of which thistles are members. Globe artichokes (*Cynara scolymus*) are the unopened flower buds of the plant. Although traditionally harvested in the spring, artichokes are now available year-round in some places, with peak seasons being spring and fall. The Jerusalem artichoke, also known as sunchoke, is a tuber and not suitable for canning.

Good Preserving Varieties
Big Heart: Conical with a wide base, this artichoke is thornless and easy to prepare for preserving; available early spring, summer and fall.
Desert Globe: Winter and early spring availability; plump heavy hearts.
Green Globe: From California and available year-round, the roundish globe-shaped varieties are prevalent in winter and spring; the conical, thornier varieties are available in summer and fall.

Purchasing/Storing
- 1 globe artichoke weighs about 1 lb (500 g), about half that when trimmed.
- You will need 3 to 4 lb (1.5 to 2 kg) for each quart (1 L) jar.

Artichokes are actually flower buds, and the bracts (green petal-like leaves) should be tightly closed when you buy them. Select artichokes that are firm and heavy for their size because that indicates a large edible heart. Winter harvests may show frost damage (bronze or brown tinges) on the outer bracts, a cosmetic defect only (many people prefer the nuttier flavour of frost-damaged artichokes). Keep moist: store in the refrigerator wrapped in a damp towel for up to 1 week, but try to preserve them as soon as possible.

Good With
- Lemon herbs such as lemon balm, lemongrass, lemon verbena.
- Savoury seasonings such as coriander, cumin, parsley, raspberry vinegar.
- All cheeses, especially Parmesan, Gruyère, pecorino and goat cheese.
- Sauces such as aïoli, tartar sauce, Asparagus Sauce (page 88).
- Other vegetables, such as eggplant, asparagus, tomatoes, onions, zucchini.
- Veal, beef, tuna, swordfish, shrimp, chicken.
- Toasted pine nuts, sunflower seeds, sesame seeds, almonds.
- Often served as appetizers or starters.

Preparation

1. To prevent discolouration, in a large canner or soup pot, mix 1/2 cup (125 mL) fresh lemon juice or 1 tsp (5 mL) crystalline ascorbic acid or six 500 mg vitamin C tablets in 1 gallon (4 L) cool water.

2. Trim: Snap off the dark green outer leaves, leaving the pale, tender inner leaves on the stem. Trim off all but 1/2 inch (1 cm) of the stem. Trim away the top third of the artichoke leaves. As you trim each artichoke, place in the pan of acidulated water.

3. Blanch: Place a pie plate on the artichokes to submerge them in the water in order to blanch them evenly. Bring the water to a boil over high heat. Cover and simmer for 5 minutes. Remove pie plate and lift artichokes out of the water. Immerse in cold water for 5 minutes. Drain and pat dry.

4. Quarter and Cut Away Choke: Use a paring knife to peel away the tough outer layer of the stem and to remove the base of the leaves. Cut the artichoke in half, then in half again. Use a spoon to scoop away and discard the hairy choke at the centre of each quarter. Using scissors, clip and discard thorny tops of inner leaves of each quarter. As the artichokes are cut and trimmed, pack them into hot quart jars (see step 4).

Canning Artichokes

Commercially canned artichokes are preserved in a marinade of oil and vinegar with some herbs added. Home pressure canners cannot reach the temperatures required to kill spore-forming bacteria, and home canning in oil is not safe. This sweet vinegar brine adds enough acid to the non-acid artichokes to enable you to safely process them using a water bath. Do not substitute water or broth for the brine; or, if you do, be sure to process using a pressure canner following the manufacturer's instructions for time at your elevation.

See detailed canning information, page 20.

1. Trim, blanch and quarter artichokes as described above.

2. Prepare Equipment: Wash and heat pint (2-cup/500 mL) or quart (1 L) jars, and scald the lids, funnel, ladle and tongs (see page 18).

3. Make Vinegar Brine to cover artichokes. You will need about 1-1/2 cups (375 mL) per quart (1 L) jar quartered artichokes. In a large saucepan, combine 1 cup (250 mL) white wine vinegar and 1/2 cup (125 mL) packed brown sugar. Bring to a boil over high heat. Add 1 cup (250 mL) chopped onion and 2 cloves garlic, chopped, stirring frequently, for

8 minutes or until onion is translucent. Add 2 tbsp (25 mL) chopped fresh parsley and 1 tbsp (15 mL) fresh thyme leaves and boil for 1 minute. Keep simmering until ready to use. Makes 1-1/2 cups (325 mL).

4. Pack artichokes into jars: Fill hot jars with prepared artichokes, packed fairly tightly. Cover with hot Vinegar Brine, leaving a 1-inch (2.5 cm) headspace. Run a non-metallic utensil around the inside of the jar to allow air to escape. Add hot brine, if necessary, to leave a 1-inch (2.5 cm) headspace. Wipe rims, top with flat lids and screw on metal rings. Return jars to the hot water bath, topping up with hot water if necessary. Bring to a full rolling boil and process jars for 15 minutes (see page 19).

OR

Process artichokes in a Pressure Canner according to the chart below for Dial-Gauge or follow manufacturer's instructions.

Processing Times at Different Altitudes for Artichokes in a DIAL-GAUGE PRESSURE Canner

Pack Style	Jar Size	0–2000 ft	2001–4000 ft	4001–6000 ft	6001+ ft
HOT	Pints	15 min	20 min	25 min	30 min
	Quarts	20 min	25 min	30 min	35 min
RAW	Pints	20 min	25 min	30 min	35 min
	Quarts	25 min	30 min	35 min	40 min

5. Cool, Label and Store: Lift jars from canner and place on a clean towel or rack. Do not re-tighten screw bands. Let the jars cool to room temperature. This may take from 12 to 24 hours. Remove and store screw bands. Check lid seals (see page 19). Wipe and label sealed jars. Store in a cool, dark place.

roasted chicken thighs, artichokes and new potatoes

The really great thing about having artichokes preserved in vinegar brine is that with the addition of olive oil, the vinegar makes an easy sauce or vinaigrette for salads and blanched vegetables. Garlic greens are the grass-like new shoots of garlic (see page 93). Similar to chives but with more of a garlic flavour, garlic greens can be harvested for a week or two in the spring, dried using a drying machine, and powdered for use in seasonings later.

In the spring, when new potatoes appear, this dish is the one I usually make. In the photo, I have used blue, yellow and red potatoes for colour and interest. The canned artichokes make a convenient sophisticated addition to what is essentially roasted chicken and spring vegetables.

Rimmed baking sheet, lightly oiled
Heated platter
Preheat oven to 400°F (200°C)
MAKES 4 SERVINGS

4 large bone-in chicken thighs, trimmed of skin and excess fat
sea salt and pepper
1 quart (1 L) artichokes packed in vinegar brine, drained, brine reserved
1 lb (500 g) small new potatoes or fingerlings, halved

4 carrots, cut into 2-inch (5 cm) pieces, halved lengthwise if thick
3 tbsp (45 mL) olive oil
2 cups (500 mL) chopped garlic greens or chives, divided
3 tbsp (45 mL) fresh thyme leaves
1/4 cup (50 mL) olive oil, optional, for dressing

1. On prepared baking sheet, arrange chicken thighs, well spaced, and sprinkle with salt and pepper. Drizzle 1/4 cup (50 mL) of the artichoke brine over top. Bake in preheated oven for 12 minutes.

2. Meanwhile, in a bowl, toss together potatoes, carrots and olive oil. Add to baking sheet, spreading vegetables around chicken pieces in single layer. Bake for 20 minutes. Stir in 1 cup (250 mL) of the garlic greens and thyme and bake for 10 minutes or until juices run clear when chicken is pierced and potatoes are tender and browned. Chicken and vegetables may be a bit charred.

3. Transfer chicken and vegetables to a heated platter, cover with foil and set aside. Add artichokes to the same baking sheet, toss with pan juices and bake for 5 minutes or until heated through. Transfer to platter with chicken and other vegetables. Garnish with remaining garlic greens.

4. If desired, in a clean jar with tight-fitting lid, combine olive oil with 3 tbsp (45 mL) of the reserved vinegar brine. Cover with lid and shake well. Drizzle over chicken and vegetables.

pan-seared artichokes with raspberry vinegar

This would be time-consuming if you had to trim fresh artichokes, but having them in the pantry ready to use makes this an easy appetizer or light lunch if served over a bed of spring greens. Homemade or store-bought raspberry vinegar is what makes the dish special; however, you can use vinegar brine if you want to make it without the raspberry flavour.

MAKES 4 SERVINGS

3 tbsp (45 mL) olive oil, divided
1 red onion, halved and thinly sliced
3 cloves garlic, slivered

1 quart (1 L) artichoke quarters, drained,
  brine reserved if desired (see above)
sea salt and freshly ground pepper
1/4 cup (50 mL) Sweet Raspberry
  Vinegar (page 48)

1. In a skillet, heat 2 tbsp (25 mL) of the olive oil over medium-high heat. Add onion and garlic and sauté for 5 to 6 minutes or until soft and translucent.

2. Add remaining olive oil and artichokes. Season to taste with salt and pepper. Drizzle raspberry vinegar over top. Heat through and toss to mix well.

Freezing Artichokes

1. Select Equipment: Select suitable-size freezer containers, bags or Mason jars (see page 24).

2. Dry-Pack: Fill pint (2-cup/500 mL) or quart (1 L) freezer containers with trimmed, blanched halved or quartered artichokes to 1 inch (2.5 cm) of the top. Squeeze out air; leave 1-inch (2.5 cm) headspace. Seal, label and freeze.

Asparagus

ASPARAGUS (*ASPARAGUS OFFICINALIS*) is a tall, feathery-leaf perennial plant that grows well in northern climates. In the spring, when temperatures rise above 55°F (13°C), it sends up stalks from the thick roots. When the stalks emerge and meet with sunlight, their colour turns from white to purple-green as the chlorophyll is activated.

Asparagus stalks grow 2 to 3 inches (5 to 8 cm) per day in cool weather, 7 or 8 inches (18 to 20 cm) in warm weather, and are cut once they reach 10 inches (25 cm). Once a stalk is cut, the plant begins to send up another stalk and will keep doing so until its energy reserves in the root are exhausted. Top right, an all-male hybrid, 'OAC Millennium,' emerges from the ground at Barrie's Farm Market in Hanover, Ontario.

Good Preserving Varieties

Asparagus plants are male or female, with both producing edible stalks. Stalks are graded by size: colossal, jumbo, large, standard and small. It is a myth that the thinner stalks are more tender. Actually, the opposite is true because as the stalks mature, the strong, tough cells needed to keep the shoot upright are not as much in abundance, making the fat stalks more tender. The thinner, tougher spears are the best choice for pickling and canning, though, because they stand up to the processing better.

When gardeners discovered that emerging asparagus stalks would remain white or pale green if covered and shielded from sunlight, a delicacy was born. Still popular in Europe—France in particular (the photo below right was taken at the market in La Forêt, Brittany)—white asparagus is usually milder in taste and recommended for fresh eating, not preserving.

Jersey Giant: Thicker in diameter than other varieties, their size makes them a good choice for grilling on the barbecue; they hold their shape and firmness and are ideal for canning, as well as for stewing and roasting.

Jersey Knight: Average length is 8 to 10 inches (20 to 25 cm); size and texture make them ideal for stir-fry dishes and for freezing or pickling.

Purple Passion: A plump spear (not as thick as Jersey Giant) that is purple in colour. The colour is lost in cooking, but if added

raw to a vegetable crudité platter, the purple colour is spectacular. Nutty flavour; good for canning or freezing.

Purchasing/Storing
• 1 lb (500 g) asparagus yields 15 to 20 medium-size stalks or about 3 cups (750 mL) 1- to 2-inch (2.5 to 5 cm) pieces.
• You will need about 1 lb (500 g) for each quart (1 L) jar.

Young, thin asparagus produces an abundance of crude fibre that is tough, a quality that makes them best for canning. Older, fatter, mature stalks contain more soft soluble fibre, which is sweet and tender, making them best for eating fresh.

For pickling and canning whole, select Fancy or Grade A (in Canada, No. 1) asparagus because it will be straight, bright green (possibly tinged with purple) and have tightly closed tips. At my local asparagus farm, I choose Utility or Grade B (in Canada, No. 2) asparagus for making soups or for my Asparagus Sauce (page 88) because the misshapen stems and tips are not an issue.

Transfer asparagus from market to home in a cooler. Keep the ends of the spears moist by wrapping in a damp towel or stand them upright in 2 inches (5 cm) of water. Refrigerate and use immediately or within 3 days because the quality deteriorates quickly after harvesting.

Good With
• Lemon herbs such as lemon balm, lemongrass, lemon verbena.
• Savoury seasonings such as coriander, parsley, raspberry or rice vinegar.
• All cheeses, especially Parmesan, Gruyère, pecorino and goat cheese.
• Sauces such as aïoli, hollandaise, Béarnaise, tartar, and Sweet Raspberry Vinegar (page 48).
• Other vegetables, such as eggplant, artichokes, tomatoes, onions, zucchini.
• Egg dishes and custards.
• Veal, beef, chicken; tuna, scallops, shrimp and most fish.
• Toasted pine nuts, sunflower seeds, sesame seeds, almonds.
• Often served as appetizers or starters.

Preparation

Wash by swishing in a sink full of clean, cool water. If particularly sandy, wash two or three times. Rinse well and pat dry.

Canning Asparagus

There is no doubt that canning asparagus can produce some less than optimum results. Be sure to start with fresh-harvested, early and thin, first-quality stalks. Try a small batch to see if you are happy with the product; if not, freeze the remaining stalks. See detailed canning information, page 20. Photo, bottom right: This jar of asparagus and hot pepper pickles was commercially produced using asparagus from the farm of Andrew Barrie, for farm gate sales.

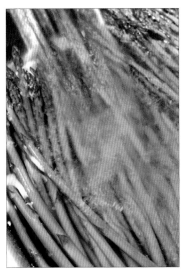

1. Cut spears 1-1/2 inches (3.5 cm) shorter than the height of the jar, or cut into 1- or 2-inch (2.5 or 5 cm) pieces, reserving the tips for a fresh dish, such as Spring Salad (page 97).

2. Prepare Equipment: Wash and heat pint (2-cup/500 mL) or quart (1 L) jars, and scald the lids, funnel, ladle and tongs (see page 18).

3. Pack asparagus into jars either hot or raw (I prefer the Raw Pack Method for asparagus because of the fragility of the tips).

Make a Raw Pack: Fill jars with whole asparagus spears, tips down and packed fairly tightly; or fill with asparagus pieces (shake the jar to pack them). Cover with boiling water or broth, leaving a 1-inch (2.5 cm) headspace. Run a non-metallic utensil around the inside of the jar to allow air to escape. Add more boiling water, if necessary, to leave a 1-inch (2.5 cm) headspace. Wipe sealing edge of jars with a clean, damp, lint-free cloth. Position flat lids over the tops of jars and hand-tighten screw bands.

OR

Make a Hot Pack: This works best with pieces. Add asparagus pieces to gently boiling water and boil for 2 or 3 minutes. Loosely fill hot jars with asparagus. Cover with boiling water, leaving a 1-inch (2.5 cm) headspace. Run a non-metallic utensil around the inside of the jar to allow air to escape. Add more hot water, if necessary, to leave a 1-inch (2.5 cm) headspace. Wipe sealing edge of jars with a clean, damp, lint-free cloth. Position flat lids over the tops of jars and hand-tighten screw bands.

4. Process asparagus in a canner: Use a Pressure Canner according to the chart below for Dial-Gauge or follow manufacturer's instructions.

Processing Times at Different Altitudes for Asparagus in a DIAL-GAUGE PRESSURE Canner

Pack Style	Jar Size	0–2000 ft	2001–4000 ft	4001–6000 ft	6001+ ft
HOT	Pints	15 min	20 min	25 min	30 min
	Quarts	20 min	25 min	30 min	35 min
RAW	Pints	20 min	25 min	30 min	35 min
	Quarts	25 min	30 min	35 min	40 min

5. Cool, Label and Store: Lift jars from canner and place on a clean towel or rack. Do not re-tighten screw bands. Let the jars cool to room temperature. This may take from 12 to 24 hours. Remove and store screw bands. Check lid seals (see page 19). Wipe and label sealed jars. Store in a cool, dark place.

Freezing Asparagus

1. Select Equipment: Select suitable-size freezer containers, bags or Mason jars (see page 24).

2. Blanch or Roast Asparagus: I personally prefer to have roasted asparagus for use in recipes because of the flavour, and roasting seems to keep the texture firm.

To Blanch: Cut spears 1-1/2 inches (3.5 cm) shorter than the height of the jar, or cut into 1- or 2-inch (2.5 or 5 cm) pieces. Bring a large saucepan of water to a boil over high heat. Add asparagus, bring back to a boil and boil for 1 minute. Lift out and immerse in ice water for 1 minute. Drain and pat dry.

To Roast: Roasting works best with whole, fat asparagus spears. Wash and trim spears; leave whole. Preheat oven to 375°F (190°C). Lightly oil a rimmed baking sheet. Arrange spears in single layer on prepared sheet and roll in oil to coat evenly. Roast in preheated oven for 15 minutes or until almost tender (a sharp knife should meet with some resistance when inserted into the centre of a spear). Spears may be lightly charred. Grind salt and pepper over top. Let cool slightly. Cut spears to fit the container, allowing for 1/2 to 1-inch (1 to 2.5 cm) headspace, or cut into 1-inch (2.5 cm) pieces.

3. Fill pint (2-cup/500 mL) or quart (1 L) freezer containers with blanched or roasted asparagus. Squeeze out air; leave 1-inch (2.5 cm) headspace. Seal, label and freeze.

asparagus sauce

Having this sauce on hand to use in fall or winter is like having a patch of crisp and sunny spring in the pantry. You can trim off the tender tips and use them fresh in a salad (see Spring Salad, page 97) and reserve the stalks for this sauce—a great way to can your asparagus and eat it too.

MAKES 9 CUPS (2.25 L)

8 cups (2 L) asparagus pieces (1-inch/2.5 cm lengths), about 4 lb (2 kg)
4 cups (1 L) chicken stock
2 tbsp (25 mL) olive oil
2 tbsp (25 mL) butter
1 cup (250 mL) chopped onion

1 cup (250 mL) finely chopped mushrooms
1/2 cup (125 mL) finely chopped green onions
3 tbsp (45 mL) chopped fresh parsley
1 tbsp (15 mL) fresh thyme leaves
grated rind and juice of 1 lemon

1. In a saucepan, combine asparagus and chicken stock. Bring to a boil over high heat. Cover, reduce the heat and simmer for 10 minutes or until tender. Remove from heat and set aside.

2. Heat nine 1-cup (250 mL) jars in boiling water, and scald the lids, lifter, funnel and tongs (see page 22).

3. Meanwhile, in a canning kettle, heat the olive oil and butter over medium heat. Add onion and sauté for 5 minutes. Stir in mushrooms and green onions. Cook, stirring frequently, for 7 minutes or until vegetables are soft. Add asparagus and stock to the vegetables and bring to a boil. Add parsley, thyme, lemon rind and lemon juice. Simmer gently for 1 minute. Using a blender or food processor, purée the asparagus mixture, in batches, until smooth. Return each batch to a clean saucepan and keep hot over medium-low heat.

4. Fill hot jars, leaving a 1-inch (2.5 cm) headspace. Run a thin non-metallic utensil around the inside of the jar to allow air to escape. Add more hot sauce, if necessary, to leave a 1-inch (2.5 cm) headspace. Wipe sealing edge of jars with a clean, damp, lint-free cloth. Position flat lids over the tops of jars and hand-tighten screw bands.

5. Place jars in pressure canner. Adjust water level (check manufacturer's instructions), lock lid and bring to a boil over medium-high heat. Vent steam for 10 minutes (check manufacturer's instructions), then close vent. Continue heating to achieve 10 lb (69 kPa) pressure and maintain pressure to process pint (2-cup/500 mL) jars for 25 minutes and quart (1 L) jars for 30 minutes. These times and pressure are based on using a weighted gauge pressure canner at 1,000 feet (305 m) or less. Check your altitude and manufacturer's instructions for variations.

6. Turn off heat; let pressure return to zero naturally. Once gauge shows 0 pressure, wait 2 minutes then open the vent. Unlock and remove canner lid. Wait 10 minutes, then lift jars from canner and place on a clean towel or rack. Do not re-tighten screw bands. Let the jars cool to room temperature. This may take from 12 to 24 hours. Remove and store screw bands. Check lid seals (see page 23). Wipe and label sealed jars. Store in a cool, dark place.

Use: As a sauce for poached eggs (as a replacement for Hollandaise sauce); drizzle over other vegetables such as potatoes and mixed vegetables; toss with cooked rice or noodles for a simple pasta sauce; or dilute with chicken or vegetable stock for a light soup, or use cream for a heavier soup.

roasted asparagus salsa

This recipe is versatile: use fresh or frozen blanched, steamed or roasted asparagus and it will be just as tasty. (I used frozen roasted asparagus for this salsa, pictured below.) Of course, you can use fresh roasted asparagus in that ever-so-brief moment in time when fresh is available locally. The salsa does freeze well, although the texture is softer than when made fresh. I don't recommend freezing this salsa if you have used frozen asparagus to make it. Either way, the asparagus should only be frozen once. Having cut roasted asparagus pieces in the freezer makes this an easy dish for entertaining later in the year.

MAKES 5 CUPS (1.25 L)

1 head roasted garlic (see page 389)
grated rind and juice of 1 lime
2 tsp (10 mL) toasted sesame oil
3 cups (750 mL) roasted asparagus pieces
   or spears, thawed if frozen
2 banana or Cubanelle hot peppers,
   roasted and diced

2 cups (500 mL) coarsely chopped
   tomatoes
6 green onions, thinly sliced
1/2 cup (125) chopped fresh cilantro or
   flat-leaf parsley
sea salt and pepper

1. Into a large bowl, squeeze the roasted garlic cloves. Mash garlic with lime juice and sesame oil.

2. Coarsely chop the asparagus, if using whole spears, and add to the bowl. Stir in peppers, tomatoes, green onions, cilantro and lime rind. Grind salt and pepper over top and toss well to combine.

3. Pack into pint (2-cup/500 mL) freezer containers or Mason jars, leaving a 1-inch (2.5 cm) headspace. Seal, label and freeze for up to 8 months.

asparagus and goat cheese flatbread

Whenever you use this delicious flatbread for an appetizer or hors d'oeuvre, or to accompany soup, it will be a tasty reminder of spring. I like the creamy goat cheese and salty prosciutto combination with that of the nutty roasted asparagus.

Rimless baking sheet
Preheat oven to 400°F (200°C)
MAKES 4 SERVINGS

**1 ball (5 oz/150 g) pizza dough, thawed
 if frozen**
olive oil for drizzling
5 oz (150 g) creamy goat cheese, crumbled
2 tbsp (25 mL) grated lemon rind, optional
**2 cups (500 mL) roasted asparagus pieces
 or Roasted Asparagus Salsa (page left),
 thawed if frozen**

**6 slices prosciutto, cut into 1-inch (2.5 cm)
 pieces**
**1 cup (250 mL) baby arugula or other
 greens**
sea salt and freshly ground pepper
shaved Parmesan cheese

1. On a lightly floured surface, roll out pizza dough to about 1/4-inch (5 mm) thickness. Transfer to baking sheet. Drizzle with olive oil. Sprinkle goat cheese and lemon rind, if using, evenly over the dough. Top with asparagus and prosciutto pieces. Drizzle with more olive oil and bake in preheated oven for 15 minutes or until crust is golden and cheese is bubbly and lightly golden.

2. Remove from oven and top with arugula. Grind salt and pepper over top and sprinkle evenly with Parmesan cheese shavings.

Spring Herbs

RURAL AND URBAN MARKETS are vibrant and alive and, most importantly, evolving to meet the sophisticated demands of their customers. Chefs and home cooks alike have come to rely on local farmers' markets, farm gate sales and market gardeners to supply them with a wide variety of fresh greens and herbs throughout the seasons. Herbs add depth and richness to your preserves. I have incorporated both common and not so well-known herbs into the recipes in each season. Some native wild plants are being cultivated in order to meet these growing demands without denuding the countryside, but to be safe, ask before purchasing "wild" plants. Poachers have stripped and continue to strip the native plant colonies, causing serious damage to wild plant habitat and actual extinction in some cases.

Fiddleheads

Fiddleheads (*Matteucia strutbiopteris*) are the unfurled fronds of the ostrich fern, found growing in the wild from the north-eastern United States to Newfoundland and west into Michigan. The season for fresh fiddleheads varies from region to region and from year to year, but generally they begin to appear in markets around the beginning of May. I do not recommend canning fiddleheads because the result is soft and brown, but freezing them is an excellent way to preserve them. To freeze fiddleheads, follow the directions for freezing green beans (page 201).

Garlic Greens

Just about the time your stock of garlic has dwindled to nothing, local garden garlic is sending up green, grassy leaves that give us the garlic flavour and a welcome hit of chlorophyll. For about two weeks in early spring, I use garlic greens in salads, egg dishes and everywhere I might be tempted to snip chives (see Roasted Chicken Thighs, Artichokes and New Potatoes, page 78).

If you own a drier, you can preserve herbs, keeping their green goodness. Store fresh dried herbs in dark airtight containers in a cool, dry place. Store for only one year, then replace with fresh dried herbs. Right: Green garlic is dried and powdered.

Sorrel

If your local market gardener is growing greens, chances are he or she will have sorrel (*Rumex acetosa*) because it is a perennial. Often puréed as a sauce for fish, sorrel can be used wherever spinach is called for in recipes. Sorrel is best preserved by freezing. The sour citrus tang of spinach and sorrel is due to oxalic acid in these greens. If you have kidney problems be careful to cook sorrel and avoid mature leaves or refrain from eating sorrel altogether.

Sweet Cicely

One of my personal favourites, delicate and lacy sweet cicely (*Myrrhis odorata*) is usually first up in my herb garden. A perennial herb, you will find it coming through the snow in early spring.

Use the chopped fresh anise-flavoured leaves with berry jams and preserves and in chutneys and salsas.

Use the whole fresh sprigs as a garnish or as lacy doilies for Strawberry Cappuccino (page 67) or Dundee Almond Cake (page 468). A piece of the whole sprig can be suspended in jam or jelly, or set on the top of a sweet preserve as a decoration. If you can get the roots in the fall, they can be candied.

Wild Leeks or Ramps

There are many plants that belong to the Allium (Latin for "garlic") family, including onions, garlic and leeks. *Allium tricoccam* is native to North America, found in deciduous forests from eastern Canada to North Carolina and Tennessee and west as far as Manitoba, Missouri and Minnesota. Good with asparagus and artichoke, wild leeks offer the green tops and white onion-like bulb for use in recipes. Use wild leeks in place of cultivated garlic cloves in the spring recipes in this chapter.

spring herb aïoli

Light, tangy citrus dressings let the peppery taste of the greens shine through, while creamy garlic tones even out bitter notes for a headier taste. And, of course, the only truly great dressing is one you make yourself. It's really not hard, especially if you have high-quality extra-virgin olive oil or nut oil and a couple of herb vinegars or fresh lemon juice on hand. Toasted sesame oil and balsamic vinegar are items to consider adding to your pantry staples if not already there.

You can make this exquisite French mayonnaise any time of year with fresh greens at your disposal as the market dictates. It absolutely has to be stored in the refrigerator, and since it does not freeze and cannot be home canned, make up very small quantities, then chill and serve within a day. Use spring herbs, such as garlic greens or wild leek leaves, or other fresh herbs, such as tarragon, thyme or sage.

Essential: You can greatly reduce the risk of botulism poisoning by gently washing eggs in cool, soapy water. Rinse well and do not return to the original carton. Store in a clean plastic egg tray in the refrigerator.

MAKES 1–1/2 CUPS (375 ML)

6 cloves garlic	**1 tbsp (15 mL) freshly squeezed lemon juice**
1 large egg + 1 egg yolk	**2 tbsp (25 mL) finely chopped fresh herbs**
1–1/4 cups (300 mL) extra-virgin olive oil	**(see above)**
or nut oil	**1/2 tsp (2 mL) sea salt**

1. In a blender or small food processor, chop garlic. Add egg and egg yolk and process until blended.

2. With the motor running, slowly add the olive oil through the opening in the lid and process just until the mixture thickens and emulsifies. (Aïoli will get even thicker upon refrigeration.) Add lemon juice. Stir in herbs and salt. Scrape into a jar or small container with a tight-fitting lid and refrigerate immediately. Keep refrigerated until ready to use. Use within 1 day.

champagne raspberry vinaigrette

In my view, spring dressings must be worthy of the spring-fresh salad greens and vegetables bursting with fresh-tasting vitality. This vibrant, sweet-tart pink vinaigrette is the perfect match for a green spring mélange. In its simplest form, vinaigrette is an emulsion made from oil, vinegar and salt, with no emulsifier used to keep the oil and vinegar from separating. Often Dijon mustard is added along with traditional herbs like tarragon, thyme and marjoram. Creative chefs and kitchen gardeners are experimenting now with different cold-pressed oils, fruited vinegars, puréed vegetables and other less traditional flavours to make exceptional vinaigrettes with zing. The ratio of vinegar to oil is usually one part vinegar to three parts oil. When lemon juice is used in place of the vinegar, the ratio changes: two parts lemon juice to three parts oil.

MAKES 1 CUP (250 ML)

3 tbsp (45 mL) Sweet Raspberry Vinegar
(page xx or store-bought)
2 tbsp (25 mL) champagne or sparkling
white wine
1 tbsp (15 mL) honey Dijon mustard
1 tbsp (15 mL) finely chopped fresh spring
herbs (see above)

1/4 tsp (1 mL) sea salt
pinch freshly ground pepper
3/4 cup (175 mL) extra-virgin olive oil
or nut oil

In a small bowl, whisk together the raspberry vinegar, champagne, mustard, herbs, salt and pepper. Whisking constantly, add the oil in a slow, steady stream until completely incorporated.

Use: Drizzle over spring greens, cooked fiddleheads, artichokes and asparagus.

spring salad

Of course, you can make this salad in the spring using all fresh ingredients. But if you have asparagus and artichokes in the pantry in January, February or March, you can celebrate spring early. The vinaigrette is sweet and sour at the same time, lending a crisp, tart balance to the fresh tastes of the asparagus and artichokes. This salad is reason enough to want to preserve some of spring's citrus green tastes for the long, dark winter ahead. Use spinach and bok choy or cabbage greens in the winter. As you can see from the photo, I leave the skin on fresh baby potatoes, but in winter, you can cook them in the skins, then peel and slice them after they are cooked. So try this salad now with fresh ingredients, then preserve your own asparagus and artichokes and enjoy it again in six months.

MAKES 4 SERVINGS

12 small new potatoes or fingerlings
1 tsp (5 mL) salt
1 cup (250 mL) baby spinach, sorrel or arugula leaves
1 pint (2-cup/500 mL) jar canned asparagus, drained, (page 85)
1 pint (2-cup/500 mL) jar canned artichokes, drained (page 76)

1/2 red onion, thinly sliced
1/4 cup (50 mL) coarsely chopped fresh spring herbs
1 cup (250 mL) Champagne Raspberry Vinaigrette (page 96)
sea salt and pepper

1. In a saucepan, cover potatoes with water. Add 1 tsp (5 mL) salt and bring to a boil over high heat. Cover, reduce heat and simmer for 12 to 15 minutes or until tender. Rinse under cool water and drain. Quarter or slice potatoes as desired.

2. Distribute spinach evenly among 4 salad plates. Divide potatoes, asparagus, artichokes, onion and herbs into 4 equal portions and pile on top of greens. Drizzle with vinaigrette and grind salt and pepper over top.

Summer

"Then followed that beautiful season . . . the Summer . . . !
Filled was the air with a dreamy and magical light; and the
landscape lay as if new-created in all the
freshness of childhood."

—HENRY WADSWORTH LONGFELLOW

Blackberries

AS MEMBERS OF THE ROSE FAMILY OF PLANTS, blackberries (*Rubus fruticosus*) and raspberries grow on brambles or canes and are sometimes called bramble fruits. You might still find them growing wild in country hedgerows because they tolerate shade. The thorns of the blackberry plant are much more dangerous to the berry picker than those of the raspberry; for this reason, thornless varieties have been cultivated and are preferred, especially by pick-your-own operators. Unlike the central core of the raspberry, that of the blackberry stays with the blackberry and can be eaten when ripe.

Good Preserving Varieties

Helen: No thorns; early variety with good flavour; popular at pick-your-own farms.
John Innes: Slightly thorny; large black, very tasty fruit.
Kotata: Thorny; excellent quality; available at the end of July.
Merton Thornless: No thorns, medium-size fruit, robust and full blackberry taste.
Silvan: Thorny; early variety; very juicy fruit with sweet-tangy and aromatic flavour.

Purchasing/Storing

- 1 lb (500 g) blackberries yields about 2-1/2 cups (625 mL).
- You will need about 1-1/2 lb (750 g) for each quart (1 L) jar.

Although they are an aggregate fruit like raspberries, blackberries do not come away from the core when picked; however, the berry should separate with no more than a gentle tug. If a hard pull is needed to separate it from the core, the fruit isn't ripe. Transport chilled, and use as soon as possible or refrigerate for up to 3 days. Wash just before using.

Good With

- Lemon herbs such as lemon balm, lemon thyme, lemon verbena; anise herbs such as sweet cicely, chervil.
- Sweet seasonings such as cinnamon, ginger, cloves, nutmeg, vanilla, almond.
- Semi-soft cheeses such as havarti, Boursin; medium-age cheddars; goat cheese.
- Other berries, such as raspberries, boysenberries, loganberries, huckleberries, cherries.
- Other fruit, such as bananas, peaches, apricots, plums, nectarines, pears.
- Toasted almonds, pecans and walnuts, hazelnuts, pistachios.
- Egg and milk products/dishes such as yogurt, crème brûlée, whipped cream, crème fraîche, custard.
- Mild fish such as tilapia, orange roughy and sole; pork, duck, goose, veal, chicken.

Preparation

Do not wash until just before using; wash in small amounts using a sieve, under gently running cool water. Pick over and remove lingering stems.

Canning Blackberries

See detailed canning information, page 14.

1. Prepare Equipment: Wash and heat pint (2-cup/500 mL) or quart (1 L) jars, and scald the lids, funnel, ladle and tongs (see page 18).

2. Make a Light Syrup: In a large saucepan, combine 1 cup (250 mL) granulated sugar with 4 cups (1 L) water; stir until dissolved. Bring to a gentle boil over high heat. Makes 4-1/2 cups (1.125 L) syrup, enough for three or four 1-quart (1 L) jars of blackberries.

Note: You can use the same amount of apple juice or white grape juice in place of the light syrup.

3. Pack Blackberries Raw (because blackberries are soft, Hot Pack is not recommended). **Make a Raw Pack:** Fill jars with blackberries, shaking the jar to pack fairly tightly. Cover with hot syrup or juice, leaving a 1/2-inch (1 cm) headspace. Run a thin non-metallic utensil around the inside of the jar to allow air to escape. Add hot liquid, if necessary, to leave a 1/2-inch (1 cm) headspace. Wipe sealing edge of jars with a clean, damp, lint-free cloth. Position flat lids over the tops of jars and hand-tighten screw bands.

4. Process blackberries in a canner: Use a Boiling Water Canner according to the chart below.

Processing Times at Different Altitudes for Blackberries in a BOILING WATER Canner					
Pack Style	Jar Size	0-2000 ft	2001-4000 ft	4001-6000 ft	6001+ ft
HOT	Pints	15 min	20 min	25 min	30 min
	Quarts	20 min	25 min	30 min	35 min
RAW	Pints	20 min	25 min	30 min	35 min
	Quarts	25 min	30 min	35 min	40 min

OR

Process blackberries in a Pressure Canner following manufacturer's directions for steam pressure and time at your altitude.

5. Cool, Label and Store: Lift jars from canner and place on a clean towel or rack. Do not re-tighten screw bands. Let the jars cool to room temperature. This may take from 12 to 24 hours. Remove and store screw bands. Check lid seals (see page 19). Wipe and label sealed jars. Store in a cool, dark place.

blackberry pudding cake

This becomes a year-round favourite if you have any type of frozen berries on hand. I have always loved the way the cake separates and the berries make a sauce. You can use drained canned blackberries in this recipe as well as fresh or frozen. For the version pictured, I used frozen blueberries, blackberries and raspberries. It is the raspberries that lighten up the sauce, making it pink instead of a deep wine colour if only blackberries had been used.

6-cup (2 L) baking or soufflé dish, lightly oiled
Preheat oven to 350°F (180°C)
MAKES 6 SERVINGS

1/4 cup (50 mL) all-purpose flour
1/2 tsp (2 mL) salt
1 cup (250 mL) granulated sugar, divided
3 tbsp (45 mL) butter, at room temperature
4 eggs, separated

grated rind and juice of 1/2 lemon
3/4 cup (175 mL) milk
2 cups (500 mL) blackberries or mixed
  berries, thawed if frozen
1 to 2 tbsp (15 to 25 mL) icing sugar, optional

1. In a bowl, sift together the flour and salt; set aside. In a mixing bowl, beat 3/4 cup (175 mL) of the sugar with butter until incorporated. Beat in egg yolks, one at a time, until light and fluffy. Stir in lemon rind and juice.

2. Using electric beaters or a wooden spoon, beat flour mixture into butter mixture alternately with milk to make a smooth thin batter.

3. In a separate bowl, with clean beaters, beat egg whites until soft peaks form. Add remaining 1/4 cup (50 mL) sugar and beat until stiff peaks form. Fold into batter. Fold in blackberries.

4. Pour pudding cake into prepared dish. Bake in preheated oven for 45 minutes or until cake is set. Cake will puff up and brown and will not jiggle when shaken. Let stand for 5 to 10 minutes before serving.

blackberry cordial

This cordial is one of a few homemade drink syrups that give my entertaining a very personal flavour. I enjoy having this on hand for mixing tall summer iced refreshers and winter cocktails. Combined with carbonated mineral water or chilled white wine, it makes a light and fruity drink. When mixed with spirits, the result is a dark and mysteriously delicious drink with panache. The brandy adds an alcohol dimension to this rich, dark syrup but is not required—especially if you want to keep your drink options open and use it in a non-alcoholic punch.

MAKES 4 CUPS (1 L)

3 lb (1.5 kg) blackberries (about 6 cups/ 1.5 L)

1-1/2 cups (375 mL) water

1 tsp (5 mL) whole cloves

1 tsp (5 mL) freshly grated or ground nutmeg

1/2 tsp (2 mL) ground cinnamon

1/4 cup (50 mL) freshly squeezed lemon juice

3 cups (750 mL) granulated sugar

1/3 cup (75 mL) brandy, optional

1. Heat four 1-cup (250 mL) jars in boiling water, and scald the lids, lifter, funnel and tongs (see page 18).

2. In a Maslin pan or canning kettle, combine blackberries, water, cloves, nutmeg and cinnamon. Cover and bring to a boil over high heat. Reduce the heat and simmer for 15 minutes or until the blackberries are very soft.

3. Strain through a cheesecloth-lined sieve, allowing the juice to drip into a non-reactive bowl or pan overnight. Combine the strained blackberry juice and lemon juice in a Maslin pan or canning kettle. Stir in sugar. Bring to a boil over high heat and boil for 1 minute.

4. Skim off and discard any foam. Stir in brandy, if using. Fill hot jars, leaving a 1/4-inch (5 mm) headspace. Run a thin non-metallic utensil around the inside of the jar to allow air to escape. Add more hot cordial, if necessary, to leave a 1/4-inch (5 mm) headspace. Wipe rims, top with flat lids and screw on metal rings. Return jars to the hot water bath, topping up with hot water if necessary. Bring to a full rolling boil and process jars for 10 minutes (see page 19).

5. Remove canner lid and wait 5 minutes before removing jars to a towel or rack to cool completely. Check seals, label and store in a cool place for up to 1 year.

Use: I have tossed this sweet, spiced syrup with fresh winter fruit for a quick dessert. It is a great base for Blackberry Granita: In the bowl of a blender, combine 1/2 cup (125 mL) Blackberry Cordial with 10 ice cubes. Process on "chop" until ice is blended with the cordial. Serve with a spoon.

black ginger marmalade

If you are looking for a preserve that is different, this is it. As with most spectacular things, it requires a bit more work, but it is so worth it, especially if you like ginger. The colour alone is stunningly unique for a preserve.

Unless you live in the tropics, fresh local ginger is probably not widely available, although it can be grown as an annual in places where the summers are long and warm. Crystallized or candied ginger and stem ginger in syrup are generally easy to find and store. Stem ginger is the term for the pink, tender stem growing out of the root; if available, use it for this recipe. If, like me, you can only find the woodier fresh gingerroot, use only the flesh around the fibrous core. In the recipe, I am assuming that you will be using fresh gingerroot, but if you are using stem ginger packed in syrup or crystallized ginger or candied ginger, measure 1-1/4 cups (300 mL) chopped and proceed to step 2.

MAKES 4 CUPS (1 L)

1 lb (500 g) fresh gingerroot, peeled
4 cups (1 L) fresh or frozen blackberries
1/2 cup (125 mL) freshly squeezed
  lemon juice

4 cups (1 L) granulated sugar
1 pouch (3 oz/85 mL) liquid pectin

1. Grate enough of the tender outer layer of the gingerroot to obtain 1 to 1-1/4 cups (250 to 300 mL), lightly packed. In a saucepan, combine ginger with 4 cups (1 L) water and bring to a boil over high heat. Boil for 5 minutes; drain and return ginger to the saucepan. Cover with 4 cups (1 L) cold fresh water and repeat the boiling and draining twice so that the ginger has been boiled a total of 3 times. Drain well after final boiling.

2. In a Maslin pan or saucepan, combine ginger with 4 cups (1 L) water. Bring to a boil over high heat. Reduce the heat and simmer gently until the shreds of ginger are tender and translucent, about 1 hour.

3. Meanwhile, in a bowl, mash the blackberries using a potato masher. Press through a cone sieve or coarse sieve lined with cheesecloth to remove the seeds, allowing the juice to collect in a non-reactive bowl or pan. Squeeze the cheesecloth to remove as much liquid as possible; discard cheesecloth and seeds. You should have about 1-1/3 cups (325 mL) blackberry juice.

4. Heat four 1-cup (250 mL) jars in boiling water, and scald the lids, lifter, funnel and tongs (see page 18).

5. When the ginger is tender and translucent, drain well and add the blackberry juice and lemon juice and bring to a boil. Stir in sugar, 1 cup (250 mL) at a time, stirring until dissolved before adding

the next cup. Bring to a hard boil and stir in the pectin. Boil, stirring constantly, for 1 minute.

6. Skim off and discard any foam. Fill hot jars, leaving a 1/4-inch (5 mm) headspace. Run a thin non-metallic utensil around the inside of the jar to allow air to escape. Add more hot marmalade, if necessary, to leave a 1/4-inch (5 mm) headspace. Wipe rims, top with flat lids and screw on metal rings. Return jars to the hot water bath, topping up with hot water if necessary. Bring to a full rolling boil and process jars for 10 minutes (see page 19).

7. Remove canner lid and wait 5 minutes before removing jars to a towel or rack to cool completely. Check seals, label and store in a cool place for up to 1 year.

Use: I like this purple-black marmalade with savoury meats and on both savoury and sweet breads. It can also be used as a topping for puddings, ices and other desserts. It is especially delicious with cheesecake and yogurt, or mixed with fresh fruits.

Freezing Blackberries

See detailed freezing information, pages 24 to 25.

1. **Select Equipment:** Select suitable-size freezer containers, bags or Mason jars (see page 24).

2. **Dry-Pack**

a) Freeze Individual Berries: Arrange washed, completely dry berries in a single layer, without touching each other, on a cookie sheet. Fast-freeze for 1 hour. Pack into freezer containers (no need to leave headspace). Squeeze out air; seal, label and return to freezer.

OR

b) Fill pint (2-cup/500 mL) or quart (1 L) freezer containers with blackberries to within 3 to 4 inches (7 to 10 cm) of the top. Pour dry granulated sugar over top; use 1/2 cup (125 mL) sugar per quart (1 L) of prepared fruit. Squeeze out air; leave 1-inch (2.5 cm) headspace. Seal, label and freeze.

OR

Pack in Syrup: In a saucepan, combine 2-1/2 cups (625 mL) granulated sugar and 4 cups (1 L) water. Bring to a gentle boil over high heat, stirring frequently. Reduce heat and gently boil for 3 minutes. Let cool. Fill pint (2-cup/500 mL) or quart (1 L) freezer containers with blackberries to within 3 to 4 inches (7 to 10 cm) of the top of the container. Pour syrup over top; use 1 cup (250 mL) syrup per 1 quart (1 L) of prepared fruit. Squeeze out air; leave 1-inch (2.5 cm) headspace. Seal, label and freeze.

OR

Crush: Using a potato masher, crush blackberries in a non-reactive bowl, or for seedless purée, press through a fine sieve into a non-reactive bowl. For every quart (1 L) of crushed blackberries, add 1 cup (250 mL) granulated sugar. Stir until the sugar is dissolved. Pack into freezer containers, leaving a 1-inch (2.5 cm) headspace. Seal, label and freeze.

Blueberries

THE LOWBUSH BLUEBERRY (*VACCINIUM ANGUSTIFOLIUM*) is a native North American species found in eastern and central Canada and the northeastern United States. Its small, dark blue berries are firm and tart-sweet—excellent for preserving. First Nations peoples dried blueberries, currants, elderberries and cranberries for use during the winter. Vaccinium is the genus of bilberry and cranberry.

Good Preserving Varieties

Lowbush blueberry plants rise up only to 18 inches (45 cm) and appear more like a ground cover than a bush or tree. They are often called "wild" because the plants are managed and encouraged from wild stock. Wild (lowbush) blueberries are excellent for preserving because they are smaller, firmer and more fragrant than the highbush or rabbiteye species. Lowbush blueberries are not available until early summer to midsummer.

Highbush (over 6 feet/1.8 m) blueberry species (*Vaccinium corymbosum*) are the most widely known because they have been commercially bred for over 100 years and appear almost exclusively in supermarkets. **Earliblue** is an early-ripening variety (from early in June) with a large berry with good flavour. **Berkeley** and **Bluecrop** are midsummer varieties that are firm and full-flavour. **Dixi**, **Darrow** and **Bluegold** are excellent-tasting, firm varieties that are available later in the season.

Half-high species blueberries are a cross between highbush and lowbush varieties and are popular in northern areas because they are hardy to Zone 3. **Northblue**, **St. Cloud**, **Northland**, **Polaris** and **Chippewa** have large fruit and are popular in northern locations.

Rabbiteye blueberries (*Vaccinium ashei*) are more common in the south (Zone 7 through 9). The plants grow to 10 feet (30 m). **Alapaha**, named for the Alapaha River in Georgia, is a new hybrid that is medium in size and excellent in flavour. **Ochlockonee** (after the Ochlockonee River, Georgia) is a large-fruit, late-season rabbiteye blueberry.

Purchasing/Storing
- 1 lb (500 g) yields about 2-1/2 cups (625 mL) blueberries.
- You will need about 1-1/2 lb (750 g) for each quart (1 L) jar.

Smaller, firmer and more flavourful blueberries are best for canning, freezing and baking. For eating fresh, choose large, plump, fully ripe blueberries that are blue-black, with a silver to white frost on the skin. There should be no greenish tinge. Avoid shrivelled berries.

Good With
- Spicy herbs such as basil, bay, thyme, chervil, tarragon.
- Sweet seasonings such as cinnamon, ginger, cloves, nutmeg, vanilla, almond.
- Full-flavour cheeses such as Emmenthal, Gruyère, Oka, Edam.
- Other fruit, such as raspberries, peaches, pears, nectarines, strawberries, cherries.
- Toasted almonds, pecans and walnuts, raisins, white chocolate, caramel.
- Egg puddings; dairy products such as yogurt, whipped cream, ice cream, crème fraîche.
- Game and wild meats such as boar, bison, venison, duck, partridge and goose.
- Full-flavoured fish such as cod, mackerel, pollock.

Preparation
Just before using, wash blueberries in small amounts. Using a sieve, hold them under gently running cool water. Pick over and remove stems.

Canning Blueberries
See detailed canning information, page 14.

1. Prepare Equipment: Wash and heat pint (2-cup/500 mL) or quart (1 L) jars, and scald the lids, funnel, ladle and tongs (see page 18).

2. Make a Light Syrup: In a large saucepan, combine 1 cup (250 mL) granulated sugar with 4 cups (1 L) water; stir until dissolved. Bring to a gentle boil over high heat. Makes 4-1/2 cups (1.125 L) syrup, enough for three or four 1-quart (1 L) jars of blueberries.

Note: You can use the same amount of apple juice or white grape juice in place of the light syrup.

3. Pack blueberries into jars either hot or raw (I prefer the Raw Pack Method for blueberries, but they are considered a firm berry and can be processed hot, if desired).

Make a Raw Pack: Fill jars with berries, shaking the jar to pack fairly tightly. Cover with hot syrup or juice, leaving a 1/2-inch (1 cm) headspace. Run a thin non-metallic utensil around the inside of the jar to allow air to escape. Add hot liquid, if necessary, to leave a 1/2-inch (1 cm) headspace. Wipe sealing edge of jars with a clean, damp, lint-free cloth. Position flat lids over the tops of jars and hand-tighten screw bands.

OR

Make a Hot Pack: Add blueberries to gently boiling syrup or juice and boil for a minute. Fill hot jars with hot fruit and cooking liquid, leaving a 1/2-inch (1 cm) headspace. Run a thin non-metallic utensil around the inside of the jar to allow air to escape. Add more hot fruit or liquid, if necessary, to leave a 1/2-inch (1 cm) headspace. Wipe sealing edge of jars with a clean, damp, lint-free cloth. Position flat lids over the tops of jars and hand-tighten screw bands.

4. Process blueberries in a canner: Use a Boiling Water Canner according to the chart below.

Processing Times at Different Altitudes for Blueberries in a BOILING WATER Canner					
Pack Style	Jar Size	0–2000 ft	2001–4000 ft	4001–6000 ft	6001+ ft
HOT	Pints	15 min	20 min	25 min	30 min
	Quarts	20 min	25 min	30 min	35 min
RAW	Pints	20 min	25 min	30 min	35 min
	Quarts	25 min	30 min	35 min	40 min

OR

Process blueberries in a Pressure Canner following manufacturer's directions for steam pressure and time at your altitude.

5. Cool, Label and Store: Lift jars from canner and place on a clean towel or rack. Do not re-tighten screw bands. Let the jars cool to room temperature. This may take from 12 to 24 hours. Remove and store screw bands. Check lid seals (see page 19). Wipe and label sealed jars. Store in a cool, dark place.

blueberry conserve

This soft conserve is just an all-round beautiful preserve. The apples and orange slices with rind add pectin, shortening the time this conserve takes to set (about 1/2 hour). If you wish to shorten the time more, use commercial fruit pectin and follow package directions.

MAKES 8 CUPS (2 L)

6 cups (1.5 L) granulated sugar
3 cups (750 mL) unsweetened apple juice
  or water
2 tbsp (25 mL) freshly squeezed lemon
  juice

2 apples, shredded
1 orange, seeded and thinly sliced
1 cup (250 mL) seedless golden raisins,
  coarsely chopped
6 cups (1.5 L) blueberries

1. Heat eight 1-cup (250 mL) jars in boiling water, and scald the lids, lifter, funnel and tongs (see page 18).

2. In a Maslin pan or canning kettle, combine sugar, apple juice and lemon juice. Bring to a boil over high heat, stirring to dissolve the sugar. Add apples, orange slices and raisins. Reduce heat and boil gently for 7 minutes. Add blueberries, increase heat to high and return to a boil. Boil hard, stirring constantly, for 15 to 20 minutes or until mixture thickens. Remove from heat and test gel (see Setting Point, below).

3. Skim off and discard any foam. Fill hot jars, leaving a 1/4-inch (5 mm) headspace. Run a thin non-metallic utensil around the inside of the jar to allow air to escape. Add more hot conserve, if necessary, to leave a 1/4-inch (5 mm) headspace. Wipe rims, top with flat lids and screw on metal rings. Return jars to the hot water bath, topping up with hot water if necessary. Bring to a full rolling boil and process jars for 15 minutes (see page 19).

4. Remove canner lid and wait 5 minutes before removing jars to a towel or rack to cool completely. Check seals, label and store in a cool place for up to 1 year.

Use: With the bits of orange floating in it, this sweet condiment is perfect with smoked meats like duck, ham or bacon. For a double whammy, I like to spoon it over blueberry scones or muffins.

Setting Point

Blueberry Conserve has reached the setting point when a candy thermometer reads 212°F (100°C).

    If you don't have a thermometer: To test for setting point, remove the conserve from the heat. Place a plate in the freezer for 2 minutes. Drop a spoonful of hot conserve onto the chilled plate (see page 9). Return the plate to the freezer for 1 minute. Push the spot of conserve with a fork. If the surface wrinkles, the conserve is set and ready to pack into hot, sterilized jars. If the conserve is not set, return to a boil and test at 3-minute intervals, using a new chilled plate each time.

potato pancake with blueberry conserve

Living as I do in beef country, with mixed farming all around me, I have made friends with many of my farming neighbours and talk food with them as often as I can. And I have come to know a bit about potatoes. For example, the russet potato and the Yukon Gold (big around here) are waxy (or low in starch) and hold their shape when shredded, so I don't make pancakes unless I have one or the other.

Some people parboil potatoes before making potato pancakes, but I have never had any luck with that method, no matter what potato I use. This method works well for me!

Rimmed baking sheet, lined with paper towels
Preheat oven to 325°F (160°C)
MAKES 4 SERVINGS

2 medium waxy potatoes, such as
  Yukon Gold
1 small sweet potato
1 carrot
1 small red onion, halved
1 tbsp (15 mL) fresh thyme leaves
2 tsp (10 mL) chopped fresh sage
  sea salt and pepper

1/4 cup (50 mL) all-purpose flour (approx)
1 large egg
2 tbsp (25 mL) olive oil
1 cup (250 mL) Blueberry Conserve (page
114) or Wild Blueberry Dipping Sauce
  (page 120)

1. Using a food processor or mandolin, shred the 2 waxy potatoes and the sweet potato; transfer to a mixing bowl. Shred the carrot and half of the onion; add to bowl. Thinly slice the remaining onion and transfer to bowl. Add thyme and sage. Grind salt and pepper over top. Mix well. Dust with flour and mix well.

2. In a small bowl, beat the egg. Add to the vegetables and mix well.

3. In a skillet, heat the olive oil over medium-high heat. Scoop out the potato mixture in 1/3 cup (75 mL) measure. Scrape out of the measuring cup into the hot oil and flatten with the back of a spoon. Add 1 or 2 more scoops of potato mixture to the skillet. Reduce heat and cook over medium heat for 5 to 8 minutes or until lightly browned on one side. Flip and cook for 3 to 5 minutes on the other side.

4. Transfer to prepared baking sheet, cover with foil and keep warm in the preheated oven while cooking the remaining potato pancakes. Serve hot with Blueberry Conserve or Wild Blueberry Dipping Sauce.

blueberry grunt

Grunts are an East Coast heritage recipe consisting of berries boiled into a sauce with sugar and water and topped with sweet dumplings. Some say the name comes from the sound the dumplings make when they are steaming in the pot. Grunts were easy, and every housewife could throw one together without consulting a written recipe, with ingredients she had on hand when the berries were ready to pick. East Coast grunts used wild blueberries, bunch-berries (Cornus canadensis), partridgeberries (Vaccinium vitis-idaea), also known widely as lingonberries, or the "bakeapple" cloudberry (Rubus chamaemorus), not really an apple at all but a golden, soft cluster berry with a musky smell. An interesting story surrounds the common name "bakeapple." It seems it is the English-sounding word for the French baie qu'appelle, which means "What is the name of this berry?"

MAKES 8 CUPS (2 L)

2 cups (500 mL) Blueberry Conserve
  (page 114)
1-1/2 cups (375 mL) all-purpose flour
1/2 cup (125 mL) granulated sugar
2 tsp (10 mL) baking powder

1/4 tsp (1 mL) salt
1/4 cup (50 mL) cold butter
2/3 to 1 cup (150 to 250 mL) buttermilk

1. In a skillet with a lid, bring the Blueberry Conserve to a boil over medium-low heat. Reduce heat and keep simmering until dumplings are ready.

2. Meanwhile, in a bowl, combine flour, sugar, baking powder and salt. Cut the butter into small pieces and add to the flour mixture. Using a pastry blender, 2 knives or your fingertips, rub the butter into the flour mixture until it resembles fine bread crumbs.

3. Make a well in the centre; using a fork, stir in the buttermilk, adding enough to make a soft biscuit dough. Drop by spoonfuls into the hot conserve. Cover with the lid and simmer over low to medium heat for 15 minutes. The dumplings should be puffed and cooked through. Transfer dumplings to serving plates and ladle hot sauce over top.

wild blueberry dipping sauce

This is a silky smooth, savory sauce for appetizers, starters and meat entrees. Wild blueberries will be the most flavorful for this sauce, but you can use any fresh or frozen blueberry available to you.

MAKES 8 CUPS (2 L)

2 tbsp (25 mL) olive oil
2 tsp (10 mL) sesame oil
2 red onions, chopped (2-1/2 cups/625 mL)
6 cups (1.5 L) fresh or frozen wild
 blueberries
2 apples, peeled, cored and quartered
3 cups (750 mL) freshly squeezed
 orange juice

2-1/2 cups (625 mL) corn syrup
1/2 cup (125 mL) rice vinegar
1/4 cup (50 mL) freshly squeezed
 lemon juice
3 tbsp (45 mL) soy sauce
1 tbsp (15 mL) Five-Spice Blend (page 216
 or store-bought), ground or powdered

1. In a skillet, heat olive oil and sesame oil over medium heat. Add onions and cook, stirring frequently, until soft, about 6 minutes. Cool.

2. In a blender or food processor, working in batches, purée the blueberries, apples and onions. Add orange juice, corn syrup, vinegar, lemon juice, soy sauce and spices. Process until smooth.

3. Pour puréed mixture into a Maslin pan or saucepan and bring to a boil over high heat. Reduce heat and boil gently, stirring occasionally for 45 minutes, or until sauce has thickened. Let cool.

4. Ladle sauce into plastic freezer containers or mason jars, leaving a 1/2-inch (1 cm) headspace. Apply lids securely and label. Freeze for up to 1 year.

Use: This is a rich and flavourful sauce. Use it as a dipping sauce for beef or chicken satay, pork ribs or vegetable/meat balls. It makes a flavourful sauce for accompanying duck, beef, veal, pork and wild meat dishes. It can be thinned with vinegar and oil for a colourful vinaigrette dressing.

Freezing Blueberries

1. Select Equipment: Select suitable-size freezer containers, bags or Mason jars (see page 24).

2. Dry-Pack

a) Freeze Individual Berries: Arrange washed, completely dry berries in a single layer, without touching each other, on a cookie sheet. Fast-freeze for 1 hour. Pack into freezer containers (no need to leave headspace). Squeeze out air; seal, label and return to freezer.

OR

b) Fill pint (2-cup/500 mL) or quart (1 L) freezer containers with blueberries to within 3 to 4 inches (7 to 10 cm) of the top. Pour dry granulated sugar over top; use 1/2 cup (125 mL) sugar per quart (1 L) of prepared fruit. Squeeze out air; leave 1-inch (2.5 cm) headspace. Seal, label and freeze.

OR

Pack in Syrup: In a saucepan, combine 2–1/2 cups (625 mL) granulated sugar and 4 cups (1 L) water. Bring to a gentle boil over high heat, stirring frequently. Reduce heat and boil gently for 3 minutes. Let cool. Fill pint (2-cup/500 mL) or quart (1 L) freezer containers with blueberries to within 3 to 4 inches (7 to 10 cm) of the top. Pour syrup over top; use 1 cup (250 mL) syrup per quart (1 L) of prepared fruit. Squeeze out air; leave 1-inch (2.5 cm) headspace. Seal, label and freeze.

OR

Crush: Using a potato masher, crush blueberries in a non-reactive bowl; or for purée, press through a fine sieve into a non-reactive bowl. For every quart (1 L) of crushed blueberries, add 2/3 cup (150 mL) granulated sugar, depending on the tartness of the berries. Stir until the sugar is dissolved. Pack into freezer containers, leaving a 1-inch (2.5 cm) headspace; seal, label and freeze.

Cherries

DEEP RED (OR BLACK OR YELLOW) and slightly heart-shaped flesh grows around a small stone (they are called "stone fruit," along with peaches, nectarines, plums and apricots). They taste sweetly fragrant . . . like, well, cherries.

Good Preserving Varieties

There are two categories of cherry (*Prunus avium*): sweet and sour. However, a hybrid of the two has been developed; sometimes called Royals or Dukes, they are slightly sweet/sour.

Sweet varieties are available from May through August and are generally eaten fresh and preserved by freezing or canning. Sour cherries are used only in jams and other preserves where sufficient sugar is added to make them palatable.

Bing: Sweet; dark red, firm flesh and large; excellent for eating and canning; ripen around the 10th of July.
Lambert: Sweet; dark red firm fruit; ripen mid-July.
Vista: Sweet; nearly black in colour and almost 1 inch (2.5 cm) in size; early July harvest.

Known as "pie cherries," sour cherries are cooked in compotes, spreads, jams and pie fillings with sugar or other sweetener. Sour varieties are smaller and more roundly plump than the sweet cherries and can be classified as having colourless juice (Montmorency, Meteor and Early Richmond) or red juice (Northstar). Sour cherries begin to ripen in June.

Early Richmond: Very sour and considered good only for jams or canning in heavy syrup; bright red with colourless juice; first available in the spring.
Montmorency: Sour; colourless juice; widely grown commercially.
Morello: Sour; perhaps the most widely known sour cherry type, Morello cherries have mahogany-colour flesh and dark juice; should be ripened on the tree for best flavour, so buy local when possible. English Morello is a very old tart cherry variety that is usually only canned in medium to heavy syrup.

Purchasing/Storing
- 1 lb (500 g) yields about 2-1/2 cups (625 mL) pitted cherries.
- You will need about 1-1/2 lb (750 g) cherries for each quart (1 L) jar.

Select large, firm and deeply coloured cherries, with no blemishes.

Good With
- Spicy herbs such as bay, tarragon, rosemary.
- Sweet seasonings such as almond, vanilla, cinnamon, nutmeg.
- Slightly sharp and tangy cheeses such as colby, Gouda, Jarlsberg, Swiss.
- Other fruit, such as redcurrants or blackcurrants, raspberries, peaches, plums, nectarines, apricots, blueberries, strawberries, oranges.
- Toasted, slivered or burnt almonds (recipe page 129), pecans and hazelnuts; raisins; dark, white or milk chocolate.
- Freshwater fish such as bass and perch, and oily fish such as mackerel; dark, rich meats like bison, venison, boar; duck, goose and other wild birds.

Preparation
Wash cherries in a sink full of cool water to which a drop of food-safe soap has been added. Discard any that float because they may be wormy. Rinse well, drain and pat dry.

Remove the stone or pit using a cherry pitter or the round end of a meat skewer.

Canning Cherries
See detailed canning information, page 14.

1. Prepare Equipment: Wash and heat pint (2-cup/500 mL) or quart (1 L) jars, and scald the lids, funnel, ladle and tongs (see page 18).

2. Make a Medium Syrup for sour varieties (light for sweet varieties, see page 15): In a large saucepan, combine 3 cups (750 mL) granulated sugar with 7 cups (1.75 L) water; stir until dissolved. Bring to a gentle boil over high heat. Makes 8 1/2 cups (2.125 L) syrup, enough for six or seven 1-quart (1 L) jars of cherries.

Note: With sour cherries, it is not advisable to substitute apple juice or white grape juice in place of syrup.

3. Pack cherries into jars either hot or raw.

Make a Raw Pack: Fill jars with pitted cherries (shake the jars to pack them tightly). Cover with hot syrup, leaving a 1/2-inch (1 cm) headspace. Run a thin non-metallic utensil around the inside of the jar to allow air to escape. Add hot syrup, if necessary, to leave a 1/2-inch (1 cm) headspace. Wipe sealing edge of jars with a clean, damp, lint-free cloth. Position flat lids over the tops of jars and hand-tighten screw bands.

OR

Make a Hot Pack: Add cherries to gently boiling syrup and boil for a minute. Fill hot jars with hot cherries and syrup, leaving a 1/2-inch (1 cm) headspace. Run a thin non-metallic utensil around the inside of the jar to allow air to escape. Add more hot cherries or syrup, if necessary, to leave a 1/2-inch (1 cm) headspace. Wipe sealing edge of jars with a clean, damp, lint-free cloth. Position flat lids over the tops of jars and hand-tighten screw bands.

4. **Process cherries in a canner:** Use a Boiling Water Canner according to the chart below.

Processing Times at Different Altitudes for Cherries in a BOILING WATER Canner					
Pack Style	Jar Size	0–2000 ft	2001–4000 ft	4001–6000 ft	6001+ ft
HOT	Pints	15 min	20 min	25 min	30 min
	Quarts	20 min	25 min	30 min	35 min
RAW	Pints	20 min	25 min	30 min	35 min
	Quarts	25 min	30 min	35 min	40 min

OR

Process cherries in a Pressure Canner following manufacturer's directions for steam pressure and time at your altitude.

5. **Cool, Label and Store:** Lift jars from canner and place on a clean towel or rack. Do not re-tighten screw bands. Let the jars cool to room temperature. This may take from 12 to 24 hours. Remove and store screw bands. Check lid seals (see page 19). Wipe and label sealed jars. Store in a cool, dark place.

amaretto black cherries

As a kid, I loved to eat maraschino cherries straight out of the jar (who didn't?), but if I ever got past that sugar high to give any thought to the underlying almond essence, I may have simply assumed that since cherries and almond flavouring were so perfect together, that almond extract was added to heighten the taste. "Maraschino" comes from "Marasca," which is the name of a small, very sour cherry that was originally grown near Zara, the capital of Dalmatia, where it was either made into my childhood obsession or something even better that I was yet to discover: maraschino liqueur. For those bright red candied orbs, the cherries are pitted and bleached, then candied in thick syrup with bitter almond oil and red or green colouring added. Had I been old enough to appreciate maraschino liqueur, now also made in Italy, I might have been keen to learn that the almond flavour of this spirit comes from the crushed cherry pits, which release the almond taste of the kernels. This recipe combines two different almond tastes to perfection. I keep Amaretto Black Cherries alongside my amaretto liqueur for winter holiday entertaining. The rich, black, sweetened Bing cherries lend a sophisticated air to desserts and drinks.

MAKES 5 CUPS (1.125 L)

4 cups (1 L) water
2 cups (500 mL) granulated sugar
1/2 cup (125 mL) amaretto or other almond
  liqueur

3 lb (1.5 kg) sweet black cherries (Bing,
  Lambert or Vista)
5 pieces (each 2 inches/5 cm long) orange
  rind

1. Heat five 1-cup (250 mL) jars in boiling water, and scald the lids, lifter, funnel and tongs (see page 18).

2. In a saucepan, combine water and sugar. Bring to a boil over high heat, stirring constantly, to dissolve the sugar. Boil rapidly for 5 minutes. Remove from heat and stir in amaretto.

3. Pack cherries into hot jars to within 1 inch (2.5 cm) of the top, shaking the jar to pack tightly. Add 1 piece of orange rind to each jar. Pour hot syrup over cherries, leaving a 1/2-inch (1 cm) headspace. Run a thin non-metallic utensil around the inside of the jar to allow air to escape. Add more hot syrup, if necessary, to leave a 1/2-inch (1 cm) headspace. Wipe sealing edge of jars with a clean, damp, lint-free cloth. Position flat lids over the tops of jars and hand-tighten screw bands.

4. Return jars to the hot water bath, topping up with hot water if necessary. Bring to a full rolling boil and process jars for 20 minutes (see page 19).

5. Remove canner lid and wait 5 minutes before removing jars to a towel or rack to cool completely. Check seals, label and store in a cool place for up to 1 year.

amaretto clafoutis with burnt almonds

One of my favourite ways to enjoy canned cherries is to make this easy eggy custard dessert or breakfast dish. This is a dish to whip up for brunch or to end a great meal with friends. It is so easy to prepare, which means you can serve it hot, right out of the oven, with whipped cream for dessert or yogurt for breakfast. You can use slivered or toasted almonds in place of the burnt almonds, but the burnt almonds really go the distance to make it extraordinary. You can make them ahead of time and keep them in an airtight container for a couple of weeks in the refrigerator or for a couple of months in the freezer.

Preheat oven to 375°F (190°C)
MAKES 6 SERVINGS

1 pint (2 cups/500 mL) Amaretto Black
Cherries, drained (page 126 or canned
  cherries), juice reserved
4 large eggs
1–1/3 cups (325 mL) milk
1/3 cup (75 mL) granulated sugar

1 tsp (5 mL) pure vanilla extract
1 cup (250 mL) all-purpose flour
1/2 tsp (2 mL) salt
1/4 cup (50 mL) icing sugar, optional
1/2 cup (125 mL) burnt almonds (recipe
  follows) or slivered almonds

1. In a heavy 10-inch (25 cm) ovenproof skillet, heat the cherries and 1/4 cup (50 mL) of the reserved juice over medium heat. Reserve remaining juice for another use.

2. Meanwhile, in a blender, combine eggs, milk, sugar and vanilla. With the blender running, add the flour and salt through the opening in the lid and process until smooth. Pour the batter over the cherries in the hot skillet. Bake in preheated oven for 20 minutes or until the clafoutis is puffed and the batter is set and golden brown around the edges.

3. Let cool slightly (custard will drop and crack) and dust with icing sugar, if using. Garnish with burnt almonds.

burnt almonds

This is actually candy, but it's a handy garnish to have in the freezer: stir it into homemade ice cream or frozen yogurt; spoon it over custards, cakes and desserts; use it to add crunch to mousse or pudding; and substitute it for natural almonds in muffins and other baked products.

**Rimmed baking sheet, greased or lined
  with parchment**
MAKES 1 CUP (250 ML)

1/3 cup (75 mL) water
1/2 cup (125 mL) granulated sugar
1 tsp (5 mL) pure vanilla extract
1/4 tsp (1 tsp) ground cinnamon
1 cup (250 mL) whole almonds (with skins)

If I don't want to use the almonds whole, instead of separating them, I let them cool, then crush them with a meat mallet.

1. In a deep-sided, heavy-bottomed saucepan, combine water, sugar, vanilla and cinnamon. Bring to a boil over high heat, stirring occasionally. Add almonds and boil lightly over medium-low heat for 5 to 8 minutes, stirring occasionally.

2. When the liquid has evaporated and the sugar covers the almonds with a dry crust, reduce the temperature to low and stir constantly until the sugar turns liquid again and coats all of the almonds evenly. The sugar will have reached the hard candy stage and will be brittle when it cools. Working quickly, pour the almond mixture onto the prepared sheet. Using 2 buttered forks, separate the almonds from each other and let cool. Store in an airtight container for up to 4 days or freeze for up to 2 months.

bay-spiked cherry currant jam

The few people who have been given this jam have flipped over it. Friends who own a bed and breakfast in our area actually wanted me to make and sell it. Could it be that cherry jam is not as common as it once was? I love this jam as well. A spoonful satisfies my maraschino-inspired cravings.

Bay adds a mysteriously subtle nutmeg and spice essence to the cherries. The almond brings out the cherry flavour in such a complementary way that if you don't know it is added, you may not detect that what you think is bright cherry flavour is actually almond enhanced. It's a perfect match, but don't be tempted to add more almond extract.

MAKES 6 CUPS (1.5 L)

2 cups (500 mL) redcurrants or cranberries
1 bay leaf
1/2 cup (125 mL) water
8 cups (2 L) pitted sour cherries
3-1/2 cups (875 mL) granulated sugar

2 tbsp (25 mL) freshly squeezed lemon juice
1 tsp (5 mL) pure almond extract

1. Combine the currants, bay leaf and water in a saucepan. Bring to a boil over medium heat, stirring occasionally. Reduce the heat and simmer gently until the currants pop, about 6 minutes. Press through a sieve, catching the juice in a non-reactive bowl. Reserve the juice and bay leaf; discard the skins, stems and seeds. Measure juice and, if necessary, add water to measure 3/4 cup (175 mL).

2. Heat six 1-cup (250 mL) jars in boiling water, and scald the lids, lifter, funnel and tongs (see page 18).

3. In a Maslin pan, combine currant juice, cherries, sugar, lemon juice and bay leaf. Heat, stirring constantly, over medium heat until sugar is dissolved. Increase heat to high and bring to a boil. Keep the mixture boiling hard for 25 to 35 minutes or until set (see Setting Point, next page), stirring occasionally.

4. Skim off and discard any foam. Stir in almond extract. Fill hot jars, leaving a 1/4-inch (5 mm) headspace. Remove air bubbles and add more hot jam, if necessary, to leave a 1/4-inch (5 mm) headspace. Wipe rims, top with flat lids and screw on metal rings. Return jars to the hot water bath, topping up with hot water if necessary. Bring to a full rolling boil and process jars for 10 minutes (see page 19).

5. Remove canner lid and wait 5 minutes before removing jars to a towel or rack to cool completely. Check seals, label and store in a cool place for up to 1 year.

Use: Serve this heavenly jam with fresh baked bread, scones, almond cake and pound cake and over cheesecake. It is very good with dark rich meats like bison, venison, duck, goose and other wild birds.

Setting Point

Cherry Currant Jam has reached the setting point when a candy thermometer reaches the jelly stage, 212°F (100°C).

If you don't have a thermometer: To test for setting point, remove the jam from the heat. Place a plate in the freezer for 2 minutes. Drop a spoonful of hot jam onto the chilled plate. Return the plate to the freezer for 1 minute. Push the spot of jam with a fork. If the surface wrinkles, the jam is set and ready to pack into hot, sterilized jars. If the jam is not set, return to a boil and test at 3-minute intervals, using a new chilled plate each time.

sour cherry pie filling

If you freeze this pie filling in a freezer bag set in a 9-inch (23 cm) pie plate so that it roughly freezes in that shape, it can be partially thawed, removed from the bag and popped right into the uncooked pie shell, topped with the pastry lattice and cooked from partially frozen. Simply allow extra time to bake at the lower temperature.

MAKES 3 PINTS (2 CUPS/500 mL) FROZEN CHERRIES, ENOUGH FOR 2 9-INCH (23 cm) PIE FILLINGS

1-1/4 cups (300 mL) granulated sugar
4 tbsp (25 mL) cornstarch
6 cups (1.5 L) fresh or frozen sour pitted cherries

2 tbsp (25 mL) melted butter
2 tbsp (25 mL) water
1 tbsp (15 mL) freshly squeezed lemon juice
1/4 tsp (1 mL) pure almond extract

1. In a large bowl, combine the sugar and cornstarch. Stir well with a fork to evenly distribute the cornstarch. Add cherries and toss well.

2. In a bowl, combine melted butter, water, lemon juice and almond extract. Mix well and drizzle over cherries. Toss well to coat the cherries.

3. Divide into two equal portions and spoon into freezer bags. Set each bag in a 9-inch (23 cm) pie plate, squeeze air out, seal, label and freeze. When frozen, lift out of the pie plates and store in freezer for up to 6 months.

OR

If freezing for Cherry Cobbler (page 134), divide into 3 and spoon into pint (2 cups/500 mL) freezer containers, leaving 1/2-inch (10 mm) headspace. Seal with lid, label and freeze.

lattice-top cherry pie

9-inch (23 cm) pie plate
Rimless baking sheet
Preheat oven to 400°F (200°C)
MAKES 1 PIE

1 bag Sour Cherry Pie Filling, (page 132)
  thawed
pastry for 9-inch (23 cm) pie, top and
  bottom (page 72)
2 tbsp (25 mL) unsalted butter

1. Divide the pastry into 2 balls. Roll out one ball to about 13 inches (32 cm) in diameter. Roll around the rolling pin and line the pie plate bottom and sides, cutting off any overhanging pastry. Roll out the second ball of pastry to the same size. Using a sharp knife, cut into 1/2-inch (1 cm) wide strips.

2. Pour (if completely thawed) or fit (if partially frozen) the pie filling into the pastry-lined pie plate. Cut the butter into small pieces and spread evenly over the top of the filling. Working from the centre of the pie, weave the strips of pastry over and under into a lattice pattern. Trim the overhanging strips and crimp all around the edge of the pie. Slide the pie onto a baking sheet. Bake in preheated oven for 10 minutes; reduce heat to 350°F (180°C) and bake for 30 to 40 minutes or until pastry is golden brown and filling is bubbly.

lori schaeffer's cherry cobbler

Last year I happened to visit my friend Lori Schaeffer at her circa 1700 home in Pennsylvania around the middle of June, and found myself up a tree the very afternoon I arrived. That day we happily pulled ripe Morello sour cherries for a few hours and dispatched 15 quarts to the freezer. With so many cherries for pies and desserts, Lori has worked out an easy and dependable recipe for making her version of this homespun dessert. She pre-cooks the filling in the microwave, which significantly reduces the baking time in the oven. Lori also has a large garden (she is a Master Gardener) with black raspberries, boysenberries and some blueberries, so sometimes she mixes any or all of those berries with the cherries.

6 oven-proof individual soufflé dishes,
  lightly oiled
1 6-well muffin tin
Preheat oven to 350° F (180° C)
MAKES 6 SERVINGS

3 pints (2 cups/500 mL) Sour Cherry Pie
  Filling (page 132), thawed
1-1/4 cups (300 mL) all-purpose flour
1/3 cup (80 mL) granulated sugar
1-1/2 tsp (7 mL) baking powder

1/4 tsp (1 mL) salt
1/3 cup (80 mL) butter
1/2 cup (125 mL) buttermilk or milk
1 egg
1/2 tsp (2 mL) pure vanilla extract

1. Combine the cherry filling in a microwaveable bowl. Microwave on high, stirring occasionally for 4 to 6 minutes or until thickened. Spoon equal portions into each of the prepared individual soufflé dishes. Set the soufflé dishes into the wells of the muffin tin. Set aside.

2. Meanwhile, in a mixing bowl, combine flour, sugar, baking powder and salt. Using a pastry blender or 2 knives, cut in the butter until the pieces are about the size of peas. Combine the buttermilk, egg and vanilla and stir until well mixed. Pour all at once into the flour mixture and stir with a fork until combined into a soft dough. If too soft and sticky, use extra flour for handling the dough. Divide the dough into 6 equal pieces and press over the cherries in the dishes. Bake in preheated oven for 15 to 20 minutes or until topping is golden and filling is bubbly. Serve warm with whipped or ice cream.

Freezing Cherries

1. **Select Equipment:** Select suitable-size freezer containers, bags or Mason jars (see page 24).

2. **Dry Pack**

a) Freeze Individual Berries: Arrange washed, completely dry pitted cherries in a single layer, without touching each other, on a cookie sheet. Fast-freeze for 1 hour. Pack into freezer containers (no need to leave headspace). Squeeze out air; seal, label and return to freezer.

OR

b) Fill pint (2-cup/500 mL) or quart (1 L) freezer containers with pitted cherries to within 3 to 4 inches (7 to 10 cm) of the top. Pour dry granulated sugar over top; use 1/2 cup (125 mL) sugar per 1 quart (1 L) of prepared fruit. Squeeze out air; leave 1-inch (2.5 cm) headspace. Seal, label and freeze.

OR

Pack in Syrup: In a saucepan, combine 2-1/2 cups (625 mL) granulated sugar and 4 cups (1 L) water. Bring to a gentle boil over high heat, stirring frequently. Reduce heat and boil gently for 3 minutes. Let cool. Fill pint (2-cup/500 mL) or quart (1 L) freezer containers with pitted cherries to within 3 to 4 inches (7 to 10 cm) of the top. Pour syrup over top; use 1 cup (250 mL) syrup per 1 quart (1 L) of prepared fruit. Squeeze out air; leave 1-inch (2.5 cm) headspace. Seal, label and freeze.

OR

Crush: Using a potato masher, crush cherries in a non-reactive bowl. For every quart (1 L) of crushed cherries, add 1-1/4 cups (300 mL) granulated sugar and 1/4 tsp (1 mL) ascorbic acid crystals. Stir until the sugar is dissolved. Pack into freezer containers, leaving a 1-inch (2.5 cm) headspace. Seal, label and freeze.

Currants

BEING A TRUE BERRY (unlike raspberries and strawberries, which are aggregate fruits), currants and gooseberries have been used for pies, jams, jellies and other preserves for ages. Native to the colder parts of North America and Europe, currants have only begun to disappear from our tables since the latter part of the 20th century, at about the same time the family garden began to decline. Almost everyone I know who is over 60—living in the city or country—can remember the currant or gooseberry patch in their grandparents' garden. Currants are bright red, round, almost translucent globes, and are filled with seeds. Their taste is sharp and tart, and I find that the best way to use them for preserving is to mash and strain them through a cone colander and use just the juice.

Good Preserving Varieties

The garden redcurrant (*Ribes rubrum*) is the most common variety, still found in country gardens.

There are wild, native North American varieties—Canadian blackcurrant (*R. hudsonianum*) and American wild currant (*R. americanum*)—but being bigger and not quite as tart, the European varieties soon replaced the wild bushes in gardens. Right: Big Ben is a European blackcurrant on display at the Hampton Court Palace Flower Show, England.

Any of the golden, red or black currant varieties grown for market today are excellent for preserving.

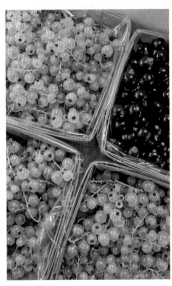

The golden currant variety is tiny, making it tedious to trim for a whole berry preserve. I would use it in a cordial where the fruit is strained. The golden syrup is a nice change from the traditional red or black drink syrups. The blackcurrants are dramatic in jam and jelly.

Purchasing/Storing
- 1 lb (500 g) fresh currants yields 4 cups (1 L).
- You will need about 3/4 lb (375 g) currants for each quart (1 L) jar.

Look for firm, fully ripe fruits that show no signs of bruising or wrinkling. Use immediately after picking. Store in a cool place or refrigerate for up to 3 days. Wash just before using.

Good With
- Spicy herbs such as basil, bay, thyme, chervil, tarragon.
- Sweet seasonings such as cinnamon, ginger, cloves, nutmeg, vanilla, almond.
- Semi-soft cheeses such as havarti, Boursin; medium-age cheddars, colby.
- Other fruit, such as raspberries, gooseberries, nectarines, peaches, pears.
- Toasted almonds, pecans and walnuts, raisins.
- Bold fish such as cod, perch.
- Dried: used in holiday fruitcakes, mincemeat and other desserts.

Preparation
Wash 1 or 2 quarts (1 or 2 L) currants at a time in cool water to which a drop of food-safe soap has been added. Rinse well. Drain, cap and stem if necessary. Pat dry.

Canning Currants
See detailed canning information, page 14.

1. Prepare Equipment: Wash and heat pint (2-cup/500 mL) or quart (1 L) jars, and scald the lids, funnel, ladle and tongs (see page 18).

2. Make a Light Syrup: In a large saucepan, combine 1 cup (250 mL) granulated sugar with 4 cups (1 L) water; stir until dissolved. Bring to a gentle boil over high heat. Makes 4-1/2 cups (1.125 L) syrup, enough for three or four 1-quart (1 L) jars of currants.

Note: You can use the same amount of apple juice or white grape juice in place of the light syrup.

3. Pack currants into jars either hot or raw.
Make a Raw Pack: Fill jars with currants, shaking the jar as you add more to pack tightly. Cover with hot syrup or juice, leaving a 1/2-inch (1 cm) headspace. Run a thin non-metallic utensil around the inside of the jar to allow air to escape. Add hot liquid, if necessary, to leave a 1/2-inch (1 cm) headspace. Wipe sealing edge of jars with a clean, damp, lint-free cloth. Position flat lids over the tops of jars and hand-tighten screw bands.

OR

Make a Hot Pack: Add currants to gently boiling syrup or juice and boil for a minute. Fill hot jars with hot fruit and cooking liquid, leaving a 1/2-inch (1 cm) headspace. Run a thin non-metallic utensil around the inside of the jar to allow air to escape. Add more hot fruit or liquid, if necessary, to leave a 1/2-inch (1 cm) headspace. Wipe sealing edge of jars with a clean, damp, lint-free cloth. Position flat lids over the tops of jars and hand-tighten screw bands.

4. Process currants in a canner: Use a Boiling Water Canner according to the chart below.

Processing Times at Different Altitudes for Currants in a BOILING WATER Canner					
Pack Style	**Jar Size**	**0–2000 ft**	**2001–4000 ft**	**4001–6000 ft**	**6001+ ft**
HOT	Pints	15 min	20 min	25 min	30 min
	Quarts	20 min	25 min	30 min	35 min
RAW	Pints	20 min	25 min	30 min	35 min
	Quarts	25 min	30 min	35 min	40 min

OR

Process currants in a Pressure Canner following manufacturer's directions for steam pressure and time at your altitude.

5. Cool, Label and Store: Lift jars from canner and place on a clean towel or rack. Do not re-tighten screw bands. Let the jars cool to room temperature. This may take from 12 to 24 hours. Remove and store screw bands. Check lid seals (see page 19). Wipe and label sealed jars. Store in a cool, dark place.

blackcurrant cordial

It's always a treat to add a splash of blackcurrant or redcurrant syrup to a drink—alcoholic or not. This light syrup will enhance white wine, champagne, soda water, smoothies, milkshakes and all sorts of fun cocktails and mocktails. Its rich, fruity and sweetly tart smooth finish is so versatile as a flavour spike in fruit dressings and sauces. Try a tablespoon (15 mL) in place of balsamic vinegar in a vinaigrette or salad dressing.

If you are expecting thick syrup, this will be too thin for you, but you can tailor the amount of sugar you use to get the degree of heaviness you desire. For medium-thick syrup, use 2 cups (500 mL) granulated sugar; for heavy syrup, use 2-1/2 cups (625 mL) granulated sugar for every 2 cups (500 mL) juice. Keep in mind that heavy syrup does not mix easily into cocktails.

MAKES ABOUT 4 CUPS (1 L)

2 lb (1 kg) blackcurrants or redcurrants
grated rind and juice of 1 orange

2 cups (500 mL) water
3 cups (750 mL) granulated sugar (approx)

1. In a Maslin pan or saucepan, combine currants with orange rind, orange juice and water. Bring to a boil over medium heat, stirring frequently. Boil for 2 or 3 minutes, crushing the berries with the back of a wooden spoon.

2. Strain the juice through a cheesecloth-lined cone (or regular) sieve into a non-reactive bowl.

3. Press the pulp to release as much of the juice as possible.

4. Heat four 1-cup (250 mL) jars in boiling water, and scald the lids, lifter, funnel and tongs (see page 18).

5. Measure the juice and reserve 1-1/2 cups (375 mL) sugar for every 2 cups (500 mL) juice. Return the juice to the saucepan and stir in the sugar. Bring to a boil over medium heat and boil for 1 minute.

6. Skim off and discard any foam. Fill hot jars, leaving a 1/4-inch (5 mm) headspace. Run a thin non-metallic utensil around the inside of the jar to allow air to escape. Add more hot syrup, if necessary, to leave a 1/4-inch (5 mm) headspace. Wipe rims, top with flat lids and screw on metal rings. Return jars to the hot water bath, topping up with hot water if necessary. Bring to a full rolling boil and process jars for 15 minutes (see page 19).

7. Remove canner lid and wait 5 minutes before removing jars to a towel or rack to cool completely. Check seals, label and store in a cool place for up to 1 year.

black forest freezer jam

This is such an easy jam, and once you have made it, you will likely remember the measurements without having to look them up. You can substitute cherries, strawberries, blackberries or redcurrants for any of the berries in the recipe.

MAKES ABOUT 5 CUPS (1.125 L)

2 cups (500 mL) blackcurrants
2 cups (500 mL) wild blueberries
2 cups (500 mL) raspberries

2 cups (500 mL) granulated sugar
**1 pkg (1–1/2 oz/45 g) freezer jam pectin
  crystals**

1. In a large non-reactive bowl, crush the currants, blueberries and raspberries using a potato masher.

2. In a separate bowl, combine sugar and pectin, stirring until well blended. Pour over berries and mix well. Stir for 3 minutes.

3. Ladle jam into plastic freezer containers or Mason jars, leaving a 1/2-inch (1 cm) headspace. Apply lids securely and label. Let jam stand at room temperature until thickened, about 30 minutes. Freeze for up to 1 year.

currant catsup

I found a wonderful recipe for Currant Catsup in Dr. Chase's Combination Recipe Book *(1917). This is my rather liberal interpretation of that "receipt."*

MAKES 3 CUPS (750 mL)

6 to 8 cups (1.5 to 2 L) fresh or frozen red currants or blackcurrants (5 cups/1.25 L strained juice)

2-1/2 cups (625 mL) lightly packed brown sugar

1/2 cup (125 mL) malt vinegar

1 tbsp (15 mL) salt

1 cinnamon stick, 3 inches (8 cm), broken into pieces

5 whole cloves

1 nutmeg, freshly grated, or 1 tsp (5 mL) ground nutmeg

1. In a non-reactive bowl or crock, mash the currants using a potato masher.

2. Spoon the mash into a colander or cone jelly strainer suspended over a non-reactive bowl. Let the juice drip into the bowl for at least 2 hours, or as long as overnight, covered. Press the pulp using the wooden cone presser or the back of a wooden spoon. Discard seeds and skin.

3. In a Maslin pan or canning kettle, combine currant juice, brown sugar, vinegar and salt. Tie cinnamon, cloves and nutmeg in a cheesecloth square and suspend in the mixture. Bring to a boil over medium-high heat, stirring frequently. Reduce heat and boil gently for up to 45 minutes, stirring occasionally, or until thickened to a ketchup consistency.

4. Heat three 1-cup (250 mL) jars in boiling water, and scald the lids, lifter, funnel and tongs (see page 18).

5. Fill hot jars, leaving a 1/4-inch (5 mm) headspace. Run a thin non-metallic utensil around the inside of the jar to allow air to escape. Add more hot catsup, if necessary, to leave a 1/4-inch (5 mm) headspace. Wipe rims, top with flat lids and screw on metal rings. Return jars to the hot water bath, topping up with hot water if necessary. Bring to a full rolling boil and process jars for 10 minutes (see page 19).

6. Remove canner lid and wait 5 minutes before removing jars to a towel or rack to cool completely. Check seals, label and store in a cool place for up to 1 year.

Use: I am addicted to enjoying this catsup with a good old-fashioned breakfast—eggs, bacon, home fries, the works—but it is so much more useful than that. It tops baked meat loaf and brings a real home-style finish to any dish with which commercial ketchup might be served. I have not yet tried it to make baked beans, but I do believe the originator of this recipe, who claims that it is very nice with them.

black forest meat loaf

This is such a retro, comfort recipe, but with an updated twist. Where our mothers and grand-mothers might have thought that adding half a cup of commercial chili sauce to their standard ground meat and onion loaf was a daring step, our dazzling, jewel-flecked ground turkey mixture is taken to another level with the addition of Black Forest Jam. It's easy and very tasty.

**9- x 5-inch (3 L) loaf pan, lightly oiled, lined on
   the bottom with parchment paper**
Preheat oven to 375°F (190°C)
MAKES 8 SERVINGS

2 tbsp (25 mL) olive oil	1/4 cup (50 mL) chopped fresh parsley
1 cup (250 mL) chopped onions	1 tbsp (15 mL) fresh thyme leaves
1 red bell pepper, diced	1 tsp (5 mL) ground cumin
1 small zucchini, diced	1/4 tsp (1 mL) ground nutmeg
2 cloves garlic, minced	1 large egg, beaten
1–1/2 lb (750 g) lean ground turkey	salt and pepper
1/2 cup (125 mL) fine dry bread crumbs	1 cup (250 mL) Black Forest Freezer Jam
1 cup (250 mL) fresh or frozen corn kernels	(page 141), divided

1. In a skillet, heat olive oil over high heat. Add onions and sauté for 3 minutes. Add red pepper, zucchini and garlic and cook, stirring frequently, for 5 minutes or until vegetables are almost soft. Set aside to cool.

2. In a bowl, combine ground turkey, bread crumbs, corn, parsley, thyme, cumin, nutmeg and egg. Mix well to combine. Season with salt and pepper. Add onion mixture and 1/2 cup (125 mL) Black Forest Freezer Jam. Stir well to combine. Gently press the mixture into prepared loaf pan. Bake for 1 hour. Brush remaining Black Forest Jam over the top of the meat loaf and bake until the internal temperature reaches 160°F (71°C) on an instant-read meat thermometer, about 30 to 40 minutes. Remove from the oven and let stand for 15 minutes before slicing and serving. Pass extra jam.

Serve cold the next day with a green salad and a dressing made with 1/4 cup (50 mL) Black Forest Freezer Jam and 2 tbsp (25 mL) balsamic vinegar. It's perfect for a luncheon, along with crusty country bread.

Freezing Currants

1. **Select Equipment:** Select suitable-size freezer containers, bags or Mason jars (see page 24).

2. **Dry Pack, Unsweetened:** Fill pint (2-cup/500 mL) or quart (1 L) freezer containers with whole currants, leaving a 1/2-inch (1 cm) headspace. Seal, label and freeze.

OR

Dry Pack, Sweetened: Fill pint (2-cup/500 mL) or quart (1 L) freezer containers with whole currants to within 3 to 4 inches (7 to 10 cm) of the top. Pour dry granulated sugar over top; use 1/2 cup (125 mL) sugar per quart (1 L) of prepared fruit. Squeeze out air; leave 1-inch (2.5 cm) headspace. Seal, label and freeze.

OR

Crush: Using a potato masher, crush currants in a non-reactive bowl. For every quart (1 L) of crushed currants, add 1–1/2 cups (375 mL) granulated sugar. Stir until the sugar is dissolved. Pack into freezer containers, leaving a 1-inch (2.5 cm) headspace. Seal, label and freeze.

Gooseberries

THRIVING IN COOLER CLIMATES, gooseberries are an old favourite of gardeners and home preservers. Gooseberries are easy to grow, produce abundant fruit and are a cinch to transform into fruity-floral jellies, jams and other preserves. Some varieties are green when fully ripe. These are usually very tart. Other varieties ripen to translucent red (almost purple); their flavour is sweeter, and they are full of juice.

Good Preserving Varieties

There are basically two categories of gooseberry: the American (*Ribes hirtellum*), which produces smaller fruit but is disease resistant, and the larger European gooseberry (*Ribes uva-crispa*). Most gooseberries have long spines that need to be snipped off at both ends of the berry, but there are some varieties that are spineless, making them less time-consuming to prepare.

Hinnomaki Red: A good variety to grow because it is disease resistant; deep red berries that give preserves good colour.

Invicta: Good flavour; good for canning.

Leveller: A traditional gooseberry in shape; yellow to green colour and flavour that is sweet-tart with pineapple/strawberry overtones; very good in jams and other preserves.

A nip from a gooseberry thorn, shown above, can be quite painful, so it is no wonder that thornless varieties have been developed.

Purchasing/Storing

- 1 lb (500 g) yields about 3-1/4 cups (800 mL) gooseberries.
- You will need 1 lb (500 g) for each quart (1 L) jar.

Select firm, dry berries with a deep sheen. Use as soon as possible. Store in a cool place or in the refrigerator for up to 2 days. Wash just before using.

This red gooseberry variety has been picked before all the berries are fully ripe. The smooth skin and lack of stem spike make it an easy variety to clean.

- Herbs such as sweet cicely, basil, bay, thyme, chervil; spices such as cumin, coriander.
- Sweet seasonings such as cinnamon, ginger, cloves, nutmeg.
- Semi-soft cheeses such as havarti, Boursin; medium-age cheddars, colby.
- Other fruit, such as apples, pineapples, peaches, nectarines, currants.
- Toasted almonds, pecans and walnuts; raisins, currants.
- Freshwater fish such as perch, whitefish, bass, trout.

Preparation

Using scissors, snip off spiny stems and tails. Fill a sink or basin with cool water and add trimmed gooseberries. Swish and allow the leaves and other debris to float to the top to be skimmed off. Lift out berries using a sieve or slotted spoon. Pick over and remove any remaining spines and stems.

Canning Gooseberries

See detailed canning information, page 14.

1. Prepare Equipment: Wash and heat pint (2-cup/500 mL) or quart (1 L) jars, and scald the lids, funnel, ladle and tongs (see page 18).

2. Make a Heavy Syrup: In a large saucepan, combine 3 cups (750 mL) granulated sugar with 4 cups (1 L) water; stir until dissolved. Bring to a gentle boil over high heat. Makes 6 cups (1.5 L) syrup, enough for four or five 1-quart (1 L) jars of gooseberries.

Note: Use medium syrup (2 cups/500 mL sugar to 4 cups/1 L water) if the gooseberries are red and sweet.

3. Pack gooseberries into jars either hot or raw.
Make a Hot Pack: Set 4 cups (1 L) gooseberries into a metal colander or sieve. Carefully lower the colander into the gently boiling syrup and heat for 30 seconds. Lift out of the syrup and drain over an empty dish or pan. Using a slotted spoon, fill hot jar with hot gooseberries, shaking the jar to pack it. Cover gooseberries with hot syrup, leaving a 1/2-inch (1 cm) headspace. Run a thin non-metallic utensil around the inside of the jar to allow air to escape. Add more hot syrup, if necessary, to leave a 1/2-inch (1 cm) headspace. Wipe sealing edge of jars with a clean, damp, lint-free cloth. Position flat lids over the tops of jars and hand-tighten screw bands.

4. Process gooseberries in a canner: Use a Boiling Water Canner according to the chart below.

Processing Times at Different Altitudes for Gooseberries in a BOILING WATER Canner

Pack Style	Jar Size	0–2000 ft	2001–4000 ft	4001–6000 ft	6001+ ft
HOT	Pints	15 min	20 min	25 min	30 min
	Quarts	20 min	25 min	30 min	35 min
RAW	Pints	20 min	25 min	30 min	35 min
	Quarts	25 min	30 min	35 min	40 min

OR

Process gooseberries in a Pressure Canner following manufacturer's directions for steam pressure and time at your altitude.

5. Cool, Label and Store: Lift jars from canner and place on a clean towel or rack. Do not re-tighten screw bands. Let the jars cool to room temperature. This may take from 12 to 24 hours. Remove and store screw bands. Check lid seals (see page 19). Wipe and label sealed jars. Store in a cool, dark place.

berried pavlova

I keep this simple dessert in my repertoire for any season, but especially for winter when berries are so appreciated. Any preserved whole berry will be spectacular; a combination of the green gooseberries and any red berry, like currants or elderberries, makes this light dessert a festive end to holiday meals. To keep life very simple, make the meringue base up to 24 hours in advance and keep cool in a breathable container (not plastic). Better still, purchase individual meringues at a specialty food store.

The filling can also be made in advance and stored in an airtight container in the refrigerator, but keep it separate from the meringue base until just before serving. If you have access to fresh mint, any of the lime, orange, lemon or fruit varieties are particularly nice in the syllabub-like filling.

As an added bonus for an even quicker dessert, you can use the berry filling without making the meringue base. I call that combination Gooseberry Fool and serve it around April 1, for April Fool's Day. Of course, you can use whipped cream in place of the drained yogurt for a richer filling.

Rimmed baking sheet, lined with parchment
Preheat oven to 250°C (120°C)
MAKES 8 SERVINGS

4 large egg whites, at room temperature	**1 cup (250 mL) superfine sugar**
1/2 tsp (2 mL) cream of tartar	

1. Using a pencil, draw a 6-inch (15 cm) circle in the centre of the parchment paper.

2. In the bowl of an electric mixer, using the whisk attachment, beat the egg whites on medium-high speed until they hold moist but fairly stiff peaks. Sprinkle cream of tartar over the whites. Continue beating and add the sugar, 1 tbsp (15 mL) at a time, until the meringue holds very stiff peaks. The peaks should be glossy, not dry, and they should stand upright when pulled by the back of a wooden spoon or spatula. If the peaks stand up but fall over, you need to add a bit more sugar. You may not need to use all of the sugar.

3. Using a rubber spatula, spread the meringue inside the circle drawn on the parchment paper. Pile the meringue around the perimeter of the circle so that you have a slight dip on the inside. This will keep the filling from running down the sides when it is mounded on top later.

4. Bake in preheated oven for 1 hour and 15 minutes or until the meringue is dry and firm to the touch. The meringue should be a creamy pale colour, not brown. Turn off the oven, open the door and let the meringue cool completely in the oven. Wrap loosely with waxed paper and keep cool in a breathable container (not plastic).

berry filling

1 cup (250 mL) canned or frozen (thawed) gooseberries, drained

1 cup (250 mL) canned or frozen (thawed) red berries (such as raspberries, cherries, currants), drained

1-1/2 cups (375 mL) drained vanilla or plain yogurt

3 tbsp (45 mL) maple syrup

2 tbsp (25 mL) chopped fresh citrus peppermint, optional

In a bowl, combine gooseberries, red berries, yogurt, maple syrup and mint, if using. Pile in the centre of the meringue base.

gooseberry and almond relish

Even if you start with only green gooseberries, the relish will be tinged with red. I like to use this with ham and rich meats like duck and game. It is refreshing with egg dishes as well. Some gooseberries have fine hairs on the skin, but they soften in cooking.

MAKES 6 CUPS (1.5 L)

1 cup (250 mL) white wine vinegar
1-1/2 cups (375 mL) granulated sugar
1/4 cup (50 mL) lightly packed brown sugar
8 cups (2 L) gooseberries
2 cups (500 mL) chopped onions

2 cups (500 mL) slivered almonds
1 tsp (5 mL) grated fresh gingerroot
1 tbsp (15 mL) finely chopped fresh basil or
  1 tsp (5 mL) ground nutmeg

1. Heat six 1-cup (250 mL) jars in boiling water, and scald the lids, lifter, funnel and tongs (see page 18).

2. In a Maslin pan or canning kettle, combine vinegar and granulated and brown sugars. Bring to a boil over medium heat, stirring constantly. Add gooseberries and onions and boil for 30 minutes, stirring often, or until most of the liquid has evaporated and mixture is thick. Add almonds, ginger and basil and boil for 1 minute.

3. Fill hot jars, leaving a 1/4-inch (5 mm) headspace. Run a thin non-metallic utensil around the inside of the jar to allow air to escape. Add more hot relish, if necessary, to leave a 1/4-inch (5 mm) headspace. Wipe rims, top with flat lids and screw on metal rings. Return jars to the hot water bath, topping up with hot water if necessary. Bring to a full rolling boil and process jars for 15 minutes (see page 19).

4. Remove canner lid and wait 5 minutes before removing jars to a towel or rack to cool completely. Check seals, label and store in a cool place for up to 1 year.

Use: Serve this fruity, rich relish with hot or cold meats, savoury pastries, meat tarts and roasted vegetables. It makes a great hamburger relish and marinade for barbecued meats or vegetables.

gooseberry gingersnap crumble

Using gingersnap cookies in place of the usual rolled oats puts a new spin on an old favourite in our house. I think this may be closer to the original berry desserts, which were simply sugared berries with cookies or stale sweet bread crumbled and spread over top. You can use any berry or combination of berries in this simple dessert.

8-cup (2 L) baking dish, lightly oiled
Preheat oven to 375°F (190°C)
MAKES 6 SERVINGS

3 cups (750 mL) frozen (thawed) or canned
  gooseberries, drained
2 cups (500 mL) chopped apples
1/4 cup (50 mL) all-purpose flour
1/4 tsp (1 mL) ground cinnamon

1/3 cup (75 mL) butter
1/2 cup (125 mL) lightly packed brown sugar
1-1/4 cups (300 mL) crushed gingersnap
  cookies (about 18)
1/4 cup (50 mL) chopped almonds

1. In prepared dish, combine gooseberries and apples. Sprinkle flour and cinnamon over top.

2. In a bowl, cream butter with brown sugar. Stir in gingersnaps and almonds, mixing well. Spread the topping evenly over fruit in the dish. Bake in preheated oven for 40 minutes or until apples are tender and topping is bubbly and golden brown.

1. **Select Equipment:** Select suitable-size freezer containers, bags or Mason jars (see page 24).

2. **Freezing Whole Gooseberries:** If you want whole gooseberries to decorate cakes (example, Berried Pavlova, page 150) or for use in fruit salads, the best way to ensure that they hold their shape during freezing is to fast-freeze them individually. Arrange washed, completely dry berries in a single layer, without touching each other, on a parchment-lined cookie sheet. Fast-freeze for 1 hour. Pack into freezer containers (no need to leave headspace); squeeze out air. Seal, label and return to freezer.

3. **Dry Pack, Unsweetened:** Fill pint (2-cup/500 mL) or quart (1 L) freezer containers with whole gooseberries, leaving a 1/2-inch (1 cm) headspace. Seal, label and freeze.

OR

Dry Pack, Sweetened: Fill pint (2-cup/500 mL) or quart (1 L) freezer containers with whole gooseberries to within 3 to 4 inches (7 to 10 cm) of the top. Pour dry granulated sugar over top; use 1/2 cup (125 mL) sugar per quart (1 L) of prepared fruit. Squeeze out air; leave 1-inch (2.5 cm) headspace. Seal, label and freeze.

OR

Crush and Strain: Using a potato masher, crush gooseberries in a non-reactive bowl. Push the fruit through a coarse sieve to remove the seeds. For every quart (1 L) of crushed gooseberry flesh, add 1-1/4 cups (300 mL) granulated sugar (or less if the berries are ripe and sweet). Stir until the sugar is dissolved. Pack into freezer containers, leaving a 1-inch (2.5 cm) headspace. Seal, label and freeze.

Melons

AS PART OF THE GOURD FAMILY, which includes pumpkins, squash and zucchini, melons usually grow large, with tender fragrant flesh. Melons fall into one of two categories: muskmelon (*Cucumis melo*) or watermelon (*Citrullus lanatus*). Muskmelons have rind or skin that is either netted or smooth, whereas watermelon varieties are all smooth skinned with thick rinds.

Good Preserving Varieties

Available all year, with a peak in late summer, muskmelon types include cantaloupe (right), honeydew, casaba, Spanish, Persian, winter and Crenshaw varieties. Generally, the firmer and fragrant-fleshed types are best for preserves and freezing.

Watermelon varieties usually have a high water content, along with a sweet, mild taste. Watermelons vary in shape and size, in skin, seed and flesh colour, and in taste. The rind can be pickled, but because of its high water content, watermelon flesh does not can or freeze well.

Purchasing/Storing

- Melons vary in size and flesh yield.
- 1 medium cantaloupe (3 lb/1.5 kg) yields 6 to 7 cups (1.5 to 1.75 L) cubed flesh.

It's always best to buy locally grown melons because flavour and water loss occur fairly quickly after harvesting. Select firm, ripe fruits that are heavy for their size, with no cuts, bruises or soft spots. A pleasant, fruity aroma will escape from the blossom end of a ripe muskmelon. A ripe watermelon will sound hollow (a dull thump or thud) when tapped.

Good With

- Mint and peppermint, tarragon and other anise-flavoured herbs.
- Sweet seasonings such as cinnamon, ginger, cloves, nutmeg, vanilla.
- Semi-soft cheeses such as havarti, Boursin; medium-age cheddars, colby.
- Other fruit, such as raspberries, peaches, nectarines, blueberries, strawberries.
- Hazelnuts, almonds, pecans and pistachio nuts; raisins, dates, currants.
- Chicken; mild fish such as tilapia, orange roughy, sole.

Preparation

Melons grow in contact with the soil, so to reduce the risk of contaminating the flesh, always wash melons just before preparing and eating. Using a soft vegetable brush, lightly scrub melons in cool water to which a drop of food-safe soap has been added.

Pat dry and cut a 1-inch (2.5 cm) slice off the stem end.

Set the melon, cut side down, on a clean cutting board or pie plate. Cut in half using a clean knife.

Remove the seeds using a large spoon.

Clean the knife and cut halves into slices or wedges; remove the rind using a paring knife.

Slice or chop the wedges to the size recommended in the recipe. If melon balls are required, scoop the round shapes out of each seeded half and reserve the remaining flesh for use in Brandied Melon Jam.

Canning Melons

Due to their low acidic value, melons are not recommended for water bath canning. You can preserve them using the Pressure Canner Method, but since they are available throughout the year, I do not recommend this. Melons preserved following recipes that include acid in the form of vinegar or lemon juice and high amounts of sugar are safely processed using a water bath canner.

brandied melon jam

The brandy and nutmeg in this recipe take the combination from a delicately flavoured and rather plain jam to one with a rich, complex flavour. Cantaloupe melons hold their shape in this jam and lend their sunset orange colour. Of course, if you use honeydew melon, the colour of the jam will be light minty green, and I would be tempted to replace the nutmeg and brandy with 1/2 cup (125 mL) chopped fresh peppermint, stirred into the jam in step 3 and boiled for 1 minute.

MAKES 6 CUPS (1.5 L)

6 cups (1.5 L) melon chunks (roughly 1 inch/2.5 cm), see above
2 cups (500 mL) slivered dried apricots or 2 cups (500 mL) chopped fresh apricots
2 cups (500 mL) water
3 tbsp (45 mL) grated lemon rind
juice of 4 lemons

5 cups (1.25 L) granulated sugar
1/2 cup (125 mL) brandy
1 pouch (3 oz/85 mL) liquid pectin
1/2 tsp (2 mL) ground nutmeg
6 tiny hot chile peppers (cayenne or other hot chile), optional

1. Heat six 1-cup (250 mL) jars in boiling water, and scald the lids, lifter, funnel and tongs (see page 18).

2. In a Maslin pan or saucepan, combine melon, apricots, water, lemon rind and juice. Bring to a boil over medium heat, stirring occasionally. Boil gently, stirring occasionally, for 30 minutes or until melon is tender and transparent. Using a potato masher, crush to a soft, spreadable consistency.

3. Add sugar, 1 cup (250 mL) at a time, stirring to dissolve before adding the next cup. Bring to a rolling boil, stirring often. Add brandy, pectin and nutmeg; stir and return to a full rolling boil. Boil for 1 minute, stirring constantly.

4. Remove pan from heat and skim off foam. Half-fill hot jars with jam. Slide a chile pepper down the side of the jar, if desired. Finish filling the jar with jam, leaving a 1/4-inch (5 mm) headspace. Run a thin non-metallic utensil around the inside of the jar to allow air to escape. Add more jam, if necessary, to leave a 1/4-inch (5 mm) headspace. Wipe rims, top with flat lids and screw on metal rings. Return jars to the hot water bath, topping up with hot water if necessary. Bring to a full rolling boil and process jars for 5 minutes (see page 19).

5. Remove canner lid and wait 5 minutes before removing jars to a towel or rack to cool completely. Check seals, label and store in a cool place for up to 1 year.

Use: Team this bright orange jam with summer fruit sorbets and use it in bread puddings, thumbprint cookies and other recipes in which a lighter-colour jam works best.

fruit chocolate mousse

The year-round availability of avocados and cantaloupe melons makes this easy and healthy (it's non-dairy and lower in sugar) dessert one of my favourites. On its own, the mousse is a bit chalky and begs for more sweetening, so I like to team it with fresh fruit and a dollop of the same fruit jam, which acts as the perfect foil for the rich chocolate flavour. Here, I have teamed it with melon wedges and Brandied Melon Jam. In winter, it tops a pound cake or citrus fruit, along with a spoonful of Classic Dundee Marmalade (page 466) or Rhubarb Raspberry Jam (page 58) or . . . well, you get the picture.

MAKES 4 SERVINGS

3 ripe avocados
2/3 cup (150 mL) unsweetened cocoa
 powder
1/2 cup (125 mL) maple syrup or corn syrup
1/4 cup (50 mL) apple juice

1/2 tsp (2 mL) pure vanilla extract
1 cantaloupe, seeded and quartered
 (rind on)
1/4 cup (50 mL) Brandied Melon Jam
 (page 160)

1. Cut avocados in half lengthwise. Twist halves open. Remove and discard the pit. Using a spoon, separate the flesh from the peel of each half. Discard peel. In a blender or food processor, combine avocados, cocoa, maple syrup, apple juice and vanilla. Process until smooth.

2. To serve, spoon Chocolate Mousse evenly on top of cantaloupe quarters. Top each serving with 1 tbsp (15 mL) Brandied Melon Jam.

Freezing Melons

Muskmelon types are best for freezing, but keep them separate from other frozen fruit and do not freeze as long as other fruits and berries. If you grow your own melons, this is an excellent method of preserving their flesh until you have time to use it in jam and other preserves.

1. **Select Equipment:** Select suitable-size freezer containers, bags or Mason jars (see page 24).

2. **Freeze Individual Slices (or balls or cubes):** Line a baking sheet with waxed paper. Arrange melon slices, closely packed in single layer, on the sheet. Cover with waxed paper and arrange another layer of melon slices. If the baking sheet will hold another layer, add more waxed paper and melon slices. Freeze the melon slices in the coldest part of the freezer. Transfer to freezer bags or containers; label and seal. Use within 6 to 8 weeks and serve slightly frozen.

OR

Pack in Syrup: In a saucepan, combine 2-1/2 cups (625 mL) granulated sugar and 4 cups (1 L) water. Bring to a gentle boil over high heat, stirring frequently. Reduce heat and gently boil for 3 minutes. Let cool. Fill pint (2-cup/500 mL) or quart (1 L) freezer containers with melon chunks or slices to within 3 to 4 inches (7 to 10 cm) of the top. Pour syrup over top; use 1 cup (250 mL) syrup per quart (1 L) of prepared fruit. Squeeze out air; leave 1-inch (2.5 cm) headspace. Seal, label and freeze.

OR

Dry Pack: Fill pint (2-cup/500 mL) or quart (1 L) freezer containers with melon chunks or slices to within 3 to 4 inches (7 to 10 cm) of the top. Pour dry granulated sugar over top; use 1/2 cup (125 mL) sugar per quart (1 L) of prepared fruit. Squeeze out air; leave 1-inch (2.5 cm) headspace. Seal, label and freeze. Keep for up to 3 months.

Nectarines

BELONGING TO THE SAME SPECIES AS PEACHES, nectarines are actually peaches with a recessive, non-fuzzy skin gene. Just like peaches, nectarines can be clingstone or freestone, and have white or yellow flesh. Nectarines tend to be moister, sweeter and more easily bruised than peaches.

Good Preserving Varieties

Of the hundreds of varieties of nectarines (*Prunus persica nucipersica*), the clingstone types generally have the best texture and firmness for preserving. Freestone varieties are easiest to work with in large quantities because the stone is readily removed from the flesh. However, like peach varieties, many freestone nectarines are of the melting flesh type, which is not the best for canning and freezing.

Arctic Jay: Freestone; large with pale yellow skin that has a slight red blush; flesh is white; flavour is deep, fragrant and sweet; use in jams and compotes.
Fire Sweet: Clingstone, medium; bright red skin with yellow patches; firm smooth yellow flesh; rich fragrant flavour; a good canning variety.
Heavenly White: Freestone; very large fruit; creamy white skin that is deeply red blushed; white flesh has full aroma and flavour.
Le Grand: Clingstone, large; bright red and yellow skin; yellow, firm flesh that is fine textured; mild tasting; a good canning variety.

Purchasing/Storing
- 1 lb (500 g), about 3 medium nectarines, yields 2-1/2 to 3 cups (625 to 750 mL) sliced.
- You will need roughly 1 lb (500 g) for each quart (1 L) jar.

Select firm, plump fruits with no touch of green or bruising. Skin colour is a characteristic of the variety, not an indication of ripeness. Ripe nectarines have a fragrant aroma and give slightly when pressure is applied along the seam. If necessary (though it's best not to), ripen in a paper bag at room temperature, away from sunlight, checking daily. Use immediately once ripened.

Good With
- Herbs such as basil, bay, thyme, chives, rosemary; anise herbs such as chervil, tarragon.
- Sweet seasonings such as cinnamon, ginger, cloves, nutmeg, vanilla, almond.

- Semi-soft cheeses such as havarti, Boursin; medium-age cheddars, colby.
- Other fruit, such as raspberries, peaches, cherries, raspberries, blueberries.
- Hazelnuts, Brazil nuts, almonds, pecans and pine nuts; raisins, currants; dark chocolate.
- Poultry, veal; hearty fish such as cod, red snapper.

Preparation

Wash under cool running water. The thin, smooth skin of nectarines is usually left on the fruit but can be removed with a vegetable peeler. Cut lengthwise in half and remove the stone. Slice or use nectarine halves.

To prevent discolouration, acidulate: Immerse peeled fruit in water with vitamin C made by mixing 1 tsp (5 mL) crystalline ascorbic acid or six 500 mg vitamin C tablets in 1 gallon (4 L) cool water.

Canning Nectarines

See detailed canning information, page 14.

Essential: Use a firm-fleshed, clingstone variety and try a small quantity of nectarines first to see if you like the quality of the canned fruit.

1. Prepare Equipment: Wash and heat pint (2-cup/500 mL) or quart (1 L) jars, and scald the lids, funnel, ladle and tongs (see page 18).

2. Make a Light Syrup: In a large saucepan, combine 1 cup (250 mL) granulated sugar with 4 cups (1 L) water; stir until dissolved. Bring to a gentle boil over high heat. Makes 4–1/2 cups (1.125 L) syrup, enough for three or four 1-quart (1 L) jars of nectarines.

Note: You can use the same amount of apple juice or white grape juice in place of the light syrup.

3. Pack nectarines into jars either hot or raw (Hot Pack is considered the best method).
Make a Hot Pack: Add nectarines whole, halved or sliced to gently boiling syrup or juice and boil for 1 minute. Fill hot jars with hot fruit and cooking liquid, leaving a 1/2-inch (1 cm) headspace. Run a thin non-metallic utensil around the inside of the jar to allow air to escape. Add more hot fruit or liquid, if necessary, to leave a 1/2-inch (1 cm) headspace. Wipe sealing edge of jars with a clean, damp, lint-free cloth. Position flat lids over the tops of jars and hand-tighten screw bands.

OR

Make a Raw Pack: Fill jars with halved or sliced nectarines, cut sides down and packed fairly tightly. Cover with hot syrup or juice, leaving a 1/2-inch (1 cm) headspace. Run a thin non-metallic utensil around the inside of the jar to allow air to escape. Add hot liquid, if necessary, to leave a 1/2-inch (1 cm) headspace. Wipe sealing edge of jars with a clean, damp, lint-free cloth. Position flat lids over the tops of jars and hand-tighten screw bands.

4. Process nectarines in a canner: Use a Boiling Water Canner according to the chart below.

Processing Times at Different Altitudes for Nectarines in a BOILING WATER Canner

Pack Style	Jar Size	0–2000 ft	2001–4000 ft	4001–6000 ft	6001+ ft
HOT	Pints	15 min	20 min	25 min	30 min
	Quarts	20 min	25 min	30 min	35 min
RAW	Pints	20 min	25 min	30 min	35 min
	Quarts	25 min	30 min	35 min	40 min

OR

Process nectarines in a Pressure Canner following manufacturer's directions for steam pressure and time at your altitude.

5. Cool, Label and Store: Lift jars from canner and place on a clean towel or rack. Do not re-tighten screw bands. Let the jars cool to room temperature. This may take from 12 to 24 hours. Remove and store screw bands. Check lid seals (see page 19). Wipe and label sealed jars. Store in a cool, dark place.

nectarine conserve

How often, I wonder, have great new inventions been the result of sheer chance or luck or accident? It happens to me so often that I am convinced it is actually part of the creative process. When I set out to design this summer conserve, I had no idea that the result would be two exquisite and completely different products. Having just tested the Blackcurrant Cordial (page 140), I was thinking through other possible fruit syrups when I put the ingredients for this shimmering preserve together. What resulted was a recipe for nectarine slices floating in syrup and—bonus—nectarine raspberry cordial to use in drinks, over fruit and in vinaigrette dressings.

With its vanilla- and cinnamon-infused syrup, this has a rich and complex taste, worthy of your best desserts. Let it shine on pound cake or warm crêpes. You can give it away with confidence and pride. And even when the last jar of nectarine slices has disappeared, you will still have their lingering memory captured in the velvety syrup.

No matter how careful you are when straining the syrup, there will be raspberry seeds that cling to the nectarine slices, so if you don't want those tiny pips in the conserve, use pitted cherries or chopped pitted red plums. And even if you don't mind the seeds in the conserve, be sure to strain them out of the syrup, because you don't want them floating in drinks. If you don't have whole vanilla bean, do not substitute vanilla extract; just omit the bean.

**MAKES 8 CUPS (2 L) CONSERVE
AND 4 CUPS (1 L) SYRUP**

**2 cups (500 mL) dry white wine or
  unsweetened white grape juice
grated rind and juice of 1 lemon
3 cinnamon sticks, each 3 inches (8 cm)
1 vanilla bean**

**5 cups (1.25 L) granulated sugar
8 cups (2 L) nectarine slices
6 cups (1.5 L) raspberries, fresh or
  frozen**

1. Heat six 1-pint (2-cup/500 mL) jars in boiling water, and scald the lids, lifter, funnel and tongs (see page 18).

2. In a Maslin pan or canning kettle, combine white wine, lemon rind, lemon juice, cinnamon sticks and vanilla bean.

3. Bring to a boil over high heat. Add sugar, 1 cup (250 mL) at a time, stirring to dissolve before adding the next cup. Bring to a boil, stirring constantly. Reduce heat and simmer gently, stirring occasionally, for 10 minutes or until the mixture turns to a medium-thick syrup. Using tongs, remove the cinnamon sticks and reserve.

4. Add nectarines and raspberries and bring to a boil over high heat, stirring constantly. Reduce heat and boil gently, stirring frequently, for about 10 minutes or until nectarines are soft but still holding their shape.

5. Meanwhile, cut the vanilla bean into 3 equal pieces. Set aside along with cinnamon sticks.

6. Skim off and discard any foam. Using a slotted spoon, fill four hot jars with fruit, leaving a 1-inch (2.5 cm) headspace. Slide a vanilla piece or cinnamon stick down the inside of the jar.

7. Pour hot syrup through a small sieve over fruit, leaving a 1/2-inch (1 cm) headspace.

8. Run a thin non-metallic utensil around the inside of the jar to allow air to escape. Add more syrup, if necessary, to leave a 1/2-inch (1 cm) headspace. Wipe rims, top with flat lids and screw on metal rings. Return jars to the hot water bath.

9. Fill remaining two hot jars with hot syrup, pouring through a strainer to catch the raspberry seeds.

10. Leave a 1/2-inch (1 cm) headspace. Slide a reserved vanilla piece or cinnamon stick down the inside of the jar. Wipe rims, top with flat lids and screw on metal rings. Return jars to the hot water bath, topping up with hot water if necessary. Bring to a full rolling boil and process jars for 15 minutes (see page 19).

11. Remove canner lid and wait 5 minutes before removing jars to a towel or rack to cool completely. Check seals, label and store in a cool place for up to 1 year.

curried summer stone fruit preserve

Sometimes when the bounty of the orchard and garden seems boundless, the most I can do to keep up is to prepare stone fruits for freezing. This has the advantage of providing more time to enjoy summer pursuits while allowing for further processing once the rush is over. Here is a favourite recipe for a delicate all-fruit curried preserve using frozen fruit. For freezing, I simply measure the acidulated fruit slices into 4-cup (1 L) portions and dry pack them. If, like me, you make your own curry and garam masala spice blends, you will know whether you would like to add more or less than the amounts given here.

Of course, you can use fresh fruit or a combination of fresh and frozen fruit in this delicious preserve.

While I call this a preserve, it is more like fruit floating in thick, lightly curried sauce, which makes it perfect for vegetable and chicken stir-fry recipes. Don't be tempted to add more liquid. Once the fruits release their juice, there is more than enough to cover the fruit in the jars. I suggest that you use 1-cup (250 mL) jars because that is the most useful amount for recipes. Naturally, you can fill pint (2-cup/500 mL) or even quart (1 L) jars if you happen to have a large-quantity recipe in mind for feeding a crowd.

MAKES ABOUT 10 CUPS (2.5 L)

1–1/2 cups (375 mL) water
grated rind and juice of 1 lemon
1–1/2 cups (375 mL) granulated sugar
1 tbsp (15 mL) curry powder
2 tsp (10 mL) garam masala spice blend
pinch salt

6 cups (1.5 L) nectarine slices, frozen
  or fresh
4 cups (1 L) peach slices, frozen or fresh
4 cups (1 L) apricot quarters or slices,
  frozen or fresh

1. Heat ten 1-cup (250 mL) jars in boiling water, and scald the lids, lifter, funnel and tongs (see page 18).

2. In a Maslin pan or canning kettle, combine water, lemon rind and lemon juice. Bring to a boil over high heat. Add granulated sugar, stirring constantly to dissolve. Stir in curry powder, garam masala and salt. Reduce heat and boil gently, stirring occasionally, for 10 minutes. Add nectarines, peaches and apricots. Increase heat and boil for 1 minute, stirring constantly.

3. Skim off and discard any foam. Using a slotted spoon, fill hot jars with hot fruit. Ladle hot syrup into jars, covering the fruit and leaving a 1/2-inch (1 cm) headspace. Run a thin non-metallic utensil around the inside of the jar to allow air to escape. Add more hot syrup, if necessary, to leave a 1/2-inch (1 cm) headspace. Wipe rims, top with flat lids and screw on metal rings. Return jars to the hot water bath,

topping up with hot water if necessary. Bring to a full rolling boil and process jars for 20 minutes (see page 19).

4. Remove canner lid and wait 5 minutes before removing jars to a towel or rack to cool completely. Check seals, label and store in a cool place for up to 1 year.

Use: This beautiful golden preserve shimmers as a sweet-savoury accompaniment to fish, meats and vegetable dishes. If you add a few tablespoons of the syrup to gravy or white sauce, it will lightly flavour them.

curried summer salad

I have to admit that, like all artists and writers, I take inspiration from everyone and everything around me. It's a natural process, I guess. So when my niece served this delicious salad for a family pool party, it was so fresh, so colourful, so . . . well, summery, I knew that it had to be included in this book. In fact, before anyone could dig in, I picked up my camera and took the shot below!

What I like about these kinds of recipes is that they are expandable. You can add any fresh summer fruit and use almost any compote, chutney or preserve* in this book for the dressing. In fact, I have slightly tweaked the original version, adding red onion and taking away the fresh dill and rosemary. Frozen cooked shrimp are easy to keep on hand, making this a great last-minute lunch at the cottage or on the patio. I particularly like the light-handed curry flavour with the seafood and mango in this version, but would be happy with any fruit-flavoured vinaigrette.

MAKES 6 SERVINGS

juice of 1 lemon
3 mangoes
3 avocados
2 cups (500 mL) sliced mushrooms
1/2 red onion, thinly sliced

2 lb (1 kg) cooked jumbo shrimp, thawed
  (or fresh jumbo shrimp, peeled, deveined,
  cooked and cooled)
1 cup (250 mL) Curried Summer Stone Fruit
  Preserve (page 170)

1. Strain lemon juice into a large mixing or salad bowl. Peel and dice the mangoes, one at a time, into the lemon juice, tossing to coat after each addition. Peel, pit and cut the avocados into cubes, one at a time, into the mango mixture, tossing to coat with lemon juice after each addition.

2. Stir in mushrooms and onion. Add shrimp. Pour half of the Curried Summer Stone Fruit Preserve over the salad and toss well. Taste and add remaining preserve if desired.

* If you use a thicker homemade preserve, thin it a little to a thick sauce consistency by adding a small amount of orange or apple juice.

Freezing Nectarines

1. **Select Equipment:** Select suitable-size freezer containers, bags or Mason jars (see page 24).

2. **Freeze Individual Slices:** Line a baking sheet with waxed paper. Arrange nectarine slices, closely packed, in a single layer on the sheet. Cover with waxed paper and arrange another layer of nectarine slices. Freeze the slices in the coldest part of the freezer. Transfer to freezer bags or containers, label and seal. Use within 6 to 8 weeks and serve slightly frozen.

OR

Pack in Syrup: In a saucepan, combine 2-1/2 cups (625 mL) granulated sugar and 1/2 tsp (2 mL) crystalline ascorbic acid or three 500 mg vitamin C tablets. Stir in 4 cups (1 L) water. Bring to a gentle boil over high heat, stirring frequently. Reduce heat and gently boil for 3 minutes. Let cool. Fill pint (2-cup/500 mL) or quart (1 L) freezer containers with halved or sliced nectarines to within 3 to 4 inches (7 to 10 cm) of the top. Pour syrup over top; use 1 cup (250 mL) syrup per quart (1 L) of prepared fruit. Squeeze out air; leave 1-inch (2.5 cm) headspace. Seal, label and freeze.

OR

Dry Pack: Fill pint (2-cup/500 mL) or quart (1 L) freezer containers with halved or sliced nectarines to within 3 to 4 inches (7 to 10 cm) of the top. Pour dry granulated sugar over top; use 1/2 cup (125 mL) sugar per quart (1 L) of prepared fruit. Squeeze out air; leave 1-inch (2.5 cm) headspace. Seal, label and freeze.

Peaches

PEACHES (*PRUNUS PERSICA*) are divided into two categories: clingstone and freestone. However, there are two different flesh types that occur in both of the categories: melting flesh and non-melting flesh types. For canning, it is advantageous to choose non-melting peach varieties whenever possible since they are less subject to bruising and will remain firm after canning. Melting flesh varieties are best eaten fresh.

Good Preserving Varieties

Non-melting, yellow-fleshed canning peaches: **Babygold 5, Triogem, Redhaven, Redskin, Sunhigh, Vulcan, Vinegold, Virgil, Venture**.
White-fleshed varieties: **White Lady, Blushingstar, Carolina Belle, China Pearl**.

Best Varieties for Eating Fresh

Melting varieties: **Red Haven, Redskin, Canadian Harmony, Loring**.

Purchasing/Storing

- 1 lb (500 g), about 3 medium peaches, yields 2-1/2 to 3 cups (625 to 750 mL) sliced.
- You will need 2 to 2-1/2 lb (1 to 1.25 kg) for each quart (1 L) jar.

Select firm, plump fruits with no touch of green or bruising. Peaches should give slightly when gently pressed and should not be soft. It is best to purchase peaches at their peak of ripeness and use immediately. If necessary, ripen in a paper bag at room temperature, away from sunlight, checking daily. Use immediately once ripened.

Good With

- Herbs such as rosemary, basil, bay, thyme.
- Sweet seasonings such as cinnamon, ginger, cloves, nutmeg, vanilla, almond.
- Semi-soft cheeses such as havarti, Boursin; medium-age cheddars, colby.
- Other fruit, such as raspberries, blueberries, nectarines, strawberries, cherries.
- Toasted almonds, pecans and walnuts; raisins; dark chocolate.
- Freshwater fish such as whitefish, trout, perch, bass, or light saltwater fish such as red snapper.

Preparation

Blanch peaches in boiling water for 45 seconds until skins loosen; plunge into cold water and slip off the skins. Cut lengthwise in half and remove the stone.

To prevent discolouration, acidulate: Immerse peeled fruit in water with vitamin C made by mixing 1 tsp (5 mL) crystalline ascorbic acid or six 500 mg vitamin C tablets in 1 gallon (4 L) cool water. Drain before using in recipes.

Canning Peaches

See detailed canning information, page 14.

1. Prepare Equipment: Wash and heat pint (2-cup/500 mL) or quart (1 L) jars, and scald the lids, funnel, ladle and tongs (see page 18).

2. Make a Light Syrup: In a large saucepan, combine 1 cup (250 mL) granulated sugar with 4 cups (1 L) water; stir until dissolved. Bring to a gentle boil over high heat. Makes 4-1/2 cups (1.125 L) syrup, enough for three or four 1-quart (1 L) jars of sliced or halved peaches.

Note: You can use the same amount of apple juice or white grape juice in place of the light syrup.

3. Pack peaches into jars either hot or raw (Hot Pack Method is considered the best).
Make a Hot Pack: Add peach slices or halves to gently boiling syrup or juice and boil for 1 minute. Fill hot jars with hot fruit and cooking liquid, leaving a 1/2-inch (1 cm) headspace. Run a thin non-metallic utensil around the inside of the jar to allow air to escape. Add more hot fruit or liquid, if necessary, to leave a 1/2-inch (1 cm) headspace. Wipe sealing edge of jars with a clean, damp, lint-free cloth. Position flat lids over the tops of jars and hand-tighten screw bands.

OR

Make a Raw Pack: Fill jars with peeled sliced or halved peaches, cut sides down and packed fairly tightly. Cover with hot syrup or juice, leaving a 1/2-inch (1 cm) headspace. Run a thin non-metallic utensil around the inside of the jar to allow air to escape. Add hot liquid, if necessary, to leave a 1/2-inch (1 cm) headspace. Wipe sealing edge of jars with a clean, damp, lint-free cloth. Position flat lids over the tops of jars and hand-tighten screw bands.

4. Process peaches in a canner: Use a Boiling Water Canner according to the following chart.

Processing Times at Different Altitudes for Peaches in a BOILING WATER Canner

Pack Style	Jar Size	0–2000 ft	2001–4000 ft	4001–6000 ft	6001+ ft
HOT	Pints	15 min	20 min	25 min	30 min
	Quarts	20 min	25 min	30 min	35 min
RAW	Pints	20 min	25 min	30 min	35 min
	Quarts	25 min	30 min	35 min	40 min

OR

Process peaches in a Pressure Canner following manufacturer's directions for steam pressure and time at your altitude.

5. Cool, Label and Store: Lift jars from canner and place on a clean towel or rack. Do not re-tighten screw bands. Let the jars cool to room temperature. This may take from 12 to 24 hours. Remove and store screw bands. Check lid seals (see page 19). Wipe and label sealed jars. Store in a cool, dark place.

peach and onion chutney

Of course, peach pies, peach jams and peach cobblers are traditional favourites, but this savoury chutney brings all of the rich peach and citrus attributes to a condiment that can be used for entrées. All kinds of ocean and freshwater fish team well with it. I have also used it on a dessert fruit-and-cheese platter to finish a meal.

MAKES ABOUT 10 CUPS (2.5 L)

2 cups (500 mL) orange sections
grated rind and juice of 2 oranges
5 cups (1.25 L) peach slices
1–2/3 cups (400 mL) granulated sugar
1 medium onion, chopped
1–1/2 cups (375 mL) rice vinegar
3/4 cup (175 mL) golden raisins

1 tbsp (15 mL) grated fresh gingerroot or
  2 tsp (10 mL) ground ginger
1 tsp (5 mL) ground cinnamon
1–1/2 tsp (7 mL) salt
1/2 tsp (2 mL) ground allspice
1 pkg (2 oz/57 g) fruit pectin crystals
1/2 cup (125 mL) slivered almonds
5 star anise

1. Heat five 1-pint (2-cup/500 mL) jars in boiling water, and scald the lids, lifter, funnel and tongs (see page 18).

2. In a Maslin pan or canning kettle, combine orange sections, rind and juice. Measure and add peaches to the pan as they are sliced. Bring to a simmer over medium heat, stirring constantly. Add granulated sugar, stirring to dissolve. Stir in onion and bring mixture to a boil. Boil for 5 minutes or until onion is soft.

3. Add vinegar, raisins, gingerroot, cinnamon, salt and allspice. Bring to a boil, stirring constantly, and boil for 5 minutes. Stir in pectin and boil for 1 minute. Remove from heat and let stand for 10 minutes. Add almonds and stir well.

4. Skim off and discard any foam. Fill hot jars, leaving a 1-inch (2.5 cm) headspace. Run a thin non-metallic utensil around the inside of the jar to allow air to escape. Slide one whole star anise down the side of the jar so that it shows through the glass. Add more hot chutney, if necessary, to leave a 1/2-inch (1 cm) headspace. Wipe rims, top with flat lids and screw on metal rings. Return jars to the hot water bath, topping up with hot water if necessary. Bring to a full rolling boil and process jars for 20 minutes (see page 19).

5. Remove canner lid and wait 5 minutes before removing jars to a towel or rack to cool completely. Check seals, label and store in a cool place for up to 1 year.

Use: The tangy citrus and sweet spices perk up the milder peach flavour of this savoury condiment and extend its use from fish and chicken to pork and beef. Combine up to 1 cup (250 mL) of this chutney with ground beef or chicken and cooked noodles for a quick pasta dish.

sweet-sour sauce

One of the great rewards of pickling and canning is that you always have a stock of flavoured vinegar and sauces on hand for quick and flavourful glazes and other finishing touches. I save all of the spiced vinegar brines and strained sauces from the preserves I've opened and substitute them in recipes that call for vinegar or liquid—soup stock, stews, casseroles, salad dressings, vinaigrette.

MAKES 1/2 CUP (125 mL)

1/2 cup (125 mL) pickle brine, strained liquid or chutney (for example, strain the sauce from Peach and Onion Chutney, left)

2 tbsp (25 mL) soy sauce
2 tbsp (25 mL) cornstarch
1 tsp (5 mL) Worcestershire sauce

1. In a jar with a tight-fitting lid, combine brine, soy sauce, cornstarch and Worcestershire sauce. Shake well and add to cooked stir-fry ingredients in wok or pan. Stir and cook over medium-high heat for 3 to 5 minutes or until sauce is thickened.

For a tangy dipping sauce, combine sweet-sour sauce ingredients and pour into cast-iron skillet. Heat over grill, stirring occasionally, until thickened.

peach chutney fish cakes

Make these flavourful fish cakes as spicy as you like by adding 1 tsp (5 mL) Dijon mustard or horseradish or hot sauce, or even chopped hot chile pepper to your desired heat level. For convenience, you can make the cakes a day in advance.

Panko is the name for Japanese bread crumbs. I like to use panko for these fish cakes because the crumbs are light, very dry and larger than regular bread crumbs. There is sugar added to panko crumbs, which is why foods coated in them brown and crisp so nicely. Panko gives a crunchy coating to fried or baked fish cakes, but you can use dried bread crumbs if you cannot find panko. If you prefer, broil these cakes in the oven on a lightly oiled rimmed baking sheet until brown and crisp on both sides, about 3 minutes per side.

Some summer herbs you can use are parsley, savory, marjoram, thyme or sage.

MAKES 4 SERVINGS

1/2 cup (125 mL) prepared mayonnaise
3 tbsp (45 mL) Peach and Onion Chutney
   (page 178), drained
1 tbsp (15 mL) chopped fresh summer herbs
1 lb (500 g) fresh or frozen (thawed)
   whitefish, cod or perch
1/2 cup (125 mL) milk
2 bay leaves
3 cups (750 mL) roughly cubed potatoes

1/2 tsp (2 mL) salt
1 tbsp (15 mL) chopped fresh chives or
   onion
sea salt and freshly ground pepper
1 cup (250 mL) panko or dry bread crumbs
all-purpose flour
1 egg
1/4 cup (50 mL) olive or sunflower oil,
   for frying

1. In a bowl, combine mayonnaise, chutney and herbs. Cover and set aside in the refrigerator.

2. In a skillet, lay out the fish so that it fits the pan, cutting in half if necessary. Add milk, bay leaves and enough water to cover the fish (about 1/2 cup/125 mL). Cover and bring to a boil over medium-high heat. Reduce heat and simmer gently, covered, for 4 minutes. Remove from heat and let stand for 10 minutes. Using tongs or a slotted spoon, lift out of milk and let cool in a colander over a sink.

3. Meanwhile, in a saucepan, cover potatoes with water. Add 1/2 tsp (2 mL) salt. Bring to a boil over high heat and simmer for 10 minutes or until tender but not soft and broken up. Drain well and tip back into the hot saucepan to dry over the still-hot element or over low heat, watching carefully. Using a potato masher or fork, mash the potatoes. Add 1 tbsp (15 mL) of the mayonnaise-chutney sauce and chives. Mix well, taste and add a few grinds of salt and pepper to taste.

4. Pat the fish dry and, using a fork or your hands, break it into large flakes into the potato mixture. Using your hands, gently mix together the fish and potatoes, being careful to keep the fish in large flakes. Add more mayonnaise-chutney mixture by the tablespoon (15 mL), only if required. Taste and add salt and pepper as required.

5. On a sheet of waxed paper, spread out panko. Lightly flour another sheet of waxed paper. In a pie plate or shallow dish, beat egg. Divide the fish cake mixture into 4 equal portions. On the floured paper and using floured hands, gently shape 4 cakes, each about 3/4 to 1 inch (2 to 2.5 cm) thick. Use a wide metal lifter to move cakes; do not try to pick them up with your hands. Working with one fish cake at a time, set each in the egg and brush over top and sides. Transfer to the panko and pat crumbs on top and sides. Transfer to a waxed paper–lined plate; cover and refrigerate for at least 30 minutes or overnight.

6. In a skillet, heat the oil over high heat. Reduce heat to medium; add chilled fish cakes, 1 or 2 at a time, and fry for about 4 minutes or until crisp and golden on the bottom. Turn once and fry for another 4 minutes. Serve with remaining mayonnaise-chutney sauce.

honeyed peach freezer salsa

I wanted a real fruit salsa that was as close to a traditional southwestern salsa as possible. These zippy vegetable or fruit mixtures consist of little more than diced fruit, lime juice, chile peppers and herbs (definitely no thickener added). I also wanted a reliable mixture that could be frozen and thawed and still hold a firm texture, showing little or no weeping or watery sauce. Was I asking for the moon? Apparently I was— until I decided to try adding a small amount of freezer jam pectin. This version is the result of a few trials. It's close to an authentic fruit salsa: it's aromatic, thanks to the cantaloupe, and fruity and saucy all at the same time. Even though most salsas are thick only with fruit or vegetables, not sauce, I like the cohesiveness of the mixture, and yet it isn't like a jam. I think I have hit just the right balance, thanks to this newfangled no-cook pectin product. It's easy to find, especially in summer preserving season.

The cinnamon is optional and could be replaced by up to 1/2 cup (125 mL) chopped fresh cilantro, added just before serving. If you wish to use the salsa as a condiment for ice cream, cakes and other desserts, omit the onion and garlic, but keep the chipotle peppers; they add a mildly hot and smoky element to the mixture.

You may be able to tell that I used fresh cantaloupe and frozen peaches in the salsa, pictured above.

MAKES 6 CUPS (1.5L)

3 cups (750 mL) diced peaches, nectarines or apricots (1/4 inch/5 mm)
3 cups (750 mL) diced cantaloupe (1/4 inch/5 mm)
1/4 cup (50 mL) diced red onion (1/4 inch/5 mm)
2 cloves garlic, finely chopped

2 chipotle peppers in adobo sauce, drained and chopped
3 tbsp (45 mL) liquid honey or agave nectar
2 tbsp (25 mL) freshly squeezed lime juice
2 tbsp (25 mL) chopped candied ginger
1 tsp (5 mL) ground cinnamon, optional
2 tbsp (25 mL) freezer jam pectin

1. Combine the peaches, cantaloupe, red onion, garlic, chipotle peppers, honey, lime juice, candied ginger and cinnamon, if using. Add pectin and stir for 3 minutes.

2. Ladle jam into freezer containers (bags or jars), leaving a 1/2-inch (1 cm) headspace. Apply lids tightly. Let salsa stand at room temperature for 15 to 20 minutes. It will not thicken as much as a jam. Freeze for up to 9 months. Refrigerate after opening for up to 2 weeks.

Freezing Peaches

1. **Select Equipment:** Select suitable-size freezer containers, bags or Mason jars (see page 24).

2. **Pack in Syrup:** In a saucepan, combine 2–1/2 cups (625 mL) granulated sugar and 1/2 tsp (2 mL) crystalline ascorbic acid or three 500 mg vitamin C tablets. Stir in 4 cups (1 L) water. Bring to a gentle boil over high heat, stirring frequently. Reduce heat and gently boil for 3 minutes. Let cool. Fill pint (2-cup/500 mL) or quart (1 L) freezer containers with halved or sliced peaches to within 3 to 4 inches (7 to 10 cm) of the top. Pour syrup over top; use 1 cup (250 mL) syrup per quart (1 L) of prepared fruit. Squeeze out air; leave 1-inch (2.5 cm) headspace. Seal, label and freeze.

OR

Dry Pack: Fill pint (2-cup/500 mL) or quart (1 L) freezer containers with halved or sliced peaches to within 3 to 4 inches (7 to 10 cm) of the top. Pour dry granulated sugar over top; use 1/2 cup (125 mL) sugar per quart (1 L) of prepared fruit. Squeeze out air; leave 1-inch (2.5 cm) headspace. Seal, label and freeze.

Plums

SMOOTH-SKINNED AND HEART-SHAPED, oblong or round, plums have a flat seed that is difficult to remove in most varieties. Plums (*Prunus*) have dark blue, pink, red, purple, green, gold or black skins, and their flesh may be red or yellow. Get to know the variety of plum that suits your needs, because there is a wide range in flavour (very sweet and fragrant to acidic and tart), texture (firm to mealy and soft) and colour. You may start to see plums in your area as early as May and as late as October, but the peak harvest is in late summer.

Good Preserving Varieties

Even with over 2,000 varieties of plums in the world today, most can be traced to three important species: Japanese (*Prunus salicina*), native to China, not Japan; American (*Prunus Americana*); and European (*Prunus domestica*).

European Plums

Damson (*P. insititia*): Wild European native with a long history, named after Damascus in Syria; blue skin, firm, tart flesh with less water content than other varieties; keeps its texture and shape when canned. Mirabelles are a Damson-type plum grown mostly in France; excellent for jams, jelly, stewing and canning.

Gages or Greengages (Britain), Reine Claude (France): Green, European-type plums; round, green or golden skinned; used for canning. Dennistons Superb and Jefferson are good Gage varieties.

Italian Prune and **Bradshaw** are other European varieties.

Japanese Plums: Santa Rosa, Gold (fruit is golden yellow), **Red Heart** (large fruit, red skin and flesh) and **Methley** (juicy, red plum) are all good preserving varieties.

American Plums: Best of All, **Black Hawk** (freestone), **Brittlewood** (clingstone), **Cheney** (clingstone) and **Cottrell** are all good preserving varieties.

Purchasing/Storing

- 1 lb (500 g) yields 2 to 2-1/2 cups (500 to 625 mL) plum halves.
- You will need 1 to 1-1/2 lb (500 to 750 g) for each quart (1 L) jar.

Select firm fruits with a pleasant aroma and that are heavy and firm yet yield to gentle pressure. Ripe plums will be slightly soft at the stem end, and the skin should have a powdery "bloom." Avoid hard or mushy, bruised, stained plums. Plums with cracks, blemishes or broken or shrivelled skin should not be used for preserving.

Umeboshi Plums

Ume is the Japanese word for a fruit in the *Prunus* genus that is called a plum, but which is more like an apricot. The fruit is dried and then pickled. I have often thought that I would like to try to make my own umeboshi paste because it is used by Asian herbalists to treat sugar addiction and cravings. Perfect. Perhaps I can shake my maraschino cherry obsession. Before the paste is made, the plums are laid out on bamboo mats to dry in the sun. The cycle of drying, softening slightly with dew, and drying again is repeated until the fruit are shrivelled and deeply wrinkled (and very ugly).

The next step on the ume's journey is to be layered with crude sea salt and packed into barrels. Often perilla—a herb that tints the fermenting ume a light pink and adds iron—is added. The dried salted plums are pressed with weights, causing them to give up a salty, sour liquid called umezu (ume vinegar), which is used like vinegar, but is not true vinegar.

Once fermentation is complete, the plums are dried or made into a paste. Along with their reputation for curbing "expansive" conditions like my sweet tooth, ume plums are highly valued as a digestive and for their antibacterial properties—sort of like the Asian equivalent of the North American "apple a day."

Good With

- Spices such as allspice, black pepper, cardamom, cinnamon, nutmeg.
- Herbs such as basil, bay, thyme, ginger.
- Yogurt, sour cream, crème fraîche, honey.
- Nutty, semi-soft cheeses such as Oka, Bel Paese, Emmenthal, Port Salut, Esrom.
- Other fruit, such as oranges, nectarines, peaches, apricots.
- Port, white wine, red wine, orange liqueur, balsamic vinegar.
- Full-flavoured fish such as red snapper, cod.

Preparation

Stem and wash plums in cool water to which a drop of food-safe soap has been added. Rinse well, drain and pat dry. For most canning recipes, the pits and skins are not removed. Prick skins of whole plums with a fork to prevent splitting. Freestone varieties may be halved and pitted.

If a recipe requires plum skins to be removed, blanch in boiling water for 30 to 45 seconds. Immerse in cold water for 1 minute and slip off the skins. Cut lengthwise in half and remove the stone.

Canning Plums

See detailed canning information, page 14.

1. Prepare Equipment: Wash and heat pint (2-cup/500 mL) or quart (1 L) jars, and scald the lids, funnel, ladle and tongs (see page 18).

2. Make a Light Syrup: In a large saucepan, combine 1 cup (250 mL) granulated sugar with 4 cups (1 L) water; stir until dissolved. Bring to a gentle boil over high heat. Makes 4-1/2 cups (1.125 L) syrup, enough for three or four 1-quart (1 L) jars of plums.

Note: You can use the same amount of apple juice or white grape juice in place of the light syrup.

3. Pack plums into jars either hot or raw.

Make a Hot Pack: Add whole plums or halves to gently boiling syrup or juice and boil for 2 minutes. Fill hot jars with hot fruit and cooking liquid, leaving a 1/2-inch (1 cm) headspace. Run a thin non-metallic utensil around the inside of the jar to allow air to escape. Add more hot fruit or liquid, if necessary, to leave a 1/2-inch (1 cm) headspace. Wipe sealing edge of jars with a clean, damp, lint-free cloth. Position flat lids over the tops of jars and hand-tighten screw bands.

OR

Make a Raw Pack: Fill jars with whole or halved plums. Shake the jar to pack fairly tightly. Cover with hot syrup or juice, leaving a 1/2-inch (1 cm) headspace. Run a thin non-metallic utensil around the inside of the jar to allow air to escape. Add hot liquid, if necessary, to leave a 1/2-inch (1 cm) headspace. Wipe sealing edge of jars with a clean, damp, lint-free cloth. Position flat lids over the tops of jars and hand-tighten screw bands.

4. Process plums in a canner: Use a Boiling Water Canner according to the chart below.

Processing Times at Different Altitudes for Plums in a BOILING WATER Canner

Pack Style	Jar Size	0–2000 ft	2001–4000 ft	4001–6000 ft	6001+ ft
HOT	Pints	15 min	20 min	25 min	30 min
	Quarts	20 min	25 min	30 min	35 min
RAW	Pints	20 min	25 min	30 min	35 min
	Quarts	25 min	30 min	35 min	40 min

OR

Process plums in a Pressure Canner following manufacturer's directions for steam pressure and time at your altitude.

5. Cool, Label and Store: Lift jars from canner and place on a clean towel or rack. Do not re-tighten screw bands. Let the jars cool to room temperature. This may take from 12 to 24 hours. Remove and store screw bands. Check lid seals (see page 19). Wipe and label sealed jars. Store in a cool, dark place.

spiced golden plum jam

Masala is the Indian word for a blend of spices. A masala may be hot or sweetly fragrant, ground fine or crushed. It is added at different stages in the cooking process. Garam masala is the most common ground spice blend and is usually added toward the end of the cooking time. You can make your own garam masala or purchase one already blended and ground. If you make your own, you will know if you want to add more than the amount called for here.

MAKES 6 CUPS (1.5 L)

4 cups (1 L) yellow plums, sliced
1/2 cup (125 mL) freshly squeezed
 orange juice
2 tbsp (25 mL) freshly squeezed
 lemon juice
5 cups (1.25 L) granulated sugar

1 pkg (2 oz/57 g) fruit pectin crystals
1 tbsp (15 mL) garam masala spice blend
 (see above)
2 tsp (10 mL) ground nutmeg

1. Heat six 1-cup (250 mL) jars in boiling water, and scald the lids, lifter, funnel and tongs (see page 18).

2. In a Maslin pan or canning kettle, crush the plums using a potato masher. Add orange juice and lemon juice and bring to a boil over medium-high heat, stirring frequently. In a bowl, combine sugar and pectin. Add sugar mixture, 1 cup (250 mL) at a time, stirring to dissolve after each addition. Add garam masala and nutmeg. Bring to a rolling boil and boil for 1 minute.

3. Remove pan from heat and skim off any foam. Fill hot jars, leaving a 1/4-inch (5 mm) headspace. Wipe rims, top with flat lids and screw on metal rings. Return jars to the hot water bath, topping up with hot water if necessary. Bring to a full rolling boil and process jars for 5 minutes (see page 19).

4. Transfer to a cooling rack to cool completely. Check seals, label and store in a cool place for up to 1 year.

asian plum sauce

I've always wanted my own recipe for plum sauce—real Asian plum sauce. I think this is close to an authentic Thai or Korean plum sauce. If you can, try to locate an Asian food store that sells tamarind. It is packaged similar to dates. Be sure to chop the flesh very fine because the small, smooth tamarind seeds are very hard, and the only way to find and discard them is to chop the flesh fine. The sharp citrus taste of tamarind is part of the authentic taste of the plum sauce, but if you can't find tamarind, simply omit it or substitute 1 tbsp (15 mL) grated lemon rind.

MAKES 6 CUPS (1.5 L)

10 cups (2.5 L) chopped red or black plums
1-1/2 cups (375 mL) chopped onions
1/2 cup (125 mL) chopped dates
3 cloves garlic, finely chopped
1 dried cayenne pepper, crushed
2 tbsp (25 mL) finely chopped candied
  ginger
1 tbsp (15 mL) finely chopped tamarind
  (see above)

1 cup (250 mL) water
1/4 cup (50 mL) freshly squeezed
  lemon juice
1 cup (250 mL) packed brown sugar
2/3 cup (150 mL) rice vinegar
1 tsp (5 mL) ground cinnamon
1/2 tsp (2 mL) salt

1. In a Maslin pan or canning kettle, combine plums, onions, dates, garlic, cayenne pepper, ginger and tamarind. Add water and lemon juice and bring to a boil, stirring constantly, over high heat. Reduce heat to low, cover and simmer, stirring occasionally, for 30 minutes or until plums are soft.

2. Meanwhile, sterilize six 1-cup (250 mL) jars, and scald the lids, lifter, funnel and tongs (see page 18).

3. Press plum mixture through a food mill or sieve and return the purée to a clean pan. Bring to a simmer over medium heat. Stir in the sugar, vinegar, cinnamon and salt. Bring to a boil, stirring constantly. Reduce heat to low and simmer for about 40 minutes, stirring occasionally, until the mixture reaches a thick consistency.

4. Fill hot jars, leaving a 1/4-inch (5 mm) headspace. Wipe rims, top with flat lids and screw on metal rings. Return jars to the hot water bath, topping up with hot water if necessary. Bring to a full rolling boil and process jars for 15 minutes (see page 19).

5. Transfer to a cooling rack to cool completely. Check seals, label and store in a cool place for up to 1 year.

Use: This tart-sweet sauce excels as a condiment for stir-fried dishes, meatballs and egg rolls. Use it as a dipping sauce for pork, beef or chicken satay.

grilled salmon with asian plum sauce

Pink and plump, salmon is complemented by the lightly spiced and delicately fragrant Asian Plum Sauce. The plum sauce gives a professional finish to the grilled fish. Trout and whitefish are excellent in place of salmon here. When I want a change from grilled fish, I poach it (see serving suggestion below) and chill it for a delicious light lunch.

You can use either Spiced Golden Plum Jam (page 188) or any of the stone fruit preserves in this book (for example, Peach and Onion Chutney, page 178) in place of the Asian Plum Sauce.

Grill or barbecue heated to high
MAKES 2 OR 4 SERVINGS

2 or 4 fresh salmon fillets
2 or 4 tbsp (25 or 50 mL) olive oil

**1/2 or 1 cup (125 or 250 mL) Asian Plum
Sauce (page 189 or store-bought)**

1. Brush both sides of salmon fillets with olive oil. Arrange fish in a grilling basket or directly on the grill. Cook for 4 minutes. Turn and cook for 3 minutes longer, then check for doneness. Salmon is done when the flesh turns from translucent to opaque and flakes easily with a fork. Cook second side longer if required.

2. Transfer salmon to a shallow dish and cover with plum sauce. Let stand at room temperature for 5 to 10 minutes before serving.

Serving Suggestion: For a change, try combining 1 cup (250 mL) Asian Plum Sauce with up to 1/2 cup (125 mL) orange juice. Bring to a boil and poach the fish for about 12 minutes or until the flesh flakes easily with a fork. Chill the salmon in the pan with the poaching liquid. Serve over a salad of fresh nectarine slices and sliced red onion. In a clean jar with tight-fitting lid, combine 1/3 cup (75 mL) olive oil and 1/4 cup (50 mL) of the poaching liquid. Drizzle the dressing over the poached salmon and the salad.

Grilled Salmon accompanied by Asian Plum Sauce.

Freezing Plums

1. **Select Equipment:** Select suitable-size freezer containers, bags or Mason jars (see page 24).

2. Pack in Syrup: In a saucepan, combine 2–1/2 cups (625 mL) granulated sugar and 1/2 tsp (2 mL) crystalline ascorbic acid or three 500 mg vitamin C tablets. Stir in 4 cups (1 L) water. Bring to a gentle boil over high heat, stirring frequently. Reduce heat and gently boil for 3 minutes. Let cool. Fill pint (2-cup/500 mL) or quart (1 L) freezer containers with halved or sliced plums to within 3 to 4 inches (7 to 10 cm) of the top. Pour syrup over top; use 1 cup (250 mL) syrup per quart (1 L) of prepared fruit. Squeeze out air; leave 1-inch (2.5 cm) headspace. Seal, label and freeze.

OR

Dry Pack: Fill pint (2-cup/500 mL) or quart (1 L) freezer containers with halved or sliced plums to within 3 to 4 inches (7 to 10 cm) of the top. Pour dry granulated sugar over top; use 1/2 cup (125 mL) sugar per quart (1 L) of prepared fruit. Squeeze out air; leave 1-inch (2.5 cm) headspace. Seal, label and freeze.

Beans

AS PART OF THE LEGUME (LEGUMINOSAE) FAMILY OF PLANTS, beans are one of the most important human foods, second only to cereals. This is because the protein in some varieties substitutes for animal protein in our diet; plus, beans are easy to grow, dry, store and cook. Almost every continent has a native variety.

If you grow soybeans, kidney beans, black beans, turtle beans or any of the lentils, you have the choice of using them fresh, or drying or canning them. Since most home gardeners do not grow these types of beans and since they are readily available in both their dried and canned states, I am focusing here on the fresh green and wax (or yellow) beans (*Phaseolus vulgaris*). Green and wax beans are grown, bought, stored and cooked in the same manner. They differ from other varieties in that their bean seeds are not grown to maturity and the pods are tender and edible. Available all year, their peak season comes in late June, July and August.

Good Preserving Varieties

Bush beans are a cultivar that stands erect without support. Sometimes referred to as string beans or snap beans, most varieties of bush beans grown in North America are in fact now stringless. When snapped in half, there is a resounding, crisp snapping sound that indicates freshness.

Pole beans describes the cultivars that climb supports, such as corn stalks, teepee poles or other lattice devices. This spread-out growth makes them easy to harvest, and they are popular with gardeners. Both bush and pole varieties are usually harvested when the pods are young and tender so that the whole green or yellow bean is eaten.

Shell beans are harvested when the pods are bulging but before they start turning brown. The pods are split to release the large, dense and meaty beans. The pod is discarded and the mature beans are eaten fresh.

Dry beans are left on the plant until the seeds are hard and the pods are dry. The seeds are then released and the pods discarded. Further drying may take place before the beans are stored.

Green bean varieties: **Improved Tendergreen**, **Contender**, **Provider** and **Strike** are most common fresh at markets; **Bush Blue Lake 247** is a variety used by commercial processors.

Yellow (wax) bean varieties: **Cherokee Wax** and **Honey Gold** are most common fresh at markets; **Eureka** and **Gold Rush** are commercial processing varieties.

Purchasing/Storing
• 1 lb (500 g) yields about 3 cups (750 mL) cut beans.
• You will need 1 to 1-1/4 lb (500 to 625 g) for each quart (1 L) jar.

Look for smooth, crisp pods that snap easily and are free from blemishes and spots. Avoid shrivelled, discoloured, fibrous pods. The actual bean seeds should not be bulging through the pod because this indicates a tough, mature pod. It's best to preserve them immediately, but you can keep them refrigerated for up to 3 days.

Good With
• Herbs such as mint, basil, bay, thyme, chervil, tarragon, dill.
• Spices such as cardamom, cumin, curry spice blends.
• Other vegetables, such as asparagus, tomatoes, onions, garlic, zucchini.
• Bacon or pancetta.
• Almonds, walnuts, sesame seeds, sunflower seeds.
• Mild fish such as tilapia, orange roughy and sole; chicken.

Preparation
Snap off stems and tops if tender. I leave the pointy end on and trim only the blossom end where the stem is attached. That gives a restaurant finish to whole beans. Wash fresh beans just before using in cool water to which a drop of food-safe soap has been added. Rinse well. After trimming, beans can be left whole, "Frenched" (cut lenghtwise on a diagonal), snapped in half or cut into 1- to 2-inch (2.5 to 5 cm) lengths.

Canning Green or Yellow (Wax) Beans
See detailed canning information, page 20.

1. Prepare Equipment: Wash and heat pint (2-cup/500 mL) or quart (1 L) jars, and scald the lids, funnel, ladle and tongs (see page 22).

2. For every 3 cups (750 mL) cut beans, bring 2 cups (500 mL) water or broth to a boil.

3. Pack whole or cut beans into jars either hot or raw.
Make a Hot Pack: Add beans to gently boiling water or broth and boil for 4 minutes. Drain, reserving cooking liquid. Fill hot jars with hot beans, shaking the jar to pack fairly tightly. Pour hot cooking liquid over beans, leaving a 1-inch (2.5 cm) headspace. Run a thin non-metallic utensil around the inside of the jar to allow air to escape. Wipe sealing edge of jars with a clean, damp, lint-free cloth. Position flat lids over the tops of jars and hand-tighten screw bands.

OR

Make a Raw Pack: Fill jars with whole or cut beans, shaking the jar to pack fairly tightly. Cover with hot water or broth, leaving a 1-inch (2.5 cm) headspace. Run a thin non-metallic utensil around the inside of the jar to allow air to escape. Wipe sealing edge of jars with a clean, damp, lint-free cloth. Position flat lids over the tops of jars and hand-tighten screw bands.

4. Place jars in pressure canner. Adjust water level (check manufacturer's instructions), lock lid and bring to a boil over medium-high heat. Vent steam for 10 minutes (check manufacturer's instructions), then close vent. Continue heating to achieve 10 lb (69 kPa) pressure and maintain pressure to process pint (2-cup/500 mL) jars for 20 minutes and quart (1 L) jars for 25 minutes. These times and pressure are based on using a weighted gauge pressure canner at 1,000 feet (305 m) or less. Check your altitude and manufacturer's instructions for variations.

5. Cool, Label and Store: Turn off heat; let pressure return to zero naturally. Once gauge shows 0 pressure, wait 2 minutes then open the vent. Unlock and remove canner lid. Wait 10 minutes then lift jars from canner and place on a clean towel or rack. Do not re-tighten screw bands. Let the jars cool to room temperature. This may take from 12 to 24 hours. Remove and store screw bands. Check lid seals (see page 23). Wipe and label sealed jars. Store in a cool, dark place.

french beans in tomato sauce

I try to make a large batch of these delicious beans for use all winter, but if I run out and want to make this for a meal in the wintertime, I use 1 lb (500 g) fresh winter beans and a jar of home-canned tomatoes in place of the fresh tomatoes. To serve four to six people, use one-third of the ingredients and a quart (1 L) jar of tomatoes (never fresh winter tomatoes).

The technique of passing fresh green beans through a device with several blades that cuts them into long slivers is called Frenching the beans. You can purchase bean Frenchers that are electric or hand-cranked, and some potato peelers have a square end with blades that sliver one bean at a time. I remember my mother using just such a peeler while we sat together on the front porch. It seemed to take hours to split enough for our small family. Even with an electric Frenching tool, it's very tedious, but the result is exceptionally nice with this tomato sauce. While I am in slow motion Frenching the beans one by one, I also like to take the time to sliver (dare I say shave?) the garlic for this recipe as well.

You can use 2 quarts (2 L) home-canned tomatoes in place of the fresh tomatoes in this recipe. Drain well before adding to the onions and garlic.

MAKES 10 CUPS (2.5 L)

3 lb (1.5 kg) young fresh green or
   yellow beans
3 tbsp (45 mL) olive oil
3 cups (750 mL) chopped onions
4 to 6 cloves garlic, thinly slivered or
   finely chopped
4 lb (2 kg) fresh tomatoes, skinned
2 tbsp (25 mL) freshly squeezed
   lemon juice
3 tbsp (45 mL) brown sugar
1 tsp (5 mL) ground nutmeg
1 tsp (5 mL) salt

1. Cut the beans in the French style by passing through a Frenching utensil or by slicing lengthwise using a paring knife. Immerse beans in cold water and set aside.

2. Heat five 1-pint (2-cup/500 mL) jars in boiling water, and scald the lids, lifter, funnel and tongs (see page 22).

3. In a Maslin pan or canning kettle, heat olive oil over medium-high heat. Add onions and cook for 5 minutes. Add garlic and cook, stirring frequently, for 2 minutes or until onion and garlic are soft but not browned.

4. Add tomatoes, lemon juice, brown sugar, nutmeg and salt. Bring to a boil and boil gently for 15 minutes, stirring frequently. Sauce should be slightly thick.

5. Drain beans and add to the pan. Cover and simmer gently for 4 minutes, turning beans with tongs to heat them evenly.

6. Using tongs, lift beans out of sauce and fill hot jars, shaking the jar to pack fairly tightly. Pour hot tomato sauce over beans, leaving a 1-inch (2.5 cm) headspace. Run a thin non-metallic utensil around the inside of the jar to allow air to escape. Wipe sealing edge of jars with a clean, damp, lint-free cloth. Position flat lids over the tops of jars and hand-tighten screw bands.

7. Place jars in pressure canner. Adjust water level (check manufacturer's instructions), lock lid and bring to a boil over medium-high heat. Vent steam for 10 minutes (check manufacturer's instructions), then close vent. Continue heating to achieve 10 lb (69 kPa) pressure and maintain pressure to process pint (2-cup/500 mL) jars for 20 minutes and quart (1 L) jars for 25 minutes. These times and pressure are based on using a weighted gauge pressure canner at an altitude of 1,000 feet (305 m) or less. Check your altitude and manufacturer's instructions for variations.

8. Cool, Label and Store: Turn off heat; let pressure return to zero naturally. Once gauge shows 0 pressure, wait 2 minutes then open the vent. Unlock and remove canner lid. Wait 10 minutes then lift jars from canner and place on a clean towel or rack. Do not re-tighten screw bands. Let the jars cool to room temperature. This may take from 12 to 24 hours. Remove and store screw bands. Check lid seals (see page 23). Wipe and label sealed jars. Store in a cool, dark place.

Use: Heat and eat French Beans in Tomato Sauce—they are divine. You can add them to stew or soup, and they are also a very nice side dish for winter roasts and chops or combined with cooked meatballs.

dilled beans

Versatile, colourful and nutritious, these beans add "snap" to winter meals and salads. You can pack them into the jars whole, in long strips or cut into 1-inch (2.5 cm) pieces. The pieces are used in Three-Bean Salad (page 199), and the whole beans are used in Niçoise Salad (page 201) with tuna, spinach and potatoes, so I usually try to make up a batch each of cut and whole dilled beans.

MAKES ABOUT 12 CUPS (3 L)

2 lb (1 kg) yellow and/or green beans
1 red bell pepper
3 cups (750 mL) apple cider vinegar
3 cups (750 mL) water
3 tbsp (45 mL) pickling salt

18 French Rosé or Brazilian green
  peppercorns
6 sprigs fresh dillweed or 3 tsp (14 mL)
  dill seed
6 cloves garlic

1. Trim beans and leave whole or cut into 1-inch (2.5 cm) pieces. Core and seed red pepper and cut into 1/4-inch (5 mm) strips or 1/4-inch (5 mm) dice.

2. Meanwhile, heat six 1-pint (2-cup/500 mL) jars in boiling water, and scald the lids, lifter, funnel and tongs (see page 18).

3. In a Maslin pan or canning kettle, combine vinegar, water and salt. Bring to a boil over high heat. Add beans and peppers and boil for 1 minute.

4. Into each hot jar, place 3 peppercorns, 1 dill sprig (or 1/2 tsp/1 mL dill seed) and 1 clove garlic. Pack hot beans and peppers snugly into the jar, leaving a 3/4-inch (2 cm) headspace. Pour hot brine over vegetables, leaving a 1/2-inch (1 cm) headspace. Run a thin non-metallic utensil around the inside of the jar to allow air to escape.

Add more hot brine, if necessary, to leave a 1/2-inch (1 cm) headspace. Wipe rim, top with flat lid and screw on metal ring. Return jars to the hot water bath. Top up the canner with hot water if necessary. Bring to a full rolling boil and process jars for 10 minutes (see page 19).

5. Transfer to a cooling rack to cool completely. Check seals, label and store in a cool place for up to 1 year.

three salads using beans

Around the time that the fresh beans are dangling in the sunlight, everything is bursting with summer activity. School is out and cottages are open; boats are on the water; and there is a general air of relaxed and peaceful enjoyment. To me, beans are the icon of summer vegetables. Blanched just until tender-crisp and tossed with the goodness the garden has to offer, their sweet flavour defines all that is best about summer food.

Beans are the prince of the garden, and I have included three recipes for using them. The first is a very simple version of the now famous three-bean salad. With Dilled Beans (page 198) in your pantry, this salad is a year-round reminder of the salad days of summer. The second bean salad is one of my "expandable" salads: it can be the inspiration for any number of fresh ingredient combinations throughout the year. The last bean salad in this medley is my personal favourite: Niçoise. Again, we see flexibility with the choice of fresh, frozen or canned tuna for this Mediterranean specialty.

dilled three-bean salad

While there are so many variations of this nutrient-dense salad, I still wanted to add my own, rather simple recipe here. I always make this salad at least once during picnic and barbecue season because it travels well (with no mayonnaise) and is so delicious with grilled foods. You can add chopped olives, nuts, grilled vegetables like asparagus, eggplant or artichokes, and red and green bell peppers. In fact, it is the kind of salad that you can make your own, depending on the various ingredients you add to it. I sometimes include sliced fennel or chopped garlic scapes, but mostly I enjoy the following simple combination, which celebrates the flavours of the genus Phaseolus. *Serve it on a bed of shredded lettuce, baby greens or finely chopped cabbage in the winter.*

MAKES 6 TO 8 SERVINGS

1 pint (2 cups/500 mL) cut Dilled Beans (page 198), drained, brine reserved
1 can (19 oz/540 mL) kidney beans, drained and rinsed
1 can (19 oz/540 mL) chickpeas, drained and rinsed
1/2 red onion, thinly sliced
1/2 cup (125 mL) olive oil

1. In a salad bowl, combine Dilled Beans (and peppers), kidney beans, chickpeas and red onion.

2. Measure 1/4 cup (50 mL) of the reserved brine and set aside the remaining brine for another use. In a clean jar with a tight-fitting lid, combine brine and olive oil. Shake and pour over bean mixture. Toss well to coat the beans.

expandable bean salad

Basically, you combine seasonal ingredients with fresh, frozen or canned beans for a dish that revolves around the prince of the garden. Add crisp crumbled bacon; diced zucchini; sliced, blanched new potatoes, broccoli, cauliflower or Brussels sprouts; chopped raw fennel; bell pepper; and any green of the season.

MAKES 4 SERVINGS

3 cups (750 mL) fresh greens (lettuce, spinach,
  herbs, shredded cabbage, bok choy)
4 fresh tomatoes, when in season
1/2 red onion, thinly sliced

1 pint (2 cups/500 mL) cut Dilled Beans
  (page 198), drained, brine reserved
3 hard-boiled eggs, shredded or quartered
1/2 cup (125 mL) olive or nut oil
2 tbsp (25 mL) Dijon mustard

1. In a salad bowl, combine greens, tomatoes, red onion and Dilled Beans (and peppers). Toss to combine. Sprinkle shredded egg over top.

2. Measure 1/4 cup (50 mL) of the reserved brine and set aside the remaining brine for another use. In a clean jar with a tight-fitting lid, combine brine, olive oil and mustard. Shake and pour over bean mixture. Toss well to coat the beans.

niçoise salad

If you live near a fresh fish market, fresh grilled tuna is really the best choice for making this famous Mediterranean salad. The next best choice is frozen tuna steaks. That is because fish today is flash-frozen right on the boat, within minutes of being caught. That makes it much better than ever before, but frozen tuna will still have a coarser texture, and its colour and flavour will not be as intense as fresh. As a last resort, canned tuna will suffice. If you can get fresh tuna, buy yellowfin, also called ahi tuna (not blue fin), because yellowfin is caught in ecologically sound ways.

MAKES 6 SERVINGS

1 lb (500 g) ahi tuna steak or 1 can
  (15 oz/425 g) chunk tuna
3/4 cup (175 mL) olive oil, divided
sea salt and freshly ground pepper
3 cups (750 mL) baby spinach leaves
1/2 red onion, thinly sliced

12 small potatoes, cooked and halved
3 small tomatoes, halved
1/4 cup (50 mL) pitted kalamata olives
1 pint (2 cups/500 mL) whole Dilled Beans
  (page 198), drained, brine reserved
3 hard-boiled eggs, cut into wedges

1. Heat a grill or skillet over medium-high heat. Wash the tuna and pat dry. Brush each side with olive oil and season with salt and pepper. Grill the tuna until just seared on the outside but pink in the centre, about 2 minutes on each side. Using a spatula, transfer the tuna to a cutting board and let rest for 5 minutes. If using canned tuna, drain and set aside.

2. Meanwhile, on a platter, arrange a bed of spinach leaves. In a bowl, combine red onion, potatoes, tomatoes and olives. Measure 1/4 cup (50 mL) of the reserved brine and set aside the remaining brine for another use. In a clean jar with a tight-fitting lid, combine brine and 1/2 cup (125 mL) of the remaining olive oil. Shake well and toss with onion and potatoes.

3. Pile potato mixture over the spinach on the platter. Using a sharp knife, cut the tuna across the grain and on a bias into 1/2-inch (1 cm) slices. Arrange Dilled Beans, tuna slices and egg wedges on top and around the platter.

Freezing Beans
1. **Select Equipment:** Select suitable-size freezer containers, bags or Mason jars (see page 24).

2. **Blanch whole or cut beans in boiling water for 3 minutes.** Lift out and plunge into cold water for 3 minutes. Drain and pat dry. Pack into containers, leaving a 1-inch (2.5 cm) headspace. Remove air, label and seal. Freeze for up to 9 months.

Carrots

OUR MODERN FLESHY, SWEET AND BRIGHT ORANGE CARROT (*Daucus carota*) is the flashy descendant of a mean and tough, pale and bitter taproot that most likely originated in Middle Asia sometime before 3000 BC.

Good Preserving Varieties
Carrot varieties are grouped as early or main-crop, and short-root or long-root.

Artist: Grows to about 8 inches (20 cm); sweet and juicy.
Chantenay Red-Cored: Broad, short root; orange-red colour; good flavour; often pulled early as baby carrots, which are perfect for pickling.
Nantes: Sweet, orange, cigar-shaped; old French variety good to grow for preserving because it is not usually grown commercially.

Purchasing/Storing
- 1 lb (500 g) yields 3 cups (750 mL) sliced or 4 cups (1 L) lightly packed shredded carrots.
- You will need about 1 lb (500 g) for each quart (1 L) jar of sliced carrots.

While purple, white and yellow "designer" carrots are starting to show up at market gardens and farmer's markets, the orange varieties still account for most of the carrots grown and preserved today.

Select small, thin, smooth carrots without blemishes. It is best if the tops are intact when purchasing because they are an indication of freshness. You can store carrots unwashed, with tops removed, for up to 3 weeks, but it is best to preserve them as soon as possible after harvesting.

Good With
- Herbs such as parsley, basil, bay, thyme, chervil, dill.
- Spices such as cinnamon, ginger, cloves, nutmeg, cardamom, curry blends, coriander.
- Other vegetables, such as parsnips, rutabaga, turnips, onions, garlic, cabbage, peas.
- Toasted almonds, pecans and walnuts; raisins; oranges.

Carrots sweeten vegetable smoothies, soup, stews and other mixed vegetables.

Small, bunching "finger" carrots are excellent for pickling or canning whole. Bunching carrots are short and may be slender or fat. Either way, they are very good for pickling. One example of a small bunching finger carrot is Amsterdam Forcing (above).

Preparation

Immerse carrots in a sink full of cool water to which a drop of food-safe soap has been added. Scrub, rinse and drain. Pat dry. Blanch whole or cut carrots in boiling water for 4 minutes. Lift out and plunge into cold water. Let stand for 4 minutes. Drain and pat dry. Shred, slice or dice carrots, or cut into uniform sticks.

Canning Carrots

See detailed canning information, page 20.

1. **Prepare Equipment:** Wash and heat pint (2-cup/500 mL) or quart (1 L) jars, and scald the lids, funnel, ladle and tongs (see page 22).

2. **For every 3 cups (750 mL) cut carrots, bring 2 cups (500 mL) water or broth to a boil.**

3. **Pack whole or cut carrots into jars either hot or raw.**
Make a Hot Pack: Add carrots to gently boiling water or broth and boil for 5 minutes. Drain, reserving cooking liquid. Fill hot jars with hot carrots, shaking the jar to pack fairly tightly. Pour hot cooking liquid over carrots, leaving a 1-inch (2.5 cm) headspace. Run a thin non-metallic utensil around the inside of the jar to allow air to escape. Wipe sealing edge of jars with a clean, damp, lint-free cloth. Position flat lids over the tops of jars and hand-tighten screw bands.

OR

Make a Raw Pack: Fill jars with whole or cut carrots, shaking the jar to pack fairly tightly. Cover with hot water or broth, leaving a 1-inch (2.5 cm) headspace. Run a thin non-metallic utensil around the inside of the jar to allow air to escape. Wipe sealing edge of jars with a clean, damp, lint-free cloth. Position flat lids over the tops of jars and hand-tighten screw bands.

4. **Place jars in pressure canner.** Process carrots in a Pressure Canner following manufacturer's directions for steam pressure and time at your altitude.

5. **Cool, Label and Store:** Turn off heat; let pressure return to zero naturally. Once gauge shows 0 pressure, wait 2 minutes then open the vent. Unlock and remove canner lid. Wait 10 minutes then lift jars from canner and place on a clean towel or rack. Do not re-tighten screw

bands. Let the jars cool to room temperature. This may take from 12 to 24 hours. Remove and store screw bands. Check lid seals (see page 23). Wipe and label sealed jars. Store in a cool, dark place.

carrot jam

It's not Dundee Marmalade (page 466), but it does give that delicious comestible a run for the money. If you are patient and let the jars sit in the cupboard for a few weeks before opening, you will be rewarded with a jam that is worthy of homemade scones and waffles. I like the good use of carrots, and the way it complements both sweet and savoury dishes.

I can't stress enough how important a heavy-bottomed pan is for preserving, and this jam is a case in point. When testing this recipe, at step 3 I totally ignored the covered pan, and by the time I checked, given the amount of steam escaping out from under the lid, I thought I had lost the batch. To my amazement, the mixture was not scorched, and I thanked the high-quality Maslin pan.

A good French knife makes short work of the orange and lemon shreds. Don't try to use a shredder or slicing blade of a food processor because those tools will mangle the citrus.

MAKES 6 CUPS (1.5 L)

1 orange, unpeeled
1 lemon, unpeeled
6 cups (1.5 L) lightly packed shredded carrots (1–1/2 lb/750 g)
1 cup (250 mL) freshly squeezed orange juice
1 tsp (5 mL) ground coriander
1/2 tsp (2 mL) ground allspice
1/2 tsp (2 mL) ground cumin
1/2 tsp (2 mL) salt
1 pkg (1–3/4 oz/49 to 57 g) fruit pectin crystals
5 cups (1.25 L) granulated sugar

1. Heat six 1-cup (250 mL) jars in boiling water, and scald the lids, lifter, funnel and tongs (see page 18).

2. Trim the ends off orange and lemon. Cut each into thin slices and remove the seeds. Stack 2 or 3 slices and cut into shreds. Repeat until all slices are shredded. (I prefer the citrus fruits to be shredded rather

than coarsely chopped because that distributes the citrus "hit" more evenly throughout.

3. In a Maslin pan or canning kettle, combine orange and lemon shreds, carrots, orange juice, coriander, allspice, cumin and salt. Bring to a boil over high heat, stirring constantly. Reduce heat, cover and boil gently for 20 minutes, stirring occasionally. The liquid may almost be evaporated, but that is fine. The important thing at this step is that the carrots and citrus peel are tender. If not, keep boiling, even if you have to add 1/2 cup (125 mL) water to keep the mixture from scorching. Stir frequently after 20 minutes of covered simmering.

4. Remove from heat and stir in pectin until dissolved. Bring to a boil over high heat, stirring constantly. Add sugar all at once and return to a full rolling boil, stirring constantly. Boil hard, stirring constantly, for 1 minute.

5. Remove from heat. Skim off and discard any foam. Fill hot jars, leaving a 1/4-inch (5 mm) headspace. Run a thin non-metallic utensil around the inside of the jar to remove air bubbles and add more hot jam, if necessary, to leave a 1/4-inch (5 mm) headspace. Wipe rims, top with flat lids and screw on metal rings. Return jars to the hot water bath, topping up with hot water if necessary. Bring to a full rolling boil and process jars for 10 minutes (see page 19).

6. Remove canner lid and wait 5 minutes before removing jars to a towel or rack to cool completely. Check seals, label and store in a cool place for up to 1 year.

Use: Carrot jam can be used as any other fruit jam, but I particularly like it on quick bread nut loaves and with savoury meat pies or wraps. Use it as a glaze for cooked vegetables: toss grilled or steamed vegetables in up to 1 cup (250 mL) of the jam while hot, just before serving. This is also a flavourful topping for fresh yogurt, or you can add a couple of tablespoons (25 mL) to a Vinaigrette Dressing or Salsa Verde.

pickled baby carrots

The small, thin baby carrots are best in this recipe. Use them whole. Cut stump, long-root or fat carrots into uniform sticks. Sometimes it's nice to have these different pickled carrots for a sandwich platter or salad accompaniment.

MAKES 10 CUPS (2.5 L)

4 lb (2 kg) fresh carrots, with tops attached
6 cups (1.5 L) apple cider vinegar
3 cups (750 mL) granulated sugar
2 tsp (10 mL) pickling salt

2 tbsp (25 mL) Classic Pickling Spice Blend
 (page 213 or store-bought), tied in a
 cheesecloth bag
2 star anise

1. Using a measure (such as a metal spatula), trim tops off carrots, leaving about 1 inch (2.5 cm) of the stems attached. Soak carrots in a sink full of cool water and scrub using a vegetable brush, being careful not to break off stems at the crown. Trim the tiny rootlets at the tip of the carrots, leaving the point intact.

2. Bring a large saucepan of water to a boil over high heat. Add carrots and cook for 4 minutes. Immerse in cold water for 4 minutes. Drain and set aside until needed.

3. Heat five 1-pint (2-cup/500 mL) jars in boiling water, and scald the lids, lifter, funnel and tongs (see page 18).

4. In a Maslin pan or canning kettle, combine vinegar, sugar and salt. Bring to a boil over high heat. Add spice bag, star anise and carrots. Cover, reduce heat and keep the mixture boiling for 5 minutes. Remove and discard spice bag and star anise.

5. Remove from heat. Using a slotted spoon, fill hot jars with carrots, shaking the jar to pack fairly tightly. Leave a 1-inch (2.5 cm) headspace. Pour hot brine over carrots through a cheesecloth-lined funnel to within 1/2 inch (1 cm) of the top. Wipe rims, top with flat lids and screw on metal rings. Return jars to the hot water bath, topping up with hot water if necessary. Bring to a full rolling boil and process jars for 10 minutes (see page 19).

6. Remove canner lid and wait 5 minutes before removing jars to a towel or rack to cool completely. Check seals, label and store in a cool place for up to 1 year.

Freezing Carrots

1. **Select Equipment:** Select suitable-size freezer containers, bags or Mason jars (see page 24).

2. **Blanch and cut carrots as directed on page 204.** Pack into containers, leaving a 1-inch (2.5 cm) headspace. Remove air, label and seal. Freeze for up to 9 months.

Clockwise *from top right:* Asian Lime Pickles, Dilled Beans, Pickled Carrots, Turnips and Peppers, Bread and Butter Pickles and Classic Dill Spears.

Pickles

THE CELEBRATED ROMAN FARMER, COLUMELLA (AD 4 to circa AD 70), whose agricultural writings in twelve volumes titled, *De Re Rustica*, wrote, "vinegar and hard brine are essential for making preserves." It's true—both pickles and chutneys use brine (salt and water) along with vinegar to preserve them and both are seasoned with herbs and spices. But while chutney can trace its lineage straight back to the *chatni* of India, pickles are truly international in their pedigree.

Almost every country boasts a pickle (or several), that is to say, a brined or corned vegetable. The Indian *Achar*; Indonesian acar, and achara from the Philippines; Vietnamese cai chua and the carrot, date and onion *achcharu* of Sri Lanka are all pickles featuring local papaya, pineapple, and/or vegetables. Korea, Japan and China have several pickled dishes, each with their own ingredients and in some cases, special uses. The *beni shoga* pickled ginger of Japan has been served with sushi and other raw fish dishes for centuries.

In Turkey, pickles are called tursu and in Greece, they say *toupai*. Some Arab countries still use the Persian word, *torshi*, and the word for Albanian, Bulgarian, Serbian and Macedonian mixed pickles is *turshi*. In these countries, cabbage, eggplant, turnips, beets, peppers and cucumber are the vegetables most often pickled. Local fish such as salmon, pike and eel along with cockles, mussels and winkles in vinegar began showing up on tables in 16th century London. All over Scandinavia to this day, vinegar-pickled herring appear on every smorgasbord.

When North Americans use the word *pickle* they mean pickled cucumber almost exclusively. For them, olives and okra may be pickled and pickled peppers, pickled onions, pickled eggs and even pickled watermelon rind is eaten, but these are not usually referred to as *pickles*.

It is thought that *pekel*, a Dutch word for brine, is the root for the English term pickle but its use as a food predates recorded history. It's not by chance that every sea-faring nation developed their own pickled foods, because pickling was an efficient way to preserve food for long voyages. It was thought that sauerkraut and pickles were an antidote for scurvy. From the builders of China's Great Wall to Julius Caesar, Napoleon and Queen Elizabeth I, pickles were valued as a healthy food and a secret of beauty.

I, for one, agree with Thomas Jefferson, who wrote, "On a hot day in Virginia I know of nothing more comforting than a fine spiced pickle, brought up trout-like from the sparkling depths of that aromatic jar, below the stairs in Aunt Sally's cellar."

pickling spice

If you make your own pickles, you should consider making your own pickling spice blends. The point is that fresh whole spices impart the zip and complex essence to the brine. Be sure to purchase the ingredients from a busy spice seller who keeps a fresh stock of whole spices and turns them over quickly. Make up enough for the preserving season and discard any left over after six months. Bay is now available fresh in the produce section of many supermarkets; that is the best choice, so look there first. Tellicherry whole black pepper-corns from the Malabar Coast of India are left on the vine longer to develop large, mature berries with a deep, rich flavour. Choose green (not white) cardamom pods: green indi-cates the freshness of the pods, and their seeds will be full of camphor. Brown mustard seeds are smaller than the yellow ones and are hotter in taste.

Store these exceptionally fragrant blends in a dark glass container away from heat and light (definitely not over the stove!). If you must use a clear glass container, cover it with a strip of brown/Kraft paper. You can purchase commercial blends of pickling spice, but try to get a package from a recent shipment, not one that has lingered on the shelf from the previous year (although that doesn't guarantee it hasn't been wintering on the distributor's shelves).

You will need cheesecloth for the spice bags and for straining some of the jams, so purchase at least a yard (3 ft/1 m) or more at a time.

classic pickling spice blend

MAKES ABOUT 1 CUP (250 ML)

6 fresh bay leaves
1 whole nutmeg
1 cinnamon stick, 3 inches (8 cm)
2 tbsp (25 mL) whole brown or yellow
   mustard seeds
2 tbsp (25 mL) whole allspice berries
1 tbsp (15 mL) coriander seeds
1 tbsp (15 mL) whole Tellicherry black
   peppercorns

1 tbsp (15 mL) ground ginger
1 tbsp (15 mL) dill or fennel seeds
1 tbsp (15 mL) hot red pepper flakes
2 tsp (10 mL) cardamom seeds
   (from green pods)
2 tsp (10 mL) cumin seeds
1 tsp (5 mL) whole cloves

Stack the bay leaves and, using scissors, snip thin strips crosswise through the stack.

Using a mortar and pestle or rolling pin, crush the nutmeg.

Using a mortar and pestle or rolling pin, crush the cinnamon.

In a bowl, combine spices. From the green bay strips, top centre, clockwise: yellow mustard seeds, allspice berries, coriander seeds, Tellicherry black peppercorns, ground ginger, dill seeds, hot pepper flakes, cardamom seeds, cumin seeds, whole cloves, cinnamon pieces, and whole nutmeg in the centre.

Mix well and spoon the spices into a dark glass jar with a tight-fitting lid.

How to Make a Spice Bag

Cut a 10-inch (25cm) square of doubled cheesecloth and a 24-inch (60 cm) length of thin string. Spoon the specified amount of pickling spice into the centre of the square.

Bring up the edges of the cloth around the spices to make a pouch. Secure with the string, leaving one long end to tie around the handle of the pot for easy removal after boiling with the pickling liquids.

curry pickling spice blend

Being blends of several different spices, curries reflect the personal preferences of each individual who combines them. Some are very hot, some are red, some are yellow, some are green, and some are slightly sweet with anise overtones. For this pickling spice blend, I have included more fragrant and anise-flavoured spices than hot ones. You can change the amounts and add other spices, according to your own whims, to make it your own.

Fenugreek (between the coriander, left, and allspice, right) is the pyramid-shaped (or tri-corn, hence the name) herb labelled *Trigonella foenum-graecum*. It gives curry its characteristic essence, so it is essential to any curry blend.

I find that curry spices are richer in flavour if dry-roasted before using. To prepare, combine the whole seeds in a spice wok for dry roasting over medium-high heat until fragrant. When roasting spices, stir constantly and remove before they begin to smoke. Let cool and combine with turmeric and ginger. Store in a cool, dark place for up to 6 months. Pictured here, clockwise from top left: red cayenne pepper strips, star anise, crushed cinnamon, whole mustard seeds, whole allspice berries, fenugreek seeds, coriander seeds, Brazilian green peppercorns and cumin seeds.

MAKES 1 CUP (250 mL)

6 dried cayenne pepper pods
2 star anise
1 cinnamon stick, 3 inches (8 cm)
2 tbsp (25 mL) whole brown or yellow
   mustard seeds
2 tbsp (25 mL) whole allspice berries

2 tbsp (25 mL) ground turmeric
2 tbsp (25 mL) fenugreek seeds
1 tbsp (15 mL) coriander seeds
1 tbsp (15 mL) whole Brazilian green
   peppercorns
1 tbsp (15 mL) ground ginger
2 tsp (10 mL) cumin seeds

1. Stack the cayenne pepper pods and, using scissors, snip thin strips crosswise through the stack.

2. Using a mortar and pestle or rolling pin, crush the star anise pod and seeds. Below, I am using a cast iron mortar and pestle for crushing a small amount of bark spices.

3. Using a mortar and pestle or rolling pin, crush the cinnamon.

4. In a bowl, combine cayenne strips, crushed star anise, crushed cinnamon, mustard seeds, allspice berries, turmeric, fenugreek, coriander, peppercorns, ginger and cumin seeds. Mix well and spoon the spices into a dark glass jar with a tight-fitting lid. Label and store away from heat and light.

five-spice blend

It is said that the traditional spices in this blend represent the five tastes: sweet, sour, bitter, pungent and salty. Make at least 1/2 cup (125 mL) of the blend and use in stir-fry dishes or with rice casseroles. There are more than a few variations for this spice blend, but most use the five basic spices I list here. Some recipes use fagara instead of peppercorns and some add cardamom, ginger or licorice to the basic five. You can dry-roast the whole spices before combining them or simply crush with a mortar and pestle, or with a rolling pin. Once the spices are crushed and combined, store in a dark glass container in a cool spot.

MAKES 1/2 CUP (125 mL)

2 tbsp (25 mL) fennel seeds
2 tbsp (25 mL) crushed star anise
1 tbsp (15 mL) crushed cinnamon

1 tbsp (15 mL) whole cloves
1 tbsp (15 mL) whole black peppercorns

1. In a bowl, combine fennel seeds, star anise, cinnamon, cloves and peppercorns. Transfer to a dark glass jar; cover, label and store in a cool spot.

Cucumbers

COLUMBUS INTRODUCED THE CUCUMBER (*CUCUMIS SATIVUS*) to North America in 1494 on the island of Haiti. As waves of Europeans came to the New World—first the Spanish, French and English—they brought their own seeds and grew them in settlement gardens. Strictly speaking, cucumbers are the fruit of the plant, although we think of them as vegetables.

Good Preserving Varieties

There are many varieties of cucumbers, including the large, smooth greenhouse-grown English cucumber—not for preserving, but a great table cucumber thanks to its delicate flavour and tender, seedless flesh. For fresh summer salads, I like the English cucumber because it fits the tube of my food processor and can be sliced into very thin rounds.

There are many varieties of cucumbers: small pickling varieties; Japanese cucumbers, which may be round or pointed, with soft spines; and seedless types. These are just a few of the many excellent pickling varieties: **Ballerina**, **Boston Pickling**, **Pioneer**, **Miss Pickler Hybrid**, **County Fair Hybrid**, **Bush Pickle Hybrid** and **Eureka Hybrid**.

Purchasing/Storing

- 1 lb (500 g) pickling cucumbers yields 3-1/2 cups (875 mL) crosswise slices.
- You will need 1 lb (500 g) for each quart (1 L) jar of sliced cucumber, more for spears or lengthwise slices.

Fresh pickling cucumbers should not be waxed, but if they are, they must be peeled since washing will not remove the wax. Look for fresh, firm, well-shaped cucumbers that are not too large or overmature. Cucumbers are usually bright green, with white tips.

Good With

- Herbs such as dill, basil, bay, thyme, chervil.
- Spices such as cinnamon, ginger, cloves, nutmeg, cumin, coriander, mustard, cardamom.
- Sour cream; all flavours of vinegar.
- Other vegetables, such as fennel, peppers, celery, radish, leeks, daikon, zucchini.

Preparation

Scrub in cool water to which a drop of food-safe soap has been added. Rinse and pat dry.

bread and butter pickles

Some pickle recipes take seven days; others are quick and just need to be refrigerated after a quick boil. This recipe can be completed in a day, but start in the morning or at least by early afternoon, and don't skip the soaking stage. These are sweet pickles meant to accompany sandwiches, light meals and lunches. I always look forward to seeing them on picnic tables, at barbecues and on paper plates all summer. In winter, they bring back memories of all those alfresco meals.

I love garlic but never add it to my bread and butter pickles, preferring the sweetness on its own, with just a hint of the ginger and fennel. If you like garlic, you can add 4 or more cloves, thinly sliced, in step 1. The brown sugar gives a dark tinge to the brine; if you want a lighter, clear brine, use granulated sugar in its place.

This recipe is a good example of how having the right tools to do the job can really save time and effort. In the photo above, I used a continuous slicer attachment on the KitchenAid stand mixer to quickly dispatch 12 cups (3 L) of cucumber slices.

MAKES 10 CUPS (2.5 L)

3-1/2 lb (1.75 kg) pickling cucumbers, sliced (1/4 inch/5 mm), about 12 cups (3 L)
4 onions, thinly sliced
1/2 cup (125 mL) pickling salt
3 cups (750 mL) white vinegar
1 tbsp (15 mL) grated fresh gingerroot
1 tsp (5 mL) fennel seeds
1 cup (250 mL) granulated sugar
1 cup (250 mL) lightly packed brown sugar

1. In a non-reactive bowl or crock, combine cucumbers, onions and salt. Mix well, cover with cold water and let stand at room temperature for 2 hours. Drain in a colander over a sink. Rinse with cold running water and drain well.

2. Heat five 1-pint (2-cup/500 mL) jars in boiling water, and scald the lids, lifter, funnel and tongs (see page 18).

3. In a Maslin pan or canning kettle, combine vinegar, ginger and fennel seeds. Bring to a boil over high heat, stirring constantly. Add granulated and brown sugars, stirring to dissolve before adding

the next cup. Stir in cucumbers and onions and return to a boil. Boil for 1 minute and remove from heat.

4. Pack hot jars with cucumber and onions, leaving a 1/2-inch (1 cm) headspace. Ladle hot pickling liquid over vegetables, leaving a 1/2-inch (1 cm) headspace. Run a thin non-metallic utensil around the inside of the jar to allow air to escape. Add more hot brine, if necessary, to leave a 1/2-inch (1 cm) headspace. Wipe rims, top with flat lids and screw on metal rings. Return jars to the hot water bath, topping up with hot water if necessary. Bring to a full rolling boil and process jars for 10 minutes (see page 19).

5. Remove canner lid and wait 5 minutes before removing jars to a towel or rack to cool completely. Check seals, label and store in a cool place for up to 1 year.

classic dill spears

Just about the time that cucumbers are perfect for pickling, along comes dill blooming and looming tall in the garden. The first gardener or cook who looked out over the plot and thought to marry the cool, crisp, mildly clear taste of "cukes" with that of the warm, pungent, slightly sharp old Norse herb and its hint of caraway must have been a culinary genius.

Note: These amounts fill four 1-pint (2-cup/500 mL) jars. If you wish to fill four 1-quart (1 L) jars, you cannot simply double the amounts. For four 1-quart (1 L) jars, increase the amounts by roughly 2-1/4 times the measures below, and use large cucumbers, cut into eighths.

MAKES 8 CUPS (2 L)

3 lb (1.5 kg) small to medium cucumbers
  (see note above)
1 head fresh dill
2 cups (500 mL) white vinegar
1 cup (250 mL) cider vinegar
3 cups (750 mL) water
2/3 cup (150 mL) granulated sugar

1/3 cup (75 mL) pickling salt
2 tbsp (25 mL) Classic Pickling Spice Blend
  (page 213 or store-bought), tied in a
  cheesecloth bag
4 cloves garlic
8 allspice berries

1. Wash and drain cucumbers following directions on page 219. Cut one end off each cucumber so that it is 1 inch (2.5 cm) shorter than the jars, and quarter each lengthwise, so that you have 4 spears from each length of cucumber. Reserve cut-off cucumber ends for Bread and Butter Pickles (page 220) or for Asian Lime Pickles (page 224).

2. Snip the stems of the dill florets close to the point where they all join the stem, leaving them long. The stems act like a handle for inserting and removing the dill from the jars. You will need about 4 florets per jar, 16 in total.

3. Heat four 1-pint (2-cup/500 mL) jars in boiling water, and scald the lids, lifter, funnel and tongs (see page 18).

4. In a Maslin pan or canning kettle, combine white and cider vinegars, water, sugar, salt and spice bag. Bring to a boil over high heat, stirring constantly, until sugar and salt are dissolved. Reduce heat and boil gently, stirring occasionally, for 15 minutes.

5. Pack cucumber spears into hot jars and add up to 4 florets of dill, using the stem to pack them between the spears. Add 1 clove of garlic and 2 allspice berries to each jar.

6. Ladle hot brine into jar to cover cucumbers, leaving a 1/2-inch (1 cm) headspace. Run a thin non-metallic utensil around the inside of the jar to allow air to escape. Add more brine if necessary to maintain a 1/2-inch (1 cm) headspace. Wipe rims, top with flat lids and screw on metal rings. Return jars to the hot water bath, topping up with hot water if necessary. Bring to a full rolling boil and process jars for 15 minutes (see page 19).

7. Remove canner lid and wait 5 minutes before removing jars to a towel or rack to cool completely. Check seals, label and store in a cool place for up to 1 year.

asian lime pickles

Easy to make and store, these pickles can be frozen in convenient 1- or 2-cup (250 or 500 mL) freezer containers or bags. Developing a freezer pickle was a new adventure for me—as far as I know, there are no recipes for them. I wondered if they would be too soft; while there is no doubt that the cucumber is softer than in traditional pickle recipes, the texture held up amazingly. I think the key is to thaw the pickles in the refrigerator.

You can make and use these pickles almost immediately without freezing them—they will store for up to 2 weeks in the refrigerator. Either way, do not skip the salting process as explained in step 1 because it draws out the water, which makes for a crisper pickle.

MAKES 8 CUPS (2 L)

8 cups (2 lb/1 kg) cucumber coins (about 1/4 inch/5 mm thick)
2 tbsp (25 mL) coarse salt
1-1/3 cups (325 mL) rice vinegar
2/3 cup (150 mL) granulated sugar
2/3 cup (150 mL) freshly squeezed lime juice

1/2 cup (125 mL) nuoc nam (Vietnamese fish sauce)
1 red bell pepper, diced (1/4 inch/5 mm)
2 tbsp (25 mL) hot red pepper flakes
2 tbsp (25 mL) finely chopped candied ginger
2 stalks lemongrass, cut to fit the container, optional

1. In a large non-reactive container, combine cucumbers and salt. Toss to mix well. Cover with cold water and let stand at room temperature for 3 hours.

2. Meanwhile, in a saucepan, combine vinegar and sugar. Bring to a light simmer over medium heat, stirring constantly. When sugar has completely dissolved, remove from heat and let cool.

3. Using a colander and working in batches, if necessary, drain and rinse the cucumbers well under cold water. Drain well. In a large non-reactive container, combine cucumbers, vinegar solution, lime juice, fish sauce, peppers, hot pepper flakes and ginger. Pack into two 1-quart (1 L) freezer bags and add 1 stalk of lemongrass, if using. Leave a minimum 1-inch (2.5 cm) headspace; press out air. Seal and freeze.

Thaw in the refrigerator for about 8 hours or overnight before serving. Store thawed pickles in the refrigerator for up to 1 week.

Freezing Cucumbers

Due to their high water content, I do not recommend freezing cucumbers as a viable method for preserving them.

Eggplant

A MEMBER OF THE NIGHTSHADE FAMILY, which includes potatoes, tomatoes and peppers, eggplant (*Solanum melongena*) bears fruit that is actually a berry, but which we eat as a vegetable.

Good Preserving Varieties

Eggplants vary in length (from 2 to 12 inches/5 to 30 cm) and shape—they can be round, oblong or pear-like. Most North Americans expect that the skin of an eggplant will be deep purple and shiny, but eggplants can range from pure white to pink, burgundy, violet, blue, red and green, to black; they can also be striped. Any of the varieties can be frozen, but the best ones for canning or pickling are those that are small and either round, long or oblong. There are excellent small types among the Japanese, Asian and, especially, Thai varieties.

Teardrop Types

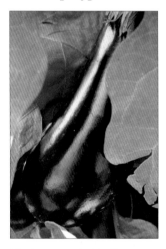

Most common in North America are glossy purple-black eggplants in the shape of a teardrop. Classy Chassis is a good example of this type.

Thai Types

Kurume Long is a long and thin Thai eggplant, good for pickles.

Round Types

A great eggplant for pickling and roasting whole, Violet Prince is small and round with pink to light purple skin.

Other Thai Varieties: **Thai Green**; **Thai Round Green** (small, light green skin); **Hybrid White Ball** (small, round, white skin); **Hybrid Tiger** (small, round with dark green striped shoulder); **Hybrid Green Doll** (small, egg-shaped, crisp and good for pickling); **Petch Siam** (round, green with dark green stripes).

Indian Types: Some Indian-type eggplant cultivars include **Hybrid Chu-Chu**, which is tiny and pear-shaped with burgundy skin; **Hybrid Southern Pink**, which is round and has purple-pink skin.

Japanese Types: **Hybrid Mangan**, high-gloss black; **Kurume Long**, glossy purple-black skin, long.

Chinese Types: **Ping-Tung Long** is a Taiwan variety that is long, with purplish glossy skin. It adds colour and interest to pickles, especially if you can get it when tiny.

Other Chinese Varieties: **Long White Angel** (long white hybrid); **Purple Ball** (small, round, dark blue skin); **Purple Excel** (long, tender, burgundy-purple skin); **Ma-Zu Purple** (very long, purple skin).

Purchasing/Storing
- 1 lb (500 g) yields about 2 cups (500 mL) diced eggplant.
- You will need 1-1/2 lb (750 g) for each quart (1 L) jar, less if using mini whole eggplant.

Select firm fruits with a uniform glossy colour and that are heavy for their size. Choose small rather than large fruit. Avoid eggplants with spongy or dark brown spots. Store in the refrigerator for up to 3 days.

Good With
- Herbs such as basil, bay, thyme, sage, rosemary; spices such as cumin, curry blends, garam masala, cinnamon, cloves, allspice, nutmeg.
- Other vegetables, such as onions, garlic, hot and sweet bell peppers, tomatoes.
- Pistachios, Brazil nuts and walnuts; sesame seeds.
- Parmesan and other hard Italian cheeses; mozzarella.
- Poultry, lamb, pork, fish.

Preparation
Remove the stem end. The skin of the tiny or immature eggplant is tender and edible, so leave it on, especially if pickling. As eggplants mature, the skin toughens and becomes bitter, so peel the large mature ones. For canning or freezing, blanch eggplant cubes or slices in boiling water for 4 minutes. To prevent discolouration, add 1/2 cup (125 mL) lemon juice per 1 gallon (4 L) of water. Immerse in cold water for 4 minutes. Drain and pat dry.

In addition to blanching, eggplants can be salted in order to draw out excess water. Use 2 tbsp (25 mL) salt for every eggplant. Peel or leave peel on; trim away blossom ends and slice eggplants lengthwise or crosswise into 1/4- to 1/2-inch (5 mm to 1 cm) slices. Lay slices on clean, lint-free towels or several layers of paper towels. Sprinkle salt over top and let stand at room temperature for 1 to 3 hours. Rinse, drain and immediately blanch for 3 minutes following instructions above.

Canning Eggplant
See detailed canning information, page 20.

1. **Prepare Equipment:** Wash and heat pint (2-cup/500 mL) or quart (1 L) jars, and scald the lids, funnel, ladle and tongs (see page 22).

2. **Prepare eggplant by blanching or by salting and blanching following instructions.**

3. **Pack eggplant slices or cubes hot.**
Hot Pack Method: Fill hot jars with hot eggplant cubes or slices, shaking the jar to pack fairly tightly. Pour hot water over top, leaving a 1-inch (2.5 cm) headspace. Run a thin non-metallic utensil around the inside of the jar to allow air to escape. Add more hot water, if necessary, to leave a 1-inch (2.5 cm) headspace. Wipe sealing edge of jars with a clean, damp, lint-free cloth. Position flat lids over the tops of jars and hand-tighten screw bands.

4. **Place jars in pressure canner.** Use a Pressure Canner according to the chart below for Dial-Gauge or follow manufacturer's instructions.

Processing Times at Different Altitudes for Eggplant in a DIAL-GAUGE PRESSURE Canner					
Pack Style	Jar Size	0–2000 ft	2001–4000 ft	4001–6000 ft	6001+ ft
HOT	Pints	15 min	20 min	25 min	30 min
	Quarts	20 min	25 min	30 min	35 min
RAW	Pints	20 min	25 min	30 min	35 min
	Quarts	25 min	30 min	35 min	40 min

5. **Cool, Label and Store:** Turn off heat; let pressure return to zero naturally. Once gauge shows 0 pressure, wait 2 minutes then open the vent. Unlock and remove canner lid. Wait 10 minutes then lift jars from canner and place on a clean towel or rack. Do not re-tighten screw bands. Let the jars cool to room temperature. This may take from 12 to 24 hours. Remove and store screw bands. Check lid seals (see page 23). Wipe and label sealed jars. Store in a cool, dark place.

eggplant caponata

In Italy, this thick dip is most often served with garlic bread as antipasto, but can also be spread on vegetables in hors d'oeuvres or with greens as a starter. I find that it is also very good when tossed with cooked pasta or rice.

Don't rush the cooking of the vegetables, especially the egg-plant. Use a heavy-bottomed covered saucepan or skillet over medium-low heat. If you sweat the onions and garlic over very low heat with a lid on the pan, you don't have to stir as often, and the onions will caramelize to become sweet. You can add shred-ded carrots, chopped red or green bell peppers, pine nuts or raisins to this basic recipe.

MAKES 4 CUPS (1 L)

1/3 to 1/2 cup (50 to 125 mL) olive oil, divided
4 cups (1 L) fresh or frozen (thawed) eggplant cubes
3 onions, chopped
4 cloves garlic, finely chopped
2 cups (500 mL) skinned, seeded and chopped plum (or Roma) tomatoes

1/2 cup (125 mL) chopped celery
1/4 cup (50 mL) shredded fresh basil
20 black olives, pitted and roughly chopped (1 can, 14 oz/398 mL, drained)
1 tbsp (15 mL) drained capers
2 tbsp (25 mL) freshly squeezed lemon juice or balsamic vinegar
2 tsp (10 mL) granulated sugar, optional

1. Heat 2 tbsp (25 mL) of the olive oil in a large, deep heavy-bottomed saucepan or skillet over medium-low heat. Add just enough eggplant so that it cooks in single layer. Cook, stirring frequently, placing the lid on the pan between stirring. Cook in batches, transferring the soft, brown cubes to a plate. Add more oil to the pan as needed. Set browned eggplant aside.

2. Add 2 tbsp (25 mL) more oil to the saucepan and heat. Add onions and garlic and cook, stirring fre-quently, for 7 minutes or until soft and golden. Add tomatoes and celery and cook over medium heat, stirring frequently, for 5 minutes or until celery is tender. Add basil, olives, capers and fried eggplant. Cook for 1 minute, stirring constantly. Stir in lemon juice and mix well. Taste and add sugar if required.

3. Freeze in 1/2- to 1-cup (125 to 250 mL) containers for up to 4 months.

Use: Spread caponata on slices of French bread or toasted bagels for an hors d'oeuvre (see Beef Bites, page 231); toss with cooked rice or pasta for a main dish. Serve over steamed or grilled vegetables. Combine with cooked rice and use as a stuffing for zucchini, tomatoes or bell peppers.

beef bites

If you have Eggplant Caponata (page 230) prepared and frozen, you can make these elegant appetizers or hors d'oeuvres in no time. For a cocktail party, they are hearty and easy to manage on a cocktail napkin. When made with bagels or ciabatta bread and hard-boiled egg or tuna, they make a delicious sandwich for lunch.

MAKES 12 SLICES

1 cup (250 mL) Eggplant Caponata (page 230), thawed if frozen

1 stick French bread, cut diagonally into 12 slices

1 cup (250 mL) fresh baby spinach leaves

12 slices grilled beef

12 Parmesan cheese curls

Spread caponata on bread slices. Layer with spinach leaves and top with grilled beef. Garnish with Parmesam cheese curls.

pickled baby eggplant

Use whole tiny round, oblong or long (finger) eggplants. If you are close to an Asian market, it is quite possible that you will be able to get several different varieties and colours of mini eggplants for this recipe. For this pickle mix, tiny hot or sweet chile peppers add colour and nip to the pickles. You can also combine eggplants with other miniature vegetables, like baby corn or carrots, or any of the dwarf squash varieties. Sometimes market gardeners grow dwarf vegetables; they are beautiful in this recipe with small finger eggplants.

MAKES 8 CUPS (2 L)

8 cups (2 L) miniature eggplants or mixed
   vegetables (see above)
1/4 cup (50 mL) freshly squeezed
   lemon juice
3 cups (750 mL) rice vinegar

1/2 cup (125 mL) water
1 cup (250 mL) granulated sugar
3 tbsp (45 mL) Classic Pickling Spice Blend
   (page 213 or store-bought), tied in a
   cheesecloth bag

1. Bring a large pot of water to a boil. Add lemon juice and eggplants (or eggplants and other baby vegetables). Cook vegetables for 5 to 7 minutes or until tender-crisp. Remove eggplants when tender, which may be before other vegetables are done. Drain and rinse with cold water. Drain and pat dry.

2. Heat four 1-pint (2-cup/500 mL) jars in boiling water, and scald the lids, lifter, funnel and tongs (see page 18).

3. In a Maslin pan or canning kettle, combine vinegar and water. Add sugar and spice bag. Bring to a boil over high heat, stirring constantly. Reduce heat and boil gently, stirring occasionally, for 10 minutes. Remove spice bag and add vegetables. Boil gently, stirring occasionally, for 3 minutes.

4. Skim off and discard any foam. Using tongs or a slotted spoon, fill hot jars with vegetables, leaving a 1/2-inch (1 cm) headspace. Pour hot brine over top, leaving a 1/2-inch (1 cm) headspace. Run a thin non-metallic utensil around the inside of the jar to allow air to escape. Add more hot brine, if necessary, to leave a 1/2-inch (1 cm) headspace. Wipe rims, top with flat lids and screw on metal rings. Return jars to the hot water bath, topping up with hot water if necessary. Bring to a full rolling boil and process jars for 10 minutes (see page 19).

5. Remove canner lid and wait 5 minutes before removing jars to a towel or rack to cool completely. Check seals, label and store in a cool place for up to 1 year.

Freezing Eggplant

1. **Select Equipment:** Select suitable-size freezer containers, bags or Mason jars (see page 24).

2. **Blanch cubed or sliced eggplant as directed on page 228.** Pack into containers, leaving a 1-inch (2.5 cm) headspace. Remove air, label and seal. Freeze for up to 9 months.

Fennel

AN AROMATIC PLANT THAT IS NATIVE TO THE MEDITERRANEAN, fennel (*Foeniculum vulgare*) produces fennel seed and the essential oil, but this plant does not grow an edible swollen bulb. *Foeniculum vulgare dulce* is the plant that produces a bulbous end at the bottom of its leaf stalks. Known in various parts of Europe as sweet, Roman or Florence fennel, or finocchio in Italy, this fennel cultivar produces a vegetable composed of thick, hollow leaf stalks; they overlap each other at the base of the stem to form an edible, fat bulb. The white, crisp, slightly anise-tasting bulb is most often sliced thin and added to salads or cooked au gratin.

Good Preserving Varieties

Rather than canning fennel on its own, it is more often pickled or added to other vegetables and canned in a sauce. All varieties listed below are *F. vulgare dulce*.

Romanesco: A late-summer fennel, which forms large, succulent bulbs that are tasty and sweet.

Zefa fino: Large bulb; sweetly anise.

Purchasing/Storing

1 large fennel bulb yields about 3 cups (750 mL) firmly packed chopped fennel.

Choose bulbs that are firm and show no signs of drying out. Some slight yellowing or bruising is acceptable since the outer layers can be removed during preparation. Store fennel tightly wrapped in the refrigerator for several days.

Good With

- Seeds: Marjoram, thyme, summer savory, basil, rosemary and lavender to make herbes de Provence.
- Bulb fennel: Vegetables such as onions, leeks, tomatoes, garlic, eggplant; fruits such as oranges, blueberries.
- Mild fish such as tilapia sole whitefish.

Preparation

Trim away and discard the round hollow stalks at the top of the bulb. Cut out and discard the hard white core. Quarter, slice or chop the bulb and immerse in cool water to which up to 1/4 cup (50 mL) lemon juice has been added.

Canning Fennel

Fennel does not produce a good canned product on its own, but when canned in tomato sauce, the result is very good as with Roasted Tomato, Fennel and Basil Relish (page 238).

finocchio à la grecque

If this recipe could decide what it is—Italian, French or Greek—it could be claimed by one country. No matter where you live, once you have this in your pantry, you will find that it adds an international flair to any dish. You can divide the recipe by 4 and use 1 fresh fennel bulb for a great summer side dish.

MAKES 4 QUARTS (4 L)

4 fennel bulbs
1 gallon (4 L) water
1/4 cup (50 mL) lemon juice
4 cups (1 L) canned, drained or fresh
  skinned tomatoes, halved or chopped
grated rind and juice of 1 lemon

1-1/4 cups (300 mL) packed brown sugar
1-1/4 cups (300 mL) white wine
3 tbsp (45 mL) fresh thyme leaves
4 cloves garlic, peeled
4 bay leaves
8 coriander seeds

1. Cut fennel bulbs into quarters. In large pot, combine water and 1/4 cup (50 mL) lemon juice. Immerse fennel in water. Set aside.

2. Heat four 1-quart (1 L) jars in boiling water, and scald the lids, lifter, funnel and tongs (see page 18).

3. In a Maslin pan or canning kettle, combine tomatoes, lemon rind and juice, sugar, wine and thyme leaves. Bring to a boil over high heat, stirring constantly. Boil, stirring frequently, for 5 minutes. Drain fennel quarters and add to pan. Boil gently, stirring occasionally, for about 7 minutes or until fennel is tender-crisp but still intact.

4. Using tongs, lift fennel quarters out of tomato sauce and fill hot jars, leaving a 1-inch (2.5 cm) headspace. Add 1 garlic clove, 1 bay leaf and 2 coriander seeds to each jar. Ladle tomato sauce over fennel, leaving a 1/2-inch (1 cm) headspace. Run a thin non-metallic utensil around the inside of the jar to allow air to escape. Add more hot sauce, if necessary, to leave a 1/2-inch (1 cm) headspace. Wipe rims, top with flat lids and screw on metal rings. Return jars to the hot water bath, topping up with hot water if necessary. Bring to a full rolling boil and process jars for 15 minutes (see page 19).

5. Remove canner lid and wait 5 minutes before removing jars to a towel or rack to cool completely. Check seals, label and store in a cool place for up to 1 year.

Use: For an elegant side dish, empty the contents of a quart (1 L) jar into a casserole dish. Combine 1-1/2 cups (375 mL) fresh or dry bread crumbs, 1/2 cup (125 mL) chopped walnuts, 2 cloves garlic, chopped, and 3 tbsp (45 mL) olive oil. Pat over the top of the fennel and bake in a 350°F (180°C) oven for 15 to 25 minutes or until top is golden and bubbly and fennel is heated through. Alter-

natively, you can divide the finnochio among 4 small casserole dishes, top with the bread crumbs, bake and serve as a starter.

Add finocchio to cooked potatoes or carrots, or combine with more canned tomatoes for a great winter soup. It can be used to poach fish or vegetables for a winter stew.

Make a carrot confit: Shave thin ribbons from 2 carrots. In a deep saucepan, heat 1 cup (250 mL) olive oil over low heat until warm. Add carrots and cook gently, stirring occasionally, for 15 to 20 minutes or until tender-crisp. Drain well. Meanwhile in another saucepan, heat finocchio. Add carrots and mix well. Serve warm or at room temperature.

Drying Fennel Leaves

Snip the feathery leaves from stalks and set aside in a warm, dark spot to dry. When dry, transfer to an airtight and dark container and use as a seasoning for salsas and tomato sauces and as a pickle brine for preserves.

roasted tomato, fennel and basil relish

I have always marvelled that tomatoes and basil, such a perfect match, ripen at the same time, as if the two were divinely ordained. Combined in this richly aromatic sauce, they help to make it extraordinary. There is no doubt about it—this is a sophisticated sauce.

Be sure to use plum or Roma tomatoes because they are meaty and can stand up to the roasting.

2 rimmed baking sheets, lightly oiled
Preheat oven to 400°F (200°C)
MAKES ABOUT 6 CUPS (1.5 L)

2-1/2 lb (1.25 kg) ripe plum tomatoes, halved and seeded (9 or 10)
1 red bell pepper, halved
10 cloves garlic, peeled
1 onion, cut into eighths
4 tbsp (50 mL) olive oil
2 fennel bulbs (about 2 lb/1 kg), cut into 1/4-inch (5 mm) dice

1/2 cup (125 mL) balsamic or red wine vinegar
1/3 cup (75 mL) packed brown sugar
1 cup (250 mL) loosely packed shredded basil leaves
1/2 cup (125 mL) chopped fresh flat-leaf parsley
1 tbsp (15 mL) pickling salt
1 tsp (5 mL) ground nutmeg

1. On one of the prepared baking sheets, arrange tomato halves in a single layer, cut side down. On the other baking sheet, arrange red pepper halves cut side down and place the garlic cloves and onions around them. Drizzle each pan with 2 tbsp (25 mL) olive oil.

2. Roast in preheated oven for 12 to 15 minutes or until tomatoes are soft and wrinkled and garlic is lightly browned and tender. Onions may be slightly charred. Let the vegetables cool on the sheets.

3. Meanwhile, heat six 1-cup (250 mL) jars in boiling water, and scald the lids, lifter, funnel and tongs (see page 18).

4. In a Maslin pan or canning kettle, combine fennel, vinegar and brown sugar. Stir in basil, parsley, salt and nutmeg. Bring to a boil over high heat. Reduce heat and simmer for 9 minutes.

5. Slip skins off tomatoes and peppers and discard. Roughly chop the tomatoes, peppers, onions and garlic. Add chopped roasted vegetables

and any juices that have accumulated on the baking sheets. Boil for 1 minute.

6. Skim off and discard any foam. Fill hot jars, leaving a 1/2-inch (1 cm) headspace. Run a thin non-metallic utensil around the inside of the jar to allow air to escape. Add more hot relish, if necessary, to leave 1/2-inch (1 cm) headspace. Wipe rims, top with flat lids and screw on metal rings. Return jars to the hot water bath, topping up with hot water if necessary. Bring to a full rolling boil and process jars for 15 minutes (see page 19).

7. Remove canner lid and wait 5 minutes before removing jars to a towel or rack to cool completely. Check seals, label and store in a cool place for up to 1 year.

Use: As a pasta sauce and in recipes where canned or stewed tomatoes are called for. Serve as an accompaniment with grilled shrimp, fish or pork.

grilled scallops with roasted tomato, fennel and basil relish

A hearty and easy entrée when accompanied by pasta or rice, this dish can also be served as an appetizer. Sea scallops are plumper and larger than bay scallops. For a vegetarian dish, you can substitute grilled peppers and eggplant for the scallops.

MAKES 4 CUPS (1 L)

4 tbsp (50 mL) olive oil, divided
2 tsp (10 mL) freshly squeezed lemon juice
1 tsp (5 mL) Cajun seasoning

1 lb (500 g) fresh sea scallops
2 cups (500 mL) Roasted Tomato, Fennel and Basil Relish (page 238)

1. In a bowl, combine 2 tbsp (25 mL) olive oil, lemon juice and Cajun seasoning. Add scallops and toss well to coat.

2. In a skillet, heat remaining oil over high heat. Add scallops and cook for about 2 minutes on each side or until done. Scallops are done when they turn from translucent to opaque.

3. Add relish and heat through.

> The key to cooking scallops is to sear each side on very high heat. This seals in the moisture and actually poaches the tender meat. Overcooking turns all seafood tough and rubbery, so when using high heat, pay attention to the time the scallops are in the pan—it's critical.

For an appetizer, serve in small pots. Top spaghetti with 1 large sea scallop tossed in Roasted Tomato, Fennel and Basil Relish.

Freezing Fennel

1. Select Equipment: Select suitable-size freezer containers, bags or Mason jars (see page 24).

2. Blanch sliced or diced fennel bulb in boiling water to which 1/4 cup (50 mL) lemon juice has been added for 3 minutes. Lift out and plunge into cold water. Let stand for 3 minutes. Drain and pat dry. Pack into containers, leaving a 1-inch (2.5 cm) headspace. Remove air, label and seal. Freeze for up to 9 months.

Garlic Scapes

NOT LONG AGO, SCAPES WERE FAIRLY RARE IN NORTH AMERICA. Now, with more market gardeners growing garlic, we are seeing more of the fresh green flower stalks showing up around the end of June or beginning of July. Scapes are tender and very tasty stems that are cut from the garlic in order to allow the plant to put all of its energy into growing the bulbs that will be harvested in the fall. These lightly garlic-scented vegetables can be grilled, steamed or poached. Treat them as you would asparagus or green beans, and use them in casseroles, soups and stews.

Good Preserving Varieties

If you can get scapes, no matter what variety of garlic they were cut from, they will make great relishes, salsa and pesto. Use them fresh, freeze them or pickle them.

Purchasing/Storing

- 1 lb (500 g) yields 2-1/2 to 3 cups (625 to 750 mL) sliced garlic scapes.
- You will need about 1 lb (500 g) for each quart (1 L) jar.

Even though scapes keep well for up to 5 days in the refrigerator, like everything else, they are best if used immediately after they are cut from the plant.

Good With

- Herbs such as basil, bay, thyme, parsley, sage, rosemary.
- Other vegetables, such as asparagus, green and wax beans, potatoes, fennel, eggplant.
- Toasted almonds, pecans and walnuts; sesame seeds, sunflower seeds, flaxseeds.
- Most fish; beef, lamb, chicken, pork.

Preparation

Cut off and discard the flower head (only if it is hard) and the straight piece that grows out of it. Swish scapes in a sink full of cool water to which a drop of food-safe soap has been added. Rinse well, drain and pat dry. Cut the thin, green, tender stalks into 1- or 2-inch (2.5 or 5 cm) pieces or chop roughly.

Canning Garlic Scapes

I don't recommend canning garlic scapes because they turn brown and lose their texture. They freeze easily and stay green and firm, so this is by far the best way to preserve them.

garlic scape relish

Surprisingly, this summer relish is not actually green because the turmeric tints it a sunny, golden colour. The mild garlic flavour from the scapes combines nicely with the classic pickling spices in this favourite relish. If you don't tell anyone that it has cabbage in it, they won't know. I use this relish to thin the consistency of commercial mayonnaise for potato and other summer salads.

MAKES 10 CUPS (2.5 L)

5 cups (1.25 L) finely chopped garlic scapes
5 cups (1.25 L) shredded green cabbage
2 cups (500 mL) chopped red bell pepper
1 cup (250 mL) finely chopped onion
3 cups (750 mL) champagne or white
   wine vinegar
1-1/2 cups (375 L) lightly packed
   brown sugar

3 tbsp (45 mL) finely chopped fresh
   gingerroot
1-1/2 tbsp (22 mL) salt
1 tbsp (15 mL) ground turmeric
3 tbsp (45 mL) Classic Pickling Spice Blend
   (page 213 or store-bought), tied in a
   cheesecloth bag

1. In a Maslin pan or canning kettle, combine garlic scapes, cabbage, red pepper and onion. Add vinegar, brown sugar, ginger, salt, turmeric and spice bag. Cover and bring to a boil over medium heat, stirring frequently. Uncover and boil hard for 5 minutes, stirring frequently. Reduce heat and boil gently, stirring occasionally, for about 20 minutes. Liquid will be reduced and relish will be thick. Discard spice bag.

2. Meanwhile, heat five 1-pint (2-cup/500 mL) jars in boiling water, and scald the lids, lifter, funnel and tongs (see page 18).

3. Fill hot jars, leaving a 1/2-inch (1 cm) headspace. Run a thin non-metallic utensil around the inside of the jar to allow air to escape. Add more hot relish, if necessary, to leave a 1/2-inch (1 cm) headspace. Wipe rims, top with flat lids and screw on metal rings. Return jars to the hot water bath, topping up with hot water if necessary. Bring to a full rolling boil and process jars for 10 minutes (see page 19).

4. Remove canner lid and wait 5 minutes before removing jars to a towel or rack to cool completely. Check seals, label and store in a cool place for up to 1 year.

Use: A tangy and sweet relish with just a hint of garlic, it is great with grilled hot dogs and hamburgers, sausages and lamb kebabs. It adds a pickle flavour to meat loaf and can be combined with mayonnaise for coleslaw and other salad mixes.

garlic scape pesto

When I first learned about garlic scapes 20 years ago and tried them in recipes, I was hooked. Now, with all the people around me who grow garlic, I could be buried in them by mid to late June when everyone is taking them off the plant. At that time of year, I'm busy making Garlic Scape Relish as well as this pesto. I make a lot and use it fresh, but also freeze it in 1- or 2-cup (250 or 500 mL) amounts.

Fresh local garlic is still not available when the scapes are harvested, so I omit the garlic cloves. The result is a mildly garlic-tasting green sauce for meat and vegetables. I have included the cloves in the recipe as an option for people who want a strongly garlic pesto. I don't use a whole cup (250 mL) of olive oil for this pesto because I like it on the dry side and rather chunky. Use more or less oil to suit your preference for pesto consistency.

MAKES 4 CUPS (1 L)

4 cups (1 L) roughly chopped garlic scapes
3 to 5 cloves garlic, optional
**1/3 cup (75 mL) pine nuts or sunflower
  seeds**

1/3 cup (75 mL) shaved Parmesan cheese
1 cup (250 mL) olive oil (approx)
sea salt

1. In a food processor, combine scapes, garlic cloves, if using, and nuts and process for 30 seconds. Add Parmesan cheese and process for 10 seconds to blend. With the motor running, add olive oil in a steady stream through the opening in the lid until the pesto reaches the desired consistency. Add salt to taste.

2. Scrape into a clean jar with a lid and refrigerate for up to a week or freeze in measured amounts for up to 6 months.

garlic scape pesto potatoes

Use any root vegetable with or in place of the potatoes in this recipe. It's one of those recipes you don't need a recipe for. Just combine pesto with enough vegetables to serve the number of guests and roast. I count on it as a great impromptu side dish that everyone loves.

Rimmed baking sheet, lightly oiled
Preheat oven to 375°F (190°C)
MAKES AS MANY SERVINGS AS YOU LIKE

2 or 3 small new potatoes or vegetable cubes
  per person
2 tbsp (25 mL) Garlic Scape Pesto per serving
  (or more if you wish)
sea salt and pepper

On prepared baking sheet, combine vegetables and pesto. Toss well to combine. Grind salt and pepper over top. Roast in preheated oven for 20 minutes or until potatoes are tender.

1. **Select Equipment:** Select suitable-size freezer containers, bags or Mason jars (see page 24).

2. **Blanch whole scapes or 1- to 2-inch (2.5 to 5 cm) pieces in boiling water for 3 minutes.** Lift out and plunge into cold water for 3 minutes. Drain and pat dry. Or raw-pack chopped scapes in 1- or 2-cup (250 to 500 mL) measures. Pack into containers, leaving a 1-inch (2.5 cm) headspace. Remove air, label and seal. Freeze for up to 9 months.

Kohlrabi

NATIVE TO NORTHERN EUROPE, KOHLRABI (*BRASSICA OLERACEA*) is a relative of cabbage, Brussels sprouts, broccoli, cauliflower and kale. Its name is derived from the apt German term "cabbage (*kohl*) turnip (*rabi*)." While the turnip-like globe of the kohlrabi appears to be a root, it is actually the swollen base of the plant's stem, which, like any stem, sprouts leaves. Both the green, cabbage-like leaves and the swollen globe at the bottom of the stems are eaten. The leaves have been trimmed off the kohlrabi in the photograph on the left.

Good Preserving Varieties

There are a number of white (pale green) and purple cultivars. Both of these have white flesh. Any of the white varieties are excellent for canning:

Early White Vienna: Few leaves, harvested about 55 days after planting.

Elder: A tender and fast-maturing (38 days) white type; good for northern climates.

Express Forcer: A white type that is heat-tolerant; often "forced" by covering the emerging plant and keeping it from turning green in the sunlight.

Gigante: Produces an extremely large bulb that stays tender and is excellent for canning.

Granlibakken: Non-woody; sweet, mild flavour.

Logo: A white forcing type used in Europe for baby vegetable production; excellent for pickling.

Purple Vienna is a Kohlrabi variety with a mild, sweet flavour. The skin is crisp and white. I prefer to use all the purple vegetables raw in order to retain their deep colour.

Purchasing/Storing

- 1 lb (500 g) yields about 1-3/4 to 2 cups (425 to 500 mL) diced kohlrabi.
- You will need 2 to 2-1/2 lb (1 to 1.25 kg) for each quart (1 L) jar of cubed kohlrabi.

Select firm, young, small globes (no more than 3 inches/8 cm in diameter). Except for Gigante and Kossak, most large, mature kohlrabi is woody and may have an off flavour.

Cut off leaves and use in salads or braise with other greens. While kohlrabi bulb may be stored wrapped in plastic in the refrigerator for up to 2 weeks, it is best to preserve it as soon as possible after harvesting.

- Dill, fennel, basil, bay, thyme, savory.
- Cinnamon, ginger, cloves, nutmeg.
- Apples.
- Other vegetables, such as potatoes, onions, leeks, celery, cabbage.
- Béchamel or cheese sauces (cooked in them au gratin).

Preparation

For canning and freezing, wash, peel, slice or cut into 1/2-inch (1 cm) dice and blanch in boiling water for 2 minutes. Immerse in cold water for 2 minutes. Drain and pat dry.

Canning Kohlrabi

See detailed canning information, page 20.

1. Prepare Equipment: Wash and heat pint (2-cup/500 mL) or quart (1 L) jars, and scald the lids, funnel, ladle and tongs (see page 22).

2. For every 3 cups (750 mL) diced kohlrabi, bring 2 cups (500 mL) water or broth to a boil.

3. Pack diced kohlrabi into jars either hot or raw.
Make a Hot Pack: Add diced kohlrabi to gently boiling water or broth and boil for 2 minutes. Drain, reserving cooking liquid. Fill hot jars with hot kohlrabi cubes, shaking the jar to pack fairly tightly. Pour hot cooking liquid over kohlrabi cubes, leaving a 1-inch (2.5 cm) head-space. Run a thin non-metallic utensil around the inside of the jar to allow air to escape. Add hot liquid, if necessary, to leave a 1-inch (2.5 cm) headspace. Wipe sealing edge of jars with a clean, damp, lint-free cloth. Position flat lids over the tops of jars and hand-tighten screw bands.

OR

Make a Raw Pack: Fill jars with blanched kohlrabi cubes, shaking the jar to pack fairly tightly. Cover with hot water or broth, leaving a 1-inch (2.5 cm) headspace. Run a thin non-metallic utensil around the inside of the jar to allow air to escape. Wipe sealing edge of jars with a clean, damp, lint-free cloth. Position flat lids over the tops of jars and hand-tighten screw bands.

4. Place jars in pressure canner. Use a Pressure Canner according to the following chart for Dial-Gauge or follow manufacturer's instructions.

Processing Times at Different Altitudes for Kohrabi in a DIAL-GAUGE PRESSURE Canner

Pack Style	Jar Size	0–2000 ft	2001–4000 ft	4001–6000 ft	6001+ ft
HOT	Pints	15 min	20 min	25 min	30 min
	Quarts	20 min	25 min	30 min	35 min
RAW	Pints	20 min	25 min	30 min	35 min
	Quarts	25 min	30 min	35 min	40 min

5. Cool, Label and Store: Turn off heat; let pressure return to zero naturally. Once gauge shows 0 pressure, wait 2 minutes then open the vent. Unlock and remove canner lid. Wait 10 minutes then lift jars from canner and place on a clean towel or rack. Do not re-tighten screw bands. Let the jars cool to room temperature. This may take from 12 to 24 hours. Remove and store screw bands. Check lid seals (see page 23). Wipe and label sealed jars. Store in a cool, dark place.

kohl relish

Cabbage and kohlrabi combine nicely in this tasty relish, and the horseradish provides a piquant perk. If you use your own dill seed, it will have a lustier taste and aroma than anything you can buy.

MAKES 8 CUPS (2 L)

5 cups (1.25 L) diced kohlrabi
3 cups (750 mL) finely chopped green cabbage
3 cups (750 mL) apple cider vinegar
1-1/2 cups (375 L) granulated sugar
1 cup (250 mL) chopped onion

1 cup (250 mL) chopped celery
1 tbsp (15 mL) prepared horseradish
1 tbsp (15 mL) pickling salt
1 tbsp (15 mL) dill seed

1. In a saucepan, cover kohlrabi with water. Bring to a boil over high heat. Reduce heat and boil gently for about 10 minutes, to soften it slightly.

2. Heat four 1-pint (2-cup/500 mL) jars or 2 quart (1 L) jars in boiling water, and scald the lids, lifter, funnel and tongs (see page 18).

3. In a Maslin pan or canning kettle, combine kohlrabi, cabbage, vinegar, sugar, onions, celery, horse-radish, salt and dill. Bring to a boil over high heat, stirring constantly. Reduce heat and boil gently, stirring occasionally, for about 20 minutes or until vegetables are tender and liquid is reduced some-what.

4. Fill hot jars with hot relish, leaving a 1/2-inch (1 cm) headspace. Run a thin non-metallic utensil around the inside of the jar to allow air to escape. Add more hot relish, if necessary, to leave a 1/2-inch (1 cm) headspace. Wipe rims, top with flat lids and screw on metal rings. Return jars to the hot water bath, topping up with hot water if necessary. Bring to a full rolling boil and process jars for 15 minutes (see page 19).

5. Remove canner lid and wait 5 minutes before removing jars to a towel or rack to cool completely. Check seals, label and store in a cool place for up to 1 year.

Use: Barbecued meats, hot dogs and hamburgers are enlivened by this relish. Use it as you would sauerkraut: in Reuben sandwiches, with corned beef and melted Swiss cheese, and with German sausages.

manhattan clam chowder

Using the Kohl Relish as the base for this hearty soup makes preparation a snap. It's easy, and yet the homemade relish gives it a restaurant finish. I like to use cod fillets, but they can be a bit strong for some people, so tilapia or sole is a good choice.

MAKES 4 SERVINGS

2 potatoes, cut into 1/2-inch (1 cm) dice
2 cups (500 mL) chicken broth
1 pint (2 cups/500 mL) Kohl Relish (page 252)

4 boneless, skinless fish fillets (14 oz/400 g total), see above
1 can (5 oz/142 g) whole baby clams (with their juices)

1. In a saucepan, combine potatoes and chicken broth. Bring to a boil over high heat. Reduce heat and simmer for 5 minutes or until almost tender.

2. Add relish, fish pieces and clams; return to boil. Reduce heat and simmer gently for 4 to 6 minutes or until the fish turns opaque and flakes easily with a fork.

sweet pickled kohlrabi and beets

Here, kohlrabi is extended with pickled beets, once a farm table staple, which turns the kohlrabi red. This pickle mixture reminds me of church suppers and old-fashioned Sunday picnics, but its bright colour and taste make it every bit a contemporary condiment.

MAKES 12 CUPS (3 L)

6 cups (1.5 L) diced kohlrabi
4 cups (1 L) diced beets
2-1/2 cups (625 mL) cider vinegar
1 cup (250 mL) water
1 cup (250 mL) granulated sugar
1/2 cup (125 mL) lightly packed brown sugar

2 tbsp (25 mL) Classic Pickling Spice Blend
    (page 213 or store-bought), tied in a
    cheesecloth bag
3 or 6 cinnamon sticks, each 3 inches (8 cm)
3 or 6 whole cloves
3 or 6 whole allspice berries

1. In a saucepan, cover kohlrabi and beets with water. Bring to a boil over high heat. Cover, reduce heat and boil gently for about 20 minutes or until tender. Drain and rinse under cold water. Set aside.

2. Heat six 1-pint (500 mL) jars or three 1-quart (1 L) jars in boiling water, and scald the lids, lifter, funnel and tongs (see page 18).

3. In a Maslin pan or canning kettle, combine vinegar, water, granulated and brown sugars, and spice bag. Bring to a boil over high heat, stirring constantly. Reduce heat and boil gently, stirring occasionally, for about 15 minutes to infuse the syrup with the spices. Remove and discard spice bag. Add kohlrabi and beets and boil for 1 minute.

4. Place 1 cinnamon stick, 1 clove and 1 allspice berry in each jar. Using a slotted spoon, fill hot jars with hot kohlrabi and beets to within 1 inch (2.5 cm) of the top. Pour hot syrup over vegetables, leaving a 1/2-inch (1 cm) headspace. Run a thin non-metallic utensil around the inside of the jar to allow air to escape. Add more hot relish, if necessary, to leave a 1/2-inch (1 cm) headspace. Wipe rims, top with flat lids and screw on metal rings. Return jars to the hot water bath, topping up with hot water if necessary. Bring to a full rolling boil and process jars for 30 minutes (see page 19).

5. Remove canner lid and wait 5 minutes before removing jars to a towel or rack to cool completely. Check seals, label and store in a cool place for up to 1 year.

Use: Bring out these brilliant pickles to enliven both the taste and colour of a winter lunch or dinner. They are particularly good with ham and beef. I use this relish in wraps and as a chunky spread for quesadillas.

kohlrabi and apple salad

This salad has many possibilities. With its creamy mustard dressing, it makes a light autumn lunch if teamed with hard-boiled eggs or tuna. It can be stuffed into tomatoes or blanched zucchini shells as a main or side dish. Because the dressing does not contain eggs, it's a perfect salad for brown bag lunches, and it travels well for late-season picnics and alfresco meals when autumn offers Indian summer weather.

MAKES 4 SERVINGS

2 cups (500 mL) Sweet Pickled Kohlrabi and
  Beets (page 254), drained
2 apples, coarsely chopped
1/2 cup (125 mL) plain yogurt, drained, or
  mayonnaise
2 tbsp (25 mL) freshly squeezed lemon juice

1 tbsp (15 mL) coarse-grained prepared mustard
3 tbsp (45 mL) finely chopped fresh parsley
1 cup (250 mL) shredded cabbage or spinach
  greens

1. In a bowl, combine Pickled Kohlrabi and Beets, apples, yogurt, lemon juice and mustard. Toss in the parsley and mix to combine. Serve over shredded cabbage or spinach or other greens.

Freezing Kohlrabi

1. **Select Equipment:** Select suitable-size freezer containers, bags or Mason jars (see page 24).

2. **Blanch sliced or diced kohlrabi as directed on page 250.** Pack into containers, leaving a 1-inch (2.5 cm) headspace. Remove air, label and seal. Freeze for up to 9 months.

Peas

GREEN "SHELLING" OR GARDEN PEAS (*PISUM SATIVUM*) are delicious and sweet when fresh. They freeze well, but results are less than satisfactory when home-canned.

The sugar snap pea and the snow pea, which have soft, edible pods and small pea seeds, are most often eaten raw or lightly steamed, or stir-fried with other vegetables.

Good Preserving Varieties

Southern and northern pea varieties are suited to the climate and soil conditions, so it's best to buy local where possible. Any variety that you can purchase fresh will perform well here.

Unshelled peas are graded as U.S. No. 1 and commercial. For U.S. No. 1 grade, 95 per cent of the pods must be at least 5 inches (12 cm) long. Both categories comprise pods of similar varietal characteristics: fairly well formed, fairly well filled, not overly mature or too young.

Purchasing/Storing

- 1 lb (500 g) fresh pea pods yields about 1 cup (250 mL) shelled peas.
- Fresh peas should be small, firm, evenly shaped and bright green. Store peas in the pod for up to 2 days in the refrigerator. Use freshly shelled peas immediately.

Good With

- Mint, basil, bay, thyme, chervil, tarragon.
- Other vegetables, such as onions, carrots, tomatoes, beans, dried peas and beans.
- Toasted almonds, pecans and walnuts, pine nuts, cashews; bean sprouts.

Preparation

Wash pea pods in a basin of cool water to which a drop of food-safe soap has been added. Rinse well and drain. Shell peas and rinse under gently running cool water. Blanch peas in boiling water for 2 minutes. Immerse in cold water and let stand for 2 minutes. Drain and pat dry.

Canning Peas

I don't recommend canning peas at home because the result is never as good as commercially canned products.

pea and prosciutto sauce

If you have frozen peas on hand, this is easy to make for a quick company meal. The smoky prosciutto (you can substitute side bacon) lends its mystery to this beautiful sauce. I make it at least once with fresh peas and several times throughout the winter months with frozen. Sometimes I use it over steamed greens or vegetables, other times with pasta.

MAKES 4 CUPS (1 L)

3 tbsp (45 mL) olive oil
1 cup (250 mL) chopped onion
1 cup (250 mL) finely diced prosciutto, lean
   parts only
2 cloves garlic, finely chopped
1/2 cup (125 mL) chopped fresh parsley
3 cups (750 mL) fresh or frozen peas, thawed

1/2 cup (125 mL) tomato sauce or chicken broth
1/2 cup (125 mL) heavy (whipping) cream or
   drained plain yogurt
sea salt and freshly ground pepper
1/2 cup (125 mL) freshly grated Parmesan
   cheese

In a large saucepan, heat the olive oil over medium-high heat. Add onion. Reduce heat to medium-low and cook, stirring frequently, for 7 minutes or until soft. Add prosciutto, garlic and parsley and cook, stirring occasionally, for 5 minutes. Add peas and tomato sauce. Cover, reduce heat and simmer gently for 8 minutes or until peas are tender but not mushy. Stir in the cream and season with salt and pepper. Serve over cooked pasta or braised spinach or other greens, and garnish with grated Parmesan cheese.

grilled lamb with minted pea and prosciutto sauce

Here's a great way to get the most out of frozen peas. Teaming them with mint makes them a perfect partner for lamb. I might even be tempted to serve them with some homemade mint or Parsley Jelly (page 298).

MAKES 4 CUPS (1 L)

3 tbsp (45 mL) olive oil
1 tsp (5 mL) ground cumin
1 tsp (5 mL) cayenne pepper
4 lamb loin chops (1 to 1-1/4 lb/500 to 625 g)

2 cups (500 mL) Pea and Prosciutto Sauce (page 258)
4 cups (1 L) cooked couscous or red rice
fresh mint leaves

1. In a bowl, combine olive oil, cumin and cayenne pepper. Brush on both sides of lamb chops. Heat the barbecue or oven broiler to high. Grill the lamb for 3 to 4 minutes on each side for medium-rare or until cooked to your liking.

2. Meanwhile, heat Pea and Prosciutto Sauce. Spoon over cooked couscous or rice and serve with lamb chops. Garnish with fresh mint leaves.

Freezing Peas

1. **Select Equipment:** Select suitable-size freezer containers, bags or Mason jars (see page 24).

2. **Blanch shelled peas as directed on page 257.** Pack into containers, leaving a 1-inch (2.5 cm) headspace. Remove air, label and seal. Freeze for up to 9 months.

Sweet Husk Tomatoes

BELONGING TO THE SAME FAMILY AS GARDEN TOMATOES and yet hardier, husk tomatoes are small fruit that grow encased in a paper-thin husk similar to that of corn. They produce well in marginal soils and are not affected by tomato blight, which makes them favourites for home and market gardeners. The two major types of husk tomatoes are excellent for canning and preserving: tomatillos in salsas and savoury sauces; and ground cherries in jams, sweet sauces and pie fillings.

Good Preserving Varieties

There are four basic types of sweet husk tomatoes available today; any of the varieties you can grow or purchase will preserve well.

Tomatillo (*Physalis ixocarpa*): Pronounced toh-MAH-tee-YO, this fruit is also called jamberberry; in Mexico, they are called *tomates verdes* or *tomates de cascara*, as well as *fresadillas*. The 3- to 4-foot (1 to 1.2 m) high plants produce copious amounts of 2 to 3 oz (60 to 90 g) tomatoes, which get sweeter as they mature and continue to do so even after they fall off the plants. The tomatillo is actually used when it is still green and tart. Some tomatillo varieties: **Purple de Milpa**, pictured; **Green Husk Tomatillo**; **Dr. Wych's Yellow**; **Verde**; **Pineapple**; **Grande Rio Verde**; **Michoacan**.

Ground Cherry (Physalis peruviana) is also called Strawberry Tomato (the French name means "Love in a Basket"); resembles a dwarf bush tomato, growing 18 to 24 inches (45 to 60 cm) tall. When ripe, the cranberry-size, deep yellow/orange fruits have an exquisite, sweet vanilla/strawberry/almond/pineapple flavour that blends well with other fruit for preserving and canning. Ground cherry varieties: **Aunt Molly's**; **Yellow Husk**.

Peruvian Cherry (*Physalis prunosa*), also called Cape Gooseberry, is a tender perennial that produces a deep-gold husked fruit that resembles a cherry in size and shape.

Golden Berry (*Physalis prunosa cross*) yields an average of 4 lb (2 kg) of fruit per plant. The sweet and juicy fruit is excellent for preserving and making delicious desserts.

Purchasing/Storing

- 1 lb (500 g) yields 2 cups (500 mL) peeled husk tomatoes.
- You will need about 2 lb (1 kg) for each quart (1 L) jar.

If you grow tomatillos, you can pull up the entire plant, store it in a cool, dark, dry area and remove the fruits as needed. Purchased tomatillos should be stored in their husks, if still attached, in the refrigerator; they can be kept for up to 3 weeks.

Ground cherries should be harvested after they fall off the plant or when fully ripe. Wrap both tomatillos and ground cherries loosely in paper in a single layer or place in a paper bag and keep in the coolest section of your refrigerator.

Good With
- Herbs such as oregano, basil, bay, thyme, winter and summer savory, rosemary, parsley, chives, sage.
- Savoury seasonings such as cayenne pepper, cumin, coriander; sweet seasonings like cinnamon, allspice, ginger, cloves, nutmeg.
- Other vegetables, such as garlic, onions, fennel, celery, peppers (sweet and hot), eggplant.
- Tomatillos in sauce or salsa complement roasted vegetables, fish, poultry, veal, lamb and beef.
- Ground cherries combine well with peaches and other stone fruit; pineapple, mango, cherries; blueberries and other berries.

Preparation
Remove the husk by rubbing it off. If it is stuck, soak the fruit for up to an hour and then remove. Wash husk tomatoes in a sink full of cool water to which a drop of food-safe soap has been added. Rinse well and pat dry.

Canning Husk Tomatoes
See detailed canning information, page 20.

1. **Prepare Equipment:** Wash and heat pint (2-cup/500 mL) or quart (1 L) jars, and scald the lids, funnel, ladle and tongs (see page 22).

2. **For every 3 cups (750 mL) husk tomatoes, bring 2 cups (500 mL) water (for ground cherries) or broth (for tomatillos) to a boil.**

3. **Pack whole or chopped husk tomatoes into jars either hot or raw.**
Make a Hot Pack: Add husk tomatoes to gently boiling water or broth and boil for 1 minute. Drain, reserving cooking liquid. Fill hot jars with hot husk tomatoes, shaking the jar to pack

fairly tightly. Pour hot cooking liquid over husk tomatoes, leaving a 1-inch (2.5 cm) headspace. Run a thin non-metallic utensil around the inside of the jar to allow air to escape. Wipe sealing edge of jars with a clean, damp, lint-free cloth. Position flat lids over the tops of jars and hand-tighten screw bands.

OR

Make a Raw Pack: Fill jars with halved or chopped husk tomatoes. Cover with hot water or broth, leaving a 1-inch (2.5 cm) headspace. Run a thin non-metallic utensil around the inside of the jar to allow air to escape. Add hot liquid, if necessary, to leave a 1-inch (2.5 cm) headspace. Wipe sealing edge of jars with a clean, damp, lint-free cloth. Position flat lids over the tops of jars and hand-tighten screw bands.

4. Place jars in a pressure canner: Use a Pressure Canner according to the chart below for Dial-Gauge or follow manufacturere's instructions.

Processing Times at Different Altitudes for Sweet Husk Tomatoes in a DIAL-GAUGE PRESSURE Canner					
Pack Style	**Jar Size**	**0–2000 ft**	**2001–4000 ft**	**4001–6000 ft**	**6001+ ft**
HOT	Pints	15 min	20 min	25 min	30 min
	Quarts	20 min	25 min	30 min	35 min
RAW	Pints	20 min	25 min	30 min	35 min
	Quarts	25 min	30 min	35 min	40 min

5. Cool, Label and Store: Turn off heat; let pressure return to zero naturally. Once gauge shows 0 pressure, wait 2 minutes then open the vent. Unlock and remove canner lid. Wait 10 minutes then lift jars from canner and place on a clean towel or rack. Do not re-tighten screw bands. Let the jars cool to room temperature. This may take from 12 to 24 hours. Remove and store screw bands. Check lid seals (see page 23). Wipe and label sealed jars. Store in a cool, dark place.

ground cherry jam

With so many wonderful preserve options available to me, I found it difficult to decide what to do with the 2-quart (8 L) basket of ground cherries that happened my way one beautiful early September day. A classic ground cherry jam would have to be the recipe for this book, but you can try combining them with their cousin, the tomatillo, or make a pie filling with lots of tapioca to soak up their juices and perhaps some crabapples, or even a sweet relish with mangoes or papaya. Remember, tomatoes and sweet husk tomatoes are berries, and like all berries, they are full of seeds. You can strain them out, but I leave them in.

MAKES 8 CUPS (2 L)

10 cups (2.5 L) ground cherries
1/4 cup (50 mL) freshly squeezed lemon juice
1/2 can (6 oz/175 g) frozen orange juice
  concentrate, thawed

5 cups (1.25 L) granulated sugar
1 pkg (1–3/4 oz/49 to 52 g) fruit pectin crystals

1. Heat four 1-pint (2-cup/500 mL) jars in boiling water, and scald the lids, lifter, funnel and tongs (see page 18).

2. In a Maslin pan or canning kettle, combine ground cherries, lemon juice and orange juice. Bring to a full rolling boil over medium-high heat, stirring constantly. Using a potato masher, crush the berries. Add sugar, 1 cup (250 mL) at a time, stirring to dissolve after each addition. Bring back to a full rolling boil and boil for 4 minutes.

3. Sprinkle pectin over berries and boil, stirring constantly, for 1 minute. Remove from heat; skim off and discard any foam. Let stand for 10 minutes, without stirring.

4. Fill hot jars, leaving a 1/4-inch (5 mm) headspace. Run a thin non-metallic utensil around the inside of the jar to allow air to escape. Add more hot jam, if necessary, to leave a 1/4-inch (5 mm) headspace. Wipe rims, top with flat lids and screw on metal rings. Return jars to the hot water bath, topping up with hot water if necessary. Bring to a full rolling boil and process jars for 10 minutes (see page 19).

5. Remove canner lid and wait 5 minutes before removing jars to a towel or rack to cool completely. Check seals, label and store in a cool place for up to 1 year.

Use: With its vanilla overtones and light tropical fruit notes, this jam is a perfect match for home-made vanilla ice cream. Use it as a sauce for all kinds of desserts and with natural yogurt. It tops waffles, crêpes and pancakes beautifully.

tomatillo salsa verde

The green tomatillos give this hot sauce its light green colour. I may as well confess: I don't much care for cilantro. Actually, I can't stand cilantro. Can't touch it, can't have it touch any food that I have in the grocery cart or, heaven forbid, have it on my plate. Thai food and guacamole are culinary nightmares for me. When I was hosting our Herb Walk programs from our circa 1860s log cabin on the Saugeen River, I would ask the participants if they liked cilantro. Not that I am obsessed—I just wanted to know if I was alone in a world of cilantro lovers. Over the six years, I figure I had a pretty good cross-section of respondents. Turns out that I'm not the only cilantro hater. My non-scientific study revealed that roughly one-third of all the people I surveyed have a very violent aversion to cilantro. After that, I dug deeper. The Wall Street Journal *published an article early in 2009 on cilantro hating as a modern phenomenon. The article cited several websites and blogs, including http://www.ihatecilantro.blogspot.com/. The interesting thing is that cilantro lovers simply cannot comprehend the terrible taste we ''haters'' experience when exposed to this controversial herb.*

I once grew a lonely cilantro plant in the herb garden. It was just beyond my nose, so for most of the season, I hardly knew it was there. To my surprise, when it had bolted and gone to seed, I discovered that I loved the seeds (coriander). Where I got the nerve to try them, I'm not sure, but the seeds have none of the offending essential oils of the leaves. In recipes like this, I simply use flat-leaf parsley in place of my one green nemesis.

MAKES 4 CUPS (1 L)

3 lb (1.5 kg) tomatillos
3 jalapeño peppers, chopped
3 serrano chiles, chopped
1 green bell pepper, chopped
1 cup (250 mL) chopped red onion
1/2 cup (125 mL) chopped green onion

1/2 cup (125 mL) chopped fresh cilantro or
   flat-leaf parsley
2 tbsp (25 mL) freshly squeezed lime juice
sea salt and freshly ground pepper

1. Clean and husk tomatillos. Place in a large saucepan and cover with water. Bring to a boil over high heat. Cover and reduce heat and simmer for 5 minutes. Remove with a slotted spoon and immerse in cold water for 5 minutes. Drain and pat dry. Chop by hand or using the pulse button of a food processor.

2. Meanwhile in a bowl, combine jalapeño and serrano chile peppers, green pepper, red and green onions, cilantro and lime juice. Add tomatillos and season to taste with salt and pepper.

Freezing Tomatillo Salsa Verde: Measure salsa in 1- or 2-cup (250 or 500 mL) amounts and fill freezer containers to within 1 inch (2.5 cm) of the top. Remove air, seal, label and freeze.

Canning Tomatillo Salsa Verde

4 cups (1 L) Tomatillo Salsa Verde
1/4 cup (50 mL) bottled lemon juice

1. Heat four 1-cup (250 mL) jars in boiling water, and scald the lids, lifter, funnel and tongs (see page 18).

2. In a saucepan, bring the Salsa Verde to a boil over medium-high heat. Boil for 1 minute. Spoon 1 tbsp (15 mL) lemon juice into hot jars. Fill hot jars, leaving a 1/2-inch (1 cm) headspace. Run a thin non-metallic utensil around the inside of the jar to allow air to escape. Add more hot salsa, if necessary, to leave a 1/2-inch (1 cm) headspace. Wipe rims, top with flat lids and screw on metal rings. Return jars to the hot water bath, topping up with hot water if necessary. Bring to a full rolling boil and process jars for 15 minutes (see page 19).

3. Remove canner lid and wait 5 minutes before removing jars to a towel or rack to cool completely. Check seals, label and store in a cool place for up to 1 year.

Freezing Husk Tomatoes
1. **Select Equipment:** Select suitable-size freezer containers, bags or Mason jars (see page 24).

2. **Dry Pack, Unsweetened:** Fill pint (2-cup/500 mL) or quart (1 L) freezer containers with whole husk tomatoes, leaving a 1/2-inch (1 cm) headspace. Seal, label and freeze.

OR
Chop or Crush: Coarsely chop husk tomatoes or, using a potato masher, crush husk tomatoes in a non-reactive bowl. Strain, if desired, and pack into freezer containers, leaving a 1-inch (2.5 cm) headspace. Seal, label and freeze.

Tomatoes

ONE OF THE SPECTACULAR NEW WORLD PLANT DISCOVERIES (along with corn, potatoes, peanuts, pumpkin, tobacco, lima beans and chocolate), tomatoes (*Lycopersicon esculentum*) are, botanically speaking, berries that grow on vines. Native to the South American Andes, where it still grows wild, the tiny fruit from which all of our modern varieties originate grows in clusters on a small, sparse vine. A nightshade plant, the tomato comes in many sizes, shapes and colours.

Good Preserving Varieties

Despite the proliferation of modern hybrids, most of which have been bred for ease of harvest and transportation properties and not for their taste, the heritage varieties have been making a strong comeback with small farmers and gardeners. Heritage, or heirloom, cultivars have been kept alive by individuals who save seeds and plant the old varieties every year. The best way to save true tomato plants is to plant them, eat them and save some of their seeds for next season. For heritage and heirloom vegetable seeds in Canada, visit Salt Spring Seeds (http://www.saltspringseeds.com); in the United States, go to Bountiful Gardens (http://www.bountifulgardens.org/) or Fedco Co-op Garden Supplies (http://www.fedcoseeds.com), which lists seven reasons to save seeds on this page (http://www.fedcoseeds.com/seeds/why_save_seeds.htm).

Heritage, or heirloom, tomatoes are generally late-maturing. Above: Green Brandywine tomatoes in mid-August, showing only very slight signs of ripening.

Tomato varieties fall into several groups, including the following (* indicates the very best canning varieties):

Wild Tomatoes: The South American plants from which all tomato varieties have sprung; small fruit on rambling vines; **Wild Cherry, Cuidad Victoria, Chiapas Wild**.

Currant Tomatoes: Small (1/2-inch/1 cm) tomatoes, sometimes called "midget," that grow in small bunches similar to currants; **Little Julia, Ildi, Cherry Roma*, Red Currant, Sugar Lump** and **Tiny Tim** are some currant tomato varieties available from heritage seed companies (see above).

Cherry or Grape Tomatoes: Can be small or medium in size relative to "regular" tomatoes, and some grow in clusters like grapes. Like currant tomatoes, cherry and grape tomatoes are similar to the original Mayan wild *tomatl* or *xtomatl*. **Golden Honey Bunch:** The first golden grape tomato, this vigorous plant produces vines with clusters of 10 to 20 fruits. Other examples of cherry or grape tomatoes: **Brown Berry, Chiapis Wild, Black Cherry,**

Patio Orange, Gardener's Delight, Lollipop, Tonadose des Conores, Red Cherry*.

Plum or Paste Tomatoes*: These are the very best sauce and canning tomatoes because their flesh is firm, they have fewer seeds, they are high-acid and they hold their shape during processing. **Crimson Giant, Aker's Pink Plum, Amish Paste, Pink Plum Rosa, Veeroma, San Marzano, Maria's, Mishca, Royal Chico, Roma** and **Heinz 1706** are some plum tomato varieties to consider planting. **Window Box Roma** has the classic plum or paste tomato shape and texture, and an excellent taste. This plant is a dwarf suitable for containers, planters and patio pots. You would need several in order to produce enough tomatoes for canning, but they freeze well for adding to winter soups and sauces.

Medium-Size Tomatoes: These are the standard tomatoes planted and used by cooks and gardeners alike. They are good in tomato sauce recipes. Some medium tomato varieties include **Ailsa Craig, Elizabeth Clear Pink** (a Russian heirloom), **Manitoba Red Tree*, Black Pear, Rutgers***.

Beefsteak Tomatoes: Tomatoes that grow large and stay succulent; the best are fragrant and full of sweet tomato flavour. **Brandywine*, Valencia, Giant Belgian, Sicilian Saucer, Tasmanian Yellow, Wonder Boy, Ponderosa*, Colossal** and **Crimson Giant*** are just a few of the "super" tomatoes, which can grow to over 3 lb (1.5 kg). **Big Beef***: A good example of a meaty red beefsteak tomato, it is small in this class (10 to 12 oz/300 to 375 g) but is a very good canning cultivar thanks to its outstanding flavour and good sugar-to-acid ratio.

Orange, Yellow and Tangerine Tomatoes: Often higher in vitamin C and lower in acid content (making them unsuitable for the Boiling Water Method unless acid is added). **Limmony** (very bright yellow), **Tiger Stripe** (reddish-orange with yellow streaks, very sweet), **Jubilee, Giant Oxheart, Golden Queen, Mandarin Cross, Moon Glow, Sunray, Tangella** (tangerine colour).

Pink, Purple or Blue Tomatoes: Similar to the orange/yellow type, these purplish-pink tomatoes are second lowest in acid content (unsuitable for the Boiling Water Method). **Dutchman, Early Detroit, Gulf State, Pink Lady, Ponderosa Pink, Watermelon Beefsteak, Winsall, Purple Prince.**

White Tomatoes: Like the yellow and pink types, white tomatoes are low in acid (unsuitable for the Boiling Water Method); take longer to fruit, so best grown in warmer climates. **Snowball, White Wonder, White Queen, White Beauty.**

Green Tomatoes: Green when fully ripe. **Green Zebra** (green with gold/green stripes); **Yellow Tiger Stripe** (green and yellow stripes); **Bali** (ribbed, marbled pink, yellow and red); **Evergreen** (low in acid, good for eating fresh); **Maritimer** (early green, often used for canning).

Purchasing/Storing

- 1 lb (500 g) yields 1-1/2 to 2 cups (375 to 500 mL) peeled tomatoes or 1 cup (250 mL) chopped tomato pulp.
- You will need 2-1/2 to 3 lb (1.125 to 1.5 kg) for each quart (1 L) jar.

Heavy tomatoes that are slightly firm yet yield to pressure and have bright, shiny skins are ripe and delicious. You can ripen hard tomatoes with green spots, but the flavour will not be as good as if vine-ripened. I reach for bumpy tomatoes, with growth lines or large eyes, because usually they are the heritage types with the most complex and rich tomato flavours.

Good With

- Herbs such as oregano, basil, bay, thyme, winter and summer savory, rosemary, parsley, chives.
- Savoury seasonings such as cumin, coriander.
- Sweet seasonings such as cinnamon, ginger, cloves, nutmeg.
- Other vegetables, such as garlic, onions, fennel, celery, eggplant.
- Pasta, fish, poultry, veal, lamb and beef, grilled vegetables (in sauce form).

Preparation

To Skin Tomatoes: Cut the core out of the top or blossom end and score the bottom with an X. Blanch tomatoes in boiling water for 15 to 30 seconds. The riper the tomato, the less time it should take to loosen the skin. Immerse in cold water for 1 minute and slip off the skins.

To Seed Tomatoes: Tomatoes do not need to be skinned in order to seed them, but if you are going to skin as well as seed, then skin first.

Cut on the diagonal between the stem and the bottom ends. Hold one half over a bowl or the sink and squeeze out the seeds. Repeat with the remaining half.

To Roast Tomatoes: Plum or paste tomatoes are best for this method. Rub tomato skins with olive oil and place directly on a hot grill or on a rimmed baking sheet under an oven broiler. Using tongs, turn often until skins blacken and begin to split. Place charred tomatoes in a colander over a glass bowl to catch the juices. Cover with a clean tea towel or lid. Let cool. Skin and seed (you can use the skin, juices and seeds in soup stock).

Canning Tomatoes

See detailed canning information, pages 14 and 20.

Essential: Low-acid tomatoes must be pressure canned or, if canned by the Boiling Water Canner Method, hot pack with bottled lemon juice added. If you do not know the acidity of the tomatoes, or to be safe, follow the Hot Pack Method and add 1 tbsp (15 mL) bottled lemon juice to pint (2-cup/500 mL) jars and 2 tbsp (25 mL) bottled lemon juice to quart (1 L) jars.

1. **Prepare Equipment:** Wash and heat pint (2-cup/500 mL) or quart (1 L) jars, and scald the lids, funnel, ladle and tongs (see page 18).

2. Tomatoes are packed whole, halved or quartered in their own juices; chopped and packed in their own juices; or crushed, puréed or juiced and packed.

3. Pack tomatoes into jars hot.
Make a Hot Pack: Cut peeled tomatoes into quarters or halves. In a saucepan, bring tomatoes and their juices to a hard boil over medium heat, stirring constantly to keep from scorching. Fill hot jars with hot tomatoes and their juices, leaving a 1/2-inch (1 cm) headspace. Add 1 tbsp (15 mL) bottled lemon juice and 1/2 tsp (2 mL) salt to pint (2-cup/500 mL) jars and 2 tbsp (25 mL) bottled lemon juice and 1 tsp (5 mL) salt to quart (1 L) jars. Run a thin non-metallic utensil around the inside of the jar to allow air to escape. Add more tomatoes, if necessary, to leave a 1/2-inch (1 cm) headspace. Wipe sealing edge of jars with a clean, damp, lint-free cloth. Position flat lids over the tops of jars and hand-tighten screw bands.

4. **Process tomatoes in a canner:** Use a Boiling Water Canner according to the chart below.

Processing Times at Different Altitudes for High-Acid Tomatoes in a BOILING WATER Canner					
Pack Style	Jar Size	0-2000 ft	2001-4000 ft	4001-6000 ft	6001+ ft
HOT	Pints	15 min	20 min	25 min	30 min
	Quarts	20 min	25 min	30 min	35 min
RAW	Pints	20 min	25 min	30 min	35 min
	Quarts	25 min	30 min	35 min	40 min

OR

Process tomatoes in a Pressure Canner following manufacturer's directions for steam pressure and time at your altitude.

5. **Cool, Label and Store:** Lift jars from canner and place on a clean towel or rack. Do not re-tighten screw bands. Let the jars cool to room temperature. This may take from 12 to 24 hours. Remove and store screw bands. Check lid seals (see page 19). Wipe and label sealed jars. Store in a cool, dark place.

green tomato chow chow

No matter how early I plant or how much of a head start with seedlings I get in the greenhouse, I always have a fair number of tomatoes that never ripen before the first frost of autumn. Using those green tomatoes is almost as important to me as the first red orb plucked from the vine and eaten up on the spot.

10 cups (4 L) skinned, seeded, chopped green
   tomatoes and their juices (6 lb/3 kg, about
   24 tomatoes)
4 tbsp (50 mL) coarse salt, divided
5 apples, chopped
4 cloves garlic, minced
2 large red onions, thinly sliced
2 hot chile peppers, chopped

2 tsp (10 mL) grated fresh ginger
2 cups (500 mL) white wine vinegar
1-1/2 cups (375 mL) lightly packed brown sugar
1-1/2 cups (375 mL) chopped raisins
3 tbsp (45 mL) dry mustard powder
1 tsp (5 mL) cumin seeds
1 tsp (5 mL) ground cinnamon
1/2 tsp (2 mL) ground cloves

1. Toss tomatoes with 2 tbsp (25 mL) of the salt and let drain in a colander for 2 hours.

2. In a Maslin pan or canning kettle, combine tomatoes, apples, garlic, onions, peppers, ginger, vinegar, sugar and raisins. Bring to a boil over high heat, stirring constantly. Reduce heat and boil gently, stirring occasionally for 1-1/2 hours until sauce begins to thicken. Add remaining salt, mustard, cumin, cinnamon and cloves. Boil gently, stirring frequently for about 30 minutes, or until thickened and sauce begins to mound on a spoon.

3. Meanwhile, heat 5 1-pint (2 cup/500 mL) jars in boiling water, and scald the lids, lifter, funnel and tongs (see page 18).

4. Fill hot jars, leaving a 1/2-inch (1 cm) headspace. Run a thin non-metallic utensil around the inside of the jar to allow air to escape. Add more hot chili if necessary, to leave a 1/2-inch (1 cm) headspace. Wipe rims, top with flat lids and screw on metal rings. Return jars to the hot water bath, topping up with hot water if necessary. Bring to a full rolling boil and process jars for 20 minutes (see page 19).

5. Remove canner lid and wait 5 minutes before removing jars to a towel or rack to cool completely. Check seals, label and store in a cool place for up to 1 year

Use: Serve as a tomato condiment where ketchup is used; or in place of chili sauce in recipes and with ham or eggs.

aunt ruth's heritage chili sauce

Growing up in Sutton, Ontario, on Lake Simcoe in the 1960s, my husband, Gary McLaughlin, experienced what can only be described as an idyllic childhood: summers in, on and about the lake; winters playing ice hockey or snowmobiling; living in the family home built by his great-grandfather Martin McLaughlin. One of his earliest memories is of the large vegetable garden tended by his Aunt Ruth and Uncle Keith Dunn. Like many families in those days, the Dunns filled their pantry with preserves and canned fruits and vegetables. Gary loved his Aunt Ruth's Chili Sauce. When I started on this book, Ruth's daughter Darla took out her mother's recipe box and dictated this recipe, written in her mother's hand. If you like your chili sauce with some heat, add fresh or dried hot cayenne pepper (crushed or chopped) or hot sauce to taste. Use organic fruits and vegetables whenever possible, especially for the apple in this recipe, which should not be peeled.

MAKES 18 CUPS (3.5L)

16 cups (4 L) skinned, seeded, chopped paste tomatoes and their juices (10 lb/5 kg, about 38 tomatoes)

8 large onions, chopped

5 red bell peppers, chopped

4 stalks celery, chopped

1/4 apple (unpeeled), chopped

2 cups (500 mL) white wine vinegar

1 cup (250 mL) granulated sugar

1 cup (250 mL) lightly packed brown sugar

3 tbsp (45 mL) salt

1 tbsp (15 mL) whole mustard seeds, crushed

1-1/2 tsp (7 mL) ground cinnamon

1 tsp (5 mL) ground cloves

1/2 tsp (2 mL) ground ginger

pinch chile powder, or to taste

1. In a Maslin pan or canning kettle, combine tomatoes, onions, peppers, celery, apple, vinegar, granulated and brown sugars, salt and mustard seeds. Bring to a boil over high heat, stirring constantly. Reduce heat and boil gently, stirring occasionally, for 1-1/2 hours or until sauce begins to thicken. Add cinnamon, cloves, ginger and chile powder. Boil gently, stirring frequently, for about 30 minutes or until sauce is thickened and begins to mound on a spoon.

2. Meanwhile, heat nine 1-pint (2-cup/500 mL) jars in boiling water, and scald the lids, lifter, funnel and tongs (see page 18).

3. Fill hot jars, leaving a 1/2-inch (1 cm) headspace. Run a thin non-metallic utensil around the inside of the jar to allow air to escape. Add more hot chile, if necessary, to leave a 1/2-inch (1 cm) headspace. Wipe rims, top with flat lids and screw on metal rings. Return jars to the hot water bath, topping up with hot water if necessary. Bring to a full rolling boil and process jars for 20 minutes (see page 19).

4. Remove canner lid and wait 5 minutes before removing jars to a towel or rack to cool completely. Check seals, label and store in a cool place for up to 1 year.

Use: Homemade chili sauce complements eggs, prepared any style, and bacon or sausage like no other condiment. If you get beyond breakfast, use this heritage chili sauce to top meat loaf, to lend the hint of cinnamon and spice to skillet dinners (see Country-Style Chicken, page 320), and to serve with roast beef or chicken at Sunday dinners.

fire-roasted pepper and tomato sauce

Here we are at the end of the summer, and four of the most flavourful ingredients to come out of the garden (tomatoes, garlic, red peppers and basil) are at the markets in full splendour. I have always roasted red peppers—it's a fall thing at our house. One year, when I secured a green garbage bag full of the crimson orbs, I stuffed them with rice and smoked them using our charcoal smoker. So it is only natural that I would roast my favourite fall vegetables for this incredibly rich and complex-tasting sauce. This sauce is as much about the roasted red peppers as the tomatoes.

Roasting has a lot going for it. I guess it gets my vote for the nutty, caramelized flavour it imparts, but high on my list of benefits is that it is easy: the skin pops up and can simply be plucked off both the tomatoes and the peppers. When roasting the peppers and garlic, check after about 10 minutes. The garlic may be soft and caramelized about 5 minutes before the peppers are charred, so transfer them to a dish to cool. When you see the skin on the peppers blister and turn black, they are ready. Some pepper varieties are meatier than others. If you can find peppers that are thick fleshed, use them in this recipe.

2 rimmed baking sheets, lightly oiled
Preheat oven to 400°F (200°C)
MAKES ABOUT 10 CUPS (2.5 L)

2 lb (1 kg) red bell peppers, halved and seeded	1/4 cup (50 mL) red wine, optional
10 cloves garlic, peeled	1 tbsp (15 mL) salt
4 tbsp (50 mL) olive oil, divided	1 cup (250 mL) chopped fresh flat-leaf parsley
4 lb (2 kg) ripe plum tomatoes (about 12), halved and seeded	1/2 cup (125 mL) loosely packed shredded basil leaves
2 cups (500 mL) chopped onions	1 tbsp (15 mL) chopped fresh oregano
1/2 cup (125 mL) packed brown sugar	1 tbsp (15 mL) chopped fresh rosemary
1/2 cup (125 mL) red wine vinegar	5 tbsp (65 mL) bottled lemon juice

1. On one of the prepared baking sheets, arrange red pepper halves in a single layer, cut sides down. Place garlic cloves between the peppers. Drizzle with 2 tbsp (25 mL) of the olive oil. On the other baking sheet, arrange tomatoes cut sides down. Drizzle with remaining olive oil.

2. Roast in preheated oven for 15 to 20 minutes. Check garlic and tomatoes. If garlic is soft, remove it.

3. Remove the skin from the tomatoes and roughly chop, reserving flesh and juices. Roast peppers for another 10 minutes or until they are blistered and partly charred. Transfer to a colander over a bowl to catch the juices and cover with a clean tea towel. When peppers are cool enough to handle, rub off the skins and chop roughly. Chop roasted garlic.

4. In a Maslin pan or canning kettle, combine tomatoes and juices, red pepper and juices, garlic, onions, brown sugar, vinegar, red wine, if using, and salt. Bring to a boil over high heat. Boil for 30 minutes. Add parsley, basil, oregano and rosemary and stir well to combine. Bring to a full rolling boil. Reduce heat and boil gently, stirring occasionally, for 1 hour or until sauce is thick.

5. Meanwhile, heat five 1-pint (2-cup/500 mL) jars in boiling water, and scald the lids, lifter, funnel and tongs (see page 18).

6. Remove hot jars from the canner and fill each with 1 tbsp (15 mL) lemon juice. Ladle hot sauce into hot jars, leaving a 1/2-inch (1 cm) headspace. Wipe rims, top with flat lids and screw on metal rings. Return jars to the hot water bath, topping up with hot water if necessary. Bring to a full rolling boil and process jars for 35 minutes (see page 19).

7. Remove canner lid and wait 5 minutes before removing jars to a towel or rack to cool completely. Check seals, label and store in a cool place for up to 1 year.

thai turkey

Teenagers love this dish, and it's something they can cook for friends on their own because it only uses one dish and is so easy. If you can't find fresh (or frozen) turkey thighs, use 6 to 8 chicken thighs or chicken wings, which are great for a casual dinner. You can make this dish as spicy-hot as you like by adding red pepper flakes or harissa or chopped fresh hot peppers. Turkey thighs are very big. I have found it easier to cook them whole in the sauce and then slice the cooked meat off the bone and put it back into the sauce. It's a bit messy to slice, but the meat stays moist and the servings are easier to manage. Serve over cooked rice or pasta, or with grilled or steamed vegetables.

As for the peanut butter, apologies to all recipe testers who want every grain of salt accounted for—I'm not keen on imposing my ingredient preferences unless there is a definite benefit to the recipe. So I'm not terribly specific about ingredients when another one you have in your pantry will work. And I suspect that everyone secretly harbours a love or hate for one or the other style of peanut butter: smooth or crunchy. In this recipe, you will notice that I haven't revealed my bias—I prefer to leave that up to you and whatever happens to be in your cupboard.

8-cup (2 L) baking dish, with lid or foil
  to cover
Preheat oven to 350°F (180°C)
MAKES 4 TO 6 SERVINGS

2 cups (500 mL) Fire-Roasted Pepper and
  Tomato Sauce (page 276)
2/3 cup (150 mL) peanut butter
2 skinless turkey thighs (each 1 lb/500 g)

1. In the baking dish, combine Fire-Roasted Pepper and Tomato Sauce with peanut butter. The sauce will be thick. Place turkey thighs in the dish and spoon the sauce over top to cover. Cover and bake in preheated oven for 45 to 50 minutes or until the temperature in the thickest part of the thigh registers 170°F (77°C).

Freezing Tomatoes

Many of the grape- and cherry-type tomatoes, Red Candy for instance, freeze well.

1. Select Equipment: Select suitable-size freezer bags for whole tomatoes, or rigid plastic containers or Mason jars for chopped or crushed tomatoes (see page 24).

2. Wash tomatoes but do not skin. Pack into bags, leaving a 1-inch (2.5 cm) headspace. Remove air, label and seal. Freeze for up to 9 months.

OR

Crush or chop: Pack into containers, leaving a 1-inch (2.5 cm) headspace. Remove air, label and seal. Freeze for up to 9 months.

Turnips

MANY PEOPLE CONFUSE TURNIPS (*BRASSICA RAPA*) with rutabaga (*Brassica napo-brassica*). Turnips are small, round/oval root vegetables with white, green or purplish crowns. You can eat the green, thin leaves or cook them as a pot-herb in soups and stews. Turnips are milder than parsnips, but can be hot and peppery, depending on the variety.

Good Preserving Varieties

Some Asian varieties, while excellent raw in salads, are not the best for preserving. One exception is **Tokyo** turnip (also called **Tokyo White**, **Tokyo Market** or **Tokyo Cross**). It is hot and nippy like a radish when eaten raw, but it mellows to a buttery flavour when cooked, so it would be good in a frozen purée.

Amber Globe: An heirloom turnip that originated in Aberdeen, Scotland; it's rare, but if you can find seeds, plant and eat, saving the seeds, because the flesh is sweet, fine-grained and creamy coloured; very good for cooking and freezing.

Golden Ball: Also known as **Golden Perfection** or **Orange Jelly**; a later variety that is small, round and yellow; tasty and excellent for pickles.

Manchester Market: Round, with green skin and white flesh; stores well.

Purple Top Milan: An early variety that produces flattish roots with purple markings and white flesh; excellent flavour; good for pickles.

Purple Top White Globe or **Veitch's Red Globe:** An early, attractive, old cultivar with round or slightly flattened roots; mild, sweet-tasting; good for pickling; reddish-purple above ground and white below.

Snowball: An early, delicately flavoured white variety; good for cooking and freezing.

While you can substitute rutabaga, above, in most of the recipes here, try young, fresh turnips first, because their taste is crisp and the flesh is white, making them a better choice for pickles.

Purchasing/Storing

- 1 lb (500 g) yields 2-1/2 cups (625 mL) cubed turnips.
- You will need about 1-1/2 lb (750 g) for each quart (1 L) jar.

Look for turnips with greens still attached. Choose small to medium firm turnips with smooth, unblemished skin. Tops should be fresh and green, not wilted or yellowing.

Good With
- Culinary herbs such as basil, bay, thyme, chervil, sage, oregano.
- Seasonings such as cumin, coriander, curry blends, cinnamon, ginger, nutmeg.
- Other root vegetables, such as parsnips, rutabagas, beets, carrots, onions, garlic, potatoes, kohlrabi.

Preparation
Scrub in a sink full of cool water to which a drop of food-safe soap has been added. Trim the ends and peel using a vegetable peeler.

Canning Turnips
I do not advise canning turnips because they develop a strong flavour. They are best frozen or pickled.

pickled carrots, turnips and peppers

I like the palette of the yellow, orange and red vegetables in this pickle because it is warm and cheerful on a winter table.

MAKES ABOUT 12 CUPS (3 L)

2 cups (500 mL) water
1-1/2 cups (375 mL) white wine vinegar
1 cup (250 mL) rice vinegar
1 cup (250 mL) granulated sugar
1/4 cup (50 mL) freshly grated gingerroot
5 cloves garlic, crushed
2 tbsp (25 mL) dill seeds
2 tbsp (25 mL) celery seeds
2 tbsp (25 mL) pickling salt

2 tbsp (25 mL) mustard seeds
1 tbsp (15 mL) Dijon mustard
12 black peppercorns
3 carrots, cut into 3-1/2 x 1/2-inch (8.5 x 2 cm) sticks
2 turnips, cut into 3-1/2 x 1/2-inch (8.5 x 2 cm) sticks
2 red bell peppers, cut into 3-1/2 x 1/2-inch (8. 5 x 2 cm) strips

1. Heat six 1-pint (2-cup/500 mL) jars in boiling water, and scald the lids, lifter, funnel and tongs (see page 18).

2. In a Maslin pan or canning kettle, combine water, white wine vinegar and rice vinegar. Bring to a boil over medium-high heat. Stir in the sugar and boil lightly, stirring constantly, for 3 minutes or until the sugar is dissolved. Stir in the ginger, garlic, dill, celery seeds, salt, mustard seeds, Dijon mustard and peppercorns. Reduce heat and keep simmering, stirring occasionally, for 10 to 15 minutes or until the liquid thickens slightly.

3. Fill hot jars with carrot sticks, turnip sticks and red pepper strips, shaking the jar to pack fairly tightly. Cover with hot vinegar brine, leaving a 1/2-inch (1 cm) headspace. Run a thin non-metallic utensil around the inside of the jar to allow air to escape. Add more hot brine, if necessary, to leave a 1/2-inch (1 cm) headspace. Wipe rims, top with flat lids and screw on metal rings. Return jars to the hot water bath, topping up with hot water if necessary. Bring to a full rolling boil and process jars for 15 minutes (see page 19).

4. Remove canner lid and wait 5 minutes before removing jars to a towel or rack to cool completely. Check seals, label and store in a cool place for up to 1 year.

root vegetable sauce

Just like all great tomato sauces, this one is excellent on spaghetti and in pasta dishes of all kinds, but it also excels with fish, chicken and other meats. When my daughter was small, I added chopped cabbage and carrots to as many dishes as possible in order to boost the nutritional value. This is a tasty example of how tomato sauce, which is already a healthy choice for nutrients, can be packed with even more goodness. The sauce should be on the thick side for freezing. To use immediately, you may wish to thin it slightly by adding chicken broth or tomato juice until it reaches the desired consistency. For this sauce, I don't skin the tomatoes, but you may wish to do so (see page 271).

1 or 2 rimmed baking sheets, lightly oiled
Preheat oven to 375°F (190°C)
MAKES 10 CUPS (2.5 L)

2 medium eggplants, halved lengthwise
1/3 to 1/2 cup (75 to 125 mL) olive oil, divided
3 cups (750 mL) chopped onions
1 cup (250 mL) chopped turnip
1 cup (250 mL) chopped carrot
1/2 cup (125 mL) chopped parsnip
4 cloves garlic, chopped

8 cups (2 L) chopped seeded paste tomatoes
2 tbsp (25 mL) balsamic vinegar
1 tbsp (15 mL) molasses
1/2 tsp (2 mL) salt
1/2 cup (125 mL) chopped fresh basil
1/4 cup (50 mL) chopped fresh oregano
2 tbsp (25 mL) chopped fresh parsley

1. Arrange eggplant halves on prepared baking sheet (use 2 sheets if needed), cut sides down. Drizzle each half with 1 tbsp (15 mL) of the olive oil. Bake in preheated oven for 35 minutes or until flesh is soft. Let cool and scoop flesh out of skins. Discard skins.

2. Meanwhile, in a large skillet, heat 3 tbsp (45 mL) of the olive oil over medium-high heat. Add onions, turnip, carrot and parsnip and cook, stirring constantly, for 2 to 3 minutes. Reduce heat to low, cover and gently cook the vegetables for about 10 minutes, stirring occasionally. Add more olive oil as needed to keep from scorching. Vegetables should be almost tender and lightly browned. Add garlic and cook, stirring frequently, for 5 to 6 minutes or until vegetables are cooked.

3. Add eggplant flesh, tomatoes, vinegar, molasses and salt. Bring to a light simmer. Cover and simmer gently, stirring occasionally, for 10 minutes. Stir in basil, oregano and parsley. Bring to a simmer and cook for 1 minute, stirring constantly. Remove from heat and let cool. Pack into freezer containers in 2- or 4-cup (500 mL or 1 L) amounts, leaving a 1-inch (2.5 cm) headspace. Remove air, label and seal. Freeze for up to 6 months.

Freezing Turnips

1. **Select Equipment:** Select suitable-size freezer containers, bags or Mason jars (see page 24).

2. **Blanch cubed turnips in boiling water for 2 minutes.** Lift out and plunge into cold water. Let stand for 2 minutes. Drain and pat dry. Pack into containers, leaving a 1-inch (2.5 cm) headspace. Remove air, label and seal. Freeze for up to 9 months.

OR

Purée: Cook cubes in boiling, salted water for 5 to 6 minutes or until tender. Drain and cool slightly, then mash using a potato masher. Pack into containers, leaving a 1-inch (2.5 cm) headspace. Remove air, label and seal. Freeze for up to 6 months.

Zucchini

SOMETIMES YOU WILL SEE THE WORD COURGETTE, especially when reading British or French cookbooks. Courgette is French for zucchini, a type of summer squash that was developed in Italy. Zucchini (*Cucurbita pepo*) is long and slender, and usually dark green over yellow, giving a striped, sometimes speckled effect. It can grow huge, but the smaller fruits are fresh, tender and delicate in flavour and best for preserving.

Good Preserving Varieties

Available year-round, local zucchini peaks in August. All varieties are good for preserving.

All Green Bush: Light speckles on dark green skin; early variety.

Condor: Nutty flavour; good for baking and preserving.

Costata Romanesco: Rich flavour; as a bonus, produces male blossoms that can be stuffed and cooked in addition to the fruits.

Eight Ball: Round, baseball-size fruits that are great for stuffing; easy to pickle and can.

Golden Dawn: Golden yellow skin; mild flesh.

Newer zucchini varieties are golden yellow in skin colour, and some are round or globe-shaped

Purchasing/Storing

- 1 lb (500 g) yields 3 cups (750 mL) sliced or cubed zucchini.
- You will need about 1-1/2 lb (750 g) for each quart (1 L) jar.

Choose firm, well-rounded zucchini, with tender, glossy, unblemished skin. Fruits longer than 3 to 6 inches (8 to 15 cm) will be tougher and have more fibre, but zucchini up to about 10 inches (25 cm) long can be pickled.

Good With

- Culinary herbs such as oregano, sage, chives, basil, bay, thyme, chervil, rosemary.
- Spices such as nutmeg, cumin, coriander, curry blends.
- Rice or pasta (in sauces or stuffed with rice mixtures).
- Other vegetables, such as tomatoes, garlic, onions, leeks, eggplant, peppers.

A medium-green zucchini hybrid with smooth, cylindrical fruit, Radiant is good for pickles, salsas and other preserves; smooth skin means peeling is not essential.

Preparation

Scrub in a sink full of cool water to which a drop of food-safe soap has been added. Rinse well and pat dry. Trim away the blossom end and the rounded end only if necessary. Leave the peel on if fruit is tender; peel away strips of skin if mature or damaged.

Canning Zucchini

See detailed canning information, page 20.

1. Prepare Equipment: Wash and heat pint (2-cup/500 mL) or quart (1 L) jars, and scald the lids, funnel, ladle and tongs (see page 22).

2. For every 2 cups (500 mL) of cut zucchini, bring 2 cups (500 mL) water or broth to a boil.

3. Pack quartered or cubed zucchini into jars either hot or raw.
Make a Hot Pack: Add zucchini to gently boiling water or broth and boil for 1 minute. Drain, reserving cooking liquid. Fill hot jars with hot zucchini, shaking the jar to pack fairly tightly. Pour hot cooking liquid over zucchini, leaving a 1-inch (2.5 cm) headspace. Run a thin non-metallic utensil around the inside of the jar to allow air to escape. Wipe sealing edge of jars with a clean, damp, lint-free cloth. Position flat lids over the tops of jars and hand-tighten screw bands.

OR

Make a Raw Pack: Fill jars with quartered or cubed zucchini, shaking the jar to pack fairly tightly. Cover with hot water or broth, leaving a 1-inch (2.5 cm) headspace. Run a thin non-metallic utensil around the inside of the jar to allow air to escape. Add hot liquid, if necessary, to leave a 1-inch (2.5 cm) headspace. Wipe sealing edge of jars with a clean, damp, lint-free cloth. Position flat lids over the tops of jars and hand-tighten screw bands.

4. Place jars in pressure canner: Use a Pressure Canner according to the chart below for Dial-Gauge or follow manufacturer's instructions.

Processing Times at Different Altitudes for Zucchini in a DIAL-GAUGE PRESSURE Canner					
Pack Style	Jar Size	0–2000 ft	2001–4000 ft	4001–6000 ft	6001+ ft
HOT	Pints	15 min	20 min	25 min	30 min
	Quarts	20 min	25 min	30 min	35 min
RAW	Pints	20 min	25 min	30 min	35 min
	Quarts	25 min	30 min	35 min	40 min

5. Cool, Label and Store: Turn off heat; let pressure return to zero naturally. Once gauge shows 0 pressure, wait 2 minutes then open the vent. Unlock and remove canner lid. Wait 10 minutes then lift jars from canner and place on a clean towel or rack. Do not re-tighten screw bands. Let the jars cool to room temperature. This may take from 12 to 24 hours. Remove and store screw bands. Check lid seals (see page 23). Wipe and label sealed jars. Store in a cool, dark place.

five-spice zucchini pickles

As anyone who has ever grown zucchini knows, the garden always produces an ample amount. If you can get out and harvest one good lot of the bright yellow flowers, this helps to thin the yield out slightly and provides a very nice dish when stuffed with rice and poached in tomato sauce.

MAKES ABOUT 10 CUPS (2.5 L)

9 cups (2.25 L) sliced zucchini
2-1/2 cups (625 mL) thinly sliced onions
1/3 cup (75 mL) pickling salt
3 cups (750 mL) white wine vinegar

1 cup (250 mL) granulated sugar
3 tbsp (45 mL) Five-Spice Blend (page 216 or store-bought), tied in a cheesecloth bag

1. In a stoneware crock or non-reactive bowl, combine zucchini and onions. Sprinkle with salt and cover with water. Let stand for 2 hours. Pour into a large colander and drain well, discarding the liquids. Rinse with fresh water and drain well.

2. Heat five 1-pint (2-cup/500 mL) jars in boiling water, and scald the lids, lifter, funnel and tongs (see page 18).

3. In a Maslin pan or canning kettle, combine vinegar and sugar. Tie the spice bag to a handle. Bring to a boil over high heat, stirring constantly. Add zucchini and onions and boil gently, stirring frequently, for 5 minutes.

4. Skim off and discard any foam. Using tongs, fill hot jars with zucchini and onions to within 1 inch (2.5 cm) of the top. Shake the jar to pack fairly tightly. Ladle hot brine over, leaving a 1/2-inch (1 cm) headspace. Run a thin non-metallic utensil around the inside of the jar to allow air to escape.

Try making your own authentic Chinese five-spice blend for these zippy pickles—the flavour will be clear and fresh, and you can tailor the amounts to suit your taste.

Add more hot brine, if necessary, to leave a 1/2-inch (1 cm) headspace. Wipe rims, top with flat lids and screw on metal rings. Return jars to the hot water bath, topping up with hot water if necessary. Bring to a full rolling boil and process jars for 10 minutes (see page 19).

5. Remove canner lid and wait 5 minutes before removing jars to a towel or rack to cool completely. Check seals, label and store in a cool place for up to 1 year.

mediterranean chutney

After the vegetables are in the pot, it takes a few hours to simmer and reduce this chutney to a thick, rich mixture, so it's a good recipe for a rainy summer day. I make this just before Labour Day, when I know the pace of our lives will pick up and recipes like these will be out of the question.

MAKES 8 CUPS (2 L)

2 lb (1 kg) tomatoes, skinned and chopped (about 2 cups/500 mL)

2 lb (1 kg) zucchini, roughly chopped (about 1-1/2 cups/375mL)

2 green bell peppers, chopped

2 tart apples, chopped

1 large Spanish onion (14 to 16 oz/400 to 500 g), chopped

4 cloves garlic, crushed

2 cayenne peppers, finely chopped

1 tbsp (15 mL) salt

1-1/2 cups (375 L) granulated sugar

1-1/2 cups (375 L) malt vinegar

2 tbsp (25 mL) fresh thyme leaves

2 tbsp (25 mL) chopped fresh oregano

1 tbsp (15 mL) chopped fresh rosemary

1. In a Maslin pan or canning kettle, combine tomatoes, zucchini, peppers, apples, onion, garlic, cayenne peppers and salt. Stir well. Cook over medium heat, stirring constantly, and slowly bringing to a boil. Simmer gently, stirring occasionally, for 1 to 1-1/2 hours or until the vegetables are soft and the juices from the tomatoes are almost evaporated.

2. Add sugar and vinegar, stirring to dissolve the sugar. Bring back to a light boil. Reduce heat and simmer gently, stirring occasionally, for about 1 hour or until the chutney is moist and thick. Stir in the thyme, oregano and rosemary and cook for 3 minutes.

3. Meanwhile, heat four 1-pint (2-cup/500 mL) jars in boiling water, and scald the lids, lifter, funnel and tongs (see page 18).

4. Fill hot jars, leaving a 1/2-inch (1 cm) headspace. Run a thin non-metallic utensil around the inside of the jar to allow air to escape. Add more hot chutney, if necessary, to leave a 1/2-inch (1 cm) headspace. Wipe rims, top with flat lids and screw on metal rings. Return jars to the hot water bath, topping up with hot water if necessary. Bring to a full rolling boil and process jars for 15 minutes (see page 19).

5. Remove canner lid and wait 5 minutes before removing jars to a towel or rack to cool completely. Check seals, label and store in a cool place for up to 1 year.

mediterranean chicken and potato salad

Just as the air turns crisp, even before it is officially autumn, I often switch to this warm and slightly heartier potato salad. Of course, if there is any left over, it is great cold for lunch the next day. Use a waxy potato variety such as Yukon Gold or russet so that they slice easily and don't break apart in the salad. For more heat, you can add chopped fresh or dried cayenne pepper or dried chile pepper flakes. If I have capers, I include them to carry through the Mediterranean taste, but they are not critical. More fresh oregano or thyme can also be added to suit your preference.

MAKES 4 SERVINGS

3 tbsp (45 mL) olive oil, divided

4 boneless chicken breasts

1 small red onion, halved and sliced

6 medium potatoes, cooked and sliced

1/2 cup (125 mL) Mediterranean Chutney
(page 291)

2 cups (500 mL) lightly packed baby spinach
leaves

2 tbsp (25 mL) drained capers, optional

1. In a skillet, heat 2 tbsp (25 mL) of the olive oil over medium heat. Add chicken breasts and cook for 2 to 3 minutes on each side or until lightly browned. Cover, reduce heat and cook for 10 minutes or until cooked through. Transfer to a plate and cut into shreds.

2. Add remaining oil to the pan and increase heat to medium-high. Add onion and cook, stirring frequently, for 6 minutes or until soft. Add potatoes and cook, stirring constantly, until lightly browned and heated through, 3 to 5 minutes.

3. In a bowl, toss together potato mixture, chicken and chutney. Divide the spinach among 4 plates and top with the warm potato salad mixture. Garnish with capers, if using.

Use: This salad is a natural for serving in zucchini flowers in summer and Boston lettuce cups in winter.

Freezing Zucchini

1. **Select Equipment:** Select suitable-size freezer containers, bags or Mason jars (see page 24).

2. **Blanch zucchini chunks in boiling water for 1 minute.** Lift out and plunge into cold water. Let stand for 1 minute. Drain and pat dry. Pack into containers, leaving a 1-inch (2.5 cm) headspace. Remove air, label and seal. Freeze for up to 6 months.

Summer Herbs

BY THE TIME SUMMER IS UPON US, the herb garden is producing at top speed, with plants maturing almost before our eyes. Most herbs will need to be harvested every other day to keep them from going to seed. One of the best ways to use the bounty from the herb bed is to make pesto, gremolata, pastes, salsa verde and persillade (see below and Fall Herbs, page 437, for recipes). These intense herb mixtures can be frozen in 1 tbsp (15 mL) or 1-cup (250 mL) amounts for use all winter.

Basil

Of all the summer herbs, basil is perhaps the most versatile. I grow and buy it to use when preserving tomato sauce and tomatoes, roasted red pepper sauce and, of course, pesto. My favourite basil is **Genovese**, left, which has a sweet anixe-nutmeg-cinnamon flavour and large waxy leaves and looks good as a garnish.

Some of the hundreds of varieties of basil (*Ocimum basilicum*): **Lettuce Leaf**; **Purple Ruffles**; **Queenette Thai**; **Sweet Dani Lemon**; **Spicy Globe**.

Calendula

The Romans named this plant calendula (*Calendula officinalis*) because they noticed it was always in bloom on the first day of the month, which in Latin is *calends* (or *kalends*). Also known as pot marigold, calendula is useful in the garden for companion planting, and the petals are excellent in summer salads, butter and vinaigrette dressings. The flower colour ranges from light to dark yellow, orange and variegated, like the petals. I have made pesto from calendula petals, added them to omelettes and custards, and dried them for use with sugars. The fragrance and taste are light and pleasingly floral. I actually prefer dried calendula petals over saffron.

In this photo, a summer salad is brightened with whole nasturtium flowers and calendula petals. To make a colourful summer vinaigrette: In a clean jar, add up to 1/4 cup (50 mL) fresh or dried calendula petals to 1/4 cup (50 mL) vinegar and 1/2 cup (125 mL) olive or nut oil. Cover tightly with the lid and shake well.

Dill

Both dillweed (the fresh or dried fern-like leaves) and dill seed are used in pickling. The leaves are also used in tartar sauce and in vinaigrette. Use 1/4 cup (50 mL) fresh dillweed or 2 tbsp (25 mL) dried dill in the recipe for vinaigrette (see Calendula on page 295).

It is convenient for preservers that both dill (*Anethum graveolens*) and cucumbers are harvested at the same time. Fresh, immature dill flower heads can be used in making pickles.

Mint

As this close-up of peppermint (*Mentha x piperita,* top) shows, you can always identify mint plants by their leaves, which are pointed, toothed and very fragrant. Another way to recognize mint family plants is by their square stems. Mint is used in jams, jellies and other preserves, peppermint being the most flavourful for preserving recipes.

Both peppermint and spearmint (bottom) are healthy and aggressive plants in the herb garden.

Parsley

Parsley is a great herb for preserving because it keeps its colour and freezes well. Curly parsley (*Petroselinum crispum*) and flat-leaf parsley (*P. neapolitanum*) are common.

I grow and use both varieties of parsley and find that the flat-leaf variety is stronger in flavour. Parsley is used in salsa, with bulgur and couscous, and in summer pastes and pesto.

Persillade

One of my favourite methods of preserving parsley is to make a persillade of finely chopped parsley, garlic and sunflower seeds in a 3:2:1 ratio. I freeze it in 1 or 2 tbsp (15 or 25 mL) amounts for an easy addition to soups, casseroles, marinades, sauces and stews. I lightly spray a plastic ice cube tray with olive oil and pack persillade into it. Once frozen, the persillade cubes pop out, and I store them in resealable plastic bags for easy use.

Rose

Although roses are not herbs, their flowers and fruits, like those of herbs, can be used in cooking. North American First Nations peoples used rose petals and hips to treat a variety of ailments. Rosewater is an effective way to preserve the fragrance of roses, and it is used in Middle Eastern cooking in particular.

Rich in vitamins C, A, B, E and K, tart-tasting rosehips can be dried for teas and infusions. Like crabapples, rosehips are also high in pectin and can be chopped and boiled with rose petal infusion or fruit juice to impart their beautiful colour, pectin and nutrients to jelly. Substitute rosehips for cranberries in sauce and relish dishes if you have enough after the cold weather brings them along to maturity.

parsley jelly

Parsley jelly is an old English favourite that often relied on crabapples or early tart apples to make the parsley infusion "set up," or jell. If made the traditional way, it's a very mild-tasting, soft jelly that can be used with pork, fish or poultry. Use the flat-leaf parsley if you have it, because it is stronger in flavour. This recipe can be used to make mint, sage, thyme or basil jelly by simply substituting any of those fresh herbs for the parsley. For more zip to the jelly, add up to 1/4 cup (50 mL) chopped fresh hot chile pepper or 2 tbsp (25 mL) crushed dried cayenne pepper.

MAKES 6-1/2 CUPS (1.625 L)

2 cups (500 mL) lightly packed coarsely chopped fresh parsley

3 cups (750 mL) boiling water

1 cup (250 mL) unsweetened apple juice (approx)

2 tbsp (25 mL) cider vinegar or white wine vinegar

2 tbsp (25 mL) freshly squeezed lemon juice

4-1/2 cups (1.125 L) granulated sugar

1 pkg (1-3/4 oz/49 to 52 g) fruit pectin crystals

1/4 cup (50 mL) finely chopped hot chile pepper (or to taste), optional

1. Place parsley in a non-reactive teapot or bowl with a tight-fitting lid. Pour boiling water over parsley and cover with lid. Let stand until cool, about 1 hour.

2. Heat seven 1-cup (250 mL) jars in boiling water, and scald the lids, lifter, funnel and tongs (see page 18).

3. Strain off the parsley infusion into a 4-cup (1 L) liquid measure. Discard the herbs. Add enough apple juice to bring the total liquid to 4 cups (1 L). Pour parsley/apple liquid into a Maslin pan or canning kettle. Add vinegar and lemon juice. Increase heat and bring to a boil over medium heat, stirring constantly.

4. Add sugar, 1 cup (250 mL) at a time, stirring to dissolve after each addition. Bring to a full rolling boil. Add pectin and boil for 1 minute. Remove from heat. Skim off and discard any foam. If using chile pepper, let jelly sit for up to 30 minutes before adding chile to the jelly.

5. Fill hot jars, leaving a 1/4-inch (5 mm) headspace. Run a thin non-metallic utensil around the inside of the jar to allow air to escape. Add more hot jelly, if necessary, to leave a 1/4-inch (5 mm) headspace. Wipe rims, top with flat lids and screw on metal rings. Return jars to the hot water bath, topping up with hot water if necessary. Bring to a full rolling boil and process jars for 10 minutes (see page xx).

6. Remove canner lid and wait 5 minutes before removing jars to a towel or rack to cool completely. Check seals, label and store in a cool place for up to 1 year.

summer herb brown mayonnaise

I make up lots of this tangy purée and use it to replace real mayonnaise, as a spread for grilled fish, to toss with rice or to mix with anchovies for crackers. It's one of those condiments that will prove to be very versatile in the kitchen. It makes a great picnic spread.

Rimmed baking sheet, lightly oiled
Preheat oven to 450°F (230°C)
MAKES 3 CUPS (750 mL)

2 onions, quartered	**2 tbsp (25 mL) chopped fresh parsley**
1 leek, trimmed, washed and coarsely chopped	**1/2 tsp (2 mL) salt**
4 cloves garlic, halved	**1/4 cup (50 mL) balsamic vinegar**
3/4 cup (175 mL) olive oil, divided	
3 tbsp (45 mL) chopped fresh basil	

1. On prepared baking sheet, arrange onions, leek and garlic in single layer. Drizzle with 1/4 cup (50 mL) of the olive oil. Roast in preheated oven, stirring frequently, for 15 to 20 minutes or until browned and tender.

2. Transfer vegetables to a small bowl. Stir in remaining olive oil, basil, parsley and salt. Cover and let stand overnight or for at least 4 hours to blend flavours.

3. In a food processor, purée vegetable mixture, adding vinegar in a slow stream through the opening in the lid. Process until smooth. Transfer to an airtight container and store in the refrigerator for up to 1 week.

To Use as a Dressing: Whisk together 3 tbsp (45 mL) Summer Herb Brown Mayonnaise with 1/2 cup (125 mL) orange juice.

basil pesto

Pesto turns from a beautiful bright green to black very quickly, almost before you can get it spooned into the jar or freezer bag. For this reason, I have included a few tablespoons of lemon juice to prevent oxidation, which turns cut herbs black. Personally, I do not use the lemon juice in pesto for my own use (it does change the taste slightly, although not in a bad way), but I offer it here as an option because it would be a shame for your family to shy away from this fabulous aromatic, nutmeg-flavoured sauce just because of its blackish colour. The benefit of making your own pesto is that you can use as much or as little oil as you like and, in turn, will get a fairly dry or a wet pesto. My husband, who uses gobs of pesto on everything, even breakfast omelettes, likes it smooth and paste-like, but not oily. I process his pesto longer than I do mine but use the same amount of oil for both. I like my pesto on the dry side and with definite small bits of the ingredients still discernible (that's my pesto in the photograph, below).

MAKES ABOUT 12 CUPS (3 L)

4 large cloves garlic
1/2 cup (125 mL) pine nuts or sunflower seeds
3 oz (90 g) hard Italian cheese (Parmesan, Parmigiano-Reggiano or pecorino), cut into small cubes

3 cups (750 mL) lightly packed fresh basil leaves
2 tbsp (25 mL) freshly squeezed lemon juice, optional (see above note)
3/4 cup (175 mL) olive oil (approx)
sea salt

1. In the bowl of a food processor, process garlic using the pulse button or an on-off technique until coarsely chopped. Add pine nuts and cheese. Process, using the pulse button or an on-off technique, until nuts and cheese are coarsely chopped. Add basil to the bowl. Drizzle lemon juice over top, if using. Process for 30 seconds or just until leaves are coarsely chopped.

2. With the motor running, add olive oil in a steady stream through the opening in the lid. Keep adding oil and blending until the pesto has reached the desired consistency. Stir in salt to taste.

Fall

"For man, autumn is a time of harvest, of gathering together.
For nature, it is a time of sowing, of scattering abroad."
—EDWIN WAY TEALE

Apples

THOUGHT TO BE THE FIRST FRUIT ever cultivated, the apple (*Malus*) is older than its depictions on prehistoric cave walls. Although there were four major North American species native to much of eastern and western North America, the first European species were brought to Port Royal and the fertile Annapolis Valley in Nova Scotia by French settlers in the early 1600s. It would be another 150 years or so before Johnny Appleseed would begin spreading apple seeds all over Ohio, Michigan, Indiana and Illinois.

Good Preserving Varieties

The best fresh eating apples are not always the best for cooking, freezing and preserving. Good pie apples are varieties that are juicy, firm and hold the shape of the slice when baked, which makes them very good for preserving, stewing and baking. Sauce apples have a softer texture and are full of juice, so they melt down into a homogenous, pourable sauce.

Crabapples, which are native to North America, and the sour apple varieties are both high in pectin and acid, two important considerations for making jelly. For other preserves, the very best apples are the early September-ripening cooking apples that are tart, juicy and barely ripe. If you can, try to combine one or two tart types with two or three sweet apples in jams, compotes and other preserves.

For preserving, look for apples that are freshly harvested, not stored. With the hundreds of varieties of apples available, the best way to know what suits your recipes is to talk to your local orchard owner and experiment with the local varieties that she or he grows. Here is a short list of good preserving apples and the optimum time to preserve them.

Lodi: Large, greenish yellow; tart-sweet; good sauce and preserve apple; September.
Gravenstein: Red with yellow stripes; sweet, tart and crisp; an excellent preserve, pie and sauce variety; not great baked; September through November.
Wealthy: Red with green stripes and splashes; excellent preserve and cooking apple; September through December.
Ripson: Yellow, overspread with dull red; October to January.
Greening: Tart, juicy; excellent cooking and preserving apple, flavour intensifies on cooking; bright greenish yellow; November to February.

Wagener: Light red; fine-grained flesh; tender and juicy; good sauce and preserve apple; November to February.

Golden Delicious: Sweet, tender; excellent pie apple; good sauce and preserving apple; rich golden colour; November to March.

Northern Spy: Large, red striped; excellent pie and preserve apple; December to March.

Rome Beauty: Large, round, striped red and green with tiny pin dots; slightly tart; good for pies and sauces, excellent for baked desserts; December to March.

Winesap: Bright red, firm; slightly tart, spicy; good for pies, preserves, sauces; December to May.

Crabapples are small, wild apples native to North America. They are tart and loaded with pectin, which makes them great for preserving; September.

Purchasing/Storing
- 1 lb (500 g) yields 2-1/2 cups (625 mL) sliced apples.
- You will need about 1-1/4 lb (625 g) for each quart (1 L) jar.

Select firm fruits with no sign of bruising. Store apples in a cool place and use for preserving as soon as possible.

Essential: Apples emit a natural gas that speeds up ripening of fruits such as pears and stone fruit, so keep them in a separate container.

Duchess (left): Light green with red stripes and splashes of red; slightly tart; great preserving, pie and cooking apple; not for baking; August, September. McIntosh (right): Red with some green splotches and tiny yellow dots; tart, tender; cooks soft and smooth; good for pies and sauce, jams, soft preserves; not good for baking; September, October (see sidebar, next page).

Good With
- Meats, poultry, cheese and vegetable dishes.
- Culinary herbs such as parsley, chives, sage, rosemary, basil, bay, thyme, savory, tarragon.
- Sweet seasonings such as cinnamon, ginger, cloves, nutmeg, vanilla, caramel.
- Old and medium-age cheddars, Asiago, colby, Gouda.
- Other fruit, such as raspberries, peaches, pears, nectarines, bananas, berries.
- Vegetables such as onions, peppers, squash.
- Toasted almonds, pecans and walnuts; raisins; chocolate.
- Pork, sausage, duck and goose, poultry, lamb and beef.

Preparation

Wash apples in a sink full of cool water to which a drop of food-safe soap has been added. Rinse well and pat dry. Apples are cored and most often peeled and halved or sliced for preserving.

To prevent discolouration, acidulate: Immerse peeled sliced fruit in water with vitamin C, made by mixing 1 tsp (5 mL) crystalline ascorbic acid or six 500 mg vitamin C tablets in 1 gallon (4 L) cool water.

Canning Apples

See detailed canning information, page 14.

1. **Prepare Equipment:** Wash and heat pint (2-cup/500 mL) or quart (1 L) jars, and scald the lids, funnel, ladle and tongs (see page 18).

2. **Make a Light Syrup:** In a large saucepan, combine 1 cup (250 mL) granulated sugar with 4 cups (1 L) water; stir until dissolved. Bring to a gentle boil over high heat. Makes 4-1/2 cups (1.125 L) syrup, enough for three or four 1-quart (1 L) jars of sliced apples.

Note: You can use the same amount of apple juice or white grape juice in place of the light syrup.

3. **Pack sliced apples into jars hot** (Raw Pack Method makes poor-quality canned apples).

The McIntosh apple tree was first found growing on the farm of John McIntosh, a United Empire Loyalist who settled in McIntosh's Corners (now called Dundela), Dundas County, Ontario. Its parents are thought to be Snow and possibly St. Lawrence. With a monument commemorating the actual site of its "birth" as a sapling in 1796, the McIntosh apple is the most commercially important Canadian apple ever grown and one of the world's most prominent varieties, particularly popular in North America.

Make a Hot Pack: Add apple slices to gently boiling syrup or juice and boil for 5 minutes, stirring frequently to prevent scorching. Fill hot jars with hot fruit. Add hot syrup to cover, leaving a 1/2-inch (1 cm) headspace. Run a thin non-metallic utensil around the inside of the jar to allow air to escape. Add more hot fruit or syrup, if necessary, to leave a 1/2-inch (1 cm) headspace. Wipe sealing edge of jars with a clean, damp, lint-free cloth. Position flat lids over the tops of jars and hand-tighten screw bands.

4. Process apples in a canner: Use a Boiling Water Canner according to the chart below.

Processing Times at Different Altitudes for Apples in a BOILING WATER Canner					
Pack Style	Jar Size	0–2000 ft	2001–4000 ft	4001–6000 ft	6001+ ft
HOT	Pints	15 min	20 min	25 min	30 min
	Quarts	20 min	25 min	30 min	35 min
RAW	Pints	20 min	25 min	30 min	35 min
	Quarts	25 min	30 min	35 min	40 min

OR

Process apples in a Pressure Canner following manufacturer's directions for steam pressure and time at your altitude.

5. Cool, Label and Store: Lift jars from canner and place on a clean towel or rack. Do not re-tighten screw bands. Let the jars cool to room temperature. This may take from 12 to 24 hours. Remove and store screw bands. Check lid seals (see page 19). Wipe and label sealed jars. Store in a cool, dark place.

crabapple chutney

When crabapples are plenty, this savoury applesauce is my favourite way to preserve them. I like a thicker consistency with chopped raisins for hors d'oeuvres, but if you're using it as a condiment—it is excellent with baked ham and pork—a thinner chutney with whole raisins and some syrup is better than the thicker version. If you don't have crabapples, use a tart apple like McIntosh or Lodi.

MAKES ABOUT 8 CUPS (2 L)

1 lemon, halved
3 lb (1.5 kg) crabapples, cored and chopped
1-1/2 cups (375 mL) apple cider vinegar
1-1/2 tsp (7 mL) salt
1 tsp (5 mL) ground cinnamon
1/4 tsp (1 mL) ground cloves
3 cups (750 mL) lightly packed brown sugar
1 cup (250 mL) granulated sugar

1 onion, chopped
2 cloves garlic, finely chopped
1-1/2 cups (375 mL) golden raisins, whole or
   coarsely chopped (see headnote)
1/3 cup (75 mL) chopped candied ginger
3 tbsp (45 mL) chopped fresh tarragon or 1 tbsp
   (15 mL) crushed dried tarragon

1. Squeeze the lemon halves, remove seeds and pour juice into a Maslin pan or canning kettle. Discard any remaining seeds in the lemon halves and chop remaining flesh and rind and add to juice in pan. Add chopped apples to the pan and stir well. Add vinegar, salt, cinnamon and cloves. Bring to a boil over high heat. Add the brown sugar and granulated sugar, 1 cup (250 mL) at a time, stirring to dissolve before adding the next cup. Stir in onion and garlic and boil lightly, stirring occasionally, for 45 minutes.

2. Meanwhile, heat four 1-pint (2-cup/500 mL) jars in boiling water, and scald the lids, lifter, funnel and tongs (see page 18).

3. Add raisins, ginger and tarragon to the boiling mixture and return to a boil. Simmer, stirring often, for 15 to 20 minutes or until fruit mixture and syrup are thick (see headnote).

4. Remove pan from heat and skim off any foam. Fill hot jars, leaving a 1/4-inch (5 mm) headspace. Run a thin non-metallic utensil around the inside of the jar to allow air to escape. Add more hot chutney, if necessary, to leave a 1/4-inch (5 mm) headspace. Wipe rims, top with flat lids and screw on metal rings. Return jars to the hot water bath, topping up with hot water if necessary. Bring to a full rolling boil and process jars for 10 minutes (see page 19).

5. Remove canner lid and wait 5 minutes before removing jars to a towel or rack to cool completely. Check seals, label and store in a cool place for up to 1 year.

Use: This hearty apple chutney can stand up to sausages, bacon, ham, pork chops, liver pâté, duck and game with real flavour because its acidic tartness cuts through the heaviness of these foods.

rosemary-spiked apple jelly

Jellies are made from fruit and from some vegetables and herbs by boiling them in water (or mashing raw soft fruit) and allowing the juice to drip through a strainer, preferably a cone strainer. The key to making sparkling clear jelly is to resist the urge to press the fruit through the strainer. If you do, more of the flesh comes through into the juice and makes the jelly cloudy. This is actually fine if chunks of fruit or herbs will be added to the jelly or if catsup will be made from the juice.

If I'm making apple jelly or pectin from apples, I try to use at least 2 different varieties of tart apples—perhaps Newton, McIntosh, Pippin, Jonagold, Jonathan, Winesap or Gala—because this tart combination contributes to the overall complex apple taste and ensures a good amount of pectin for setting the jelly.

MAKES ABOUT 6 CUPS (1.5 L)

**3 lb (1.5 kg) mixed tart apples, peeled, cored
and seeds intact,
   cut into chunks (about 10 to 12)
4 cups (1 L) water
10 sprigs fresh rosemary, divided**

**3 cups (750 mL) granulated sugar
2 tbsp (25 mL) freshly squeezed lemon juice
1 tbsp (15 mL) rice vinegar**

1. In a Maslin pan or canning kettle, combine apples, water and 4 sprigs of rosemary. Bring to a boil over high heat. Cover, reduce heat to low and simmer for 20 to 25 minutes or until apples are soft.

2. Set a cheesecloth-lined cone strainer over a 6-cup (1.5 L) bowl and pour in apple mixture. Cover with a clean towel and set aside for at least 4 hours or overnight. Allow juice to drip through without pressing.

Probably the most popular jelly is apple. The best method for obtaining clear juice is to set up a cone strainer over a non-reactive bowl and let the cooked apple mash (or raw mashed soft fruit) drip without pressing on it. This takes some time—it's best to leave it overnight. Pioneers and old-time preservers would hang a pillowcase or a large cheesecloth bag from the legs of an overturned stool and let the juice drip into a bowl positioned on the underside of the seat.

3. The next day, heat six 1-cup (250 mL) jars in boiling water, and scald the lids, lifter, funnel and tongs (see page 18). Discard the cheesecloth with apple and rosemary solids. Apple juice should measure roughly 4 cups (1 L).

4. In a Maslin pan or canning kettle, bring the strained apple juice to a boil over high heat. Add sugar, 1 cup (250 mL) at a time, stirring until it dissolves before adding the next cup. Add lemon juice and vinegar and bring to a rolling boil, stirring often. Boil, uncovered, until the syrup sheets off a cool metal spoon (see sidebar), about 15 to 18 minutes.

Sheeting Test: Dip a cool metal spoon into the boiling liquid and allow it to run off into the pan. If 2 drops of jelly hang off the edge of the spoon and then run together, the jelly is sheeting and is ready to be processed in jars.

5. Remove pan from heat and skim off any foam. Fill hot jars, leaving a 1/4-inch (5 mm) headspace. If desired, add a sprig of rosemary to each jar. Wipe rims, top with flat lids and screw on metal rings. Return jars to the hot water bath, topping up with hot water if necessary. Bring to a full rolling boil and process jars for 5 minutes (see page 19).

6. Remove canner lid and wait 5 minutes before removing jars to a towel or rack to cool completely. Check seals, label and store in a cool place for up to 1 year.

chocolate apple mousse conserve

Rich tasting, and yet not loaded with fat, this conserve makes a sweet-tart chocolate sauce and topping for all sorts of desserts. The keys to this textural delight are: start with cooking apples; cook them until they are soft; and purée in a food processor or blender until silky smooth. A fine sieve or a food mill both work in place of a food processor for this purpose. You can double the recipe, but be sure to use a very deep and heavy-bottomed pot because when you return the puréed mixture to the pan, it will spit when it bubbles.

MAKES 3-1/2 CUPS (875 mL)

1 lemon
6 cups (1.5 L) chopped apple (about 2 lb/1 kg)
3 cups (750 mL) granulated sugar

1/2 cup (125 mL) unsweetened cocoa powder
1/2 tsp (2 mL) salt
1 tsp (5 mL) pure vanilla extract

1. Grate the rind of half of lemon, then juice it. In a Maslin pan or canning kettle, combine lemon juice, lemon rind and apples. Stir well to coat the apples with the lemon juice.

2. In a bowl, combine sugar, cocoa powder and salt. Stir into apples and bring to a boil over medium heat, stirring constantly. Lower the heat and simmer gently, stirring frequently, for 20 to 30 minutes or until apples are soft. Using a food processor and working in one or two batches, purée the apple mixture until smooth.

3. Meanwhile, heat four 1-cup (250 mL) jars in boiling water, and scald the lids, lifter, funnel and tongs (see page 18).

4. Return the purée to a clean Maslin pan or canning kettle. Add vanilla and bring to a light boil over medium heat, stirring constantly. Cook the mixture, stirring constantly, for 15 minutes or until thickened enough to mound on a wooden spoon.

5. Fill hot jars, leaving a 1/4-inch (5 mm) headspace. Run a thin non-metallic utensil around the inside of the jar to allow air to escape. Add more hot conserve, if necessary, to leave a 1/4-inch (5 mm) headspace. Wipe rims, top with flat lids and screw on metal rings. Return jars to the hot water bath, topping up with hot water if necessary. Bring to a full rolling boil and process jars for 15 minutes (see page 19).

6. Remove canner lid and wait 5 minutes before removing jars to a towel or rack to cool completely. Check seals, label and store in a cool place for up to 1 year.

Use: As a dessert sauce for puddings, tarts, gingerbreads and other baked desserts; as a filling for layer cakes and crêpes.

crabapple and goat cheese barquettes

One of the many rewards for preserving the best of the harvest is that it makes entertaining super easy. I love it when impromptu opportunities for serving casual snacks, meals and even desserts present themselves because I have a pantry of homemade gems to draw on. For this zesty hors d'oeuvre, a fruit chutney, relish, salsa or even a fruit jelly (Rosemary-Spiked Apple Jelly (page 310) works beautifully. Choose creamy goat cheese or brie and either fresh endive boats (barquettes) or whole wheat crackers. The baguettes require very little prep time. Soft creamy goat cheese will be easier to cut into rounds if it is partially frozen.

A barque is a three-masted French sailing vessel. Samuel de Champlain used one in 1605 to explore and chart the New England coast. From this ancient French word comes the term barquettes, for small, boat-shaped pastry tarts made of short crust pastry or puff pastry, baked blind and then filled with sweet or savoury fillings. Barquettes are almost always served as hors d'oeuvres or appetizers. In this version, the individual endive leaves are actually shaped like the hull of a barque; hence the term barquettes is applied.

MAKES 12 BARQUETTES

5 oz (150 g) goat cheese, brie or cream cheese
2 bunches endive, leaves separated, or 12 whole
  wheat crackers

1 cup (250 mL) Crabapple Chutney (page 309)
  or other fruity-savoury preserve

Slice cheese into rounds or cut into 12 portions and position one portion on each of 12 endive leaves. Add about 1–1/2 tbsp (20 mL) Crabapple Chutney on top or to the side of the cheese.

Freezing Apples

1. Select Equipment: Select suitable-size freezer containers, bags or Mason jars (see page 24).

2. Pack in Syrup: In a saucepan, combine 2–1/2 cups (625 mL) granulated sugar and 1/2 tsp (2 mL) crystalline ascorbic acid or three 500 mg vitamin C tablets. Stir in 4 cups (1 L) water. Bring to a gentle boil over high heat, stirring frequently. Reduce heat and gently boil for 3 minutes. Let cool. This is enough syrup to cover 12 cups (4 L) sliced apples.

Fill pint (2-cup/500 mL) or quart (1 L) freezer containers with halved or sliced apples to within 3 to 4 inches (7 to 10 cm) of the top. Pour syrup over top; use 1 cup (250 mL) syrup per quart (1 L) of prepared fruit. Squeeze out air; leave 1-inch (2.5 cm) headspace. Seal, label and freeze.

OR

Dry Pack: Fill pint (2-cup/500 mL) or quart (1 L) freezer containers with halved or sliced apples to within 3 to 4 inches (7 to 10 cm) of the top. Pour dry granulated sugar over top; use 1/2 cup (125 mL) sugar per quart (1 L) of prepared fruit. Squeeze out air; leave 1-inch (2.5 cm) headspace. Seal, label and freeze.

Cranberries

IN THE NORTHERN UNITED STATES AND CANADA, cranberries are the last fruit of the season. They have a significant place in our history, being one of the gifts from First Nations peoples to European settlers that may have saved many of them from the fatal disease scurvy. Cranberries are the fruit of perennial evergreen trailing vines or dwarf shrubs, depending on the species.

Good Preserving Varieties

There are some native North American plants of a different species that are often confused with cranberries because they bear red fruit that look similar to cranberries and their common names—American Cranberrybush or Highbush Cranberry—are misleading. In fact, this plant (*Viburnum trilobum*) is a deciduous shrub that grows up to 13 feet (4 m) tall and is not a true cranberry.

Today, there are over 100 cranberry cultivars that grow in North America, and all of them are excellent for preserves. Not many wild cranberry vines have survived, yet some commercial cranberry beds contain vines that are over 100 years old. Massachusetts, Wisconsin, Oregon, New Jersey and Washington are the big cranberry-producing states. British Columbia, Ontario and Nova Scotia produce the most cranberries in Canada. Some popular cranberry varieties include the following:

Cranberries grow in acidic peat bogs (above, a bog near Bala, Ontario) or acidic sand beds throughout the cooler parts of the Northern Hemisphere. *Vaccinium macrocarpon* is the cranberry species that is native to North America. The *Vaccinium* species is the true cranberry; all are low-growing plants.

Early Black: The first to ripen in eastern North America; sweet-tasting; deep, dark red colour.
Howes: Big, firm berries that store well.

Purchasing/Storing
• 1 lb (500 g) yields 4 cups (1 L) cranberries.
• A 12-oz (340 g) pkg of whole cranberries yields 3 cups (750 mL).

Select firm, dry berries with clear colour. Berries may be light pink, speckled or bright crimson, depending on the variety. Avoid wet, crushed berries or those that show signs of mildew. The higher cranberries bounce the fresher they are. Fresh or frozen cranberries can be used interchangeably in all preserving, dessert or sauce recipes.

Good With
- Citrus flavours (orange, lemon, lime, grapefruit) in traditional jelly, sauce or relish.
- Sweet seasonings such as cinnamon, ginger, cloves, nutmeg, vanilla, almond.
- Whole grains such as oats and oatmeal, in baked products and desserts.
- Aged cheeses such as old cheddar, Asiago, Gruyère.
- Other fruit, such as apples, raspberries, peaches, pears, plums, raisins.
- Roast turkey, chicken or duck; lamb, beef and wild game.

Preparation
Wash cranberries in a sink full of cool water to which a drop of food-safe soap has been added. Rinse well, drain and pat dry.

Canning Cranberries
Cranberries are so easily frozen that I don't recommend canning them.

country-style chutney

I love this chutney because it is the colour of fall. It's nice to have bright red chutney on the pantry shelf that isn't tomato or beet. You can make this using frozen cranberries in the late summer when stone fruits are abundant; it makes a very nice Thanksgiving condiment for roast turkey. Of course, it is the heart-healthy and cancer-preventing anthocyanins that give cranberries their deep red colour and health benefits. The curry spice blend is not overwhelming in this chutney, but you can use any of the pickling spice blends (pages 213 to 216) in its place if you wish.

MAKES ABOUT 8 CUPS (2 L)

1/4 cup (50 mL) apple cider vinegar
2 tbsp (25 mL) balsamic vinegar
3 cups (750 mL) fresh or frozen cranberries
 (12-oz/340 g bag)
3 cups (750 mL) chopped onions
2 cups (500 mL) chopped apples
2 cups (500 mL) chopped pears
2 cups (500 mL) chopped plums

2 tbsp (25 mL) Curry Pickling Spice Blend (page
 214 or store-bought), tied in a cheesecloth
 bag
2 cups (500 mL) granulated sugar
1/2 cup (125 mL) packed brown sugar
1/2 cup (125 mL) chopped candied pineapple
 (6 oz/175 g)
1/2 cup (125 mL) chopped dried apricots
2 tbsp (25 mL) finely chopped candied ginger

1. In a Maslin pan or canning kettle, combine cider vinegar, balsamic vinegar and cranberries. Place over medium heat and add onions, apples, pears, plums and spice bag. Bring to a boil over medium high heat, stirring constantly. Add granulated sugar, 1 cup (250 mL) at a time, stirring to dissolve before adding the next cup. Add brown sugar. Adjust heat and boil gently, stirring frequently, for 30 minutes. Add pineapple, apricots and ginger. Boil gently, stirring frequently, for about 40 minutes or until fruit is tender and mixture thickens enough to mound on a wooden spoon. You may find it necessary to add up to 1 cup (250 mL) water to keep the mixture from sticking to the bottom of the pan.

2. Meanwhile, heat four 1-pint (2-cup/500 mL) jars in boiling water, and scald the lids, lifter, funnel and tongs (see page 18).

3. Fill hot jars, leaving a 1/4-inch (5 mm) headspace. Run a thin non-metallic utensil around the inside of the jar to allow air to escape. Add more hot chutney, if necessary, to leave a 1/4-inch (5 mm) headspace. Wipe rims, top with flat lids and screw on metal rings. Return jars to the hot water bath, topping up with hot water if necessary. Bring to a full rolling boil and process jars for 10 minutes (see page 19).

4. Remove canner lid and wait 5 minutes before removing jars to a towel or rack to cool completely. Check seals, label and store in a cool place for up to 1 year.

Use: Serve as an accompaniment to roasted meats and toss with roasted vegetables. For a fruity vinaigrette dressing, mix 1/3 cup (75 mL) with 3 tbsp (45 mL) olive oil and 1 tbsp (15 mL) red wine vinegar.

country-style chicken

This is a super-fast, down-home, warm skillet-salad dinner. The cucumber and red onion can be replaced by baby spinach or thinly sliced radishes or baby zucchini. The point is that when the garden is really going in the summer and harvest vegetables are plentiful in the fall, there are all sorts of tender young vegetables that can be tossed into the mix and eaten mostly raw with the cooked chicken. Then in the winter, when shredded carrots and beets are easy to fix, it reappears on busy weeknight menus. It is the spicy chutney that pulls this dish together and gives it a professional flair.

MAKES 4 SERVINGS

2 tbsp (25 mL) olive oil
1 lb (500 g) boneless chicken pieces or ground chicken or turkey
1/2 cup (125 mL) Country-Style Chutney (page 319)

1/4 English cucumber, thinly sliced
1/4 red onion, thinly sliced

1. In a skillet, heat olive oil over medium-high heat. Add chicken and cook, stirring frequently, for 10 minutes or until cooked through and lightly browned.

2. Stir in the chutney and heat through. Divide evenly into 4 portions and mound each on a plate.

3. Divide cucumber and red onion evenly among plates and top with the chicken.

cranberry orange conserve

North American Thanksgiving dinner would not be the same without roasted turkey and its one key accompaniment, cranberry sauce. There are hundreds of cranberry jelly and wholeberry sauce recipes from which to choose, and most families have their favourite. This is our family's preference, the orange being a complementary ingredient that offers a refreshing balance to the tart cranberries. It is not sweet, so you might want to add more sugar to suit your taste. If you like more spice, add up to 1/2 tsp (2 mL) each ground cinnamon and nutmeg or allspice. Over the years, I've adapted the recipe so that it conveniently uses one package of cranberries. You can double the recipe if you wish.

Photo by Kate Carlsen

If you are making this tart, citrusy holiday condiment a week before using, there is no need to process in a water bath or freeze the jars. Simply fill clean or sterilized jars, then cap and refrigerate until ready to serve. If you wish to keep the conserve longer, I have given the instructions for canning, but you can opt to freeze it if you won't be using it for a few months.

MAKES ABOUT 3 CUPS (750 mL)

3 cups (750 mL) fresh or frozen cranberries (12-oz/375 g bag)
2 oranges, sectioned and chopped
1-1/2 cups (375 mL) granulated sugar
1/2 cup (125 mL) water
1 tbsp (15 mL) grated orange rind
1/2 cup (125 mL) freshly squeezed orange juice
2 tbsp (25 mL) freshly squeezed lemon juice

1. Heat three 1-cup (250 mL) jars in boiling water, and scald the lids, lifter, funnel and tongs (see page 18).

2. In a Maslin pan or canning kettle, combine cranberries, orange sections, sugar, water, orange rind, orange juice and lemon juice. Bring to a boil over high heat, stirring con-

stantly. Boil gently, stirring frequently, for about 25 minutes or until mixture thickens enough to mound on a wooden spoon.

3. **To can:** Skim off and discard any foam. Fill hot jars, leaving a 1/4-inch (5 mm) headspace. Run a thin non-metallic utensil around the inside of the jar to allow air to escape. Add more hot conserve, if necessary, to leave a 1/4-inch (5 mm) headspace. Wipe rims, top with flat lids and screw on metal rings. Return jars to the hot water bath, topping up with hot water if necessary. Bring to a full rolling boil and process jars for 15 minutes (see page 19).

4. Remove canner lid and wait 5 minutes before removing jars to a towel or rack to cool completely. Check seals, label and store in a cool place for up to 1 year.

To freeze instead of can: Omit steps 3 and 4 above. After step 2, remove the compote from the heat and let cool. This could take up to 2 hours. Stir occasionally as the mixture cools. Spoon into Mason jars or plastic containers, leaving a 1-inch (2.5 cm) headspace. Seal, label and freeze for up to 6 months.

Freezing Cranberries

The easiest way to freeze fresh cranberries is in their original, unopened bag. If you happen to live near a cranberry farm and can get them in bulk, wash (see page 318), pat dry and freeze in 2- or 4-cup (500 mL or 1 L) amounts in resealable freezer bags.

Pears

See also Winter Pears, page 505.

ORIGINATING IN WESTERN ASIA and known to the ancient Greeks and Romans—Homer mentions them in his *Odyssey*—pears (*Pyrus communis*) have been cultivated in the Mediterranean region for over 3,000 years.

Good Preserving Varieties

Our juicy, butter-textured, fragrant varieties are hybrids that were developed around the middle of the 18th century. Firm varieties that are sweet and richly flavoured are best for preserving. Some varieties, such as Red and Green Anjou, Bosc and Comice are in the winter section.

Bartlett: Clear yellow skin is a sign of ripeness (it turns from bright green to golden yellow); white, creamy, juicy flesh that cooks down easily; sweet; often used for preserves because it keeps its flavour after heating; August to February.

Red Bartlett: Similar to the yellow-skinned Bartlett except that the skin turns bright red when ripe; smooth, sweet and juicy flesh makes a beautiful jelly; August to January.

Concorde: Long, slender variety that is a **Comice/Conference** cross; dense, firm-textured flesh; full-flavoured and juicy; like **Comice**, it is a good variety for preserves; September to February.

Seckel: Small size; olive green with maroon blush; crunchy, firm flesh and ultra-sweet flavour; holds it shape very well in canning, preserves, pickles and poaching; September to February.

Purchasing/Storing

- 1 lb (500 g) yields 2 cups (500 mL) sliced pears.
- You will need about 1-1/2 lb (750 g) for each quart (1 L) jar.

Look for smooth, wrinkle-free skin, free of blemishes. Ripe pears are firm but give a little when pressed gently at the stem end. Ripe pears are sweet, buttery, tender and filled with juice. Use just-ripe pears in preserves. To ripen pears at home, place them in a paper bag and store in a dry area at room temperature for 2 to 3 days. Do not store near apples, which emit a natural gas that speeds up their ripening. Preserve pears as soon as possible after harvest or, if you must, store ripe pears in the crisper drawer of the refrigerator.

- Spicy herbs such as basil, bay, thyme, chervil, tarragon, rosemary, sage.
- Sweet seasonings such as cinnamon, licorice, cloves, nutmeg, vanilla.
- Creamy cheeses such as Camembert, Danish blue, gorgonzola.
- Other fruit, such as raspberries, apples, apricots, stone fruit.
- Toasted pecans, almonds and walnuts; raisins; chocolate.
- Chicken, pork, veal.

Preparation

Wash pears in a sink full of cool water to which a drop of food-safe soap has been added. Rinse well and pat dry. For preserving, pears are cored and, most often, peeled. Cut in half lengthwise and remove core using a melon baller or metal measuring spoon.

To prevent discolouration, acidulate: Immerse peeled pears in water with vitamin C made by mixing 1 tsp (5 mL) crystalline ascorbic acid or six 500 mg vitamin C tablets in 1 gallon (4 L) cool water.

Canning Pears

See detailed canning information, page 14.

1. Prepare Equipment: Wash and heat pint (2-cup/500 mL) or quart (1 L) jars, and scald the lids, funnel, ladle and tongs (see page 18).

2. Make a Light Syrup: In a large saucepan, combine 1 cup (250 mL) granulated sugar with 4 cups (1 L mL) water; stir until dissolved. Bring to a gentle boil over high heat. Makes 4-1/2 cups (1.125 L) syrup, enough for three or four 1-quart (1 L) jars of sliced pears.

Note: You can use the same amount of apple juice or white grape juice in place of the light syrup.

3. Pack sliced pears into jars hot.

Make a Hot Pack: Add acidulated pear slices or halves to gently boiling syrup or juice and boil for a minute. Fill hot jars with hot fruit and syrup, leaving a 1/2-inch (1 cm) headspace. Run a thin non-metallic utensil around the inside of the jar to allow air to escape. Add more hot fruit or syrup, if necessary, to leave a 1/2-inch (1 cm) headspace. Wipe sealing edge of jars with a clean, damp, lint-free cloth. Position flat lids over the tops of jars and hand-tighten screw bands.

4. Process pears in a canner: Boiling Water Canner according to the chart below.

Processing Times at Different altitudes for Pears in a BOILING WATER Canner					
Pack Style	Jar Size	0–2000 ft	2001–4000 ft	4001–6000 ft	6001+ ft
HOT	Pints	15 min	20 min	25 min	30 min
	Quarts	20 min	25 min	30 min	35 min
RAW	Pints	20 min	25 min	30 min	35 min
	Quarts	25 min	30 min	35 min	40 min

OR

Process pears in a Pressure Canner following manufacturer's directions for steam pressure and time at your altitude.

5. Cool, Label and Store: Lift jars from canner and place on a clean towel or rack. Do not re-tighten screw bands. Let the jars cool to room temperature. This may take from 12 to 24 hours. Remove and store screw bands. Check lid seals (see page 19). Wipe and label sealed jars. Store in a cool, dark place.

vanilla pears in orange wine syrup

Whole pears are suspended in a sweet vanilla-tinged orange and wine syrup for easy, elegant poached pear desserts later in the year. Use a dry, light white wine—Chablis, Pinot Blanc, Chardonnay—for the syrup or reduce the amount of sugar if using a sweet wine. Once I have used the pears, I save the leftover pear and wine-flavoured syrup to use as simple syrup in cocktails or as a glaze for cut fresh fruit.

In the photograph on the right, I used whole, unpeeled Bosc pears; however, Concord or Seckel also work well in this recipe.

MAKES 24 PEARS IN SYRUP

24 small to medium just-ripe pears
4 cups (1 L) white wine (see above)
2 tbsp (25 mL) grated orange rind
2 cups (500 mL) freshly squeezed
  orange juice

2 cups (500 mL) granulated sugar
1 cup (250 mL) packed brown sugar
1 vanilla bean, cut into 4 pieces
4 sprigs fresh tarragon

1. Wash pears. Peel, if desired, leaving the core and stem intact. Immerse in ascorbic acid water (see page 326) if peeled. Set aside.

2. In a Maslin pan or heavy-bottomed saucepan, combine wine, orange rind and juice, granulated sugar and brown sugar. Bring to a gentle boil over high heat, stirring occasionally. Reduce heat, add vanilla pieces and gently boil for 5 minutes. Using tongs or a slotted spoon, ease pears gently into the syrup. Cover and simmer for 8 to 10 minutes, gently rolling pears over a couple of times. Pears should not be soft but should show some resistance when pierced with the tip of a knife. Remove saucepan from the heat and let cool.

3. Pack 6 pears, 1 piece of vanilla bean and 1 tarragon sprig into a freezer bag and cover with about 1 cup (250 mL) syrup. Squeeze out air. Seal, label and place on a baking sheet so that pears remain in single layer in the bag. Repeat for remaining pears, arranging 2 bags side by side on each baking sheet, and freeze. Remove from baking sheets once frozen hard.

Use: Thaw and place syrup in a saucepan. Bring to a boil over medium-high heat. Reduce heat and gently boil until thick and slightly reduced, about 7 minutes. Add pears and warm through. Remove vanilla bean. Serve as a poached pear dessert with a tray of assorted cheeses. Or spoon over sponge cake, or serve with sweetened mascarpone cheese or candied almonds.

vanilla pears and gingerbread

This is a traditional gingerbread that fills the kitchen with its spice and warmth. Pairing it with the vanilla and orange in the pears and syrup adds an unusual and modern twist. The ginger-bread freezes well if leftover squares are tightly wrapped and sealed in an airtight bag. Thaw and warm in the microwave oven and serve with any homemade canned whole fruit or fruit preserve and perhaps a dollop of freshly whipped cream.

If you have made the Chocolate Mousse (page 162), use it in this recipe because it adds a dark and richly chocolate flavour. If not, use a thick applesauce.

9-inch (2.5 L) square baking pan or 9- x 5-inch (23 x 13 cm) loaf pan, lightly oiled
Preheat oven to 350°F (180°C)
MAKES 6 SERVINGS + LEFTOVER GINGERBREAD

3 Vanilla Pears in Orange Wine Syrup (page 328), thawed and drained, syrup reserved
1 cup (250 mL) whipped cream, optional
6 orange rind knots for garnish, optional

GINGERBREAD
2–1/3 cups (575 mL) all-purpose flour
1/2 cup (125 mL) packed brown sugar
2 tsp (10 mL) baking soda
1 tsp (5 mL) ground ginger
1 tsp (5 mL) ground cinnamon
1/2 tsp (2 mL) salt
3/4 cup (175 mL) dark molasses
1/2 cup (125 mL) hot water
1/2 cup (125 mL) Chocolate Mousse (page 162) or applesauce
1 egg, lightly beaten
1/2 cup (125 mL) butter, softened

1. To make gingerbread: In bowl of a stand mixer or in large mixing bowl, stir together flour, sugar, baking soda, ginger, cinnamon and salt.

2. In a batter bowl or large measuring cup, combine molasses, hot water and mousse. Using mixer on low speed or hand mixer, pour molasses mixture into the dry ingredients all at once and beat. Add egg and butter and beat until combined. Increase speed to medium and beat for 2 minutes.

3. Scrape gingerbread batter into prepared baking pan. Bake in preheated oven for 45 to 55 minutes if using a square baking pan, for 55 minutes to 1 hour if using a loaf pan, or until cake tester inserted in centre of gingerbread comes out clean. Let cool for 15 minutes on a wire rack.

4. To serve: Cut gingerbread into squares or slices. Place 6 pieces onto dessert plates. Wrap remaining gingerbread tightly and reserve for another use. Cut pears in half, if whole, and remove core. Slice thinly, leaving the stem end intact. Arrange a pear half in a fan on top of each piece of gingerbread and drizzle with 3 tbsp (45 mL) syrup. If using, top with a dollop of whipped cream and garnish with orange rind knots.

gingered autumn conserve

With so much produce in abundance in early fall, I find that my pantry has odd small amounts of fruit and vegetables—it seemed that I needed a preserve that would use up the most popular ones. This richly fruity conserve was my answer. Make it and use it for a cheese platter or meat dish, or to add a sweet-savoury note to puddings and other baked desserts.

MAKES 8 CUPS (2 L)

3 cups (750 mL) chopped cored pears (about 4)
2 cups (500 mL) chopped cored green or very
    tart apples (2 or 3)
1 cup (250 mL) chopped celery
1 cup (250 mL) chopped red bell pepper
1/3 cup (75 mL) chopped candied ginger
grated rind and juice of 2 large lemons
4 cups (1 L) granulated sugar

2-1/2 cups (625 mL) lightly packed brown
    sugar
1 tsp (5 mL) ground cinnamon
1/2 tsp (2 mL) ground coriander
2 pouches (each 3 oz/85 mL) liquid pectin
8 cinnamon sticks, each 2 inches (5 cm),
    optional

1. Heat eight 1-cup (250 mL) jars in boiling water, and scald the lids, lifter, funnel and tongs (see page 18).

2. In a Maslin pan or canning kettle, combine pears, apples, celery, red pepper, ginger, lemon rind and lemon juice. Stir in granulated sugar, brown sugar, cinnamon and coriander. Bring to a full rolling boil over high heat, stirring constantly. Stir in pectin and boil hard, stirring constantly, for 1 minute. Remove from heat and skim off any foam.

3. Half-fill hot jars. Slide a cinnamon stick down the side of the jar, if using. Finish filling jar, leaving a 1/4-inch (5 mm) headspace. Run a thin non-metallic utensil around the inside of the jar to allow air to escape. Add more hot conserve, if necessary, to leave a 1/4-inch (5 mm) headspace. Wipe rims, top with flat lids and screw on metal rings. Return jars to the hot water bath, topping up with hot water if necessary. Bring to a full rolling boil and process jars for 10 minutes (see page 19).

4. Remove canner lid and wait 5 minutes before removing jars to a towel or rack to cool completely. Check seals, label and store in a cool place for up to 1 year.

Use: I like to toss roasted vegetables or stir-fried chicken strips in this lightly spiced, sweet and fruity conserve.

1. **Select Equipment:** Select suitable-size freezer containers, bags or Mason jars (see page 24).

2. **Pack in Syrup:** In a saucepan, combine 2-1/2 cups (625 mL) granulated sugar and 1/2 tsp (2 mL) crystalline ascorbic acid or three 500 mg vitamin C tablets. Stir in 4 cups (1 L) water. Bring to a gentle boil over high heat, stirring frequently. Reduce heat and boil gently for 3 minutes. Let cool. Fill pint (2-cup/500 mL) or quart (1 L) freezer containers with halved or sliced pears to within 3 to 4 inches (7 to 10 cm) of the top. Pour syrup over top; use 1 cup (250 mL) syrup per quart (1 L) of prepared fruit. Squeeze out air; leave 1-inch (2.5 cm) headspace. Seal, label and freeze.

OR

Dry Pack: Fill pint (2-cup/500 mL) or quart (1 L) freezer containers with halved or sliced pears to within 3 to 4 inches (7 to 10 cm) of the top. Pour dry granulated sugar over top; use 1/2 cup (125 mL) sugar per quart (1 L) of prepared fruit. Squeeze out air; leave 1-inch (2.5 cm) headspace. Seal, label and freeze.

Persimmons

ONE OF THE NEWEST RISING STARS at many local food and farmer's markets is the persimmon (the genus *Diospyros*). Of course, they aren't new at all. In fact, ancient Greeks referred to them as "the fruit of the Gods," and the wood from the persimmon tree has been used for centuries as ebony. Today more North American market farmers are growing these exotic fruits. Because it takes years before the plants produce fruit, it is hoped that many more growers will have persimmons for sale in the future.

Good Preserving Varieties

There are many species of persimmon, but the Japanese (*Diospyros kaki*) is the most widely cultivated and commercially available. Of the *D. kaki* varieties, only two (listed below) are widely available in North American markets and supermarkets. The native American (*D. virginiana*) species is edible and has been gathered for years from the wild in the eastern United States. Because of the tannins that occur in the fruit, this species is astringent, which means that it is mouth-puckeringly tart and inedible until the fruit is completely ripe.

Fuyu: A square, squat, flat-bottomed fruit that is called "non-astringent" because it is less astringent before ripening. May be eaten while still firm but is best when orange and slightly soft. This is the best variety for canning when a sliced or chopped fruit texture is desired, as for a chutney, or for using whole, halved or sliced in syrup.

Hachiya: Looks very similar to the Fuyu on the top, but the bottom end comes to a rounded point, making it heart-shaped rather than square and squat. Hachiya persimmons cannot be eaten before they turn a deep red-orange (similar to blood oranges in colour) and completely soft and ripe. Their tartness comes from unpalatable tannins, which are highly astringent in the immature fruit. Wait for the fruit to be soft (almost squishy), then spoon the soft pulp out of the skin for jam and jelly.

Purchasing/Storing

- 1 lb (500 g) yields 1-1/2 cups (375 mL) sliced Fuyu persimmons.
- You will need about 2 lb (1 kg) for each quart (1 L) jar.

Select fruit that is fully ripe, especially Hachiya. Both varieties may ripen at home at room temperature, but it is always best to buy tree-ripened fruit if possible.

Good With

- Mediterranean herbs such as basil, bay, thyme, sage, oregano.
- Sweet seasonings such as cinnamon, cloves, nutmeg, vanilla.
- Creamy cheeses such as Camembert, Danish blue, gorgonzola.
- Other fruit, such as raspberries, mangoes, oranges and tangerines.
- Toasted pecans, almonds and walnuts; raisins; chocolate.
- Chicken and fish.

Preparation

Treat persimmons gently. Wash in a sink full of cool water to which a drop of food-safe soap has been added. Rinse well and pat dry.

Cut away the calyx and the leaves at the top of the fruit and discard.

Cut persimmons in half and peel with a paring knife.

Slice or chop persimmons for canning or preserves.

Cut Hachiya persimmons in half lengthwise and scoop out the soft flesh.

Canning Persimmons

Only Fuyu persimmons are firm enough to be canned in syrup. See detailed canning information, page 14.

1. Prepare Equipment: Wash and heat pint (2-cup/500 mL) or quart (1 L) jars, and scald the lids, funnel, ladle and tongs (see page 18).

2. Make a Medium Syrup: In a large saucepan, combine 2 cups (500 mL) granulated sugar with 4 cups (1 L mL) water; stir until dissolved. Bring to a gentle boil over high heat. Makes 5 cups (1.25 L) syrup, enough for three or four 1-quart (1 L) jars of sliced or cubed Fuyu persimmons.

Note: You can use the same amount of apple juice or white grape juice in place of the medium syrup.

3. Pack sliced or cubed Fuyu persimmons into jars either hot or raw.
Make a Raw Pack: Fill jars with prepared fruit. Cover with hot syrup or juice, leaving a 1/2-inch (1 cm) headspace. Run a thin non-metallic utensil around the inside of the jar to allow air to escape. Add hot liquid, if necessary, to leave a 1/2-inch (1 cm) headspace. Wipe sealing edge of jars with a clean, damp, lint-free cloth. Position flat lids over the tops of jars and hand-tighten screw bands.

OR

Make a Hot Pack: Add persimmon slices to gently boiling syrup or juice and boil for 45 seconds. Fill hot jars with hot fruit and cooking liquid, leaving a 1/2-inch (1 cm) headspace. Run a thin non-metallic utensil around the inside of the jar to allow air to escape. Add more hot fruit or liquid, if necessary, to leave a 1/2-inch (1 cm) headspace. Wipe sealing edge of jars with a clean, damp, lint-free cloth. Position flat lids over the tops of jars and hand-tighten screw bands.

4. Process persimmons in a canner: Use a Boiling Water Canner according to the chart below.

Processing Times at Different Altitudes for Persimmons in a BOILING WATER Canner					
Pack Style	Jar Size	0–2000 ft	2001–4000 ft	4001–6000 ft	6001+ ft
HOT	Pints	15 min	20 min	25 min	30 min
	Quarts	20 min	25 min	30 min	35 min
RAW	Pints	20 min	25 min	30 min	35 min
	Quarts	25 min	30 min	35 min	40 min

OR

Process persimmons in a Pressure Canner following manufacturer's directions for steam pressure and time at your altitude.

5. Cool, Label and Store: Lift jars from canner and place on a clean towel or rack. Do not re-tighten screw bands. Let the jars cool to room temperature. This may take from 12 to 24 hours. Remove and store screw bands. Check lid seals (see page 19). Wipe and label sealed jars. Store in a cool, dark place.

persimmons in rosehip syrup

In this simple comestible, delicate persimmon slivers float in ruby-red syrup. I find the taste is exotic and only lightly tinged with the tartness of the rosehips.

If you grow roses and are not particular about deadheading them, you will always have a good supply of rosehips for fall and winter teas and syrup. If you don't grow roses, you can still make this syrup using chopped dried rosehips or rosehip and rose petal tea found in specialty tea shops or health food stores. I often use a combination of rosehips and hibiscus flowers; this recipe is based on using the dried rosehips. If you are using rosehips that have not yet dried out completely, double the amount given here.

MAKES 6 CUPS (1.5 L)

4 cups (1 L) water
1/2 cup (125 mL) chopped dried rosehips or
  combination (see above)
2 cups (500 mL) granulated sugar
4 lb (2 kg) Fuyu persimmons

1. Wash and heat pint (2-cup/500 mL) jars in boiling water and scald the lids, funnel, ladle and tongs (see page 18).

2. In a deep-sided, heavy-bottomed saucepan, bring water to a boil. Add rosehips and simmer gently for 10 minutes.

3. Over a large bowl, strain off and discard the rosehips. Return the rosehip infusion to the saucepan and add the sugar. Simmer gently over low heat for 4 minutes, stirring constantly, or until the sugar is completely dissolved and the mixture is clear (syrup will thicken upon cooling).

4. Add persimmon slices to gently boiling syrup and boil for 45 seconds. Fill hot jars with hot fruit and syrup, leaving a 1/2-inch (1 cm) headspace. Run a thin non-metallic utensil around the inside of the jar to allow air to escape. Add more hot syrup, if necessary, to leave a 1/2-inch (1 cm) headspace.

Wipe sealing edge of jars with a clean, damp, lint-free cloth. Position flat lids over the tops of jars and hand-tighten screw bands.

5. Process persimmons in a Boiling Water Canner (see page 18), or process in a Pressure Canner following manufacturer's directions for steam pressure and time at your altitude.

6. Cool completely. Check seals, label and store.

Use: Drain and reserve the syrup for cocktails and fruit drinks or to drizzle over sorbet. Use the persimmon slices in a layered trifle or with puddings or chocolate mousse. Substitute them for pears to add a different touch to the gingerbread (page 330).

hachiya persimmon freezer jam

Because Hachiya persimmons must be absolutely ripe before they are edible, the flesh is very soft and perfect for making freezer jam. Mango and pineapple complement the taste of persimmons; try equal amounts of either of these tropical fruits with the persimmons to boost the flavour of this jam.

MAKES ABOUT 4 CUPS (1 L)

1-1/2 cups (375 mL) granulated sugar
1 pkg (1-1/2 oz/45 g) freezer jam pectin crystals
1/2 tsp (2 mL) ground allspice
4 cups (1 L) Hachiya persimmon flesh

1. Select Equipment: Select suitable-size freezer containers, bags or Mason jars (see page 24).

2. In a bowl, combine sugar, pectin and allspice. Stir to mix well. Add persimmon flesh to sugar mixture, stirring for about 3 minutes. Let stand for 10 minutes.

3. Spoon jam into freezer containers. Squeeze out air; leave 1/2-inch (1 cm) headspace. Seal, label and freeze. This can be frozen for 4 to 5 months.

Freezing Persimmons

1. **Select Equipment:** Select suitable-size freezer containers, bags or Mason jars (see page 24).

2. **Pack in Syrup:** Use syrup for freezing Fuyu halves or slices. In a saucepan, combine 3 cups (750 mL) granulated sugar and 4 cups (1 L) water. Bring to a gentle boil over high heat, stirring frequently. Reduce heat and gently boil for 3 minutes. Let cool. Fill pint (2-cup/500 mL) or quart (1 L) freezer containers with halved or sliced Fuyu persimmons to within 3 to 4 inches (7 to 10 cm) of the top. Pour syrup over top; use 1 cup (250 mL) syrup per 1 quart (1 L) of prepared fruit. Squeeze out air; leave 1-inch (2.5 cm) headspace. Seal, label and freeze.

OR

Dry Pack: Use the Dry Pack Method for either Fuyu halves or slices, or for Hachiya pulp. Fill pint (2-cup/500 mL) or quart (1 L) freezer containers with halved or sliced Fuyu persimmons or Hachiya pulp to within 3 to 4 inches (7 to 10 cm) of the top. Pour dry granulated sugar over top; use 1/2 cup (125 mL) sugar per 1 quart (1 L) of prepared fruit. Squeeze out air; leave 1-inch (2.5 cm) headspace. Seal, label and freeze.

Beets

BEETS HAVE LONG BEEN A FAVOURITE VEGETABLE because their leafy green stalks are edible and the roots store very well for fresh eating. They also make an excellent preserve. Beets (*Beta vulgaris*) are canned in water or broth, or pickled and made into all sorts of jams and preserves. In addition to the red-bulb beet we call the garden beet, there are other edible subspecies: chard, sugar beet (a white root, used for table sugar) and mangold, which is used as a fodder crop.

Good Preserving Varieties

The fleshy red root of the beet was originally carrot-shaped, and this shape still exists in some varieties. The round beet shape was developed around the 16th century but didn't become popular until the early 1900s. Both the tankard (or canister) beet, which is oval, and the baby beet types, which remain small, are perfect for pickling. While the most widely known beet colour is red, there are purple, white and variegated varieties available.

Detroit Dark Red: Matures in 40 days.
Little Ball: A baby beet type.

Chiogga is a heritage type beet with white rings in the flesh; sometimes called Candy-stripe or Bull's Eye.

Purchasing/Storing

- 1 lb (500 g) yields 2 cups (500 mL) diced beets.
- You will need 1-1/2 lb (750 g) for each quart (1 L) jar.

If the tops are intact, cut them off, leaving 1 to 2 inches (2.5 to 5 cm) above the crown. For storing, leave the root ends intact. Although beets can be stored in the crisper drawer of the refrigerator for up to 3 weeks, it is best to use them as soon as possible for preserves.

Orange and purple beets are becoming more common at markets in the fall. Ask the grower about sweetness and texture before deciding to can large quantities.

Good With

- Vinegar, nuts and citrus (especially oranges) if beets are naturally sweet.

- Herbs such as parsley, oregano, sage, basil, bay, thyme, chervil, tarragon, rosemary.
- Spices such as cumin, garlic, coriander, cardamom, turmeric, star anise.
- Sweet seasonings such as cinnamon, ginger, cloves, nutmeg.
- Other fruit and vegetables, such as apples, pears, squash, onions.
- Toasted nuts and seeds

Preparation

Scrub beets under cool running water.

Blanch whole beets in boiling water for 15 minutes, counting from the time the water returns to the boil. Immerse in cold water for 5 minutes or until cool enough to handle. (Rubber gloves allow you to handle the beets while they are still hot so that they remain hot for canning.) Trim ends and slip off skins. Beets can be preserved whole if small (see Pickled Baby Beets, page 346), sliced or diced.

Since beets bleed when peeled and trimmed, leave 2 inches (5 cm) of stems and the whole root end intact for blanching.

Canning Beets

See detailed canning information, page 20.

1. Prepare Equipment: Wash and heat pint (2-cup/500 mL) or quart (1 L) jars, and scald the lids, funnel, ladle and tongs (see page 22).

2. For every 3 cups (750 mL) diced beets, bring 2 cups (500 mL) water or broth to a boil.

3. Pack small whole or sliced or diced beets into jars hot.
Make a Hot Pack: After blanching, trimming and cutting the beets, they will be warm or even hot. Fill hot jars, one at a time, with warm/hot beets, shaking the jar to pack fairly tightly. Pour hot water or broth over beets, leaving a 1-inch (2.5 cm) headspace. Run a thin non-metallic utensil around the inside of the jar to allow air to escape. Add more hot water, if necessary, to leave a 1/2-inch (2.5 cm) headspace. Wipe sealing edge of jars with a clean, damp, lint-free cloth. Position flat lids over the tops of jars and hand-tighten screw bands.

4. Place jars in pressure canner. Adjust water level (check manufacturer's instructions), lock lid and bring to a boil over medium-high heat. Vent steam for 10 minutes (check manufacturer's instructions) then close vent. Continue heating to achieve 10 lb (69 kPa) pressure and maintain pressure to process pint (2-cup/500 mL) jars for 30 minutes and quart (1 L) jars for 35 minutes. These times and pressure are based on using a weighted gauge pressure canner at 1,000 feet (305 m) or less. Check your altitude and manufacturer's instructions for variations.

5. Cool, Label and Store: Turn off heat; let pressure return to zero naturally. Once gauge shows 0 pressure, wait 2 minutes then open the vent. Unlock and remove canner lid. Wait 10 minutes then lift jars from canner and place on a clean towel or rack. Do not re-tighten screw bands. Let the jars cool to room temperature. This may take from 12 to 24 hours. Remove and store screw bands. Check lid seals (see page 23). Wipe and label sealed jars. Store in a cool, dark place.

Freezing Beets

1. **Select Equipment:** Select suitable-size freezer containers, bags or Mason jars (see page 24).

2. **Blanch, skin, and slice or dice beets as directed on page 344.** When beets are cool and dry, pack into containers, leaving a 1-inch (2.5 cm) headspace. Remove air, label and seal. Freeze for up to 9 months.

pickled baby beets

It's possible to halve this recipe if you can get only a couple of bunches (about 2 lb/1 kg) of beets. You know they are fresh when the greens are crisp enough to use in a salad or to braise for dinner.

MAKES 8 CUPS

4 lb (2 kg) baby beets, with greens attached
3 cups (750 mL) granulated sugar
6 cups (1.5 L) red wine vinegar
2 tsp (10 mL) pickling salt

2 tbsp (25 mL) Classic Pickling Spice Blend
(page 213 or store-bought), tied in a cheese
cloth bag
4 star anise

1. Rinse the surface soil off beets and pat dry. Using a measure (right, I am using a metal spatula), trim tops off beets, leaving about 1 inch (2.5 cm) of stem attached. Soak beets in a sink full of cool water and scrub using a vegetable brush.

2. Using a sharp paring knife, scrape the tough skin away from the crown of the beets, being careful to keep the stems intact. Trim off all but 1/2 inch (1 cm) of the root end and scrape away the tiny rootlets.

3. Heat four 1-pint (2-cup/500 mL) jars in boiling water, and scald the lids, lifter, funnel and tongs (see page 18).

4. Meanwhile, bring a large saucepan of water to a boil over high heat. Add beets and cook for 4 minutes. Immerse in cold water for 4 minutes. Drain and set aside until needed.

5. In a Maslin pan or canning kettle, combine sugar, vinegar and salt. Bring to a rolling boil over high heat, stirring constantly. Add spice bag and beets. Cover, reduce heat and keep the mixture boiling for 5 minutes. Remove and discard spice bag.

6. Remove from heat. Using a slotted spoon, half fill hot jars with beets, shaking the jar to pack fairly tightly. Add 1 star anise to the jar and fill jar with beets, leaving a 1-inch (2.5 cm) headspace. Pour hot brine over beets through a cheesecloth-lined funnel to within 1/2 inch (1 cm) of the top. Run a thin non-metallic utensil around the inside of the jar to allow air to escape. Add more hot brine, if necessary, to leave a 1/2-inch (1 cm) headspace. Wipe rims, top with flat lids and screw on metal rings. Return jars to the hot water bath, topping up with hot water if necessary. Bring to a full rolling boil and process jars for 10 minutes (see page 19).

7. Remove canner lid and wait 5 minutes before removing jars to a towel or rack to cool completely. Check seals, label and store in a cool place for up to 1 year.

honeyed beets

Unlike the vinegar-doused canned beets of my youth, these beets are tender, lightly sweet-ened and delicious. I use them with cooked grains like spelt, kasha, wheat berries, couscous and bulgur (see Beet Tabbouleh, next page), or as a bed for roasted vegetables, or tossed with other root vegetables for a fresh winter salad.

MAKES 8 CUPS (2 L)

3-1/2 lb (1.75 kg) beets (about 18 medium)
2 cups (500 mL) chicken broth
1 cup (250 mL) liquid honey
3/4 cup (175 mL) rice vinegar
1/4 cup (50 mL) freshly squeezed lemon juice

1/2 tsp (2 mL) ground cloves
1/2 tsp (2 mL) salt
2 tbsp (25 mL) chopped fresh basil

1. Prepare beets by blanching, skinning and trimming as directed on page 344. Let cool and shred.

2. Meanwhile, heat four 1-pint (2-cup/500 mL) jars in boiling water, and scald the lids, lifter, funnel and tongs (see page 22).

3. In a saucepan, combine chicken broth, honey, vinegar, lemon juice, cloves and salt. Bring to a boil over high heat. Add beets and boil for 3 or 4 minutes, stirring constantly, until heated through. Remove pan from heat and stir in basil. Fill hot jars, leaving a 1/2-inch (1 cm) headspace. Run a thin non-metallic utensil around the inside of the jar to allow air to escape. Add more brine, if necessary, to leave a 1/2-inch (1 cm) headspace. Wipe rims, top with flat lids and screw on metal rings.

4. Place jars in pressure canner. Adjust water level (check manufacturer's instructions), lock lid and bring to a boil over medium-high heat. Vent steam for 10 minutes (check manufacturer's instructions) then close vent. Continue heating to achieve 10 lb (69 kPa) pressure and maintain pressure to process pint (2-cup/500 mL) jars for 25 minutes and quart (1 L) jars for 30 minutes. These times and pressure are based on using a weighted gauge pressure canner at 1,000 feet (305 m) or less. Check your altitude and manufacturer's instructions for variations.

5. Turn off heat; let pressure return to zero naturally. Once gauge shows 0 pressure, wait 2 minutes then open the vent. Unlock and remove canner lid. Wait 10 minutes then lift jars from canner and place on a clean towel or rack. Do not re-tighten screw bands. Let the jars cool to room temperature. This may take from 12 to 24 hours. Remove and store screw bands. Check lid seals (see page 23). Wipe and label sealed jars. Store in a cool, dark place.

Use: Honeyed Beets are delicious in bean salads and as a an accompaniment to roasts and vegetarian entrées. Toss them with cooked wild rice or whole grains for a nutritious luncheon dish or dinner appetizer.

beet tabbouleh

It's not often that you will see a tabbouleh made with beets. In fact, the traditional Levantine Arab salad is generally green in colour, given the predominant ingredients—chopped fresh parsley and mint. Chopped tomatoes add hits of colour, but the overall colour is green. I like the idea of using shredded beets to add colour in the winter, when local heritage tomatoes are not available. It's an easygoing dish: you could add cubed or thinly sliced cucumber or zucchini, chopped oil-packed sun-dried tomatoes, chickpeas or other lentils, chopped green onions, chopped chives, chopped fresh thyme or cilantro, sesame or sunflower seeds, almonds, pecans or walnuts, chopped garlic, green or red onion or chopped red pepper.

In the photo above, I have used ginger mint and both flat-leaf and curly parsley. Toasting the almonds is key for heightening the flavour of the already nutty-tasting bulgur.

MAKES 4 to 6 SERVINGS

2 cups (500 mL) chicken or vegetable broth
1 cup (250 mL) fine or medium-grain bulgur
1 pint (2 cups/500 mL) Honeyed Beets (page 348), drained, liquid reserved
1 cup (250 mL) chopped fresh parsley
1/3 cup (75 mL) chopped fresh mint
1/3 cup (75 mL) crumbled feta cheese
1/3 cup (75 mL) toasted slivered almonds

VINAIGRETTE
1/4 cup (50 mL) reserved beet liquid
1/4 cup (50 mL) olive oil
1 tsp (5 mL) toasted sesame oil
1/4 tsp (1 mL) salt, optional

1. In a saucepan, bring broth to a boil. Stir in bulgur. Cover and remove from heat. Let stand for 10 minutes or until liquid has been absorbed. Remove lid, stir and let stand until cool.

2. Meanwhile, make dressing: In a jar with tight-fitting lid, combine beet liquid, olive oil, sesame oil and salt, if using. Cap and shake to combine.

3. In a salad bowl, combine bulgur, beets, parsley, mint, feta cheese and almonds. Drizzle dressing over salad and toss to coat salad ingredients.

Use: Beet Tabbouleh can be served over a bed of greens or ribboned cucumber. You can heap it in a bowl and offer radicchio leaves to scoop it out for an appetizer.

Broccoli

ONE OF THE CRUCIFEROUS VEGETABLES and a close relative to cauliflower, broccoli (*Brassica oleracea italica*) is actually a cluster of green, unopened flower buds branching from a thick green stem. Each plant produces one large central head. As its Latin name hints, broccoli originates from the Italian word *brocco*, meaning "arm" or "branch." Like all vegetables in the Brassica genus, broccoli is a native of the Mediterranean and Asia Minor, and offers cancer-fighting phytonutrients.

Good Preserving Varieties

Broccoli cultivars fall into two basic classifications. Calabrese is the most common type of broccoli in North America, producing green heads that are larger than the Broccoli types, which may be purple or white and produce smaller heads. Romanesco broccoli, or Roman Cauliflower, is grouped with cauliflower (page 371).

Calabrese Types

Arcadia: A popular and reliable plant to grow; firm green heads.

Green Comet: A quick-maturing hybrid; green heads are large and tightly formed; excellent for all forms of preserving.

Broccoli Types

Early Purple Sprouting: Hearty and prolific.

Late White Sprouting: Produces heads that look like cauliflower.

Purchasing/Storing

1 lb (500 g) broccoli yields 2 cups (500 mL) florets.

Buy broccoli with compact bud clusters. The heads should be tightly closed, without the yellow flower showing. Stalks and stem branches should be firm and tender, not split, woody or hollow.

Good With

- Herbs such as sage, rosemary, garlic, ginger, basil, bay, thyme, chervil, chives.
- Other vegetables, such as onions, cauliflower, Brussels sprouts and leafy greens.
- Walnuts, almonds, pecans, sunflower seeds, sesame seeds and flaxseeds; raisins, dried apricots, cranberries, dried cherries.
- Smoked ham and bacon, prosciutto and prosciutto di Parma.
- Hard cheeses such as Parmesan, Romano and Asiago.

Preparation

Wash broccoli by swishing it in a sink full of cool water to which a drop of food-safe soap has been added. Rinse well and pat dry. Trim away the stem and, if tender, set aside for another use.

If necessary to remove insects: in a sink or tub, combine 1 cup (250 mL) salt and 1 gallon (4 L) cold water. Soak broccoli in the solution for 30 minutes. Lift out and rinse well.

Cut the flower head into small florets. Blanch broccoli florets in boiling water for 3 minutes. Immerse in cold water for 3 minutes. Drain and pat dry.

Canning Broccoli

I don't recommend canning broccoli because processing turns it brown and intensifies strong flavours. Pickling and freezing are the best methods of preserving.

sizzling broccoli and honeyed beets

Use any lightly cooked green—sliced cabbage, kale, spinach or Swiss chard—in place of the broccoli in this recipe. If you wish to make this a substantial dish for a light lunch, add strips of chicken to the skillet along with the garlic. Cook for 7 minutes or until no longer pink inside and lightly browned outside.

MAKES 4 SERVINGS

3 tbsp (45 mL) olive oil
3 cloves garlic, thinly sliced
2 cups (500 mL) steamed or blanched broccoli florets
1 pint (2 cups/500 mL) Honeyed Beets (page 348), drained
1/4 tsp (1 mL) hot red pepper flakes

In a large skillet, heat olive oil over high heat. Add garlic and cook, stirring frequently, for 3 minutes or until browned. Add broccoli and beets. Cook, stirring constantly, until heated through. Sprinkle hot pepper flakes over top and serve immediately.

brocco-cauli mixed pickles

This is a recipe for many hands. I have a romantic vision of grandparents and grandchildren gathered together on a porch and the weather has turned suddenly hot—Indian summer! They are "putting down" the last of the garden's goodness in preparation for the long winter ahead. This scenario has never happened to me (I don't even have grandchildren), but the sight of these mixed pickles always evokes the same vignette.

Once the vegetables are prepared, the rest is easy. You can cut the recipe in half if you wish.

MAKES 12 CUPS (3 L)

3 cups (750 mL) broccoli florets

3 cups (750 mL) cauliflower florets

2 cups (500 mL) sliced carrots

2 cups (500 mL) pickling or pearl onions

2 large red or orange or yellow bell peppers, cut into 1/2-inch (1 cm) strips

6 cayenne or small hot chile peppers

1 cup (250 mL) pickling salt

6-1/2 cups (1.625 L) white vinegar

2 cups (500 mL) granulated sugar

1/4 cup (50 mL) mustard seeds

2 tsp (10 mL) celery seeds

1 tbsp (15 mL) ground turmeric

First Day

1. In a large crock or stainless steel kettle, combine broccoli, cauliflower, carrots, onions, bell peppers and hot peppers.

2. In a large glass or stainless steel bowl, combine pickling salt and 4 quarts (4 L) water. Stir well to dissolve. Pour over vegetables. Cover with a clean kitchen towel and let stand in a cool place for 12 to 18 hours.

Second Day

1. Using a large colander, drain vegetables (in batches if necessary) over a sink. Rinse under cool running water and drain well. Separate the chile peppers from the rest of the vegetables and set both aside.

2. Heat six 1-pint (2-cup/500 mL) jars in boiling water, and scald the lids, lifter, funnel and tongs (see page 18).

3. In a Maslin pan or canning kettle, combine vinegar, sugar, mustard seeds, celery seeds and turmeric. Bring to a boil over high heat, stirring constantly. Boil for 3 minutes. Add reserved vegetables (not reserved chile peppers) and return to a boil. Reduce heat and boil gently, stirring occasionally, for 5 minutes, until vegetables are heated through.

4. Half-fill hot jars with vegetables and liquid. Slide a chile pepper down the side of the jar and finish filling the jar with vegetables and liquid, leaving a 1/2-inch (1 cm) headspace. Run a thin non-metallic utensil around the inside of the jar to allow air to escape. Add more hot vegetables or brine, if necessary, to leave a 1/2-inch (1 cm) headspace. Wipe rims, top with flat lids and screw on metal rings. Return jars to the hot water bath, topping up with hot water if necessary. Bring to a full rolling boil and process jars for 15 minutes (see page 19).

5. Remove canner lid and wait 5 minutes before removing jars to a towel or rack to cool completely. Check seals, label and store in a cool place for up to 1 year.

Use: These pickles are very nice as an alternative to crudités with dip or to enliven winter salads. Save the pickling brine to use in vinaigrette or to thin commercial mayonnaise.

Freezing Broccoli
1. **Select Equipment:** Select suitable-size freezer containers, bags or Mason jars (see page 24).

2. **Wash and blanch broccoli as instructed on page 352.** Pack into containers, leaving a 1-inch (2.5 cm) headspace. Remove air, label and seal. Freeze for up to 9 months.

Brussels Sprouts

SOMETIME DURING THE MIDDLE AGES (roughly AD 500 to 1500), the common "colewort" (cabbage) plant began to be modified by people living in different geographic locations. When cabbage plants in Belgium were selected and reseeded for their clusters of tightly packed leafy buds along the main stem, they grew into what were called *Brassica oleracea gemmifera*, meaning "cabbage of the vegetable garden bearing gems"—what we know as Brussels sprouts.

Good Preserving Varieties
New hybrids have been developed in order to respond to machine harvesting, and these varieties definitely have an improved taste, some being almost sweet.

Content: Dark green; dense, with tightly wrapped leaves; October through November.
Genius: Available December through January.
Oliver: Early season; medium green; moderately dense, with a mild flavour; June through October.
Prince Marvel: Early season; tight, sweet sprouts.

Purchasing/Storing
1 lb (500 g) yields 2 cups (500 mL) whole small Brussels sprouts.

For pickles and freezing, select small, firm, tightly wrapped young heads.

Good With
- Culinary herbs such as oregano, sage, thyme, rosemary.
- Seasonings such as cumin, coriander, nutmeg, cinnamon.
- Semi-soft cheeses such as havarti, Boursin; medium-age cheddars, colby.
- Dried fruit such as raisins, apricots, prunes.
- Other vegetables, such as tomatoes, garlic, onions.
- Toasted almonds, pecans, walnuts.
- Robust meats, such as beef and lamb, roasted turkey and game.

Preparation
Trim the stem to the base of the sprout and remove coarse outer leaves. Wash in a sink full of

cool water to which a drop of food-safe soap has been added. Rinse, drain and pat dry. Sort into small, medium and large sizes. Blanch whole Brussels sprouts in boiling water: small heads for 3 minutes, medium heads for 4 minutes, and large heads for 5 minutes. Immerse in cold water for 3, 4 or 5 minutes. Drain and pat dry.

Canning Brussels Sprouts

I don't recommend canning Brussels sprouts because processing turns them brown and intensifies their strong sulphur flavour. Pickling and freezing are the best methods of preserving.

Freezing Brussels Sprouts

1. **Select Equipment:** Select suitable-size freezer containers, bags or Mason jars (see page 24).

2. **Trim, wash and blanch sprouts as directed on page 357.** Pack into containers, leaving a 1-inch (2.5 cm) headspace. Remove air, label and seal. Freeze for up to 12 months.

sweet pickled brussels sprouts

Try to find small Brussels sprouts for this pickle. If you must use larger heads, cut them in half. Pickling sweetens and mellows the flavour so that you can use them in grain salads (such as Beet Tabbouleh, page 349) and with braised winter greens. You can cut this recipe in half if you wish.

MAKES 10 CUPS (2.5 L)

8 cups (2 L) small Brussels sprouts
3 cups (750 mL) white vinegar
1-1/2 cups (375 mL) granulated sugar
1-1/2 cups (375 mL) thinly sliced onions
1 cup (250 mL) diced red bell peppers

2 tbsp (25 mL) mustard seeds
1 tbsp (15 mL) celery seeds
1 tsp (5 mL) ground turmeric
1 tsp (5 mL) hot red pepper flakes

1. Trim and blanch sprouts as directed on page 357.

2. Meanwhile, heat five 1-pint (2-cup/500 mL) jars in boiling water, and scald the lids, lifter, funnel and tongs (see page 18).

3. In a Maslin pan or canning kettle, combine vinegar, sugar, onions, red pepper, mustard seeds, celery seeds, turmeric and red pepper flakes. Bring to a boil over high heat, stirring frequently. Adjust heat and simmer for 5 minutes.

4. Distribute onion and diced pepper in hot jars. Fill jars with Brussels sprouts and hot liquid, leaving a 1/2-inch (1 cm) headspace. Run a thin non-metallic utensil around the inside of the jar to allow air to escape. Add more hot liquid, if necessary, to leave a 1/2-inch (1 cm) headspace. Wipe rims, top with flat lids and screw on metal rings. Return jars to the hot water bath, topping up with hot water if necessary. Bring to a full rolling boil and process jars for 10 minutes (see page 19).

5. Remove canner lid and wait 5 minutes before removing jars to a towel or rack to cool completely. Check seals, label and store in a cool place for up to 1 year.

raspberry-glazed brussels sprouts with pancetta

The sweetness of the raspberry and the salty pancetta balance the heady taste of the Brussels sprouts. I like the crunch of the red pepper and onion in contrast with the softened texture of the frozen and thawed Brussels sprouts.

You can use smoked side bacon or prosciutto, both cut into dice, to replace the pancetta. Some notes on the difference in the two Italian pork ingredients: Pancetta is Italian salt-cured bacon cut from the pork belly, and is not smoked. It is sold rolled or in a slab. Rolled pancetta is sliced thinly; a slab is chopped or diced before being fried and added to a dish. Prosciutto is the Italian word for "ham." It is usually sold dry-cured (uncooked) and thinly sliced. Melon and figs complement the salty taste of prosciutto.

MAKES 4 SERVINGS

2 tbsp (25 mL) olive oil, divided
3 oz (90 g) pancetta, cut into 1/4-inch (5 mm) dice
1/2 cup (125 mL) chopped red bell pepper
1/2 cup (125 mL) chopped red onion
1 clove garlic, finely chopped

1/4 cup (50 mL) whole almonds
1/4 cup (50 mL) Raspberry Vinegar (page 48 or store-bought)
2 cups (500 mL) Brussels sprouts, thawed if frozen
sea salt and pepper

1. In a skillet, heat 1 tbsp (15 mL) of the olive oil over medium-high heat. Reduce heat to medium and add pancetta. Cook for 6 to 8 minutes, stirring frequently, until crisp and browned. Using tongs, lift out to a paper towel–lined plate and set aside.

2. Add remaining oil to the skillet and heat over medium heat. Add red pepper and onion and cook for 8 to 10 minutes, stirring occasionally, until soft and translucent. Add garlic and almonds and cook for 2 minutes or until almonds are toasted and lightly browned. Remove vegetables and almonds from the skillet.

3. Add raspberry vinegar to the skillet and bring to a boil over high heat. Reduce heat and simmer for about 7 minutes or until reduced and slightly syrupy. Add Brussels sprouts and stir for about 5 minutes or until heated through. Toss with red pepper, onion, garlic and almonds. Transfer to a serving bowl. Garnish with crisp pancetta. Season to taste with a few grinds of salt and pepper.

Cabbage

BRASSICA PLANTS (kale, collards, broccoli, cauliflower, turnip, Brussels sprouts) are referred to as cruciferous due to their cross-shaped (from the Latin *crucifix*, meaning "cross") flower petals. Cabbage (*Brassica oleracea capitata*) is an old plant, once called colewort, or cole. Over the centuries, it has been selectively bred to a round ball shape with tightly wrapped leaves around a central core.

Good Preserving Varieties

Cabbage may be yellow, white, green, purple or red; round-, flat- or conical-headed; curly or fringed; tight or loose leaved. The most common varieties are round and light green or red.

Round, Green Cabbage Types

Krautkaiser: Large, slightly flattened shape, white; weighs up to 6 lb (3 kg); perfect for sauerkraut and pickled cabbage. Other round green types for preserving include **Cheers, Stonehead, Autumn Queen, January King, Minicole** and **Viking**.

Cheers is a round green variety that is perfect for cabbage rolls because the large leaves separate easily.

Oxheart Cabbage Types

The distinguishing characteristic is their enormous firm heads that grow to a point. Cultivars in this category are dark green and good to grow because they will stand in the garden for a long time (from July to December if covered) and have very good flavour. **Caramba** is an excellent Oxheart cabbage type for preserving.

Savoy Cabbage Types

With their crinkly leaves and milder taste, Savoy cabbages are considered to be the most tender and sweet. Savoy is a good choice for stuffed cabbage leaves since the leaves are more pliable and stand up better to longer cooking times. Use in Frozen Coleslaw (page 368).

Savoy types are a good choice for stuffed cabbage leaves.

Red and Purple Cabbage Types

These types take longer to mature, so they are generally not as tender as green or white varieties. Most often pickled, raw shredded red cabbage also makes a striking addition to traditional green salads. Along with green cabbage, red cabbage is the best for storing, and it preserves well. The heart-healthy compound anthocyanin,

Shredding Cabbage

Preserving recipes call for shredded cabbage, and everyone has a favourite tool for getting just the right cut. You will need a large cleaver or French knife to split dense green cabbage heads in half. I use a mandolin when I want long, thin shreds of cabbage for coleslaw. For preserved cabbage recipes such as Moroccan Cabbage (page 366), I like the 1/8-inch (2 mm) slicing disc of my food processor (above left). The 1/4-inch (5 mm) slicing disc (above middle) produces an even shred for pickles. The shredding disc (above right) is used when a finer chop is required for soups and stews.

When a few heads of cabbage are being cut, the shredding or slicing attachments for a stand mixer are ideal because they allow you to continuously shred a large amount without having to stop and empty a container bowl.

which gives red cabbage its beautiful colour, will also turn it blue when cooked with any alkaline substance (salt or baking soda).

Purchasing/Storing
- 1 medium green cabbage weighs from 5 to 6 lb (2.5 to 3 kg).
- 1 lb (500 g) yields 5 or 6 cups (1.25 or 1.5 L) shredded cabbage.

For preserving, cabbage heads should be solid and heavy, with clean outer leaves that are moist and free of discoloured veins or damage. The stem should not be dry or split.

Good With
- Herbs such as sage, basil, parsley, bay, thyme, chervil, chives, dill, savory.
- Spices such as caraway, celery seed, cumin, coriander, nutmeg, ginger.
- Other vegetables, such as celery, carrots, onions, garlic, potatoes, peppers.
- Fruit such as apples, pears, plums.
- Walnuts, almonds, pecans; raisins; sesame seeds, flaxseeds, sunflower seeds.
- Hearty and spicy meats, such as sausage, bacon, prosciutto, ham, lamb, pork, beef and corned beef.

Preparation
Cut out and discard the core with a sharp knife. Rinse leaves in cool running water. Drain and pat dry.

Canning Cabbage
I don't recommend canning cabbage—first because it is so widely available fresh all year long, and second because canning causes cabbage to become stronger in flavour. So pickling it or preparing sauerkraut is the best method of preserving.

moroccan chicken tagine

One of the things that defines the cuisine of North Africa is the subtle combination of fruit with savoury dishes. When making this ever-so-easy dish, I often add slivers of dried apricots or dates, raisins or sliced fresh peaches, or other stone fruit. I use a North African clay pot called a tagine; however, a covered casserole or Dutch oven also work well. The unique, cone-shaped tagine lid traps steam as the food cooks and changes it to liquid, causing a very moist cooking environment—it's raining inside. This means that food cooked in a tagine is very tender and moist.

Tagine or Dutch oven with lid, lightly oiled
Preheat oven to 375°F (190°C)
MAKES 4 SERVINGS

4 cups (1 L) Moroccan Cabbage (page 366) with
  juices, bay leaf and cinnamon stick
1/4 cup (50 mL) sliced red bell pepper or
  apricots
3 tbsp (45 mL) golden raisins

4 pieces (2 lb/1 kg) skinless chicken
2 tbsp (25 mL) olive oil or butter
salt and pepper
1 tbsp (15 mL) garam masala spice blend
1 tbsp (15 mL) chopped fresh parsley

In the bottom of a tagine or Dutch oven, combine cabbage with juices, red pepper and raisins. Arrange chicken in a single layer over cabbage. Brush with oil and season with salt and pepper. Cover and bake in preheated oven for 1 hour or until chicken is done. Garnish with garam masala and parsley.

moroccan cabbage

Moroccan spices in the Five-Spice Blend complement the nutty flavour of cabbage in this pickle. Don't let the 2 days in the procedure deter you. It's not hard to make, and I think you will find it convenient and delicious for winter meals. I think of it as a quick and easy version of sauerkraut. You can cut the recipe in half and use pint (2-cup/500 mL) jars.

MAKES 12 CUPS (3 L)

2 heads green cabbage, shredded (about 10 cups/2.5 L)
1/3 cup (75 mL) pickling salt
3 cups (750 mL) white wine vinegar
1 cup (250 mL) lightly packed brown sugar
2 tbsp (25 mL) Five-Spice Blend (page 216 or store-bought), tied in a cheesecloth bag

4 apples, shredded
2 red onions, thinly sliced
3 or 6 bay leaves
3 or 6 cinnamon sticks, each 2 inches (5 cm)

First Morning

1. In a large crock or stainless steel kettle, layer cabbage and salt. Cover and let stand in a cool place for 24 hours.

Second Morning

1. Using a large colander, drain cabbage (in batches if necessary) over a sink. Rinse with cool running water and drain well. Set out on towel-lined trays to drain thoroughly for at least 4 hours.

2. Heat three 1-quart (1 L) or six 1-pint (2-cup/500 mL) jars in boiling water, and scald the lids, lifter, funnel and tongs (see page 18).

3. In a Maslin pan or canning kettle, combine vinegar and brown sugar. Tie spice bag to the handle of the pan. Bring to a boil over high heat, stirring constantly. Boil for 5 minutes to infuse the liquid with the spices. Add apples and onions. Reduce heat and boil gently, stirring occasionally, for 7 minutes or until onions are cooked. Remove and discard spice bag.

4. Half-fill hot jars with cabbage. Slide a bay leaf and a cinnamon stick down the side of the jar and loosely fill the jar with cabbage, leaving a 3/4-inch (2 cm) headspace. Ladle hot pickling liquid and vegetables into the jar to cover the cabbage, leaving a 1/2-inch (1 cm) headspace. Run a thin non-metallic utensil around the inside of the jar to allow air to escape. Add more hot brine, if necessary, to leave a 1/2-inch (1 cm) headspace. Wipe rims, top with flat lids and screw on metal rings. Return jars to the hot water bath, topping up with hot water if necessary. Bring to a full rolling boil and process jars for 20 minutes (see page 19).

5. Remove canner lid and wait 5 minutes before removing jars to a towel or rack to cool completely. Check seals, label and store in a cool place for up to 1 year.

Use: Try Moroccan Cabagge as a base for vegetarian and vegan dishes by adding chickpeas or other cooked peas, lentils or beans, other steamed vegetables, or nuts and seeds. As a side dish, it can be served at room temperature or gently heated.

frozen coleslaw

Cabbage is brimming with cancer-fighting endoles and other phytonutrients, and since discovering its cancer-protecting attributes, I have made it a regular in my diet. I try to have raw or cooked cabbage (or other Brassica vegetables) at least twice a week.

Coleslaw is the one salad that I can make in any season or order on almost any restaurant menu when dining out. If I take a container out of the freezer the night before, I have a great salad for lunch on the go the next day, especially if I toss in a handful of nuts, seeds or some shredded cheese.

This frozen coleslaw is made with sugar syrup, which is necessary for keeping the cabbage crisp. You can drain off the syrup before serving the coleslaw. Add shredded apple or pear and more shredded carrot or red onion if you like.

MAKES 6 CUPS (1.5 L)

1 medium head cabbage, shredded (about 5 cups/1.25 L)	1 cup (250 mL) apple cider vinegar
2 carrots, shredded	2 cups (500 mL) granulated sugar
1 red bell pepper, diced	1 tsp (5 mL) mustard seeds
1 tbsp (15 mL) pickling salt	1 tsp (5 mL) celery seeds

Morning (or night before)

1. In a large crock or in a glass or stainless steel bowl, combine cabbage, carrots and pepper. Sprinkle salt over top and toss well to combine. Cover and let stand in a cool place for 4 to 6 hours or overnight.

Afternoon

1. Using a large colander, drain cabbage (in batches if necessary) over a sink. Rinse with cool running water and drain well. Set out on towel-lined trays to drain thoroughly for at least 4 hours.

Evening

1. In a saucepan, combine vinegar, sugar, water, mustard seeds and celery seeds. Bring to a boil over medium-high heat, stirring constantly. Adjust heat and simmer for 5 minutes, stirring occasionally. Remove from heat and cool completely.

2. In a large bowl, combine cabbage and vegetables and spiced syrup. Toss to mix well. Pack in 2- or 4-cup (500 mL or 1 L) measures into containers, leaving a 1-inch (2.5 cm) headspace. Remove air, label and seal. Freeze for up to 9 months.

Freezing Cabbage

Freezing raw cabbage causes it to become limp and lose flavour. Except for the frozen cole-slaw recipe (previous page), I do not recommend freezing cabbage

Cauliflower

ANOTHER BRASSICACEAE FAMILY PLANT, cauliflower (*Brassica oleracea botrytis*) is a cultivated plant with a single stalk bearing a large round, tightly packed mass of white (or creamy), green, purple, brown or yellow flower buds (called "curd").

Good Preserving Varieties

There are five main groups into which all varieties of cauliflower can be classified.

Italian: These are the ancestral varieties from which all the modern varieties have developed. This type includes white and Romanesco varieties, as well as various green, purple, brown and yellow cultivars.

Purple Cape: A heritage Italian variety with the same anthocyanins found in red cabbage; best steamed and eaten fresh; the purple colour turns green when processed by canning.

Asian: Developed in India, now used mainly in China and India, the Asian varieties include old and vintage varieties such as **Early Patna** and **Early Benaras**.

Northwest European biennial: This type of cauliflower was developed in France and was cultivated in Europe for winter and early spring harvest. It includes such old cultivars as **Roscoff** and **Angers**.

Northern European annual: Most popular in Europe and North America and harvested in summer and fall, this cauliflower type includes such old cultivars as **Erfurt** and **Snowball**.

Romanesco varieties resemble a light green cauliflower except that the buds grow in perfect logarithmic spirals, making the vegetable a work of geometric art. Romanesco is best steamed and eaten fresh.

Orange cauliflower makes an excellent preserving cultivar since it is higher in antioxidants and vitamin A and is milder in flavour than traditional white cauliflower.

Purchasing/Storing

- A medium-size head of cauliflower weighs about 2 to 3 lb (1 to 1.5 kg).
- 1 lb (500 g) yields 2-1/2 cups (625 mL) cauliflower florets.

Buy clean, firm, white or creamy white, tightly packed heads without loose or spreading florets. Leaves should be green, moist and fresh looking, with no drying, yellowing or withering. Smudgy and speckled surfaces indicate aphids (plant lice).

- Herbs such as sage, chives, rosemary, basil, bay, thyme, chervil, tarragon.
- Spices such as cardamom, cumin, coriander, curry blends, mustard, garlic, cinnamon, ginger, cloves, nutmeg.
- Other vegetables, such as celery, onions, broccoli, cabbage, potatoes, carrots, peas.
- Cheddar, Swiss, Parmesan, Romano or Asiago cheese.
- Béchamel sauce, hollandaise and cheese sauce.
- Walnuts, almonds, pecans; sunflower seeds, sesame seeds and flaxseeds; raisins and dried apricots.
- Smoked ham and bacon, prosciutto and prosciutto di Parma.

Preparation

To wash cauliflower, swish it in a sink full of cool water to which a drop of food-safe soap has been added. Rinse well and pat dry. Trim away the outer leaves and core stalk.

If necessary to remove insects: In a sink or tub, combine 1 cup (250 mL) salt and 1 gallon (4 L) cold water. Soak cauliflower in the solution for 30 minutes. Lift out and rinse.

Cut the flower head into small florets. Blanch cauliflower florets in boiling water for 3 minutes. Immerse in cold water for 3 minutes. Drain and pat dry.

Canning Cauliflower

I don't recommend home canning cauliflower. Pickling and freezing are the best methods to preserve it.

frozen purée of cauliflower

If you have this light and healthy substitution for mashed potatoes in the freezer, you have a delicious base for fish and chicken or roasted vegetable entrées. Add curry or garam masala spice blend, Dijon mustard, herb pesto, chopped fresh chives, roasted garlic, crumbled blue cheese or grated Parmesan cheese to tailor this basic recipe to your menu. This recipe makes enough for 4 servings and can be doubled or tripled. It is easiest to process the cauliflower in batches.

MAKES 6 CUPS (1.5 L)

1 head cauliflower
2 cups (500 mL) chicken broth or water or milk
3 tbsp (45 mL) butter, olive oil or herb pesto
sea salt and freshly ground pepper

1. Wash and trim cauliflower as directed on page 372 (do not blanch). In a large saucepan, combine cauliflower florets and chicken broth. Cover and bring to a light boil over medium-high heat. Simmer gently for 15 to 20 minutes or until cauliflower is tender.

2. Using a slotted spoon, lift out half of the cauliflower and process in the blender with 1/4 cup (50 mL) of the cooking broth until smooth. Add remaining cauliflower, 1/4 cup (50 mL) of the cooking broth, butter and salt and pepper. Process until smooth, adding more cooking broth as needed to make a thick, smooth purée.

3. Spoon into freezer container, leaving a 1-inch (2.5 cm) headspace. Remove air, label and seal. Freeze for up to 9 months.

Use: Combine with milk or cream to make a soup; or use in place of mashed potatoes or as a savory "coulis" in main dishes.

rainbow fruited chow chow

This is one of the last pickle recipes of the fall, and it uses up the last of the produce on hand. It is pretty in the jar and on the table with its different shapes and colours. The recipe is easy and forgiving—you can use more or less of almost any fruit or vegetable you happen to have on hand. I have used apple cider vinegar in place of the rice vinegar, but I prefer the rice vinegar flavour with the curry pickling spice, which is only mildly spicy.

If you want to leave the beans whole, use about a handful each of green and yellow. The peppers can be cut into strips or diced, and that goes for both the celery and the carrots, too. If I don't have pearl onions, I use a whole cooking onion, cut into eighths. If I have broccoli, I use half cauliflower and half broccoli florets, but I never omit the cauliflower because it is what defines this pickle.

MAKES 10 CUPS (2.5 L)

3 cups (750 mL) cauliflower florets

2 cups (500 mL) pickling or pearl onions

1 cup (250 mL) cut green beans

1 cup (250 mL) cut yellow beans

3 stalks celery, cut into matchsticks

2 red bell peppers, cut into 1/2-inch (1 cm) strips

2 carrots, cut into matchsticks

3 cups (750 mL) rice vinegar

1 cup (250 mL) lightly packed brown sugar

1 cup (250 mL) granulated sugar

1 tbsp (15 mL) chopped candied ginger or grated fresh gingerroot

1 tbsp (15 mL) salt

2 tbsp (25 mL) Curry Pickling Spice Blend (page 214 or store-bought), tied in a cheesecloth bag

2 apples

2 pears

1. In a large bowl or pot, combine cauliflower, onions, green beans, yellow beans, celery, peppers and carrots. Set aside.

2. Heat five 1-pint (2-cup/500 mL) jars in boiling water, and scald the lids, lifter, funnel and tongs (see page 18).

3. In a Maslin pan or canning kettle, combine vinegar, brown sugar, granulated sugar, ginger and salt. Bring to a boil over high heat, stirring constantly. Add spice bag and vegetables and return to a boil. Boil gently, stirring occasionally, for 10 minutes. Core and peel apples and pears and slice into the boiling vegetable mixture. Boil for about 2 minutes or until vegetables are tender-crisp.

4. Fill hot jars with hot vegetables, fruit and brine, leaving a 1/2-inch (1 cm) headspace. Run a thin non-metallic utensil around the inside of the jar to allow air to escape. Add more hot brine, if necessary, to leave a 1/2-inch (1 cm) headspace. Wipe rims, top with flat lids and screw on metal rings.

Return jars to the hot water bath, topping up with hot water if necessary. Bring to a full rolling boil and process jars for 15 minutes (see page 19).

5. Remove canner lid and wait 5 minutes before removing jars to a towel or rack to cool completely. Check seals, label and store in a cool place for up to 1 year.

Freezing Cauliflower

1. **Select Equipment:** Select suitable-size freezer containers, bags or Mason jars (see page 24).

2. **Wash and blanch cauliflower as directed on page 372.** Pack into containers, leaving a 1-inch (2.5 cm) headspace. Remove air, label and seal. Freeze for up to 12 months.

Corn

NATIVE TO THE AMERICAS, corn is the second most cultivated food plant in the world, after wheat. First Nations peoples called it maize, colonists called it corn (from the Anglo-Saxon for "small particles" or the German for "wheat"), and its Latin name is *Zea mays*. Corn held significant practical and religious importance for Incan, Mayan and Aztec cultures.

Good Preserving Varieties

Standard: The oldest type of sweet corn; sugar turns to starch at peak of maturity, or harvest; best eaten fresh immediately (within hours of picking). These cultivars are not best for preserving unless you grow or buy them and process within hours of picking. "Golden Cross Bantam" is a yellow heirloom variety.

Sugary Extender: Has more sugar than Standard types; retains sweetness for 2 to 4 days; delicate texture, fine for preserving; the popular "Peaches and Cream" variety belongs to this group.

Supersweet: These varieties have up to three times the sugar content of standard and can be stored for up to 10 days without the sugar turning to starch; varieties preserve well.

Synergistic: A new breed, combining genetically differing kernels on the same ear; fine for preserving.

Augmented Supersweet: The newest breed, combining multiple gene types on Supersweet ears; fine for preserving.

Sweet corn is a general class of corn that is grown for human consumption (as opposed to "field corn," which is intended for livestock). With some exceptions, mostly in the **Standard** group, nearly all corn sold today is a hybrid.

Purchasing/Storing

- 1 lb (500 g) corn in the husks yields about 1 cup (250 mL) kernels.
- You will need about 3 lb (1.5 kg) for each quart (1 L) jar.

Look for heavy cobs with fresh green leaves that have not turned yellow and dried out. The silk, or fine strands at the top of the ear, should be moist and full. The kernels should not be bulging or split because this indicates over-maturity.

The sugars in eating varieties of corn begin to change into starch immediately after harvesting, although some sweet corn hybrids hold the sugars longer. Ideally, corn should be cooked and eaten within hours of picking. Transport and store in the husk, in a cool place until ready to cook. Bring a large pot of water to a boil and remove the husk just before plunging into the water. Cover and cook for 5 minutes.

Good With
- Herbs such as parsley, chives, rosemary, basil, bay, thyme, chervil, dill.
- Spices such as cumin, coriander, chile powder, cinnamon, cloves, nutmeg.
- Other vegetables, such as onions, potatoes, celery, carrots, peas, peppers, tomatoes, zucchini, garlic.
- Chicken, beef, fish, seafood, pork, lamb.
- Milk and cream, especially in chowders.

Preparation
Remove husk and silk; trim stalk ends to about 1 inch (2.5 cm). Wash ears under cool running water. Blanch whole baby corn "fingers" in boiling water for 3 minutes for canning. Immerse in cold water for 3 minutes. Drain and pat dry.

Blanch whole medium-size ears in boiling water for 4 minutes, counting from when the water comes back to the boil.

Immerse in ice water for 4 minutes. Drain and pat dry.

Remove kernels from the cob: Stand the ear on its wide stem end over a pie plate. Run a sharp knife down the cob, cutting the kernels off and letting them fall onto the plate.

To prepare cream-style corn: Blanch and cool for 4 minutes as directed above. Set the ear over a pie plate and run a sharp knife down the cob, removing the kernels at about one-half of their depth. Turn the knife and run the blunt end down the cob to remove the remainder of the kernels and collect the watery "milk" in the pie plate.

See detailed canning information, page 20.

1. Prepare Equipment: Wash and heat pint (2-cup/500 mL) or quart (1 L) jars, and scald the lids, funnel, ladle and tongs (see page 22).

2. For every 4 cups (1 L) corn kernels or baby corn fingers, bring 2 cups (500 mL) water or broth to a boil.

3a. Pack corn kernels into jars either hot or raw.

Make a Hot Pack: Add kernels (see previous page) to boiling water or broth and boil for 5 minutes, stirring constantly. Remove from heat. Fill hot jars one at a time with hot corn kernels and cooking liquid, leaving a 1-inch (2.5 cm) headspace. Run a thin non-metallic utensil around the inside of the jar to allow air to escape. Add corn or liquid, if necessary, to leave a 1-inch (2.5 cm) headspace. Wipe sealing edge of jars with a clean, damp, lint-free cloth. Position flat lids over the tops of jars and hand-tighten screw bands.

OR

Make a Raw Pack: Fill jars with kernels (see previous page). Cover with hot water or broth, leaving a 1-inch (2.5 cm) headspace. Run a thin non-metallic utensil around the inside of the jar to allow air to escape. Add corn or liquid to keep the 1-inch (2.5 cm) headspace. Wipe sealing edge of jars with a clean, damp, lint-free cloth. Position flat lids over the tops of jars and hand-tighten screw bands.

3b. Pack cream-style corn into jars hot.

Use only 1-cup (250 mL) or pint (2-cup/500 mL) jars and only pack using the Hot Pack Method.

Make a Hot Pack: Add cream-style corn (see previous page) to gently boiling water or broth and boil for 5 minutes. Fill hot jars with hot corn kernels and cooking liquid, leaving a 1-inch (2.5 cm) headspace. Run a thin non-metallic utensil around the inside of the jar to allow air to escape. Add corn and liquid to keep the 1-inch (2.5 cm) headspace. Wipe sealing edge of jars with a clean, damp, lint-free cloth. Position flat lids over the tops of jars and hand-tighten screw bands.

3c. Pack whole baby corn fingers into jars hot.

Make a Hot Pack: Add whole unblanched baby corn fingers to boiling water or broth and boil for 3 minutes, stirring constantly. Remove from heat. Using tongs, fill hot jars one at a time with hot baby corn fingers, shaking the jar to pack tightly. Ladle cooking liquid over top, leaving a 1-inch (2.5 cm) headspace. Run a thin non-metallic utensil around the inside of the jar to allow air to escape. Add hot liquid, if necessary, to leave a 1-inch (2.5 cm) headspace.

Wipe sealing edge of jars with a clean, damp, lint-free cloth. Position flat lids over the tops of jars and hand-tighten screw bands.

4. Place jars in pressure canner. Adjust water level (check manufacturer's instructions), lock lid and bring to a boil over medium-high heat. Vent steam for 10 minutes (check manufacturer's instructions) then close vent.

For kernels and baby corn fingers: Continue heating to achieve 10 lb (69 kPa) pressure and maintain pressure to process pint (2-cup/500 mL) jars for 55 minutes and quart (1 L) jars for 85 minutes.

For cream-style corn: Continue heating to achieve 10 lb (69 kPa) pressure and maintain pressure to process 1-cup (250 mL) and pint (2-cup/500 mL) jars for 85 minutes.

These times and pressure are based on using a weighted gauge pressure canner at 1,000 feet (305 m) or less. Check your altitude and manufacturer's instructions for variations.

5. Cool, Label and Store: Turn off heat; let pressure return to zero naturally. Once gauge shows 0 pressure, wait 2 minutes then open the vent. Unlock and remove canner lid. Wait 10 minutes then lift jars from canner and place on a clean towel or rack. Do not re-tighten screw bands. Let the jars cool to room temperature. This may take from 12 to 24 hours. Remove and store screw bands. Check lid seals (see page 23). Wipe and label sealed jars. Store in a cool, dark place.

peaches and cream relish

Each time I open a jar of this sweetly fragrant and delicious relish, I am taken back to the farmer's market, where heaps of just-picked ears are stacked. The first fresh local corn of the season is always an event at our house. It's not surprising, then, that of all the preserves in my pantry, this is the one that disappears first. This is perhaps my favourite of them all.

MAKES ABOUT 16 CUPS (4 L)

12 ears peaches and cream corn, husked
3 cups (750 mL) rice vinegar
1-1/2 cups (375 mL) granulated sugar
1 cup (250 mL) packed brown sugar
2 bay leaves
2 tbsp (25 mL) mustard seeds
2 tsp (10 mL) salt

1 tsp (5 mL) ground turmeric
5 cups (1.25 L) chopped green cabbage
3 red bell peppers, diced
2 red onions, finely diced
1 or 2 hot green chile peppers, finely diced,
   optional
1 pkg (1–3/4 oz/49 to 52 g) low-sugar pectin

1. Prepare corn kernels as directed on page 378; do not blanch. You should have about 8 cups (2 L).

2. Heat eight 1-pint (2-cup/500 mL) jars in boiling water, and scald the lids, lifter, funnel and tongs (see page 18).

3. In a Maslin pan or Dutch oven, combine vinegar, granulated sugar, brown sugar, bay leaves, mustard seeds, salt and turmeric. Bring to a boil over high heat. Add cabbage, red peppers, onions and green chile peppers, if using. Stir well and bring to a boil. Add pectin and boil for 1 minute. Turn the heat off and let the pan sit on the burner for 5 minutes.

4. Remove pan from heat and skim off any foam. Fill hot jars, leaving a 1/2-inch (1 cm) headspace. Run a thin non-metallic utensil around the inside of the jar to allow air to escape. Add more hot relish, if necessary, to leave a 1/2-inch (1 cm) headspace. Wipe rims, top with flat lids and screw on metal rings. Return jars to the hot water bath, topping up with hot water if necessary. Bring to a full rolling boil and process jars for 15 minutes (see page 19).

5. Remove canner lid and wait 5 minutes before removing jars to a towel or rack to cool completely. Check seals, label and store in a cool place for up to 1 year.

Use: There are so many ways to enjoy this relish. I often cook bacon and onion, add potatoes and milk and a pint (2-cup/500 mL) jar of corn relish for quick, homemade corn chowder. It is all you need to perk up grilled chicken and fish. It complements scallops and seafood and it makes a very good salsa with the addition of hot peppers, garlic and tomatoes. I team it with sausages for country breakfasts with eggs and toast. Of course, it is a favourite hot dog and hamburger relish at our house in the summer.

chile corn bread

The savoury corn bread rounds out a soup or salad at lunch or dinner. I sometimes bake the batter in small cast iron pans and use the mini loaves as you would crackers with spreads and dips. Slice and fill them with chopped ham or egg salad for substantial hors d'oeuvres and snacks. With the cornmeal and the corn relish, this bread is bursting with corn flavour. I like the little hits of hot green chile pepper, but don't miss out on this great bread if you don't care for hot peppers—simply substitute sweet green or red pepper. Served hot, with sharp cheddar cheese or butter, this is one of my favourite quick breads.

You can make this bread as one large loaf or, if you happen to have cast iron pans with small loaf indentations, make smaller loaves like these.

9- x 5-inch (23 x 13 cm) loaf pan, 12-cup muffin
 tin or cast iron pan, lightly oiled
Preheat oven to 425°F (220°C)
MAKES 1 LOAF

1 cup (250 mL) all-purpose flour
1 cup (250 mL) cornmeal
2 tsp (10 mL) baking powder
1/2 tsp (2 mL) baking soda
3/4 tsp (4 mL) salt
1/4 cup (50 mL) finely chopped hot chile
 peppers
1 cup (250 mL) milk
1 cup (250 mL) Peaches and Cream Relish
 (page 381)
2 eggs, beaten
3 tbsp (45 mL) melted butter

The antique cast iron pans I used are shaped like corn cobs. Muffin pans work well also.

1. Heat the prepared loaf pan in the preheating oven until ready to fill with batter.

2. Into a large bowl, sift flour, cornmeal, baking powder, baking soda and salt. Add chile peppers and mix well. In a separate bowl, combine milk, relish, eggs and butter. Add to dry ingredients all at once and stir only until the batter is mixed. Be careful not to overmix the batter.

3. Turn the batter into the heated loaf pan. Bake in preheated oven for 30 minutes or until bread shrinks away from the sides of the pan. Serve hot.

char-grilled corn and cauliflower salad with asian dressing

In late summer, I make double the recipe and freeze half. The rest makes a delicious light lunch or side dish for a barbecue. On hot summer days, it makes a colourful and different potluck contribution without heating up the kitchen. The nice thing about this salad is that you can prepare it an hour before serving and let it stand at room temperature or even make it the night before, store it covered in the refrigerator and bring it out an hour before grilling. If you have the barbecue ready for cooking meat or fish, the salad can be grilled in a grilling basket over medium coals. If you don't have a barbecue, spread the marinated vegetables in single layer on rimmed baking sheets and cook on the top shelf of the oven on broil for 3 to 5 minutes or until crisp-tender.

In the winter, use frozen corn and either fresh or frozen cauliflower. Omit the marinade and grilling steps altogether: simply steam the corn and cauliflower, then toss with onions and Asian Dressing for an incredibly easy and interesting vegetable side dish.

MAKES 8 TO 10 SERVINGS

6 ears sweet corn, blanched and cooled (see page 378) or thawed if frozen
1 head cauliflower, blanched and cooled (see page 372) or thawed if frozen

LIME AND CHILE MARINADE
1/4 cup (50 mL) olive oil
3 tbsp (45 mL) butter
6 small hot chile peppers, finely chopped
2 green onions, finely chopped
2 tbsp (25 mL) chopped fresh lemongrass or lemon verbena, optional
grated rind and juice of 2 limes

ASIAN DRESSING
1/4 cup (50 mL) peanut oil
2 tbsp (25 mL) lemon juice
2 tbsp (25 mL) soy sauce
2 tbsp (25 mL) rice vinegar
1 tbsp (15 mL) sesame oil
1 tbsp (15 mL) liquid honey
1 tsp (5 mL) finely grated fresh gingerroot
2 cloves garlic, finely chopped

1. Cut corn into 1-inch (2.5 cm) pieces. Cut cauliflower into small florets. In a bowl, combine corn and cauliflower, set aside.

2. Make Marinade: In a skillet, heat olive oil over medium heat. Add butter, chile peppers and green onions. Cook, stirring constantly, for 3 minutes or until soft. Remove pan and stir in lemongrass, if using. Cool to room temperature. Add lime rind and juice.

3. Drizzle marinade over corn and cauliflower. Cover and set aside for up to 24 hours in the refrigerator. Bring to room temperature 1 hour before grilling. Using a vegetable grilling basket, grill vegetables over medium coals, turning often and basting with marinade for 5 to 7 minutes or until tender-crisp.

4. Meanwhile, make Asian Dressing: In a jar with tight-fitting lid, combine peanut oil, lemon juice, soy sauce, vinegar, sesame oil, honey, ginger and garlic. Cover jar and shake well to combine. Set aside.

5. Tip grilled corn and cauliflower into a large bowl and toss with dressing.

Use: The marinade can be used for grilled fish, chicken and vegetables, and the Asian Dressing is lovely with both summer greens and winter root vegetable salads. Try different nut oils—peanut oil is good—in the dressing.

Freezing Corn

1. **Select Equipment:** Select suitable-size freezer containers, bags or Mason jars (see page 24).

2. **Blanch and cool medium ears as instructed on page 378.** Cut ears into 1-inch (2.5 cm) pieces or remove kernels as instructed on page 378. Pack into containers, leaving a 1/2-inch (1 cm) headspace. Remove air, label and seal. Freeze for up to 9 months.

Garlic

OFTEN THOUGHT OF ONLY AS A HERB OR A SEASONING, garlic is a member of the lily family, which also includes onions, shallots, chives and leeks.

Garlic (*Allium sativum*) can be hot and pungent when eaten raw, but when roasted, it morphs into a sweet and meltingly tender pulpy mass with a mellow flavour. All parts of the plant—bulb, tender green spring shoots and scapes (the long, green and twisted seed heads)—are eaten.

Good Preserving Varieties

There are two subspecies of garlic: hard-neck and soft-neck. All garlic varieties fall into one or the other subspecies. Unlike most other fruits and vegetables, garlic come in only five varieties: **Rocambole**, **Porcelain** and **Purple Stripe** (hard-neck); **Artichoke** and **Silverskin** (soft-neck). Of course, there are hundreds of sub-varieties.

Hard-Neck Garlic

Hard-neck varieties are easy to peel and more pungent, but the cloves are usually smaller. Hard-neck garlic does not store as well as soft-neck garlic.

Spanish Roja (left) and German Red (right) are Rocambole varieties.

Romanian Red (above) is a Porcelain variety. It has larger and fewer cloves per bulb.

Chesnok Red (above) is a Purple Stripe variety with red or purple markings.

Soft-Neck Garlic

The soft-neck garlic is milder in flavour and tends to be larger, has more cloves and keeps longer. It is likely to be the type that is available fresh in the new year, up until about late February. After that, depending on your location, the only fresh garlic available will be imported. Some Soft-Neck Garlic sub-varieties are **Inchelium Red**, **California Early and Late**, **Chet's Italian Red** and **Susanville** (Artichoke variety); and **Mild French**, **Silver White** and **Nootka Rose** (Silverskin variety).

Purchasing/Storing

1 lb (500 g) yields about 2 cups (500 mL) chopped garlic.

Choose firm, plump bulbs that are heavy for their size. Skins should be clean, dry and unbroken. Avoid bulbs that are sprouting. Store garlic in a ventilated container in a cool, dry place, not in the refrigerator. If stored properly, soft-neck garlic should keep for up to 6 months, but garlic should be preserved as soon as possible after harvesting.

Good With

- Herbs such as basil, oregano, marjoram, summer savory, bay, thyme, rosemary.
- Roasted garlic with cinnamon, ginger, cloves, nutmeg.
- Other Alliums, such as onions, leeks, shallots.
- Other vegetables, such as asparagus, fresh and dried beans, artichokes, tomatoes, eggplant, to name a few.

Preparation

For preserving raw garlic, peel and blanch whole cloves in boiling water for 1 minute. Immerse in cold water for 1 minute. Drain and pat dry. Leave whole for canning in syrup, or slice or chop for freezing.

Essential: Garlic's close contact with soil may expose it to dangerous bacteria. Garlic preserved in oil has been a popular item but cannot safely be made with home canning methods because temperatures in home pressure canners cannot achieve the high temperatures sufficient to kill the toxic spores that may be on the raw garlic. Oil is the perfect incubator for those spores.

To Roast Garlic:

Preheat oven to 400°F (200°C). Cut a 1/4-inch (5 mm) slice off the tops of the cloves in a whole head of garlic. Place, root end down, on a large square of foil or in a baking pan. Drizzle 2 tsp (10 mL) olive oil over the top of the cloves. Fold the foil into a package around the garlic head or cover the pan with foil. Bake in preheated oven for 1 hour or until cloves are soft. Let cool. Squeeze caramelized cloves out of their skin.

Canning Garlic

For centuries, herbalists have made what was known as a "rob" from plant juice and sugar—essentially infused syrup. The sugar in the syrup acted as a preservative and carrier for the medicinal components of garlic and other herbs. In the Middle Ages, garlic and elderberries were common medicinal preparations that were used to treat a wide range of health problems, especially throat and chest ailments.

1. Prepare Equipment: Wash and heat 1-cup (250 mL) or pint (2-cup/500 mL) jars, and scald the lids, funnel, ladle and tongs (see page 18).

2. Make a Medium Syrup: In a large saucepan, combine 2 cups (500 mL) granulated sugar with 4 cups (1 L) water; stir until dissolved. Bring to a rolling boil over high heat. Makes 5 cups (1.25 L) syrup, enough for 6 cups (1.5 L) whole peeled garlic.

3. Pack peeled whole garlic into jars hot.
Make a Hot Pack: Add 6 cups (1.5 L) whole peeled garlic to boiling syrup. Return to a boil and boil for 3 minutes. Remove pan from the heat and fill hot jars with hot garlic one at a time, shaking the jar to pack tightly. Add hot syrup, leaving a 1/2-inch (1 cm) headspace. Run a thin non-metallic utensil around the inside of the jar to allow air to escape. Add more hot syrup, if necessary, to leave a 1/2-inch (1 cm) headspace. Wipe sealing edge of jars with a clean, damp, lint-free cloth. Position flat lids over the tops of jars and hand-tighten screw bands.

4. Process garlic in a canner: Use a Boiling Water Canner according to the chart below.

Processing Times at Different Altitudes for Garlic in a BOILING WATER Canner					
Pack Style	**Jar Size**	**0–2000 ft**	**2001–4000 ft**	**4001–6000 ft**	**6001+ ft**
HOT	Pints	15 min	20 min	25 min	30 min
	Quarts	20 min	25 min	30 min	35 min
RAW	Pints	20 min	25 min	30 min	35 min
	Quarts	25 min	30 min	35 min	40 min

OR

Process garlic in a Pressure Canner following manufacturer's directions for steam pressure and time at your altitude.

5. Cool, Label and Store: Lift jars from canner and place on a clean towel or rack. Do not re-tighten screw bands. Let the jars cool to room temperature. This may take from 12 to 24 hours. Remove and store screw bands. Check lid seals (see page 19). Wipe and label sealed jars. Store in a cool, dark place.

garlic, onion and cherry chutney

If you are looking for a very different preserve, this is it. Using dried cherries in chutney is unusual, and if you have fresh, you can use them in this recipe as long as you reduce the amount of water. Look for the smallest pickling onions you can find. Follow the directions for peeling onions, page 398, for both the onions and garlic.

MAKES ABOUT 8 CUPS (2 L)

3 cups (750 mL) garlic cloves
3 cups (750 mL) red or white pearl or pickling
   onions
juice of 2 large lemons
2 cups (500 mL) dried cherries
3 pears, cut into 1/4-inch (5 mm) dice, divided
1-1/4 cups (300 mL) red wine vinegar
1-1/2 cups (375 mL) granulated sugar

1 tsp (5 mL) pickling salt
2 tbsp (25 mL) Classic Pickling Spice Blend
   (page 213 or store-bought), tied in a
   cheesecloth bag
1-1/2 cups (375 mL) water

1. In a Maslin pan or canning kettle, combine garlic, pearl onions, lemon juice, cherries, half of the pears, vinegar, sugar, salt, spice bag and water. Bring to a boil over high heat, stirring constantly. Reduce heat to medium-low and simmer for about 45 minutes or until most of the liquid has been absorbed and the onions and garlic are tender.

2. Meanwhile, heat four 1-pint (2-cup/500 mL) jars in boiling water, and scald the lids, lifter, funnel and tongs (see page 18).

3. Stir in remaining pears. Reduce heat to low and cook for about 5 minutes, just until pears are slightly soft but still holding their shape.

4. Skim off and discard any foam. Fill hot jars, leaving a 1/2-inch (1 cm) headspace. Run a thin non-metallic utensil around the inside of the jar to allow air to escape. Add chutney, if necessary, to leave a 1/2-inch (1 cm) headspace. Wipe rims, top with flat lids and screw on metal rings. Return jars to the hot water bath, topping up with hot water if necessary. Bring to a full rolling boil and process jars for 15 minutes (see page 19).

5. Remove canner lid and wait 5 minutes before removing jars to a towel or rack to cool completely. Check seals, label and store in a cool place for up to 1 year.

Use: The tartness of the cherries makes this chutney ideal for serving with rich foods such as pâté, pork sausages and duck. I also serve it with roast turkey as a change from cranberry sauce.

roasted garlic and artichoke spread

I call this robust Mediterranean combo a spread, but it is much more than a cocktail spread to be brought out only for canapés and hors d'oeuvres. Use it as an impromptu sauce for steamed vegetables, a substitute for mayonnaise, a dip for raw vegetables, or tossed with rice or whole wheat bread crumbs for a healthy stuffing. Once thawed, it keeps in the refrigerator, tightly covered, for up to 1 week.

MAKES 6 CUPS (1.5 L)

6 heads garlic, roasted (see page 389)
4 cups (1 L) cooked or canned artichokes, drained
4 tbsp (50 mL) chopped fresh rosemary
1-1/4 cups (300 mL) olive oil
sea salt and freshly ground pepper

1. Squeeze the soft caramelized garlic flesh out of the skins into the bowl of a blender or food processor. Add artichokes and rosemary. Blend on high, adding olive oil through opening in the lid, until soft and creamy. Season to taste with salt and pepper.

2. Pack into freezer containers in 1-cup (250 mL) measures, leaving a 1-inch (2.5 cm) headspace. Remove air, label and seal. Freeze for up to 9 months.

gremolata

Use a thick-skinned lemon variety like Eureka or Bearss for this lemony garlic garnish. Since you will likely only be using 1 or 2 tbsp (15 or 25 mL) at a time, you could easily work out how much to make for a year's supply. I have given the amounts required to make 1 cup (250 mL), but this recipe may easily be increased to produce larger amounts. Freeze in ice cube trays for 1 tbsp (15 mL) amounts or in 1/4- or 1/2-cup (50 or 125 mL) amounts.

MAKES 1 CUP (250 ML)

1/2 cup (125 mL) finely chopped fresh parsley
1/3 cup (75 mL) finely chopped garlic
1/4 cup (50 mL) grated lemon rind
1 or 2 tbsp (15 or 25 mL) olive oil

1. In a bowl, combine parsley, garlic and lemon rind. Drizzle olive oil over top, 1 tsp (5 mL) at a time, mixing and adding more oil just until the mixture holds together.

2. Fill ice cube trays or 1/4- or 1/2-cup (50 or 125 or mL) freezer containers to within 1/2 inch (1 cm) of the top. Squeeze out air; leave 1/2-inch (1 cm) headspace. Seal, label and freeze.

Use: You can add frozen Gremolata by the tablespoon (15 mL) to sauces, soups and stews as they cook. Thaw and distribute liberally over cooked vegetables, especially fried potatoes, and poached fish or poultry. Gremolata perks up scrambled eggs, savoury custards and quiche dishes.

Freezing Garlic

1. **Select Equipment:** Select suitable-size freezer containers, bags or Mason jars (see page 24).

2. **Blanch garlic as directed on page 388.** Slice or chop, then spoon into ice cube trays or 1/4- to 1/3 cup (50 to 75 mL) containers, leaving a 1-inch (2.5 cm) headspace. Remove air, label and seal. Freeze for up to 6 months.

Onions

THE COMMON ONION IS A SINGLE BULB that belongs to the lily family and grows underground. With a long history of use and many varieties, onions (*Allium cepa*) are used in almost every country in the world. It could be argued that onion and garlic, with their characteristic smell and flavour due to sulphur compounds, are indispensable vegetable flavourings.

Good Preserving Varieties

The hundreds of varieties of onions can be classified into two general categories: sweet and storage. The sweet types are mild, sweet and tender, and are usually eaten raw or lightly cooked. The storage types are more pungent and flavourful, with less water content, and are perfect for preserving.

Sweet Types: Best eaten raw, they contain more water, which makes them poor varieties for preserving. Some sweet varieties: **Vidalia** (aka Granax), **Texas 1015**, **Walla Walla**, **Oso Sweet** (up to 50% sweeter than Vidalia), **Maui Sweets**.

Storage Types:
Bermuda: Generally sweet and mild; available in the spring; fine for preserving. Some Bermuda varieties: **Yellow Bermuda**, **White Bermuda**, **Red Bermuda**.
Pearl: Also called pickling onions, they are sweet and mild, and the perfect size for pickle recipes; available late summer, early fall. Some Pearl varieties: **Crystal Wax**, **Barletta**, **Eclipse**.

Shallot: Small, hot and garlic-tasting onions with brown papery skins; often used in preserving. There are several varieties of shallot, red and yellow among them.

Spanish: Large, slightly sweet onions; good preserving varieties; available September to April. Some Spanish varieties: Red, Candy, Super Star.

White: Clean, tangy flavour, good preserving varieties, often used in salsa recipes.

Green onions (also called spring onions) are small, immature onions that have been harvested before they mature. There are various varieties, usually white or yellow; sometimes red onions are pulled early. Usually eaten fresh, cooked or raw.

Red: Sweet enough to eat raw; some varieties are classed as Sweet Types, some are more pungent than others; available March to June. Red varieties include **Italian Onion, Italian Red Onion, Burgundy, Creole Onion, Red Torpedo Onion**; good for preserving.

Yellow: Common; often called cooking onions, these varieties are high in sulphur compounds and deliver a complex onion flavour that caramelizes on long slow cooking to become mild and sweet. Some Yellow varieties: **Buffalo, Early Yellow Globe**.

Purchasing/Storing

1 lb (500 g) yields 2 cups (500 mL) chopped onion.

Choose onions that are firm and dry with a mild odour. The skins should have a shiny appearance and a papery, dry crackly feel. Onions should not be wet or show signs of sprouting or have any soft spots, which are a sign of rotting. Dark patches on the onions may indicate mould. For preserving, it is best to buy onions from farm gates and farmer's markets at harvest time. If purchasing onions that are sold in a bag, be sure to check all the onions for rotting, sprouting or bad spots.

Good With

- Culinary herbs such as chives, parsley, sage, rosemary, basil, bay, thyme, chervil, tarragon.
- Spices such as cinnamon, ginger, cloves, nutmeg, curry blends, cumin, coriander, cardamom, caraway, mustard, turmeric.
- Most other vegetables and some fruit, such as apples and pears.

Preparation

Pearl Onions: Rub the loose skin off onions. Blanch in boiling water for 1 minute. Immerse in cold water for 1 minute. Drain and pat dry. Slip off peels.

Canning Onions

Due to the year-round availability of fresh onions and their superior quality in cooking, I don't recommend canning them. However, onions are key ingredients in chutney, pickles, confit and even marmalade (see Roasted Onion and Garlic Marmalade, page 400).

curried onions

The curry is mild in this pickle. For a stronger curry taste, grind the Curry Pickling Spice fine and add it to the pan without using cheesecloth. I toss about 1/2 cup (125 mL) or more with roasted vegetables or steamed cauliflower. They can also be added to stir-fried vegetable or meat dishes. The small pearl onions are best in this pickle.

MAKES 12 CUPS (3 L)

3 lb (1.5 kg) pickling onions (about 10 cups/2.5 L)
4 cups (1 L) hot water
1/4 cup (50 mL) pickling salt
2 green bell peppers

3 cups (750 mL) white wine vinegar
1/2 cup (125 mL) granulated sugar
1 tbsp (15 mL) Curry Pickling Spice Blend (page 214 or store-bought), tied in a cheesecloth bag

First Day

Peel onions following instructions on page 398. Trim the roots close to the base but leave the hard core intact so that the onions do not break apart during cooking. Place in a large crock or glass bowl. In a jug, combine water and salt. Stir to dissolve salt. Pour brine over onions. Cover and let stand at room temperature for 2 days.

Third Day

1. In a large colander or in batches, drain onions, discarding brine. Rinse well, drain and pat dry. Cut peppers into 1/4-inch (5 mm) crosswise rings or lengthwise strips. Set aside.

2. Heat six 1-pint (2-cup/500 mL) jars in boiling water, and scald the lids, lifter, funnel and tongs (see page 18).

3. In a Maslin pan or canning kettle, combine vinegar, sugar and spice bag. Bring to a boil over medium-high heat, stirring constantly. Add onions and green pepper and boil for 1 minute.

4. Fill hot jars with onions and several green pepper rings or slices, leaving a 1/2-inch (1 cm) head-space. Run a thin non-metallic utensil around the inside of the jar to allow air to escape. Add hot liquid, if necessary, to leave a 1/2-inch (1 cm) headspace. Wipe rims, top with flat lids and screw on metal rings. Return jars to the hot water bath, topping up with hot water if necessary. Bring to a full rolling boil and process jars for 20 minutes (see page 19).

5. Remove canner lid and wait 5 minutes before removing jars to a towel or rack to cool completely. Check seals, label and store in a cool place for up to 1 year.

Use: I serve these with all sorts of different dinners. They complement enchiladas and other Mexican entrées, as well as Chinese and Indian foods.

roasted onion and garlic marmalade

With some slight adjustments to three of the ingredients, you can make a golden or a dark burgundy version of this delicately pear-flavoured marmalade. I like both and find the golden marmalade slightly more delicate in taste, so I use it with fruit, chicken and fish dishes. The heartier dark marmalade is rich and complex enough for red meats, vegetable dishes and game. I have listed the ingredients for the golden version first; those for the burgundy version follow in brackets.

MAKES 6 CUPS (1.5 L)

4 lb (2 kg) yellow cooking onions, about 10 medium (red onions, 4 or 5 large)

12 large cloves garlic

4 tbsp (50 mL) olive oil

3 tbsp (45 mL) butter

6 pears

1 cup (250 mL) granulated sugar (lightly packed brown sugar)

1 cup (250 mL) dry white wine (red wine)

1 cup (250 mL) white wine vinegar (red wine vinegar)

2 cinnamon sticks, each 2 inches (5 cm)

1. Cut the onions in half. If you have a food processor or stand mixer attachment, use the 1/8-inch (2 mm) blade to thinly slice the onions and the garlic. Or slice by hand. Set aside.

2. In a Maslin pan or heavy-bottomed saucepan, heat olive oil and butter over medium-high heat. Add onions and garlic and stir well to coat. Core and thinly slice pears by hand, one at a time, into the pan.

3. Sprinkle the sugar over top and stir until dissolved. Boil lightly, uncovered, for 40 to 50 minutes, stirring frequently. Reduce heat if the mixture begins to scorch or stick. The onions are cooked when all their juices have evaporated and they are soft and sticky.

4. Meanwhile, heat six 1-cup (250 mL) jars in boiling water, and scald the lids, lifter, funnel and tongs (see page 18).

5. Add wine, vinegar and cinnamon sticks. Bring to a light boil and keep simmering, stirring frequently, until the onions are either a golden or a dark mahogany colour and the liquid has reduced by over half. The marmalade is done when a wooden spoon drawn across the bottom of the pan leaves a path that fills in rapidly with thick syrupy juice.

6. Fill hot jars, leaving a 1/4-inch (5 mm) headspace. Run a thin non-metallic utensil around the inside of the jar to allow air to escape. Add more hot marmalade, if necessary, to leave a 1/4-inch (5 mm) headspace. Wipe rims, top with flat lids and screw on metal rings. Return jars to the hot water bath,

topping up with hot water if necessary. Bring to a full rolling boil and process jars for 15 minutes (see page 19).

7. Remove canner lid and wait 5 minutes before removing jars to a towel or rack to cool completely. Check seals, label and store in a cool place for up to 1 year.

Use: This soft and spreadable sweet-savoury confection is delicious with liver pâté and terrines, or with duck, goose, pork or sausages. It complements roasted chicken and vegetables. I often serve individual pots of it with a cheese and fruit plate after a meal. It can be brought out at breakfast or served with egg puddings and frittatas.

onion and fennel soup

Of all the soups you might make ahead and freeze, I think this is the most versatile. Freezing softens the texture and mellows the flavours. I find that I turn to this as a base and use it as a stock for other soup recipes. Of course, when I want to make French onion soup, all I need do is thaw, top with garlic toasts and lots of shredded mozzarella and Parmesan cheese, and heat in the oven for a hearty lunch or light dinner.

MAKES 12 CUPS (3 L)

4 tbsp (50 mL) olive oil, divided
2 cups (500 mL) chopped fennel bulb
6 large yellow or white onions, chopped
4 cloves garlic, chopped

5 cups (1.25 L) chicken broth
1 cup (250 mL) dry white wine
2 tbsp (25 mL) balsamic vinegar
sea salt and freshly ground pepper

1. In a Maslin pan or canning kettle, heat 2 tbsp (25 mL) of the olive oil over medium heat. Add fennel and cook, stirring, for a minute to soften slightly. Add onions and garlic and reduce heat to low. Cook, stirring frequently, for 15 to 20 minutes, adding more oil as needed to keep the vegetables from sticking to the bottom of the pan.

2. Add chicken broth, wine and balsamic vinegar. Increase heat and bring to a boil, stirring frequently. Lower heat to medium, cover the pot and cook for 7 to 10 minutes, stirring occasionally. Season to taste with salt and pepper. Let cool.

3. Pack into quart (1 L) containers, leaving a 1-inch (2.5 cm) headspace. Remove air, label and seal. Freeze for up to 9 months.

Freezing Onions

Because of the year-round availability of fresh onions and their superior quality in cooking, I do not recommend freezing them. However, onions can be the key ingredients in frozen dishes such as soups. Use dry storage-type onions for recipes that will be frozen.

Parsnips

AS ALL MARKET GARDENERS KNOW, the very best time to preserve and cook with parsnips (*Pastinaca sativa*) is in the fall, after several weeks of frost, because the starch in the root is changed into sugar, making them sweet and delicious. Once a vegetable of the very poor in Europe, tapered root varieties cultivated in North America are sweet with smooth, light skin and white flesh.

Good Preserving Varieties

Some parsnip varieties (e.g., **White Gem**) are short and stubby and not as easy to use whole for pickles, but they do slice easily into matchsticks. Examples of long, slender, fine-skinned varieties are:

Gladiator: Long, tapering; white skin and flesh.
Hollow Crown: Long and tapered; relatively free of hair-like side roots.
Lancer: A hardy variety with sweet, smooth-skinned, uniform colour; very slender, which makes them excellent for pickles.
Tender and True: Long, smooth-skinned roots; traditional yellow-white.

Purchasing/Storing

- 1 lb (500 g) yields 2 cups (500 mL) chopped parsnips.
- You will need 1-1/2 lb (750 g) for each 1-quart (1 L) jar.

Select small, thin, smooth parsnips without blemishes. It is best if the tops are intact. Avoid large, woody roots because they will be tough and tasteless. You can store parsnips unwashed, with tops removed, for up to 3 weeks, but it is best to preserve them as soon as possible after harvesting.

Good With

- Herbs such as parsley, basil, bay, thyme, sage, chervil, dill, chives.
- Sweet seasonings such as cinnamon, ginger, cloves, nutmeg, mace, cumin, coriander, curry blends.
- Other vegetables, such as garlic, onions, carrots, rutabaga, turnips, cabbage, peas, tomatoes.
- Dried fruit such as raisins, currants, apricots.
- Meat and vegetable soups and stews, giving them a sweet note.

Preparation

Immerse parsnips in a basin of cool water to which a drop of food-safe soap has been added. Scrub, rinse and drain. Pat dry. Blanch whole or cut parsnips in boiling water for 3 to 5 minutes. Lift out and plunge into cold water. Let stand for 3 to 5 minutes. Drain and pat dry. Shred, slice or dice parsnips or cut into uniform sticks.

Canning Parsnips

Canning tends to turn parsnips bitter, so pickles, jam or marmalades are best, along with freezing blanched or puréed parsnips.

Freezing Parsnips

1. **Select Equipment:** Select suitable-size freezer containers, bags or Mason jars (see page 24).

2. **Blanch and cut parsnips as directed above.** Pack into containers, leaving a 1-inch (2.5 cm) headspace. Remove air, label and seal. Freeze for up to 9 months.

cinnamon-scented parsnip pear jam

The cinnamon complements the sweetness of the parsnips in this quick jam, and the pear adds dimension. You can have this cooling in the jars in less than 1-1/2 hours, and no one will guess that you made it with parsnips. If you want to make this for your family because you like the thought of serving parsnips in a completely different way (one that doesn't involve turned-up noses), but if the thought of all that sugar is daunting, you can use "no sugar" pectin. My advice would be to use a small amount of sugar (follow the instructions with the package) rather than an artificial sweetener.

MAKES 8 CUPS (2 L)

2 cups (500 mL) chopped blanched parsnips
2 cups (500 mL) chopped ripe pears
1/3 cup (75 mL) freshly squeezed lemon juice
8 cups (2 L) granulated sugar

1 tsp (5 mL) ground cinnamon
1 pouch (3 oz/85 mL) liquid pectin
8 cinnamon stick pieces, each 1 inch (2.5 cm),
 optional

1. Heat eight 1-cup (250 mL) jars in boiling water, and scald the lids, lifter, funnel and tongs (see page 18).

2. In a Maslin pan or canning kettle, combine parsnips, pears, lemon juice, sugar and cinnamon. Bring to a full rolling boil over high heat, stirring constantly. Stir in pectin. Boil hard, stirring constantly for 1 minute.

3. Skim off and discard any foam. Fill hot jars to the halfway point with the hot jam. Slide a cinnamon stick down the side of the jar, if using. Fill jar, leaving a 1/4-inch (5 mm) headspace. Run a thin non-metallic utensil around the inside of the jar to allow air to escape. Add jam, if necessary, to leave a 1/4-inch (5 mm) headspace. Wipe rims, top with flat lids and screw on metal rings. Return jars to the hot water bath, topping up with hot water if necessary. Bring to a full rolling boil and process jars for 10 minutes (see page 19).

4. Remove canner lid and wait 5 minutes before removing jars to a towel or rack to cool completely. Check seals, label and store in a cool place for up to 1 year.

Use: I like to thin this jam with a little orange juice and use it as a glaze for carrots and even for braised or steamed parsnips. The low-sugar version makes a good condiment for cheese platters and meat dishes.

frozen moroccan parsnip purée

I think the idea of vegetable purée is so sophisticated—they are popular in upscale restaurants—and yet they are so simple. With this lightly sweetened and spiced purée in the freezer, I always have a quick side dish or tasty bed for lamb shanks, beef stew or poached fish.

MAKES 8 CUPS (2 L)

8 to 10 medium parsnips (2 lb/1 kg)
2 tbsp (25 mL) olive oil
1 onion, coarsely chopped
4 cloves garlic, minced

1 tbsp (15 mL) Five-Spice Blend (page 216 or store-bought), ground
1/2 tsp (2 mL) salt
3 cups (750 mL) chicken or vegetable stock, divided (approx)

1. Blanch the parsnips as directed on page 406. Shred or chop parsnips and set aside. In a Maslin pan or heavy-bottomed saucepan, heat olive oil over medium heat. Reduce heat to medium-low. Add onions and cook, stirring frequently, for 5 or 6 minutes or until soft and slightly translucent. Add garlic and cook, stirring constantly, for 1 minute. Add parsnips, Five-Spice Blend and salt. Cook and stir for 1 minute to lightly coat in oil and spices.

2. Add enough stock to cover the vegetables (the amount depends on the depth of your pot). Cover and bring to a light boil. Reduce heat and simmer gently for 10 to 15 minutes, stirring occasionally. Add more stock to the pot if necessary to keep vegetables from scorching. Vegetables should be soft.

3. Let vegetables cool. Using a food processor or blender, purée in batches, adding stock to the food processor as needed to blend to a soft consistency. Measure 2- or 4-cup (500 mL or 1 L) amounts and pack into freezer containers, leaving a 1/2-inch (1 cm) headspace. Remove air, label and seal. Freeze for up to 9 months.

Use: This purée is brilliant! Not only is it a stand-alone vegetable dish, but it can be added to soup or stew. Be sure to freeze some in 1- or 2-cup (250 or 500 mL) amounts to make it easy to use in other dishes. Add 1 cup (250 mL) thawed Parsnip Purée to risotto for a creamy result. A recipe for using this amazing purée in soup follows.

moroccan parsnip soup

Having frozen cooked and spiced parsnip purée makes this soup easy, convenient and delicious. I serve it with lavash or pita points. If pomegranates are in season, they make a beautiful garnish, along with the homemade Pomegranate Pepper Jelly. I like mango, apple or peach chutney with it as well.

MAKES 8 CUPS (2 L)

4 cups (1 L) Moroccan Parsnip Purée
  (page 408), thawed
1 pint (2 cups/500 mL) or 1 can (14 oz/398 mL)
  crushed tomatoes with juices
1 cup (250 mL) chicken or vegetable broth
1 can (14 oz/398 mL) lentils or chickpeas,
  drained and rinsed

1/2 tsp (2 mL) ground nutmeg
sea salt and freshly ground pepper
1/2 cup (125 mL) Pomegranate Pepper Jelly
  (page 488 or store-bought), optional
1/2 cup (125 mL) pomegranate seeds, optional

In a saucepan, combine Parsnip Purée, tomatoes and juices, chicken broth, chickpeas and nutmeg. Bring to a simmer over high heat, stirring frequently. Taste and add salt and pepper as needed. Garnish with pomegranate jelly and seeds, if using.

Peppers

THE WHOLE PEPPER FAMILY (*CAPSICUM*) of sweet and hot fleshy pods is fascinating and complicated at the same time. Most popular for preserves and pickling mixtures are the sweet green, red, yellow or orange bell peppers (*Capsicum annuum*), which are large and thick fleshed, with a sweet, crisp taste. A variety of sweet bell peppers are on display at the San Francisco Ferry Building Farmers Market, left.

Chile peppers, while still of the *Capsicum* genus, may be sweet or hot and are native to Mexico and tropical America. Both sweet and hot chile peppers are preserved in salsa and jelly or pickled whole. There are many cultivars of chile peppers available, and many are sold under a confusing variety of names. Hot chile peppers are rated for their degree of heat by the amount of the capsaicin they contain.

Some hot chiles are pickled on their own or with other vegetables, and some are used in sweet herb and fruit jellies and other preserves.

Colour is not so much an indication of the cultivar as it is of maturity. Most bell peppers mature green to red, although some hybrids mature yellow, orange and even purple or chocolate colour. Here (left) we see one pepper beginning to ripen red in the basket full of green bell peppers.

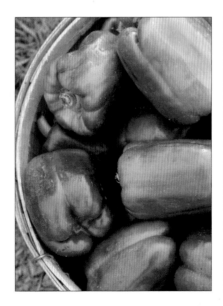

Good Preserving Varieties

The big question in deciding what variety of pepper to use in preserves is this: do you want sweet or heat? The following is a short list of some sweet pepper cultivars.

Sweet Peppers

Godfather Hybrid: A classic Italian pepper that is excellent for grilling and roasting because of its flat, elongated shape, which also makes it good for pickling.

Chocolate Belle: A hybrid tiny sweet bell pepper that is the colour of chocolate. The colour does fade when pickled, but the size makes it a good pickling choice.

Golden Baby Belle: A bright yellow, sweet little bell pepper that is perfect for stuffed hors d'oeuvres. The size and colour are ideal for pickling.

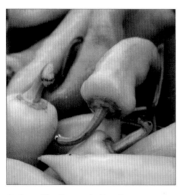

Cubanelle: Sweet Italian banana-type pepper with superb flavour; thick skinned and good for grilling; for sweet pickles and other preserves where heat is not desire.

Biscayne Sweet: Ripens from light yellow-green to red (above, we see all three stages of ripening); excellent for grilling, pickling and preserving.

Carmen Sweet: Delicious sweet taste when ripe red; excellent for roasting, grilling, canning and for red pepper sauce.

Orange Grande: A sweet bell pepper that matures to a glossy bright orange.

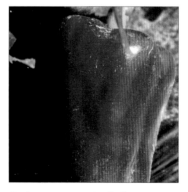

Redstart: Most sweet bell peppers are picked when green, those that are left on the plant to mature to red being more expensive. This cultivar ripens to red early, giving it the advantage over most sweet bell peppers.

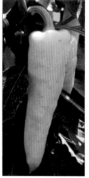

Superette Sweet (left) and **Sweet Savannah** (right) are two sweet banana-type peppers that have been developed by Stokes to grow to a size that fits canning jars.

Purchasing/Storing

- 1 large bell pepper yields 1-1/4 cups (300 mL) chopped.
- You will need about 8 large banana chile peppers for 1 quart (1 L).

Select firm, plump fruits with clear, bright skin. There should be no touch of damage or bruising.

Good With

- Spicy herbs such as rosemary, basil, bay, thyme, chervil, tarragon.
- Cinnamon, ginger, cloves, nutmeg (hot chiles).
- Other vegetables, such as onions, potatoes, leeks, garlic, tomatoes, fennel.
- Cucumber and yogurt, which can be cooling for dishes containing hot chile peppers.
- Peaches, pears, plums, raisins.
- Chocolate.

Preparation

Wash peppers in a sink full of cool water to which a drop of food-safe soap has been added. Rinse well, drain and pat dry. Roast peppers for canning.

Essential: Use Gloves When Handling Hot Chiles

The active components that give chiles their heat are the capsaicinoids. These irritating elements transfer easily from the chiles to your hands, the basket or harvest container, the knife and the cutting surface—anything that they come in contact with. To avoid painful burning of your eyes, lips and other mucus areas, use disposable gloves to harvest and prepare hot chiles for recipes and don't touch your face.

In their *Big Book of Herbs* (see Resources), Arthur Tucker and Thomas DeBaggio recommend that if you get capsaicin on your hands, you should wash with a small amount of chlorine bleach or ammonia because these household products change the irritants into water-soluble salts. Capsaicin is also alcohol soluble, so for burning in the mouth, "cheap vodka makes a good mouthwash."

Tucker and DeBaggio go on to clear up the misinformation about what parts of the chile pepper are hottest. Some sources claim that the seeds are the hottest part, but that is not quite the case. As Tucker and DeBaggio note, "The pure seeds themselves contain none or up to 10 percent of the total capsaicinoids; the heat on the seeds primarily arises from contamination from the placenta." According to these experts, it is the thin membrane (the placenta) on the inside of the chile pepper that holds the highest concentration of the fiery elements, and anything that touches this heat centre will be tainted with the heat from the capsaicinoid essences.

To Roast Bell, Sweet and Chile Peppers

Roasting peppers not only provides an easy method of peeling peppers, it intensifies their nutty flavours, caramelizes their sugars and makes them soft and tender. Choose thick-walled fresh peppers for roasting. Roasted peppers can be canned or frozen to preserve them for future use.

1. Wash and dry peppers. If roasting bell peppers, cut in half lengthwise and remove stem, membrane and seeds. If using chile peppers, leave whole with stem intact. Arrange on a lightly oiled rimmed baking sheet, cut side down. Brush lightly or drizzle with olive oil.

2. Roast on the top rack in an oven set to broil (or 500°F/260°C) for 10 to 12 minutes or until skins blacken and blister. You will need to turn whole chile peppers once or twice during roasting.

3. Cover with a clean kitchen towel or place in a paper bag and let cool. If you are planning to freeze the roasted peppers, cool and seal in a freezer bag without removing the skin, which will slip off easily upon thawing. Skin should rub away or pull off easily. Cut off stem end of chile peppers and remove seeds, if desired, but leave chile peppers whole. Slice bell peppers, quarter or leave halved.

Canning Bell Peppers

Bell peppers lose their snappy texture and flavour and become soft and unappealing when canned. For this reason and since they are available fresh year-round, I do not recommend canning them.

Canning Chile Peppers

See detailed canning information, page 20.

1. **Roast and peel whole chiles as directed above.** You will need about 8 large banana chile peppers for 1 quart (1 L).

2. **Prepare Equipment:** Wash and heat pint (2-cup/500 mL) or quart (1 L) jars, and scald the lids, funnel, ladle and tongs (see page 22).

3. **In a Maslin pan or canning kettle, bring 6 to 8 cups (1.5 to 2 L) water to a boil over high heat.**

4. **Make a Hot Pack:** Loosely pack peeled chiles into 1 hot jar at a time. For pints (2 cups/500 mL), add 1-1/2 tsp (7 mL) vinegar and 1/4 tsp (1 mL) salt. For quarts (1 L), add 1 tbsp

(15 mL) vinegar and 1/2 tsp (2 mL) salt. Pour boiling water over chiles, leaving a 1-inch (2.5 cm) headspace. Run a thin non-metallic utensil around the inside of the jar to allow air to escape. Add boiling water, if necessary, to leave a 1-inch (2.5 cm) headspace. Wipe sealing edge of jars with a clean, damp, lint-free cloth. Position flat lids over the tops of jars and hand-tighten screw bands.

5. Place jars in pressure canner: Use a Pressure Canner according to the chart below for Dial-Gauge or follow manufacturer's instructions.

Processing Times at Different Altitudes for Peppers in a DIAL-GAUGE PRESSURE Canner					
Pack Style	Jar Size	0–2000 ft	2001–4000 ft	4001–6000 ft	6001+ ft
HOT	Pints	15 min	20 min	25 min	30 min
	Quarts	20 min	25 min	30 min	35 min
RAW	Pints	20 min	25 min	30 min	35 min
	Quarts	25 min	30 min	35 min	40 min

6. Cool, Label and Store: Turn off heat; let pressure return to zero naturally. Once gauge shows 0 pressure, wait 2 minutes then open the vent. Unlock and remove canner lid. Wait 10 minutes then lift jars from canner and place on a clean towel or rack. Do not re-tighten screw bands. Let the jars cool to room temperature. This may take from 12 to 24 hours. Remove and store screw bands. Check lid seals (see page 23). Wipe and label sealed jars. Store in a cool, dark place.

green giant chutney

You can use tomatoes that have not ripened and are still hard and green, or the variety of tomatoes that mature green if you have them. Green peppers and green beans combine to make this a unique and great-looking preserve. If the tomatoes are unripe, they may take longer than 1 minute in boiling water to shrink away from the skin, so test this before blanching a whole batch.

MAKES 10 CUPS (2.5 L)

5 lb (2.2 kg) green tomatoes
1 tbsp (15 mL) salt
3 lb (1.5 kg) green bell peppers
1 lb (500 g) green beans
3 tbsp (45 mL) olive oil
4 onions, thinly sliced
5 cloves garlic, finely chopped
3 cups (750 mL) white wine vinegar

1 cup (250 mL) packed brown sugar
1/2 cup (125 mL) granulated sugar
1 cup (250 mL) Thompson raisins
1 tbsp (15 mL) Five-Spice Blend (page 216 or
   store-bought), finely ground
5 bay leaves
5 hot green chile peppers, optional

1. Blanch tomatoes for 1 to 2 minutes. Using a slotted spoon, lift out of water, reserving water for peppers and beans. Immerse in cold water for 1 to 2 minutes. Peel and coarsely chop. In a bowl, toss chopped tomatoes with salt. Transfer to a colander and let drain for 2 hours.

2. Meanwhile, cut green peppers into 1/2-inch (1 cm) dice. Cut beans into 1/2-inch (1 cm) pieces. Bring the reserved water back to a boil and blanch the green peppers for 3 minutes. Using tongs or a slotted spoon, lift out and immerse in cold water for 3 minutes. Drain and pat dry. Bring the water back up to a boil and blanch the beans for 1 minute. Immerse in cold water for 1 minute. Drain and pat dry.

3. In a Maslin pan or canning kettle, heat the olive oil over medium-high heat. Add onions and cook for 5 minutes, stirring frequently. Add garlic and cook for 5 minutes, stirring frequently, until vegetables are soft. Add vinegar and bring to a boil. Stir in brown sugar and white sugar and bring back to a boil, stirring constantly.

4. Heat five 1-pint (2-cup/500 mL) jars in boiling water, and scald the lids, lifter, funnel and tongs (see page 18).

5. Meanwhile, rinse and thoroughly drain the tomatoes. Add tomatoes, green peppers, green beans, raisins and spice to the boiling mixture. Boil gently for 1 hour, stirring frequently, until thick.

6. Half fill a hot jar. Slide 1 bay leaf and 1 hot chile pepper, if using, down the side of the jar. Fill the

jar, leaving a 1/2-inch (1 cm) headspace. Run a thin non-metallic utensil around the inside of the jar to allow air to escape. Add chutney, if necessary, to leave a 1/2-inch (1 cm) headspace. Wipe rims, top with flat lids and screw on metal rings. Return jars to the hot water bath, topping up with hot water if necessary. Bring to a full rolling boil and process jars for 15 minutes (see page 19).

7. Remove canner lid and wait 5 minutes before removing jars to a towel or rack to cool completely. Check seals, label and store in a cool place for up to 1 year.

Use: This green chutney is perfect for serving on a Ploughman's Lunch dish of cold meats, cheddar cheese and homemade bread. It is substantial, the beans and peppers lending a solid presence, so it is very good with roasted meats.

roasted red pepper dip

Use freshly roasted peppers or peppers that you have roasted and frozen in 2-cup (500 mL) measures. This dip is delicious tossed with cooked pasta and rice, mixed into salads, or served with raw vegetables. I use it as a glaze for roasted or steamed vegetables.

MAKES 2 CUPS (500 ML)

2 cups (500 mL) roasted sliced red peppers (see page 414)
1/2 cup (125 mL) Basil Pesto (page 301)

In a bowl, combine roasted red pepper slices and pesto. Transfer to the bay of a food processor or blender, purée until smooth.

Freezing Bell and Chile Peppers

In my view, the very best way to freeze peppers is to roast them first (directions on page 414), but if you do not wish to roast them, here is the method.

1. **Select Equipment:** Select small freezer containers, bags or Mason jars (see page 24).

2. **Wash and dry peppers; do not blanch.** Cut bell peppers in half and remove membrane and seeds. Leave chile peppers whole (remove stem, membrane and seeds, if desired). Pack into containers, leaving a 1-inch (2.5 cm) headspace. Remove air, label and seal. Freeze for up to 9 months.

Pumpkin

PUMPKINS ARE GOURDS, which are native to the Western Hemisphere. Like their relatives—melons, cucumbers and squash—pumpkins grow on long trailing vines. Technically they are berries, which we use mostly as scary lanterns at Halloween, but sometimes as vegetables. Pumpkins (*Cucurbita pepo*) may be round or oblong, with thick or moderately thin walls. The thick-fleshed varieties are best for baking and preserving and are sometimes called pie pumpkins. Like squash, pumpkins are a good source of vitamins A and C.

Good Preserving Varieties

Traditional pumpkin varieties are bright orange, but some are white. When choosing pumpkins for preserving, keep in mind that carving pumpkins were bred for their fairly thin skins and strong stem. A short list of some of the most popular pumpkin varieties follows.

Autumn Gold: Medium in size; a newer hybrid that turns yellow quickly and matures to orange quickly.

Howden Field and **Connecticut Field:** Two large pumpkins grown for Halloween.

Baby Boo, Jack-Be-Little, Munchkin and **Sweetie Pie:** All miniature; often used as soup bowls and candleholders.

Small Sugar (also called New England Pie or **Sugar Pie):** is the standard baking pumpkin with thin skin and thick, sweet flesh; perhaps the best pumpkin for purée.

Purchasing/Storing

- 1 lb (500 g) pie pumpkin yields 4 cups (1 L) raw cubed pumpkin.
- 1 small (5 lb/2.2 kg) pumpkin yields about 4 cups (1 L) mashed, cooked pumpkin pulp.
- You will need less than 1 lb (500 g) pumpkin for each quart (1 L) jar.

Select heavy pumpkins with no touch of green, bruising, soft spots or mould. Press the bottom of the pumpkin: if it flexes or gives, it is not fresh. A green stem indicates a freshly harvested pumpkin.

Casper (above) **Lumina** and **Snowball** are white varieties (*Cucurbita maxima*).

Good With

- Herbs such as sage, chives, thyme, savory.
- Sweet seasonings such as cinnamon, ginger, cloves, nutmeg, mace.
- Other fruit, such as apples, pears.
- Vegetables such as onions, fennel, tomatoes, garlic.
- Toasted almonds, pecans and walnuts; raisins; brown sugar.

Preparation

Scrub in a sink full of cool water to which a drop of food-safe soap has been added. Rinse well, drain and pat dry. Using a large heavy knife, cut the pumpkin in half. Use a large spoon to scrape out seeds and stringy material. Save seeds for roasting with spices. Cut into wedges or large cubes. Unless you plan to cut pumpkin flesh into 1-inch (2.5 cm) or smaller cubes, it is easier to remove the skin after boiling, steaming or baking.

Canning Pumpkin

Cube only—do not shred or mash pumpkin for canning. See detailed canning information, page 20.

1. Prepare Equipment: Wash and heat pint (2-cup/500 mL or quart (1 L) jars, and scald the lids, funnel, ladle and tongs (see page 22).

2. Cut pumpkin quarters into 1-inch (2.5 cm) wide strips and peel. Cut strips into 1-inch (2.5 cm) cubes. In a Maslin pan or canning kettle, cover pumpkin with water. Bring to a boil and boil for 30 seconds. Work quickly to fill hot jars one at a time.

3. Pack cubed pumpkin into jars hot.
Make a Hot Pack: Using a slotted spoon, lift pumpkin out of hot water and fill hot jars. Pour hot water over cubes, leaving a 1-inch (2.5 cm) headspace. Run a thin non-metallic utensil around the inside of the jar to allow air to escape. Add hot water, if necessary, to leave a 1-inch (2.5 cm) headspace. Wipe sealing edge of jars with a clean, damp, lint-free cloth. Position flat lids over the tops of jars and hand-tighten screw bands.

4. Place jars in pressure canner: Use a Pressure Canner according to the chart below for Dial-Gauge or follow manufacturer's instructions.

Processing Times at Different Altitudes for Pumpkin in a DIAL-GAUGE PRESSURE Canner					
Pack Style	Jar Size	0–2000 ft	2001–4000 ft	4001–6000 ft	6001+ ft
HOT	Pints	15 min	20 min	25 min	30 min
	Quarts	20 min	25 min	30 min	35 min
RAW	Pints	20 min	25 min	30 min	35 min
	Quarts	25 min	30 min	35 min	40 min

5. Cool, Label and Store: Turn off heat; let pressure return to zero naturally. Once gauge shows 0 pressure, wait 2 minutes then open the vent. Unlock and remove canner lid. Wait 10 minutes then lift jars from canner and place on a clean towel or rack. Do not re-tighten screw bands. Let the jars cool to room temperature. This may take from 12 to 24 hours. Remove and store screw bands. Check lid seals (see page 23). Wipe and label sealed jars. Store in a cool, dark place.

pumpkin chutney

I always try to make this beautiful bright orange chutney in time for Halloween. In my view, the very best way to cook pumpkin and other gourds is to roast them. Roasting not only makes it easy to scoop the flesh away from the skin, but I like the caramelized sugars and nutty flavour that result.

If you want a soft, spreadable mixture, use pie pumpkins and roast just until tender-crisp. For chunky chutney, any of the firmer Halloween pumpkins will work. I like the jam-like texture from the baking or pie pumpkins. For the pumpkin cubes, cut pumpkin quarters into 1-inch (2.5 cm) wide strips and peel. Cut strips into 1-inch (2.5 cm) cubes.

13- x 9-inch (3 L) baking pan, lightly oiled
Preheat oven to 400°F (200°C)
MAKES 8 CUPS (2 L)

8 cups (2 L) pumpkin cubes (1 inch/2.5 cm), see above	**1/2 cup (125 mL) golden raisins**
2 tbsp (25 mL) olive oil	**1 cup (250 mL) lightly packed brown sugar**
grated rind and juice of 2 oranges, divided	**1/3 cup (75 mL) malt vinegar**
2 Golden Delicious apples, chopped	**1 tbsp (15 mL) Five-Spice Blend (page 216 or store-bought), ground**
1 onion, chopped	**1 tsp (5 mL) salt**

1. Arrange pumpkin cubes in single layer in prepared baking dish (use 2 lightly oiled pans if necessary). In a jar with tight-fitting lid, combine olive oil and 3 tbsp (45 mL) orange juice. Shake and drizzle over pumpkin. Bake in preheated oven for 40 minutes or until soft (see above).

2. Heat four 1-pint (2-cup/500 mL) jars in boiling water, and scald the lids, lifter, funnel and tongs (see page 18).

3. About 10 minutes before pumpkin is finished roasting, heat remaining ingredients: in a Maslin pan or canning kettle, combine remaining orange juice, orange rind, apples, onion, raisins, sugar, vinegar, spices and salt. Bring to a boil over high heat, stirring constantly. Add roasted pumpkin and any pan juices. Reduce heat and boil gently, stirring occasionally, for 20 minutes or until thick.

4. Fill hot jars, leaving a 1/2-inch (1 cm) headspace. Run a thin non-metallic utensil around the inside of the jar to allow air to escape. Add more chutney, if necessary, to leave a 1/2-inch (1 cm) headspace. Wipe rims, top with flat lids and screw on metal rings. Return jars to the hot water bath, topping up with hot water if necessary. Bring to a full rolling boil and process jars for 25 minutes (see page 19).

5. Remove canner lid and wait 5 minutes before removing jars to a towel or rack to cool completely. Check seals, label and store in a cool place for up to 1 year.

Use: I like this delicately spiced chutney with curries, rice dishes and to enliven baked chicken or fish. Spoon it over the meat in the last 10 minutes of baking to add the delicious flavour, then pass extra at the table. Use it as a spread for hors d'oeuvres.

three sisters enchiladas

Native North Americans referred to beans, corn and squash as the "three sisters" and always planted them together so that the beans grew up around the corn, using it as a stake, while the squash spread out along the ground and kept the soil relatively weed-free and moist. Using your homemade preserves and either canned or frozen vegetables in this recipe makes it fast food, but good. If you have preserved either the Pumpkin Chutney (page 424) or the Peaches and Cream Relish (page 381), you are in luck because I am offering two options for filling these delicious enchiladas. Try them both!

MAKES 12 ENCHILADAS

12 large (10-inch/24 cm) corn tortillas
2 tbsp (25 mL) olive oil, divided, optional

Filling 1
2 cups (500 mL) Pumpkin Chutney (page 424)
2 cups (500 mL) cooked lima or kidney beans, or 1 can (19 oz/540 mL), drained
1 cup (250 mL) fresh, frozen or canned corn kernels, drained

Filling 2
2 cups (500 mL) cooked mashed pumpkin or squash
2 cups (500 mL) cooked lima or kidney beans, or 1 can (19 oz/540 mL), drained
1 cup (250 mL) Peaches and Cream Relish (page 381) or store-bought corn relish

Garnish
1 cup (250 mL) green taco sauce
1 cup (250 mL) sour cream

1. Heat tortillas either in the oven or in a skillet. To heat in the oven, wrap in foil and heat in a 350°F (160°C) oven for 5 to 10 minutes. To heat in a skillet, heat 1 tbsp (15 mL) olive oil over medium-high heat. Using tongs, heat tortillas on one side (about 30 seconds), turn and heat the other side. Add more oil as necessary.

2. Meanwhile, in a saucepan, combine Filling 1 ingredients or Filling 2 ingredients. Cook, stirring constantly, over medium-high heat. Divide hot pumpkin mixture into 12 portions and spread over corn tortillas. Fold up one end and fold in the sides of the tortillas toward the centre. Top with a drizzle of green taco sauce and garnish with a dollop of sour cream.

pumpkin pie

Most commercially canned "pumpkin" pie fillings are made with squash, which is fine, but the texture and taste will be different (smoother, I think) if you use pie pumpkin. You can use table cream (10% B.F.) or whipping cream (approximately 36% B.F.); the higher the butter fat, the richer the filling. Use frozen thawed or canned pumpkin in this mild and lightly spiced true pumpkin pie filling.

Preheat oven to 450°F (230°C)
MAKES 2 PIES

2 cups (500 mL) mashed cooked pumpkin	1/2 tsp (2 mL) ground nutmeg
3/4 cup (175 mL) packed brown sugar	1/4 tsp (1 mL) ground ginger
2 eggs, well beaten	2 cups (500 mL) cream (see above) or milk
1/2 tsp (2 mL) salt	2 unbaked pie shells, each 9 inches (23 cm)
1/2 tsp (2 mL) ground cinnamon	

In a bowl, combine pumpkin, sugar, eggs, salt, cinnamon, nutmeg and ginger. Beat with an egg beater. Add cream and beat until well mixed. Pour into pie shells. Bake in preheated oven for 10 minutes. Reduce heat to 325°F (160°C) and bake for 30 to 40 minutes or until a knife inserted in the middle comes out clean.

Freezing Pumpkin

1. **Select Equipment:** Select suitable-size freezer containers, bags or Mason jars (see page 24).

2. **Blanch 1-inch (2.5 cm) peeled pumpkin cubes in boiling water for 5 to 7 minutes or until soft.** Lift out and plunge into cold water. Let stand for 5 minutes. Drain and pat dry. Leave cubes whole or mash and pack into containers, leaving a 1-inch (2.5 cm) headspace. Remove air, label and seal. Freeze for up to 9 months.

certified organic

SQUASH

$2 small $3 large

Squash

THE GOURD FAMILY (CUCURBITACEAE) of vegetables includes some 700 different varieties, of which pumpkins, zucchini and cucumbers are members. There is some blurring of the words "pumpkins," "squash" and "gourds," all of them being applied in various ways. Like its relatives, the squash plant is a trailing or climbing vine (or it could be a bush) with large leaves and generally large, yellow flowers. The edible fruit (actually a berry) is sometimes called a pepo, and can grow to enormous size. Squash flowers are edible.

Good Preserving Varieties

Of the 700 or so varieties of *Cucurbita*, there are four main species, and to add to the classification confusion, most species are subdivided into two main categories: winter and summer squash. Winter squash develops a thick, hard skin and is excellent for storage (keeping for up to 1 year in a cool, dark, dry, ventilated place). Summer squash is harvested and eaten when the skin is thin and tender. Summer squash is not meant for long storage. To learn more about pumpkin, squash and zucchini, visit Jack Creek Farms (California) at its website: www.allaboutpumpkins.com. The four main *Cucurbita* species are as follows:

C. *pepo*, usually eaten before it reaches full maturity (summer squash). Most traditional carving and baking pumpkins, **Yellow Crookneck**, **Yellow Straight Neck**, **Pattypan**, the **Zucchini**, **Spaghetti Squash** and **Acorn** are part of this group.

Another great pepo-type winter squash is **Delicata**, a.k.a. **Sweet Potato**. One of the sweetest squash—it really does taste like sweet potato — this variety is creamy and thin skinned, great for roasting or baking.

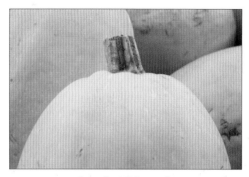

Spaghetti Squash

Acorn

Delicata

C. maxima: These gourds grow huge and store well. Their stem is spongy or cork-like. Most winter squash types fall into this category. Examples of maxima squash are **Pink Banana**, **Turban**, **Buttercup** and **Hubbard**. Generally, maxima squash have softer flesh.

C. moschata: Flesh is orange, sweet and refined. Stores extremely well and is very good in preserves. Examples of moschata squash are **Cushaw Green**, **Cushaw Gold**, **Butternut** and **Sweet Dumpling**.

C mixta: Flesh is pale yellow or cream in colour and generally not as sweet or refined as moshata or maxima; in fact, the flesh can be stringy or woody. Not many mixta cultivars have great eating qualities, most being best used for gourd crafts.

Turban

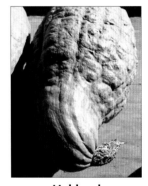

Hubbard

Purchasing/Storing

- 1 lb (500 g) yields 3-1/4 to 4 cups (800 mL to 1 L) raw cubed squash.
- You will need 1 lb (500 g) or less for each 1-quart (1 L) jar.

Select heavy squash with no touch of green, bruising, soft spots or mould. The rind on summer squash should be easily punctured with a fingernail. Winter squash should be hard, clean and heavy for its size.

Butternut

Good With

- Sweet seasonings such as cinnamon, ginger, cloves, nutmeg, anise, fennel, cardamom, maple syrup, brown sugar, honey.
- Vegetables such as tomatoes, onions, garlic, fennel.
- Apples, pears.
- Toasted almonds, pecans, walnuts; raisins.

Preparation

Scrub in a sink full of cool water to which a drop of food-safe soap has been added. Rinse well, drain and pat dry. Using a large heavy knife, cut the squash in half. Use a large spoon to scrape out seeds and stringy material. Save seeds for roasting with spices. Cut into

Sweet Dumpling

wedges or large cubes. Unless you plan to cut squash flesh into 1-inch (2.5 cm) or smaller cubes, it is easier to remove the skin after boiling, steaming or baking.

Canning Squash

Cube only; do not shred or mash squash for canning. See detailed canning information, page 20.

1. Prepare Equipment: Wash and heat pint (2-cup/500 mL) or quart (1 L) jars, and scald the lids, funnel, ladle and tongs (see page 22).

2. Cut squash quarters into 1-inch (2.5 cm) wide strips and peel. Cut strips into 1-inch (2.5 cm) cubes. In a Maslin pan or canning kettle, cover squash with water. Bring to a boil and boil for 30 seconds. Work quickly to fill hot jars one at a time.

3. Pack cubed squash into jars hot.
Make a Hot Pack: Using a slotted spoon, lift squash out of hot water and fill hot jars. Pour hot water over cubes, leaving a 1-inch (2.5 cm) headspace. Run a thin non-metallic utensil around the inside of the jar to allow air to escape. Add hot water, if necessary, to leave a 1-inch (2.5 cm) headspace. Wipe sealing edge of jars with a clean, damp, lint-free cloth. Position flat lids over the tops of jars and hand-tighten screw bands.

4. Place jars in pressure canner: Use a Pressure Canner according to the chart below for Dial-Gauge or follow manufacturer's instructions.

Processing Times at Different Altitudes for Squash in a DIAL-GAUGE PRESSURE Canner					
Pack Style	Jar Size	0–2000 ft	2001–4000 ft	4001–6000 ft	6001+ ft
HOT	Pints	15 min	20 min	25 min	30 min
	Quarts	20 min	25 min	30 min	35 min
RAW	Pints	20 min	25 min	30 min	35 min
	Quarts	25 min	30 min	35 min	40 min

5. Cool, Label and Store: Turn off heat; let pressure return to zero naturally. Once gauge shows 0 pressure, wait 2 minutes then open the vent. Unlock and remove canner lid. Wait 10 minutes then lift jars from canner and place on a clean towel or rack. Do not re-tighten screw bands. Let the jars cool to room temperature. This may take from 12 to 24 hours. Remove and store screw bands. Check lid seals (see page 23). Wipe and label sealed jars. Store in a cool, dark place.

maple nut squash

You will love this side dish—it is perfect for Thanksgiving or Christmas dinner because it can be made in advance and popped into the oven to heat while the turkey is being carved. With several cups of squash (you can also used cooked pumpkin) in the freezer or pantry, this dish is very easy. Double the recipe for a larger amount, but for a holiday meal at which several vegetable dishes are being served, count on this recipe serving 6 to 8 people.

As an alternative to butter, I have tossed the squash with 1 cup (250 mL) of Crabapple Chutney (page 309). Use applesauce or any savoury chutney in this book as an alternative. Use Hubbard, Butternut or Pink Banana squash in this recipe.

13- by 9-inch (3 L) baking pan, lightly oiled
Preheat oven to 350°F (180°C)
MAKES 4 SERVINGS (SEE ABOVE)

4 cups (1 L) cooked squash cubes, drained if canned, thawed if frozen
1 cup (250 mL) Crabapple Chutney (page 309)
3 tbsp (45 mL) maple syrup
1/2 tsp (2 mL) ground cinnamon

1/4 tsp (1 mL) ground nutmeg
sea salt and pepper
1/2 cup (125 mL) chopped toasted pecans or walnuts

In prepared baking pan, combine squash, chutney, maple syrup, cinnamon and nutmeg. Grind some salt and pepper over top. Cover with a lid or foil and heat in preheated oven for 30 to 45 minutes. Garnish with toasted pecans.

pickled baby vegetables

Some market gardeners grow mini vegetables for the restaurant trade and may have surplus available at peak times. Look for baby carrots and parsnips and the mini varieties of squash (pattypan and crookneck), eggplant, turnip and pearl onions.

MAKES 8 CUPS (2 L)

3 lb (1.5 kg) tiny whole vegetables
1/2 cup (125 mL) coarse salt
3 cups (750 mL) white vinegar
1 cup (250 mL) granulated sugar

4 to 8 sprigs fresh thyme, marjoram or oregano
4 to 16 small hot red peppers
4 to 8 star anise

1. In a large saucepan, cover vegetables with water. Bring to a boil over high heat. Reduce heat and simmer gently for 5 minutes. Drain and immerse in cold water for 5 minutes. Drain well and pat dry.

2. In a large stone crock or non-reactive container, dissolve salt in 8 cups (2 L) water. Add vegetables. Cover with a clean towel and let stand for 3 hours.

3. Meanwhile, heat eight 1-cup (250 mL) or four 1-pint (2-cup/500 mL) jars in boiling water (see page xx), and scald the lids, lifter, funnel and tongs (see page xx).

4. In a saucepan, combine vinegar and sugar. Bring to a boil over high heat and keep hot.

5. Using a colander and working in batches, if necessary, drain and rinse the vegetables well under cold water. Drain well. Pack vegetables into hot jars, adding a sprig of thyme, 1 or 2 hot peppers and 1 star anise into each jar.

6. Pour hot brine over vegetables, leaving a 1/2-inch (1 cm) headspace. Run a thin non-metallic utensil around the inside of the jar to allow air to escape. Add more hot brine, if necessary, to leave 1/2-inch (1 cm) headspace. Wipe rims, top with flat lids and screw on metal rings. Return jars to the hot water bath, topping up with hot water if necessary. Bring to a full rolling boil and process jars for 10 minutes (see page xx).

7. Remove canner lid and wait 5 minutes before removing jars to a towel or rack to cool completely. Check seals, label and store in a cool place for up to 1 year.

Use: These tiny pickled gems are delightful in salads and as a side dish for grilled chicken and fish.

Freezing Squash

1. **Select Equipment:** Select suitable-size freezer containers, bags or Mason jars (see page 24).

2. **Blanch 1-inch (2.5 cm) peeled squash cubes in boiling water for 5 to 7 minutes or until soft.** Lift out and plunge into cold water. Let stand for 5 minutes. Drain and pat dry. Leave cubes whole or mash and pack into containers, leaving a 1-inch (2.5 cm) headspace. Remove air, label and seal. Freeze for up to 9 months.

Fall Herbs

HERB PLANTS REALLY RESPOND TO PRUNING, so if you have been diligent in cutting back and using fresh herbs all summer, your plants will be very happy: dense, with small tender leaves. Fall is traditionally the time for drying herbs and making herb oils and vinegars. Herbalists gather roots from herbs such as wild ginger, chicory and echinacea once the first frost of the fall has withered the tops and the energy of the plant is concentrated in the roots. You may find parsley root for sale at your farmer's market at this time of year. With the exception of lavender, the herbs listed here are harvested from about June onward, but now is the time to bring them in for drying and using in preserves.

How to Preserve Herbs by Drying

Early in the day, after the dew has evaporated but before the full sun has hit the herb garden, clip green herbs and any flowering tops to just above the woody stems. Swish in a sink full of cool water to which a drop of food-safe soap has been added. Rinse well, drain and pat dry. Loosely gather bunches of the same herb together and tie. Label each bunch. Hang in a dry, dark spot. When partially dry, tighten the string on the bunches, because the stalks will shrink as they dry. When crackling dry, strip the leaves from their stems, but leave them whole. Store in a labelled airtight container in a cool spot (not over the stove). Keep herbs for up to one year and replace with fresh dried the next season.

Rosemary (left) and **sage** (right) from my herb garden are laid out on parchment paper to dry after cleaning. I let the herbs shrink a bit before tying in bunches and hanging in my pantry to dry completely. Sometimes I stack these sheets of partially dry herbs in a cupboard or drawer to dry completely instead.

Horseradish

Most often thought of as the roast beef condiment, the sharp and mustard-like heat of horseradish (*Armoracia rusticana*) can be used in small amounts in a wide range of dishes, from stir-fried chicken and lamb to cheese and white sauces for vegetables and fish.

To Make Horseradish Cream: Whip 1/2 cup (125 mL) whipping cream with 2 tsp (10 mL) granulated sugar; fold in 2 tsp (10 mL) white wine vinegar and 2 to 3 tbsp (25 to 45 mL) grated fresh horseradish (or more to taste). Let stand for 20 minutes before serving with roasted meats, chicken or fish. A dollop perks up steamed vegetables as well.

Oregano

Food writer Craig Claiborne called oregano (*Origanum spp.*) the "pizza herb" because it is an essential ingredient in Italian tomato sauces. There is no doubt that homemade tomato sauce is enlivened by the fresh essence of oregano. There are many oregano cultivars; at right is a variegated type. Greek oregano (*O. vulgare spp. Hirtum*) is my personal favourite. The only variety to avoid for cooking is *O. vulgare*, also called Wild Marjoram, because it is absolutely tasteless.

Rosemary

Rosemary (*Rosmarinus officinalis*) has a piny and pungent flavour, with notes of mint, citrus and ginger. These characteristics, along with its evergreen needle-like leaves, make it an excellent herb for spiking preserves and for drying. The variety on the right, which happens to be in bloom, is Corsican Blue.

Sage

Probably the most popular use of sage (*Salvia officinalis*, above left), is in bread stuffing for poultry, so it is the predominant fragrance when Thanksgiving or Christmas turkey is cooking. But sage is also used in muffins and other sweet or savoury quick breads, egg dishes, custards and bread puddings. It may be used in tomato sauces and some jelly recipes.

The purple variety (*S. officinalis purpurea*, above middle), adds colour and is used as you would garden green sage—in apple compotes and other preserves, stuffing, sausage, omelettes, soups and stews.

With its pineapple scent and deep red flowers, Pineapple Sage (*S. elegans,* above right), adds a distinctly fruity pineapple taste to jams, jelly, drinks (it is often added to syrups), and chicken and fish dishes.

A chiffonade of herbs is a thin shred made by stacking herb leaves (like the sage, left) and cutting across the stack horizontally. Finely shredded herbs, such as sage and basil, are used in jelly, jams and vinaigrette dressings.

mediterranean herb paste

Fall is the time to make this versatile flavour paste and freeze it for use as a poultry rub (see page 441) or to spice stuffing. It can form the basis for a vinaigrette, soup, dip or spread, and even as a flavouring for savoury muffins and scones. Freeze it in ice cube trays or 1/2-cup (125 mL) amounts.

MAKES 3/4 CUP (175 ML)

1 large bunch fresh sage
10 cloves garlic
1/2 cup (125 mL) fresh thyme leaves
1/4 cup (50 mL) fresh rosemary leaves
2 tbsp (25 mL) Dijon mustard
1 tbsp (15 mL) sea salt
1/4 cup (50 mL) olive oil
1 tbsp (15 mL) tarragon or white wine
    vinegar

1. Using a mezzaluna or French knife, finely chop sage leaves.

2. In a mortar and pestle, pound the garlic into a pulp.

3. Add sage, thyme and rosemary leaves. Pound and grind until well mixed into the garlic.

4. Add mustard and salt and grind to a paste, adding the olive oil by the tablespoon until a thick paste is achieved. Add vinegar just before the last of the oil is added.

Note: You can use the food processor to make this paste; the consistency will be smoother, with fewer pieces of the individual herbs.

To Make Mediterranean Herb Vinaigrette:

In a clean jar with a tight-fitting lid, combine 1 scant tablespoon (15 mL) of the Mediterranean Herb Paste, 1/4 cup (50 mL) olive oil and the juice of 1/2 a lime or lemon.

Use Mediterranean Herb Paste when roasting chicken and vegetables: Preheat oven to 375°F (190°C). Arrange chicken, fleshy part up, in a shallow roasting pan or on a rimmed baking sheet. Rub 1/4 cup (50 mL) Mediterranean Herb Paste evenly over the chicken. Distribute roughly cut carrots, onions and potatoes in single layer evenly around the chicken thighs. Drizzle olive oil over vegetables and chicken. Bake for 40 minutes or until chicken and vegetables are cooked through.

Use Mediterranean Herb Paste for roasted vegetables with pasta: Preheat oven to 375°F (190°C). Combine sliced zucchini, red pepper, onions, carrots, parsnips or other favourite vegetables in a bowl. Toss with 1/4 cup (50 mL) Mediterranean Herb Paste. Transfer to a shallow roasting pan or a rimmed baking sheet. Bake for 35 to 40 minutes or until vegetables are tender. Toss with cooked pasta and add more Mediterranean Herb Paste as desired.

Winter

"From December to March, there are for many of us three gardens—the garden outdoors, the garden of pots and bowls in the house, and the garden of the mind's eye."

—KATHERINE S. WHITE

Citrus Fruits

***CITRUS* IS THE GENUS NAME** for a group of flowering plants in the *Rutaceae* family. We group the fruit of these tropical shrubs into the category citrus, which has become a widely used common term that has expanded to include closely related fruits such as kumquats, which are actually in the genus *Fortunella*. Oranges, tangerines, minneolas (tangerine and grapefruit cross), tangelos (tangerine, grapefruit and orange cross), lemons, limes, grapefruit and ugli fruit (a popular tangelo type) are all citrus fruits.

Even though some varieties of individual citrus fruits are available year round, like all produce, citrus fruits have a definite season. In the Northern Hemisphere, there are winter fruits that peak from October to March, with December, January and February being prime months for their availability in both specialty food stores and supermarkets. This, and the fact that citrus preserving techniques create distinctive flavours that are very different from those of the fresh fruit, makes them a very good winter preserving fruit.

Citrus trees are evergreen trees that produce a wide range of oval to round fruits. The coloured outer rind (or zest) is called the "epicarp" and contains essential oil glands that give each fruit its typical fragrance. A thick, white, bitter "mesocarp," or pith, lies between the rind and the inner tart or sweet pulp. Together the coloured rind and the white pith are referred to as the peel. The inside flesh or pulp grows in sections that are divided by a thin (or thick, as in grapefruit) membrane.

Purchasing/Storing
Look for shiny fruits, with no touch of green or bruising, that are heavy in the hand for their size. Citrus fruits should smell fragrant, not fermented, and there should be no signs of shrivelling or white patches. Keep citrus fruits in a cool, dark place for 3 or 4 days or in the crisper drawer of the refrigerator for up to 1-1/2 weeks.

Good With
- Lemon or spicy herbs such as lemongrass, lemon verbena, basil, sage, thyme, tarragon.
- Sweet seasonings such as vanilla, ginger, cinnamon, dark chocolate.
- Egg and dairy dishes and bread puddings.
- Other fruit, such as strawberries, raspberries, blueberries, melon, peaches, avocado, mangoes, pomegranates.
- Mediterranean vegetables such as fennel, shallots, olives; other vegetables, such as asparagus, artichokes, beans, broccoli.
- Chicken, goose and duck; fish such as mahi-mahi, trout, salmon, perch; seafood.

Preparation

The parts of citrus fruits used for preserves include the whole fruit; the sectioned or chopped flesh; the chopped rind and flesh; the rind itself; and sometimes the rind and pith.

If the rind (or zest) is to be used, scrub the fruit with warm soapy water using a vegetable brush; rinse well and pat dry.

To section citrus fruits: Trim away stem and blossom ends. Set one flat end on a cutting surface and, using a paring knife, slice from top to bottom in a curve, cutting away the rind and the bitter white pith.

Take the peeled fruit in hand and, working over a bowl to catch the juice, slice into sections using the membrane as a cutting guide.

When sectioning grapefruit (left), cut out the flesh sections between the tougher membrane so that the sections do not include this tougher skin (right).

Equipment for Grating and Using Citrus Rind:

When the outermost coloured part of citrus rind is used in cooking, it is often referred to as the zest. Citrus rind and zest are the same thing. The oil-rich and very fragrant zest is separated from the bitter white pith that lies between it and the sweet flesh by using the following specialized tools:

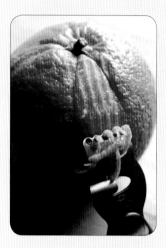

1. Use a vegetable peeler to remove 1/2-inch (1 cm) wide strips of coloured rind or zest, being careful not to include the bitter white pith. Chop or cut the zest into thin strips.

2. Use the round sharp holes on a zester to remove thin strands of zest, which are often used to garnish a dish.

3. Use the wide knife on a zester to remove a continuous, 1/4-inch (5 mm) wide strip of zest. These strips can be knotted or curled and used as a garnish.

4. Use a micro-grater or rasp to remove thin shreds of zest when grated rind or zest is called for in a recipe. Shown are two different micro-graters: a long, flat grater (left) that fits over a bowl so that the rind can fall directly into the mixture, and a hand-held grater with a handle (right).

Grapefruit

FLORIDA IS THE LARGEST PRODUCER OF GRAPEFRUIT in North America, with Texas, California and Arizona providing a mere one-quarter of the total output. Grapefruit is available year-round, but in Florida and Texas sweet, plump grapefruit are in peak season from late December through April.

Our modern varieties of grapefruit have been developed from the pomelo (*Citrus maxima* or *C. grandis*), a larger, very seedy fruit with deeply pitted, puffy and thick rinds. A pomelo (a.k.a. Shaddock, or Chinese Grapefruit, middle) is shown beside a Texas Red grapefruit (left) and a navel orange (right).

Good Preserving Varieties

Grapefruit has "white" or creamy-coloured or "red" flesh that can be pale pink to brilliant ruby red. The rind can be pale yellow, deep yellow, orange or red, with variations in between these shades.

Duncan: Perhaps the oldest variety but mostly sold for commercial use, it has white flesh, with good, sweet-tart flavour; lots of seeds; is excellent for juicing, jelly and jams.

Flame: Nearly seedless, with red flesh and a slight rind blush, making it a good variety for marmalade and jams, jelly and compotes.

Marsh (Marsh Seedless): A Duncan descendant; very juicy and aromatic with white flesh that is balanced in acidity and sweetness; tender membranes. Medium in size, with smooth yellow rind; nearly seedless. Balance of acidity and sweetness but somewhat less flavour than seeded varieties.

Rio Red: Seedless, distinctly reddish rind and deep red flesh; firmer and smoother than Redblush; sweet-tart taste; excellent for juicing and preserving.

Star Ruby: Mostly grown in Florida; seedless, with the reddest flesh; clean, sweet and crisp tasting; easy to peel; easy to separate into segments; smaller and less acidic than other varieties; a very good preserving variety.

Two red-fleshed grapefruit varieties: Ruby and **Texas Red**. The red-fleshed varieties are at their darkest red when they are at their peak, which may account for the variations in flesh colour in the same variety.

Texas Red: Mostly grown in Texas; some are seedless, some have large seeds; pale pink to red flesh, and a yellow rind lightly tinged with red. Red flesh fades to pink, then buff by end of season.

Ruby Red (**Redblush** and **Ruby**): Seedless or very few seeds; bright red flesh; medium to large, with red-orange to red rind; a good preserving variety because the flesh holds its colour.

sliced or diced citrus peel in syrup

Citrons are the citrus of choice for this traditional recipe, but they can be hard to find. You can use oranges, lemons and limes in place of the grapefruit, but be sure that the variety you choose has a high ratio of pith and rind to fruit. Spoon the peel and syrup over ice cream or pound cake, or chop the peel for use in holiday fruit pudding and fruitcake.

Note: This preserve is not water-bath processed to hermetically seal it, but the high sugar content is enough to keep it for up to 6 months if it is stored in sterilized jars in the refrigerator. Should you wish to process the jars to keep them longer or to store them in a cool cupboard, return filled and capped jars to the hot water bath, topping up with hot water if necessary. Bring to a full rolling boil and process jars for 10 minutes (see page 19). Transfer to a cooling rack to cool completely. Check seals, label and store in a cool place for up to 1 year.

MAKES 4 CUPS (1 L)

4 grapefruit or 2 pomelos
1–1/4 cups (300 mL) granulated sugar
1–1/4 cups (300 mL) water

1. Wash grapefruit following directions on page 446. Trim and discard the ends.
For slices: slice crosswise into thin slices. Remove seeds and set slices aside.
For diced peel: Follow directions on page 446. Set diced peel aside.

2. Sterilize two 1-pint (2-cup/500 mL) jars, and scald the lids, funnel and lifter (see page 18).

3. In a heavy-bottomed saucepan, combine sugar and water. Bring to a boil over medium-high heat, stirring constantly to dissolve the sugar. Stir in the grapefruit slices and bring back to the boil. Gently simmer, without stirring, for 15 minutes. Remove from heat and let slices cool in the syrup.

4. Using tongs, fill jars with slices and cover with syrup to within 1/4-inch (5 mm). Store in a very cold place or the refrigerator for up to 6 months.

Lemons

THOUGHT TO HAVE ORIGINATED IN REGIONS OF EAST INDIA, Burma and south China, the lemon that is most commonly used in North America (*Citrus limon*, syn. *C. limonium*) was brought to North Africa by Arabs and, from there, taken to the rest of Europe by returning Crusaders.

Good Preserving Varieties

Bearss: Rind is rich in oil; flesh is very juicy and acidic, with few seeds. Now thought to be the leading variety in Florida, it is good for preserving; peaks August through November.

Eureka: The most widely grown lemon in the world, it is a true "bitter lemon," with a high juice and acid content. Rind is smooth and thin; flesh is tart with few seeds. Season peaks from winter to early spring.

Femminello: One of the oldest, most popular Italian varieties, with several strains that produce fruit at different times. Fruits are medium in size, oblong with a pointed tip. Rind is yellow, finely pitted, medium-smooth, medium-thick. Flesh is juicy, very acidic, with few, mostly undeveloped seeds. One strain or another is available all year.

Villafranca: Thought to have originated in Sicily, it was the leading lemon cultivar in Florida for many years. Tart juice and few seeds. One strain is available year-round; one peaks in the summer months.

Two fruits that are closely related to lemons (in the *Citrus* genus but of the *C. medica* species) are the Citron and the Fingered Citron. Their thick rinds make both a popular choice for candying or preserving in syrup.

Citron: Larger than lemon, with a tough and warty rind that is usually pared and discarded; the inner pith is very thick, and is sliced or diced and preserved in syrup or candied. Not used for its flesh or juice, which is dry and insignificant, the citron is cultivated in the Mediterranean region, where it has naturalized (being originally from Southeast Asia). Citrons were once used for medicinal purposes.

Meyer: A hybrid, possibly lemon crossed with mandarin orange; introduced into the United States by Frank N. Meyer from a Chinese ornamental plant. Rind is smooth, dark yellow to light orange, with numerous small oil glands, and is thin, making it perfect for preserving whole. Pulp is pale orange-yellow, usually in 10 segments with tender walls; sweet, juicy, moderately acid with medium lemon flavour; seeds are small and relatively few. Season peaks from December to April in North America, with fruit coming from California, Florida and Texas.

lemon chutney

This chutney gets better and better over time. In fact, it is best when "aged" from 4 to 6 months. So if you make it in January or February, this tangy grill buddy will be ready for barbecue season in the summer, when it will lend zest to grilled vegetables, fish and chicken with its spicy, rich marmalade flavour. Don't be put off by the overnight macerating of the rind, flesh and salt, because all you do is chop the lemons, combine with salt, cover and let stand overnight.

MAKES 4 CUPS (1 L)

8 Bearss lemons (or other thick-skinned
   variety), scrubbed
2 tbsp (25 mL) pickling salt
4 large cloves garlic, minced
1/2 cup (125 mL) dried currants
1/2 cup (125 mL) chopped dried apricots
1/2 cup (125 mL) freshly squeezed lemon juice
1/2 cup (125 mL) cider vinegar
1 tbsp (15 mL) freshly grated gingerroot
1 dried cayenne pepper, crushed
1 tsp (5 mL) ground cardamom
1 tsp (5 mL) crushed coriander
1/2 tsp (2 mL) hot red pepper flakes, optional
2 cups (500 mL) + 2 tbsp (25 mL) packed
   brown sugar

One of the great rewards of home preserving is that you get familiar with a wide variety of spices and blends by using and tasting them in the preserves. For the Lemon Chutney, I recommend that you use the following spices (clockwise from top): freshly grated peeled whole ginger; one whole dried (or fresh) cayenne pepper, crushed; crushed cardamom seeds; and crushed coriander seeds (still in my spice mortar). Because I like this chutney to have extra heat for grilled foods, I add either dried chipotle or hot red pepper flakes, but you can omit these if you wish. Use a small, heavy spice mortar and pestle—mine is cast iron—or a rolling pin to crush the seeds, and a micro-grater to grate the fresh gingerroot.

1. Using a vegetable peeler, remove the rind from the lemons, being careful not to include the white pith. Using a paring knife, cut away and discard the white pith from around the lemons. Finely chop the rind. Coarsely chop the lemons, discarding the seeds.

2. In a non-reactive bowl, combine rind, lemons and salt. Cover with a clean cloth and set aside in a cool place overnight.

3. In a Maslin pan or large saucepan, combine macerated lemon mixture, garlic, currants, apricots, lemon juice, vinegar, ginger, cayenne, cardamom, coriander and hot pepper flakes. Bring to a light simmer over high heat. Reduce heat to medium and stir in the brown sugar. Stir constantly until the sugar is dissolved.

4. Adjust the heat to keep the mixture at a regular simmer and cook, stirring frequently, for 30 to 45 minutes or until the mixture becomes thick and mounds on a wooden spoon.

5. Meanwhile, heat four 1-cup (250 mL) jars in boiling water, and scald the lids, lifter, funnel and tongs (see page 18).

6. Skim off and discard any foam. Fill hot jars, leaving a 1/4-inch (5 mm) headspace. Run a thin non-metallic utensil around the inside of the jar to allow air to escape, and add more hot chutney, if necessary, to leave a 1/4-inch (5 mm) headspace. Wipe rims, top with flat lids and screw on metal rings. Return jars to the hot water bath, topping up with hot water if necessary. Bring to a full rolling boil and process jars for 10 minutes (see page 19).

7. Remove canner lid and wait 5 minutes before removing jars to a towel or rack to cool completely. Check seals, label and store in a cool place for up to 1 year.

Use: Serve Lemon Chutney once it has "aged" for at least 2 months right from the jar with baked whitefish, trout or salmon. Or mix 1 cup (250 mL) chutney with 3 tbsp (45 mL) chopped capers for a flavourful and different tartar sauce. Mix with orange juice or an equal amount of yogurt, and coat chicken before baking. Mix 1/4 cup (50 mL) chutney with the same amount of soy sauce and use for stir-fried foods. Serve as a condiment for cooked chicken or cold cuts, and with a cheese platter or over brie, cream cheese or goat cheese.

lemon chutney dressing

1/2 cup (125 mL) Lemon Chutney (page 454)
2 green onions, coarsely chopped
1/2 cup (125 mL) olive oil

In a food processor or blender, combine Lemon Chutney and onions. Process until well blended. With the motor running, add olive oil through the lid opening in a steady stream and process until combined and slightly thickened. Cover and refrigerate dressing until needed, up to 1 week.

lemon-seasoned whitefish

In this recipe, I have added the chutney after the fish has been grilled. If you like, spoon a couple of tablespoons (25 mL) over the top of the fillets after they have been turned once on the grill. Cod, perch, catfish and pickerel work well in this recipe.

**Rimmed baking sheet or grilling basket,
  lightly oiled**
**Broiler or barbecue grill preheated to broil
  or high**
MAKES 4 SERVINGS

4 whitefish fillets, about 1 inch/2.5 cm thick
1 tbsp (15 mL) olive oil
1/2 cup (125 mL) Lemon Chutney (page 454)

1. Using a paper towel, pat the fish dry. Arrange in single layer on prepared baking sheet. Brush with olive oil. If using the barbecue, set fillets into prepared grilling basket. Broil in the oven or over a medium-high flame on the barbecue for 10 minutes or until the fish turns opaque and flakes easily with a fork.

2. Arrange each fillet on a plate with grilled (or steamed) greens or rice and top each with 2 tbsp (25 mL) Lemon Chutney.

preserved lemons

Preserved lemons are essential ingredients in Middle Eastern cooking, and they are becoming more and more popular in North American dishes. If you have them in your pantry, you will happily use them in last-minute dishes.

1 large, wide-mouth jar
MAKES 10 PRESERVED LEMONS

12 small Meyer or other thin-skinned organic lemons,
   well scrubbed
pickling salt

1. Squeeze the juice from 2 lemons. Discard rinds and set juice aside.

2. Sterilize a large (8-cup/2 L) jar in boiling water, and scald the lid, lifter and tongs (see page 18).

3. Slit remaining 10 lemons: Trim and discard the top and bottom ends of the lemons. Place lemons in a shallow dish so that they are sitting upright on one of the flat cut ends.

4. Using a paring knife, make a vertical cut through the centre, from the top running three-quarters of the way to the bottom so that the 2 halves remain attached at the base; do not cut all the way through. Rotate the lemon and make a vertical cut at a right angle to the first slit, from the top running three-quarters of the way to the bottom so that the 4 pieces still remain attached at the base. Remove the seeds and set the lemon aside. Repeat, making the same slits on remaining lemons. Add any juice from the dish to the reserved juice.

5. Spoon 2 tbsp (25 mL) salt into the bottom of the sterilized jar. Fill the slits in each lemon with as much salt as the lemon will hold and pack 5 of the salted lemons into the sterilized jar. Pour reserved lemon juice over the lemons and push lemons down using a wooden spoon.

6. Pack the remaining salted lemons into the jar and pack down. Spoon 2 tbsp (25 mL) salt over the top of the lemons.

7. Secure the lid and set the jar aside in a cool, dark place. After a few days, check that the lemons are completely submerged in lemon juice. If they aren't, add freshly squeezed lemon juice until they are covered. Allow lemons to marinate for at least 6 weeks, shaking the jar from time to time. Rinse lemons before using in recipes. Store Preserved Lemons in the refrigerator for up to 6 months after curing at room temperature.

Use: Preserved lemons are meant to be used whole or chopped—the rind, pith and flesh are all edible. Great with baked fish or chicken, especially tagine dishes (see Preserved-Lemon Chicken Tagine, page 460) and with vegetables, rice and couscous. Because of the salt, preserved lemons are best in savoury dishes (remember to rinse well and add no extra salt to the recipe), but I have used them successfully in egg, bread and rice puddings.

preserved lemon chicken tagine

From as long ago as the 13th century, fruited tagine stews featuring chicken or lamb and crushed nuts, seeds, fruit and spices have been cooked in open fires throughout North Africa and the Middle East. This dish is fragrant and lightly red-tinged from the saffron. Make sure your tagine is flame-proof before using it on direct heat. Use a Dutch oven if you do not have a tagine or if your tagine is not flame-proof.

I find that only a very small amount of pure fresh saffron is as much of the floral, very unique flavour that I can tolerate, and I have made it optional in the recipe.

Flame-proof tagine or Dutch oven
MAKES 4 SERVINGS

2 tbsp (25 mL) freshly squeezed lemon juice,
   optional
10 to 15 threads saffron, optional
2 tbsp (25 mL) olive oil
1 onion, chopped
1 red or yellow bell pepper, chopped
4 cloves garlic, minced
1–1/2 cups (375 mL) chicken broth
1 preserved lemon (page 458), rinsed
   and chopped

1/4 cup (50 mL) sliced dried apricots
2 large chicken breasts, cut in half
1/2 cup (125 mL) chopped pitted green olives
1/4 cup (50 mL) ground almonds or pistachio
   nuts
1 tbsp (15 mL) Gremolata (page 394) or chopped
   fresh parsley

1. If using saffron: In a small bowl, sprinkle lemon juice over saffron and set aside for 1 hour or as long as overnight to soften.

2. In the bottom of a flame-proof tagine or Dutch oven, heat olive oil over medium heat. Add onion and pepper and sauté for 5 minutes. Add garlic and cook for 3 minutes, stirring frequently. Add broth, preserved lemon, apricots, soaked saffron, if using, and chicken. Cover, reduce heat to low and cook for 20 to 30 minutes or until chicken is tender and sauce is slightly thick.

3. Add olives, almonds and Gremolata. Stir well; cover and cook for 5 minutes.

lemon chutney chicken tagine

This top-of-the-stove version of tangine uses either the Lemon Chutney (page 454) or Classic Dundee Marmalade (page 466) in place of preserved lemons.

Dutch oven or large heavy-bottomed saucepan with lid
MAKES 4 SERVINGS

2 tbsp (25 mL) olive oil
1 onion, chopped
3 cloves garlic, finely chopped
1 tsp (5 mL) ground ginger
2 tsp (10 mL) ground cinnamon
1 roasting chicken, 3 to 5 lb (1.5 to 2.2 kg)
sea salt and freshly ground pepper

2 cups (500 mL) chicken broth
1 cup (250 mL) Lemon Chutney (page 454)
1/4 cup (50 mL) sliced green olives
1/2 cup (125 mL) chopped fresh parsley
2 tbsp (25 mL) chopped fresh oregano

1. In a Dutch oven large enough to hold the chicken, heat the olive oil over medium heat. Add onion and sauté until soft and golden in colour. Stir garlic, ginger and cinnamon into the onions and cook, stirring constantly, for 1 minute.

2. Add chicken to the pot and spoon onion mixture over the top and sides. Season with salt and pepper to taste. Add broth and chutney. Increase the heat to high and bring to a boil. Cover and reduce heat to medium-low. Simmer gently for 1-1/2 hours, turning the chicken over once or twice during cooking.

3. Add olives, parsley and oregano; cover and cook for 10 minutes or until the chicken is very tender. Transfer chicken to a warmed platter and cover. Boil the liquid in the pan for about 5 minutes or until slightly reduced. Skim off surplus fat and serve the sauce over the carved chicken or pass separately.

lemon curd

If you like lemon, as I do, this is a pantry must-have. Our book club has an annual Christmas cookie exchange, and we are always so thrilled when one of our members makes a jar of Lemon Curd for each of us. My jar is usually gone by New Year's because it can be used in so many easy desserts. Because this creamy spread is not water-or pressure-processed, the jars need to be sterilized before filling. Be sure to store the curd in the refrigerator.

MAKES 6 CUPS (1.5 L)

6 eggs, lightly beaten
6 tbsp (90 mL) finely grated lemon rind
1 cup (250 mL) freshly squeezed lemon juice

1–1/2 cups (375 mL) butter, at room temperature
2 cups (500 mL) granulated sugar

1. Sterilize three 1-pint (2-cup/500 mL) jars in boiling water, and scald the lid, lifter and tongs (see page 18).

2. In the top of a double boiler or a non-reactive bowl, combine eggs, lemon rind and lemon juice. Set the pan or bowl over a bottom pan of simmering water (top pan should not touch the water). Add butter and sugar and stir until both are dissolved. Cook, stirring constantly, for 15 to 20 minutes or until the mixture is thickened. The mixture is thickened when it coats the back of a metal spoon and mounds slightly. Be careful not to boil the mixture because it will curdle.

3. Fill hot jars, leaving a 1/4-inch (5 mm) headspace. Run a thin non-metallic utensil around the inside of the jar to allow air to escape. Add more hot curd, if necessary, to leave a 1/4-inch (5 mm) headspace. Wipe rims, top with flat lids and screw on metal rings. Let cool on a wire rack or towel. Label and store in the refrigerator for up to 1 month.

Use: Enjoy Lemon Curd as a filling in cooked pastry shells; as a custard substitute in dessert trifles; to replace whipped cream as a topping on fruit or desserts; as a pie filling with egg white meringue.

A double boiler is essential for this recipe because it gently heats the delicate egg protein and thickens the curd without curdling it. Double boiler sets can be made of glass (above), stainless steel, or ceramic with copper bottoms. If you don't have a double boiler, set a smaller saucepan or stainless steel bowl over a larger saucepan.

Oranges

CITRUS PLANTS ARE EASILY HYBRIDIZED, and sometime in antiquity the sweet orange (*Citrus* x *sinensis*) was the result of a possible cross between a pomelo and a tangerine. Except for the Seville orange, which is used in marmalade, bitter oranges (*Citrus aurantium*) are rarely used in cooking.

Good Preserving Varieties

Blood (top right): Originating in Italy, there are three popular strains: **Tarocco**, **Moro** (usually found in North America) and **Sanguigno**, but it may be difficult to know what variety is in stores. Rind is deep orange with a red or purple blush; flesh is dark (blood) red to purple, making them good for curds, jams, marmalades and other preserves. The antioxidant anthocyanin is responsible for the deep red colour. California blood oranges peak from January through late spring; Texas blood oranges peak in January and February.

Navel (middle right): Has seedless meaty flesh in segments that separate easily. All navel oranges have a round button-like circle at the blossom end that resembles a human navel. Thick rinds make them easy to peel and good for candied peel. California navel oranges peak in February, March and April; Florida navel oranges, which have a higher juice content and much thinner peel than the California ones, peak in December and January.

Seville (bottom right): A variety of the **Chinese Bitter Orange** (*Citrus aurantium*), Seville oranges are tart, with a thick skin and large seeds; naturally high in pectin, which makes them perfect for marmalade and compotes. Peak from mid-December to the end of February.

Valencia: Sweet and juicy, Valencia is the variety widely grown in Florida. Florida Valencia oranges peak in March and April.

classic dundee marmalade

In my view, the bitter Seville oranges (Citrus aurantium) *that appear in markets just before Christmas and stay for a short month or two make the finest orange marmalade in the Scottish tradition. Be warned: this is very close to the traditional marmalade method and not a quick technique, but it's not difficult—and you will be well rewarded.*

MAKES 8 CUPS (2 L)

6 Seville oranges (about 2 lb/1 kg)
1 lemon

8 cups (2 L) water
7 cups (1.75 L) granulated sugar

1. In a sink full of warm, soapy water, scrub oranges and lemon using a vegetable brush to remove any wax film. Rinse well. Cut oranges and lemons in half crosswise. Using a hand or electric citrus juicer, squeeze orange and lemon juice. Strain into a Maslin pan or canning kettle, saving the seeds and rinds.

2. On a 10-inch (25 cm) square of double-thickness cheesecloth, place seeds and membranes. Bring up sides and tie the top with cotton string. Place in pan with juice.

3. On a cutting board, stack 3 orange rind halves together and cut in half. Keeping the 3 rind quarters stacked, cut crosswise into 1/4-inch (5 mm) thick strips. Add to the pan along with any accumulated juices. Repeat with remaining orange and lemon rind halves.

4. Add water to the pan and bring to a boil over high heat. Reduce heat to medium and stir in sugar, 1 cup (250 mL) at a time, stirring to dissolve before adding the next cup. Boil lightly for 2-1/2 to 3 hours or until thickened and setting point (see note, next page) is reached, stirring occasionally. During the last 1/2 hour, skim off and discard the foam that rises to the top.

5. Meanwhile, sterilize eight 1-cup (250 mL) jars in boiling water, and scald the lids, lifter, funnel and tongs. (See page 18).

6. Fill hot jars, leaving a 1/4-inch (5 mm) headspace. Run a thin non-metallic utensil around the inside of the jar to allow air to escape. Add more hot marmalade, if necessary, to leave a 1/4-inch (5 mm) headspace. Wipe rims, top with flat lids and screw on metal rings. Return jars to the hot water bath, topping up with hot water, if necessary. Bring to a full rolling boil and process jars for 10 minutes (See page 19).

7. Remove canner lid and wait 5 minutes before removing jars to a towel or rack to cool completely. Check seals, label and store in a cool place for up to 1 year.

Setting Point

Marmalade has reached the setting point when a candy thermometer reaches the jelly stage at 222°F (110°C).

If you don't have a thermometer: To test for setting point, remove the marmalade from the heat. Place a plate in the freezer for 2 minutes. Drop a spoonful of hot marmalade onto the chilled plate.

Return the plate to the freezer for 1 minute. Push the spot of marmalade with a fork. If the surface wrinkles, the marmalade is set and ready to pack into hot, sterilized jars. If the marmalade is not set, return to a boil and test at 3-minute intervals, using a new chilled plate each time.

dundee almond cake

This is an unusual cake in that there is no grain flour as the main ingredient. For a cake that relies on nuts for its structure, it is surprisingly light.

9-inch (23 cm) springform pan, base lined with parchment and sides lightly buttered
Preheat oven to 350°F (180°C)
MAKES 1 CAKE

1-1/4 cups (300 mL) blanched almonds
4 eggs, separated
1 cup (250 mL) granulated sugar, divided
1/4 cup (50 mL) chopped fresh sweet cicely
grated rind and juice of 3 oranges (about 1-1/4
   cups/300 mL juice and 3 tbsp/45 mL grated
   rind)

1 tbsp (15 mL) Anisette or other anise-flavoured
   liqueur, optional
1/4 cup (50 mL) icing sugar
6 sprigs sweet cicely or other fresh herb,
   optional

1. Using a food processor, chop the almonds until coarse. At this stage, the almonds should not be ground or finely chopped. Remove almonds to a separate bowl. Wipe out food processor bowl and process the 1 cup (250 mL) sugar with the sweet cicely until the sweet cicely is fine. Transfer the herbed sugar to a bowl.

2. In a bowl, whisk the egg yolks with 1/2 cup (125 mL) of the herbed sugar until thick. With the motor running, add yolk mixture to the food processor through the opening in the lid, processing until the mixture is thick and smooth. Transfer the mixture to a large bowl and stir in orange rind. If the mixture is too thick, stir in 1 or 2 tablespoons (15 or 25 mL) orange juice until it is the consistency of thick cake batter.

3. In a separate bowl, beat egg whites until soft peaks form. Sprinkle 1 tbsp (15 mL) of the herbed sugar over and beat until the peaks hold their shape. Fold half of the meringue into the almond mixture until just evenly mixed. Quickly fold the other half into the mixture, being careful not to overmix in order to keep the air in the whites.

4. Gently spoon the batter into the prepared pan. Bake in preheated oven for 35 minutes or until set in the centre and a golden colour. Let cool on a cooling rack until the sides have shrunk away from the pan. Remove springform pan sides and transfer to a serving plate.

5. Meanwhile, make Orange Sauce. In a saucepan, combine orange juice and remaining herbed sugar. Bring to a boil over medium-high heat. Lower the heat and boil lightly for 10 minutes or until thickened slightly. Remove from heat and stir in the liqueur, if using. Drizzle orange sauce over the top of the cake and let stand for 20 minutes or longer before serving. Or make a puddle of orange sauce on each serving plate and arrange a slice of cake on top. Dust with powdered sugar and garnish with an herb sprig, if using.

candied citrus peel

Simmering citrus peel in a simple syrup made from granulated sugar and water is one of the oldest forms of preserving the unique fragrance and taste of citrons, oranges and lemons. This method can be used for any thick-rind citrus fruit or for fresh gingerroot.

The peel—the rind and pith—simmers slowly in heavy simple syrup that turns it to candy, but first it is simmered three times in salted water. Triple-boiling the peel helps remove some bitterness from the inner pith, but if you include the pith, this confection will still be bitter-sweet and will dance on your tongue long after the candy has disappeared.

If you like sweet and salty together in the same bite, try rolling the sugar-dusted and partly dry citrus strips in coarse sea salt, but be careful not to load it on. You want just enough to give a slight hit of salt with the sugar.

If you prefer to candy only the zest (rind), use a vegetable peeler to remove 1/2-inch (1 cm)-wide strips of zest from the fruit without any of the pith attached to it. Boil zest-only strips once in salted water and then proceed to step 3.

MAKES ABOUT 2 CUPS (500 mL)

2 navel oranges
1-1/2 tsp (7 mL) salt, divided
1-1/4 cups (300 mL) granulated sugar + 1/4
  cup (50 mL) approx, for coating
1-1/4 cups (300 mL) water

1. Wash oranges. Trim away the ends of the oranges. Cut the oranges into quarters and remove the inner flesh sections, leaving the rind and pith intact. Set the inner flesh aside for another use, such as a fruit salad. Cut the peel into strips that are roughly 1/4 inch (5 mm) by 2 inches (5 cm).

2. In a saucepan, combine peel strips with 2 cups (500 mL) cold water (the strips should be generously covered). Add 1/2 tsp (2 mL) salt and bring to a boil over medium heat. Boil gently for 2 minutes. Strain, discarding the water.

Repeat this step 2 more times. Rinse well with cold water.

3. In a heavy-bottomed saucepan, combine sugar and water. Bring to a boil over medium heat, stirring constantly to dissolve the sugar. Add drained peel strips, reduce heat and simmer gently for 1 hour. Stir the strips once to distribute them evenly in the sugar water but after that, leave them to simmer, without stirring. Check on the pan occasionally to make sure that the syrup is simmering gently and not scorching. A heavy-bottomed pan is essential. After 1 hour, check on the pan every few moments. The water should be almost evaporated and the strips should be translucent and soft but not mushy.

4. Meanwhile, prepare parchment or waxed paper by sprinkling it with 3 tablespoons (45 mL) granulated sugar. Remove the pan from the heat and using tongs, transfer the candied strips from the syrup to the sugared paper. Toss well to coat the strips and sprinkle with more sugar if needed to evenly coat them. Use a fork to separate the strips. Let cool and dry overnight on the paper over a wire rack. Store in an airtight container in a cool place for 1 week or pack into freezer containers, seal, label and store for up to 9 months.

Use: Dip the candied peel in chocolate and use as a sweet confection; use to decorate cakes or muffins, or chop and add to the batter of baked goods. I have used peel as swizzle sticks for cocktails, and it is especially nice with rich chocolate mousse or brownies.

spiced pickled oranges

I like the unusual sweet-tart flavour and decorative uses for this condiment. It complements game meats, pork (especially ham), turkey and sharp cheddar cheeses. This recipe is easy, and it uses the whole sliced fruit with only the ends and seeds removed. I've tried grapefruit but find that they are just too bitter in this recipe. Wide-mouth pint (2-cup/500 mL) jars are best for packing the slices, and smaller oranges work better than the largest ones.

Use a wide-bottomed canning kettle or saucepan (not a Maslin pan) because the slices will have to be boiled in batches—the wider the pan, the less time it will take. This is best if left to infuse for a month or so. I am always surprised at the range of flavours that this recipe generates. Sometimes the result is very sweet; other times it is very tart because it depends on the variety of oranges used.

MAKES ABOUT 8 CUPS (2 L)

6 oranges
2 cups (500 mL) white wine vinegar
1 cup (250 mL) brown sugar
1 tsp (5 mL) salt
4 allspice berries
2 cloves

2 cardamom pods, crushed
1 cinnamon stick, 3 inches (8 cm)
1 star anise
1 tsp (5 mL) pink or green peppercorns
1 tsp (5 mL) coriander seeds

1. Scrub the oranges following directions on page 446. Trim away and discard or reserve the ends for another use. Slice the trimmed fruit crosswise into 3/8-inch (1 cm) slices. Try to keep the slices the same width and thinner rather than thicker. You should get 4, possibly 5 slices from each orange depending on the size. Remove and discard seeds and set orange slices aside.

2. Heat five 1-pint (2-cup/500 mL) jars in boiling water, and scald the lids, lifter, funnel and tongs (see page 18).

3. In a wide-bottomed canning kettle or saucepan, combine vinegar, brown sugar and salt. Bring to a boil over high heat, stirring constantly until the sugar is dissolved and the brine is boil-

ing rapidly. Add allspice, cloves, cardamom, cinnamon, star anise, peppercorns, coriander seeds and 8 orange slices or enough to simmer covered by the brine. Boil the orange slices, turning once or twice with tongs, until the peel is soft but not mushy.

4. Using tongs, fill a hot jar with slices, slightly twisting them so that they fit the jar. Leave a 1/4-inch (5 mm) headspace. Run a thin non-metallic utensil around the inside of the jar to allow air to escape. Pour hot brine over slices, leaving a 1/4-inch (5 mm) headspace. Wipe rim, top with a flat lid and screw on metal ring. Return jar to the hot water bath.

5. Meanwhile, add another layer of orange slices to the boiling brine and repeat step 4.

6. When all the jars have been packed and capped, top up water bath with hot water if necessary, bring to a full rolling boil and process jars for 10 minutes (see page 19). Remove canner lid and wait 5 minutes before removing jars to a towel or rack to cool completely. Check seals, label and store in a cool place for up to 1 year.

Use: I like to use Spiced Pickled Oranges with baked ham. Set a cooked or uncooked ham in a baking dish (keep the baking instructions from the packaging). Using tongs, lift the Spiced Pickled Orange slices out of the jar and place all over the ham, securing with toothpicks. In a saucepan, combine strained brine with 1/4 cup (50 mL) orange juice. Bring to a boil, reduce heat and simmer for 10 minutes or until slightly thickened. Pour over the ham and bake according to the instructions on the packaging.

Exotic/Tropical Fruit

WITH THE GLOBAL MARKET VIRTUALLY ON OUR DOORSTEP, exotic or tropical fruit is not quite as mysterious as when our grandmothers may have cherished and preserved it. In fact, it is becoming more and more common and widely available, so I've placed this category of preserved fruit here as a salute to an age when tropical fruit was a novelty in Europe and the Northern Hemisphere—a rare and treasured extravagance on winter tables.

Technically, "tropical" means the area of earth between the Tropic of Cancer at the northern latitude of 23.4° and the Tropic of Capricorn at the southern latitude of 23.4° (south of the equator). Tropical fruits are those edible fruits that originated in that zone called "the tropics". They were considered to be "exotic" because they were unknown to Europeans until refrigerated shipping made their delivery viable in quantity. These fruits may now be grown in countries outside the tropics, but have one thing in common: they do not tolerate frost and so are only grown in frost-free regions of the world.

There are hundreds of edible tropical/exotic fruits and for most North Americans these fruits arrive by ship or airplane from frost-free southern US states, Mexico, South America or Asia.

Purchasing/Storing

Tropical fruit for sale in northern markets may have been picked when still green. Try to find tropical fruit that is ripe because most will not sweeten as they ripen. Store in a cool place and use as soon as possible.

Good With

- Aromatic herbs such as basil, rosemary, sage and thyme, and curry spices.
- A variety of cheeses including soft and medium-hard varieties.
- Sweet seasonings such as vanilla, ginger, cinnamon and nutmeg.
- All types of fish, seafood and poultry.
- With other fruit or greens in salads.

Mangoes

AN EVERGREEN TREE that is indigenous to the East Indies and Malaysia, mango (*Mangifera indica*) is one of the earliest known tropical fruits. Flavour and sweetness vary according to variety. Mangoes are eaten fresh, blended into drinks and chopped raw and added to salsa with lime juice and hot chile peppers. Mangoes have always been preserved in pickles and chutney, the Miscut pickle from Goa being particularly popular.

Good Preserving Varieties

The following is a list of fibre-free varieties that are excellent for jams and other preserves.

Ataulfo: Sweet, richly flavoured; creamy in texture, making it good for soft jams and sauces.

Kent: Flesh is smooth and creamy in texture and soft when ripe; sweet and rich-tasting for chutney, salsa and relish.

Tommy Atkins: Firmer than the above varieties but juicy and sweet; holds its shape in preserves.

Purchasing/Storing

Colour is not always an indication of ripeness since there are many mango varieties, ranging from green to yellow-orange to red and red-purple. Hold the fruit in your hand and press gently to determine if there is a slight give. Ripen in a paper bag at room temperature, away from sunlight, and check daily. Use immediately once ripened.

Good With

- Green citrus herbs such as rosemary, lemon thyme or sage.
- Sweet seasonings such as cinnamon, ginger, cloves, nutmeg, vanilla, almond.
- Fresh cheeses such as cottage cheese, Neufchâtel, goat cheese.
- Other fruit, such as raspberries, peaches, apricots, nectarines.
- Toasted almonds, pecans and walnuts; raisins; white chocolate.
- Moist, soft-textured fish such as catfish, mackerel, tilapia.

Preparation

Wash the fruit in warm water to which a drop of food-safe detergent has been added. Rinse well and pat dry.

How to Dice a Mango:

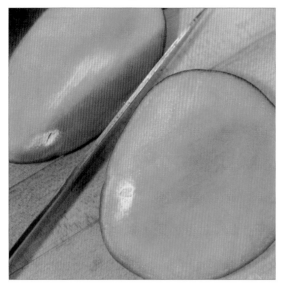

1. Slice off the hips or bulges on either side of the large flat stone or pit in the centre of the mango.

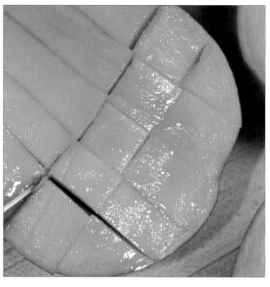

2. Place each half on the cutting board, flesh side facing up. Using a paring knife, cut the flesh into 1/2-inch (1 cm) cubes in a criss-cross pattern. Make the cuts right down to the skin.

3. Turn the diced mango half inside out. The cubes will stand up for easy trimming away from the skin.

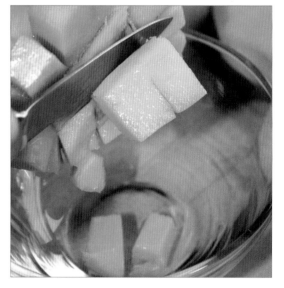

4. Cut the cubes away from the skin and into a bowl or canning pan. Repeat with the second mango half. Remove the skin from the remaining centre section (with stone in it) and carve the flesh away from the stone (the flesh will not come away in perfect cubes).

How to Slice a Mango: Use a vegetable peeler to remove the skin. Hold the mango in one hand and, using a paring knife, cut out slices down to the stone.

pan-seared moroccan cauliflower

The brilliant colour of the chutney makes this dish stand out on the table. It's a great side dish for both vegetarian and meat-based menus.

MAKES ABOUT 2 CUPS (500 mL)

1 head cauliflower, trimmed
3 tbsp (45 mL) olive oil, divided
3/4 cup (175 mL) water
1/2 cup (125 mL) Scarlet Mango Chutney (page 480)

1. Using a paring knife, separate the florets from the core of the cauliflower and cut the larger ones into 4 pieces and the smaller florets in half. Heat 2 tbsp (25 mL) of the oil in a wok over high heat. Add cauliflower pieces in a single layer, flat side down. Cook for 2 to 4 minutes or until well browned on the bottom. Transfer to a bowl. Add remaining oil to the wok and cook remaining cauliflower in the same way.

2. When second batch is browned, return first batch of cauliflower to the wok. Add water, stir, cover and reduce heat to low. Cook for 6 to 8 minutes or until stems are tender. Using a slotted spoon, remove cauliflower to the bowl and toss with chutney.

scarlet mango chutney

I wonder if most people, when they think of mango chutney (if at all), imagine an orange-yellow, soft and piquant preserve that smoothes out the hot jolt of curry dishes. While this chutney is piquant enough to stand up to the spiciest of dishes, it is not the colour one would expect: it is flaming red. I love the beet/mango combination and the way the cider vinegar, candied ginger, turmeric and pickling spice combine to transport one back to Bombay and early twentieth-century England, with its curries and chutneys.

I challenge you to try this scarlet version before going back to the traditional, glowing orange mixture, but if you really must have yellow chutney, simply substitute grated butternut or acorn squash for the beets.

MAKES ABOUT 8+ CUPS (2+ L)

4 to 6 mangoes (about 4 lb/2 kg)
1 cup (250 mL) raisins
1/2 cup (125 mL) freshly squeezed lime juice
1–1/4 cups (300 mL) apple cider vinegar
1/4 cup (50 mL) apple juice
3/4 cup (175 mL) packed brown sugar
1 tbsp (15 mL) ground turmeric

1 tbsp (15 mL) pickling salt
2 tbsp (25 mL) Classic Pickling Spice Blend
   (page 213) or commercial pickling spice,
   wrapped in cheesecloth
4 cups (1 L) shredded beets
2 cups (500 mL) chopped onions
1/2 cup (125 mL) chopped candied ginger

1. Dice mangoes following directions on page 478. You should have about 6 cups (1.5 L). Transfer mango to a large bowl and combine with raisins and lime juice.

2. Heat five 1-pint (500 mL) jars in boiling water, and scald the lids, lifter, funnel and tongs (see page 18).

3. In a Maslin pan or canning kettle, combine vinegar, apple juice and brown sugar. Bring to a boil over high heat, stirring constantly. Add turmeric and salt. Stir well and hang the pickling spice bag so that it is immersed in the boiling mixture. Add mango mixture, beets, onions and ginger. Stir and bring back to a boil. Reduce heat and boil gently, stirring occasionally, for 30 to 45 minutes or until vegetables are soft.

4. Fill hot jars, leaving a 1/4-inch (5 mm) headspace. Run a thin, non-metallic utensil around the inside of the jar to allow air to escape, and add more hot chutney, if necessary, to leave a 1/4-inch (5 mm) headspace. Wipe rims, top with flat lids and screw on metal rings. Return jars to the hot water bath, topping up with hot water if necessary. Bring to a full rolling boil and process jars for 10 minutes (see page 19).

5. Remove canner lid and wait 5 minutes before removing jars to a towel or rack to cool completely. Check seals, label and store in a cool place for up to 1 year.

Use: The beets in this chutney make it more savoury than traditional mango chutney, so it can be used liberally with grilled roasted meats, hearty winter casseroles and stir-fried dishes.

Pineapples

NATIVE TO BRAZIL, THE PINEAPPLE (*ANANAS COMOSUS*) is one of the most delicious and widely available of all the tropical fruits. Older varieties have sharp, spiny leaves; they have now been bred to have smooth leaves, which makes cultivation and use easier.

Good Preserving Varieties

Cayenne: Large, elongated fruit with light yellow scales. **Smooth Cayenne** has a relatively smooth crown of leaves. Flesh is deep yellow, sweet and juicy. Cayenne pineapples are largely grown in Hawaii; peak season is April and May.

Red Spanish: The most widely available variety, scales are a deep orange and leaves are hard and spiky. Flesh is white to light yellow and not as sweet as Cayenne. Grown mostly in Honduras, Costa Rica, Puerto Rico, Mexico and Central America. Peak seasons for Caribbean pineapples are December through February and August through September.

Purchasing/Storing

1 medium pineapple weighs about 4 lb (2 kg) and yields about 4 cups (1 L) 1/2-inch (1 cm) diced pineapple (more if coarsely chopped).

Pineapples should be firm and free of soft spots or bruises. Fresh, ripe pineapples are fragrant, without a trace of fermentation. Look for fruits that are orange or red, and if there are only green pineapples available, choose one that has started to ripen at the base, because it will finish ripening once you get it home.

To ripen a pineapple, turn it on its leaf end and let it stand at room temperature for a few days until the colour has turned to a deep orange or yellow and the aroma is fragrant.

Good With

- Spicy herbs such as basil, bay, thyme, chervil, tarragon, ginger, mustard.
- Sweet seasonings such as cinnamon, licorice, cloves, nutmeg, vanilla.
- Creamy cheeses such as Camembert, Danish blue, gorgonzola.
- Other fruit, such as raspberries, apples, apricots, peaches, nectarines, plums, strawberries, cherries, citrus.
- Toasted pecans, almonds and walnuts; raisins; chocolate.
- Chicken, veal, pork.

Twist or cut off the leaves (or crown) and discard or use them as a centrepiece decoration.

For wedges, cut the pineapple in half down the centre.

Lay one half on the cutting surface, cut side down. Cut in half. Cut one of the halves in half again so that you have 4 wedges. Trim away the inner core and outer scales and set the wedges aside. Repeat with the other half.

For slices, lay the pineapple on its side on a cutting surface. Cut crosswise slices to the desired width as you would a loaf of bread.

Using a paring knife, cut away and discard the outside scales and the inside core.

Use slices whole or chop into 1- or 1/2-inch (2.5 or 1 cm) dice as directed by the recipe. One pineapple will yield about eight 1/2-inch (1 cm) slices and 4 cups (1 L) 1/2-inch (1 cm) dice.

pineapple mustard

Every time I make this delicious condiment, it reaffirms my love affair with homemade preserves. There is nothing like this in a store. The flavour is rich and piquantly sweet-sour. Use it as you would any mustard—on its own as a glaze, as a seasoning in sauces and in small quantities on ham, chops and other grilled meats and vegetables. In my opinion, it is not hot, but you can use more or fewer cayenne peppers to suit your taste.

MAKES 6 CUPS (1.5L)

2-1/2 cups (625 mL) white wine vinegar
2 cups (500 mL) granulated sugar
1 cup (250 mL) lightly packed brown sugar
1 pineapple, cut into 1/2-inch (1 cm) dice (about
   4 cups/1 L)
1 cup (250 mL) golden raisins
1 onion, chopped
1/2 cup (125 mL) chopped dates
grated rind and juice of 2 lemons

1 tbsp (15 mL) chopped candied ginger
2 dried cayenne peppers, crushed, or to taste
1 tbsp (15 mL) mustard seeds
1 tbsp (15 mL) mustard powder
1 tbsp (15 mL) ground turmeric
1 tsp (5 mL) salt
1 tsp (5 mL) ground cinnamon
1/4 tsp (2 mL) ground nutmeg
1/4 tsp (2 mL) ground cloves

1. Heat six 1-cup (250 mL) jars in boiling water, and scald the lids, lifter, funnel and tongs (see page 18).

2. In a Maslin pan or canning kettle, combine vinegar and sugars. Bring to a boil over high heat, stirring constantly. Add pineapple (and any accumulated juice), raisins, onion, dates, lemon rind, lemon juice, ginger, cayenne peppers, mustard seeds, mustard powder, turmeric, salt, cinnamon, nutmeg and cloves. Reduce heat and simmer gently, stirring occasionally, for 60 minutes. Mixture will be reduced in liquid and thickened considerably.

3. Ladle some of the hot chunky mixture into 2 or 3 hot jars, leaving a 1/4-inch (5 mm) headspace. Run a thin non-metallic utensil around the inside of the jar to allow air to escape. Add more hot mustard, if necessary, to leave a 1/4-inch (5 mm) headspace. Wipe rims, top with flat lids and screw on metal rings. Return jars to the hot water bath.

4. Using a food processor or blender, purée the remaining mixture until it is smooth. Ladle into remaining jars, leaving a 1/4-inch (5 mm) headspace. Run a thin non-metallic utensil around the inside of the jar to allow air to escape. Add more hot mustard, if necessary, to leave a 1/4-inch (5 mm) headspace. Wipe rims, top with flat lids and screw on metal rings. Return jars to the hot water bath topping up with hot water if necessary. Bring to a full rolling boil and process jars for 10 minutes (see page 19).

5. Remove canner lid and wait 5 minutes before removing jars to a towel or rack to cool completely. Check seals, label and store in a cool place for up to 1 year.

Pomegranates

THE FRUIT ONCE CALLED "APPLE OF CARTHAGE" by Pliny has been naturalized all over the Mediterranean. With many biblical references and documented use by Moses, Solomon, the prophet Mohammed and other ancients, the pomegranate (*Punica granatum*) has a long and symbolic history. In fact, it is thought that Granada in Spain was named after the fruit. Sirop de Grenadine, or grenade, as it is know in France, is made from the juice of pomegranates, as is pomegranate molasses.

Purchasing/Storing

Select firm and heavy fruits that appear to have ripened fully yellow or deep red. Unpeeled pomegranates will keep in a cool place or the refrigerator for a few weeks.

Good With

- Sweet or savoury dishes (the juicy flesh surrounding the individual seeds has a sweet, slightly astringent flavour that complements both).
- Green citrus herbs such as rosemary, lemon thyme or sage.
- Black olives, red onion, greens, nuts, citrus fruits.
- Fresh cheeses such as cottage cheese, Neufchâtel, goat cheese.
- Other fruit, such as mangoes, raspberries, peaches, apricots, nectarines.
- Moist, soft-textured fish such as catfish, mackerel, tilapia.

Preparation

The rind and the walls, or septa, that divide the inside sections of pomegranate are very bitter, so the glistening ruby red seeds must be separated from both before using. Using a paring knife, cut off the crown. Score the fruit in quarters and pull apart the 4 sections. Peel away the inner walls covering the seeds and turn the quarters inside out so the seeds will pop out.

The photo above, taken in an open stall in Istanbul, shows the grains, or seeds of the "grain apple," or pomegranate. These seeds, encased in sacs of juice, are called arils and are held in place inside the outer skin by thin bitter membranes.

pomegranate pepper jelly

The ruby red colour of the pomegranate juice makes this a vibrant jelly for a holiday table. I also use it in the summer with grilled vegetables and chicken or fish. If you have a juice machine, you can juice fresh pomegranate by separating the seeds following the directions on page 486. I usually purchase the juice for this popular jelly because it is always readily available.

MAKES ABOUT 5 CUPS (1.25 L)

1-1/2 cups (375 mL) pomegranate juice
1 cup (250 mL) red wine vinegar
2 to 4 jalapeño peppers, halved lengthwise and seeded
5 cups (1.25 L) granulated sugar
1 pouch (3 oz/85 mL) liquid pectin
5 tiny red hot peppers, optional

1. In a saucepan, combine pomegranate juice, vinegar and jalapeno peppers. Bring to a boil over high heat. Cover, reduce heat and simmer for 10 minutes. Strain into a 4-cup (1 L) bowl, discarding peppers. Liquid should measure 2 cups (500 mL).

2. Heat five 1-cup (250 mL) jars in boiling water, and scald the lids, lifter, funnel and tongs (see page 18).

3. In a Maslin pan or Dutch oven, bring the strained pomegranate liquid to a boil over high heat. Stir in the sugar, one cup at a time, stirring until the sugar dissolves before adding the next cup. Bring to a rolling boil, stirring often. Add pectin, stir and return to a full rolling boil. Boil for 1 minute, stirring constantly.

4. Remove pan from heat and skim off foam. Fill hot jars, leaving a 1/4-inch (5 mm) headspace. If desired, add a whole tiny red pepper to each jar. Wipe rims, top with flat lids and screw on metal rings. Return jars to the hot water bath, topping up with hot water if necessary. Bring to a full rolling boil and process jars for 5 minutes (see page 19).

5. Transfer to a cooling rack to cool completely. Check seals, label and store in a cool place for up to 1 year.

Use: This jelly is delicious served over brie baked in the oven to soften it. Walnuts and almonds make a very nice accompaniment in salads, sauces or dressings, or with roasts.

pomegranate molasses

Here is another example of a homemade version being so much better than store-bought—if you can even find pomegranate molasses anywhere other than in Middle Eastern markets or online. I fell in love with the flavour on a recent visit to Istanbul. Of course, I brought a bottle back and used it as a glaze and a flavouring in drinks and lamb stew and even in salad dressing. It wasn't long before I set to work on my own recipe. I usually make half of the recipe below because I don't process the jars. You have the option of making half the recipe and storing it in the refrigerator or water-bath processing the larger amount so that you can store it in a cupboard.

MAKES ABOUT 4 CUPS (1 L)

8 cups (2 L) pomegranate juice
2 cups (500 mL) granulated sugar
grated rind and juice of 2 lemons

1. In a Maslin pan or Dutch oven, combine pomegranate juice, sugar, lemon rind and lemon juice. Bring to a boil over high heat, stirring constantly until sugar is dissolved. Reduce heat and simmer gently, stirring only occasionally, for 45 to 60 minutes. Watch the pan carefully as the time approaches the 3/4-hour mark: the liquid should be reduced by about half and the syrup should be thick but not sticky. A thermometer will register between 100 and 104°F (37.7 and 40°C).

2. Meanwhile, heat five 1-cup (250 mL) jars in boiling water, and scald the lids, lifter, funnel and tongs (see page 18).

3. Remove pan from heat and skim off foam. Fill hot jars, leaving a 1/4-inch (5 mm) headspace. Wipe rims, top with flat lids and screw on metal rings. Return jars to the hot water bath, topping up with hot water if necessary. Bring to a full rolling boil and process jars for 5 minutes (see page 19).

4. Remove canner lid and wait 5 minutes before removing jars to a towel or rack to cool completely. Check seals, label and store in a cool place for up to 1 year.

Use: As a sweetener for sauces, dressing; in drinks instead of grenadine; for a finishing glaze for roasted vegetables or meats.

grilled pomegranate pepper pork

The fruity, sweet-tart flavour of the Pomegranate Pepper Jelly cuts through the richness of the roasted pork in this dish. In addition, the colour gives an appetizing glow to the pork slices. For a casual lunch or dinner, I serve the meat sliced on pita rounds with greens and shredded or chopped fresh vegetables from the garden. Glazed pork also makes an elegant main dish for more formal dinners.

Rimmed baking sheet, lightly oiled
Preheat oven broiler or barbecue
MAKES 4 TO 6 SERVINGS

1 lb (500 g) boneless pork tenderloin or lamb loin	4 Greek-style pitas
1 tbsp (15 mL) olive oil	2 cups (500 mL) fresh baby spinach leaves
1/2 cup (125 mL) Pomegranate Pepper Jelly (page 488), divided	4 tomatoes, cut into eight wedges
1 tbsp (15 mL) freshly squeezed lemon juice	fresh mint leaves, optional

1. Arrange pork on prepared baking sheet. In a bowl, combine 1/4 cup (50 mL) of the Pomegranate Pepper Jelly with lemon juice. Pour over pork and let stand at room temperature for 15 minutes.

2. Cook pork on top rack under broiler or on the barbecue for 4 minutes each side or until done to your liking. Slice into 16 slices and toss with remaining Pomegranate Pepper Jelly.

3. On each pita, arrange 1/2 cup (125 mL) spinach leaves. Top with tomato wedges and 3 or 4 slices of pork. Sprinkle mint leaves over top, if using. Serve open-faced and let guests roll as a wrap or eat as a salad.

Dried Fruits

IT'S INTERESTING THAT A FRUIT that has already been preserved by drying should be used in preserves, but this too is a time-honoured winter tradition. Perhaps initiated by industrious cooks looking for interesting recipes at a time of year when there weren't many fresh ingredients, many recipes for jam, spreads, liqueur and even wine call for the use of dried fruits.

The drying process concentrates the flavour and sugar of the fruit, making it taste stronger and allowing it to be stored for up to a year without refrigeration. Dehydration (the removal of water) destroys most of the vitamin C, but most other nutrients—vitamins A and most Bs, as well as the minerals calcium, iron, magnesium, phosphorus, potassium, sodium, copper and manganese—are retained. Commercially dried fruit may contain added sulphur dioxide, which keeps the bright colour of the fresh fruit. Non-sulphured dried fruit is available; it tends to be darker in colour, but is favoured by individuals who may be sensitive to additives or who suffer from asthma.

Raisins, dates, figs, prunes and apricots are the long-time favourite dried fruits used in preserving, but raspberries, blackberries, cherries, blueberries, mangoes and bananas, in addition to apples, peaches and tomatoes, are popular now as well.

Purchasing/Storing

Some commercially dried fruits are dipped in sulfites, sulfates or ascorbic acid to keep them from darkening during the drying process. If you are sensitive to these chemicals, choose naturally dehydrated fruit.

When fruit is dried or dehydrated, the removal of water preserves the fruit so that it can be stored at room temperature for long periods of time. Keep dried foods in moisture-proof containers in a cool, dark place.

Good With

- Custards and baked fruit dishes such as compotes.
- Baked goods like fruitcakes, fruit puddings, buns and cookies.
- Sweet seasonings such as vanilla, ginger, cinnamon and nutmeg.
- Rich meats such as goose, duck, lamb and pork.

Denair, CA 95316
www.bellaviva.com

Why we lov
These dried plouts are
combination of sweet and
bursting with flavor. They
Grenade because each bite
explode with flavor. Add ch
salads and baked goods for ar

Dried Apricots

Apricot purée and preserves are popular with pastry chefs because they are so versatile: as a glaze, a filling, an icing and as a sweet-tart flavouring. In the winter, when fresh apricots are not available, I use the dried fruit in both sweet and savoury recipes.

To Soak Dried Apricots: In a Maslin pan or canning kettle, cover dried apricots with warm water. Let stand at room temperature for 1 hour or overnight. Bring the apricots and their steeping water to a boil over medium-high heat. Boil, stirring occasionally, for 1 hour or until the apricots are plump and about half of the water has been absorbed.

spiced apricot and orange butter

This "butter" is a modern version of an old-fashioned "fruit cheese" recipe that was boiled down until it resembled soft cheese. I like the lighter, more versatile butter result from my version; I use fruit pectin crystals to make it set without the hours of boiling and stirring. Silky smooth and tart-sweet, it may be used straight out of the jar as a filling, an icing or flavouring, or thinned with orange juice and used as a glaze. It serves as a tasty and nutritious spread for breakfast scones. If I have a jar of this in the pantry, I find I use it often in savoury dishes, as well as in baking.

MAKES 7 CUPS (1.75 L)

1 lb (500 g) dried apricots
  (3-1/2 cups/875 mL)
4 cups (1 L) water
grated rind and juice of 2 oranges
1 tbsp (15 mL) freshly squeezed lemon juice
1/2 tsp (2 mL) ground cinnamon
1/4 tsp (1 mL) ground allspice
1 pkg (2 oz/57 g) fruit pectin crystals
4 cups (1 L) granulated sugar

1. Soak apricots following the directions on page 495.

2. Heat seven 1-cup (250 mL) jars in boiling water, and scald the lids, lifter, funnel and tongs (see page 18).

3. In a food processor, working in batches, purée the apricots with their cooking liquids.

4. Measure the apricot purée and round out to the full cup, reserving leftover purée for another use. You should have 4 cups (1 L) apricot purée; if not, use 1 cup (250 mL) sugar for every 1 cup (250 mL) purée. Return the purée to the Maslin pan. Add orange rind, orange juice, cinnamon, allspice and pectin. Bring to a boil, stirring constantly. The mixture will be very thick and must be stirred constantly to keep it from scorching. Stir in the sugar, 1 cup (250 mL) at a time, stirring to dissolve before adding the next cup. Bring to a boil or an intense bubble, stirring constantly and using a long-handled spoon so as not to burn yourself because the thick mixture spits.

5. Fill hot jars, leaving a 1/4-inch (5 mm) headspace. Run a thin non-metallic utensil around the inside of the jar to allow air to escape. Add more hot butter, if necessary, to leave a 1/4-inch (5 mm) headspace. Wipe rims, top with flat lids and screw on metal rings. Return jars to the hot water bath, topping up with hot water if necessary. Bring to a full rolling boil and process jars for 10 minutes (see page 19).

6. Remove canner lid and wait 5 minutes before removing jars to a towel or rack to cool completely. Check seals, label and store in a cool place for up to 1 year.

Photo by L. Dearie-Bruce

Dried and Fresh Figs

With some 700 varieties, figs (*Ficus carica*) are one of the earliest fruits cultivated. The medical use of figs was already being noted as early as 2900 BC in Sumeria. Every inhabitant of Athens was a *philosykos*, which literally translated means "a friend of the fig." Thought to be native to western Asia, figs spread to all the countries around the Mediterranean and quickly became a staple there. The Spaniards brought figs to the Americas in the early 16th century, and Mission Figs travelled to California with missionary fathers.

Although considered a fruit, the fig is actually a receptacle that encloses many tiny flowers that grow and mature inside the fruit.

Fresh and dried figs for sale in an open stall in Turkey. The fresh variety is likely **Kalamata Black** or **Large Greek Black**, which splits when ripe and is sweet with dark red pulp.

Clockwise from foreground are **Adriatic**: widely available, its sugar content makes it a good preserving fig; **Calimyrna**: actually a Smyrna fig that was imported by a San Joaquin Valley grower around the turn of the last century and simply renamed in honour of its new home; **Mission**: matures to a deep purple-black and dries to a rich black.

orange fig spread

Orange and rosemary combine in this honeyed and chunky spread to give it both a nip and an aromatic spike, which is useful for sweet and savoury dishes. It may seem tedious to chop the walnuts twice, but it is the combination of fine and coarse nuts that keeps the texture of this spread interesting. Make extra for gifts at holiday time.

MAKES 5 CUPS (1.25 L)

2 cups (500 mL) finely chopped walnuts
2 cups (500 mL) coarsely chopped walnuts
2 cups (500 mL) chopped dried or fresh figs
2 cups (500 mL) liquid honey
1/2 cup (125 mL) freshly squeezed orange juice

2 tbsp (25 mL) grated orange rind
2 tsp (10 mL) crushed dried rosemary
1/2 tsp (2 mL) coarse sea salt

1. Heat five 1-cup (250 mL) jars in boiling water, and scald the lids, lifter, funnel and tongs (see page 18).

2. In a bowl, combine walnuts, figs, honey, orange juice, orange rind, rosemary and sea salt. Mix well.

3. Fill hot jars, leaving a 1/4-inch (5 mm) headspace. Run a thin non-metallic utensil around the inside of the jars to allow air to escape, and add more spread, if necessary, to leave a 1/4-inch (5 mm) headspace. Wipe rims, top with flat lids and screw on metal rings. Return jars to the hot water bath, topping up with hot water if necessary. Bring to a full rolling boil and process jars for 10 minutes (see page 19).

4. Remove canner lid and wait 5 minutes before removing jars to a towel or rack to cool completely. Check seals, label and store in a cool place for up to 1 year.

Use: Spoon over brie or other soft cheese and warm gently in the oven or leave out at room temperature and serve with crackers or baguette slices. Serve with an assortment of cheeses and fruit at the end of a meal. Toss with soy sauce or orange juice and use as a sauce for stir-fry dishes (see Honeyed Fig Chicken Stir-Fry, next page). Serve as a spread for cinnamon toast, waffles or French toast.

honeyed fig chicken stir-fry

The fig spread keeps the chicken from drying out in this fast and tasty dish. Served over rice and with braised winter greens, a green salad or fresh fruit (depending on the season), this is a recipe that I have used many times for entertaining. I have also grilled and roasted chicken, meat, fish and vegetables using the fig mixture combined in step 1 of this recipe.

MAKES 4 SERVINGS

1/4 cup (50 mL) Orange Fig Spread (page 500)
2 tbsp (25 mL) soy sauce
2 tbsp (25 mL) chicken broth or orange juice
1 tbsp (15 mL) olive oil
2 tsp (10 mL) toasted sesame oil
2 cloves garlic, thinly sliced
1 piece (1 inch/2.5 cm) fresh gingerroot,
   thinly sliced
2 chicken breast filets, sliced in half and cut
   into strips

1. In a bowl, combine fig spread, soy sauce and chicken broth. Set aside.

2. In a wok, heat olive oil and sesame oil over high heat. Add garlic and ginger and cook for 30 seconds. Using tongs, remove and reserve. Add chicken slices and cook, stirring constantly, for 2 minutes or until chicken is browned on all sides.

3. Add reserved garlic and ginger and Orange Fig Spread mixture and heat through.

mincemeat

Once made with minced or ground beef (sometimes mutton), suet and dried fruit—with sugar, spices and brandy or sherry added for flavour—mincemeat is a traditional holiday sweet tart or pie filling dating from as early as 15th-century England. At first, vinegar and wine, and later alcohol and sugar, served to preserve the meat. Modern adaptations omit both the meat and the suet, but I have retained the latter to give a rich, moist texture and flavour to my version.

This recipe uses the Winter Pear Chutney (page 506), but you can substitute the same amount of any of the following preserves from this book: Crabapple Chutney (page 309), Country-Style Chutney (page 319), Gingered Autumn Conserve (page 332), Cinnamon-Scented Parsnip Pear Jam (page 407), Blueberry Conserve (page 114), Gooseberry and Almond Relish (page 152), Brandied Melon Jam (page 160) or Peach and Onion Chutney (page 178).

It's easy to make this mincemeat because every ingredient is simply measured and added to a large glass or stainless steel mixing bowl and macerated or allowed to sit and meld before packing into sterilized jars. If stored in the refrigerator, the mixture will keep for a couple of months.

MAKES 8 CUPS (2 L)

2 cups (500 mL) coarsely chopped apples
2 cups (500 mL) Winter Pear Chutney
  (page 506 or see substitutions above)
1 cup (250 mL) dark raisins
1/2 cup (125 mL) chopped dried apricots
1/2 cup (125 mL) chopped dried figs or dates
1/2 cup (125 mL) dried cranberries or cherries
1/4 cup (50 mL) dried currants
1/4 cup (50 mL) whole mixed chopped
  candied peel

4 oz (125 g) chopped or shredded suet
1 cup (250 mL) lightly packed brown sugar
grated rind and juice of 1 orange
grated rind and juice of 1 lemon
2 tsp (10 mL) ground allspice
1/2 tsp (2 mL) ground cinnamon
1/4 tsp (1 mL) ground nutmeg
1/4 cup (50 mL) sherry or brandy

1. In a large mixing bowl or stainless steel pot, combine apples, pear chutney, raisins, apricots, figs, cranberries, currants, candied peel, suet, brown sugar, rind and juice of orange and lemon, allspice, cinnamon and nutmeg. Stir well and drizzle sherry over top. Let the mixture macerate in a cool place, stirring every other day, for 1 week. If it gets too dry, add more sherry to keep it moist.

2. After the week, sterilize four 1-pint (2-cup/500 mL) jars (page 18). Pack the mincemeat and juices into the hot jars, leaving a 1/4-inch (5 mm) headspace. Wipe rims, top with flat lids and screw on metal rings. Cool the jars, label and store in the refrigerator for 2 to 3 months.

Winter Pears

SOME VARIETIES OF PEARS need at least 2 months in cold storage in order to ripen properly when brought out of the cold; we call those varieties winter pears. Most are late-fall-harvesting pears that are immediately put into cold storage. Winter pears may require some ripening at home after being held in cold storage: place them in a paper bag and store in a dry area at room temperature for 2 to 3 days. Do not store near apples, which emit a natural gas that speeds up their ripening.

Good Preserving Varieties

Anjou: A large, plump, egg-shaped variety with abundant juice and flavour. Sweet and juicy; best for jams and preserves. Green and Red Anjou pears do not change colour as they ripen; both are grown in Oregon and Washington.

Anjou

Bosc: Long and lean, with an elongated neck topped by a long, curved stem. Ripe Bosc pears are a cinnamon colour with a russet blush. Slightly firm, dense and spicy-tasting flesh make Bosc pears a good canning variety.

Bosc

Comice: Some green with a red blush; plump and round with a very short, protruding neck. Considered the sweetest and juiciest pear; sweet, buttery and abundantly juicy flesh makes it best for chutneys and sauces.

Comice

winter pear chutney

One of the nice things about this chutney is the cheerful colour in the jars. This recipe is easy and makes enough to give away at holiday time. Sometimes I use the chutney in place of my traditional cranberry sauce at Christmas, and it is good with many other winter sweet and savoury dishes during the long winter months.

MAKES 8 CUPS (2 L)

3 cups (750 mL) chopped winter pears
  (Anjou, Bosc or Comice)
2 cups (500 mL) chopped pineapple
grated rind and juice of 1 lemon
1 tbsp (15 mL) Five-Spice Blend (page 26 or
  store-bought), ground

6 cups (1.5 L) granulated sugar
1 pkg (2 oz/57 g) fruit pectin crystals
1-1/2 cups (375 mL) slivered almonds
1 cup (250 mL) dried cherries or cranberries
1 tsp (5 mL) pure almond extract

1. Heat four 1-pint (2-cup/500 mL) jars in boiling water, and scald the lids, lifter, funnel and tongs (see page 18).

2. In a Maslin pan or canning kettle, combine pears, pineapple, lemon rind and juice and spice blend. Bring to a light boil over medium-high heat, stirring frequently. Add sugar, one cup (250 mL) at a time, stirring to dissolve before adding the next cup. Add fruit pectin and bring to a boil, stirring constantly. Hold at a full rolling boil for 4 minutes.

3. Remove from heat and skim off any foam. Stir in almonds, cranberries and almond extract. Fill hot jars, leaving a 1/4-inch (5 mm) headspace. Run a thin non-metallic utensil around the inside of the jar to allow air to escape. Add more hot chutney, if necessary, to leave a 1/4-inch (5 mm) headspace. Wipe rims, top with flat lids and screw on metal rings. Return jars to the hot water bath, topping up with hot water if necessary. Bring to a full rolling boil and process jars for 10 minutes (see page 19).

4. Remove canner lid and wait 5 minutes before removing jars to a towel or rack to cool completely. Check seals, label and store in a cool place for up to 1 year.

squash stuffed with rice and winter pear chutney

Roasting the squash brings out the sweet and nutty flavour and makes it easy to remove the seeds. This easy recipe makes a filling vegetarian main dish or a very impressive side dish. If you have cooked rice, couscous or barley, the preparation is even easier. Sometimes I add toasted almonds or fresh herbs as a garnish, but it's not necessary.

Rimmed baking sheet, lightly oiled
Preheat oven to 350°F (180°C)
MAKES 4 SERVINGS

2 acorn or dumpling squash, cut in half crosswise
4 tbsp (50 mL) melted butter
sea salt and pepper

2 cups (500 mL) Winter Pear Chutney (page 506)
1/2 cup (125 mL) cooked wild rice

1. Arrange squash halves, cut side up, on a rimmed baking sheet. Brush with butter and grind salt and pepper over each half. Cover with foil and bake in preheated oven until moist and tender, about 45 minutes.

2. Meanwhile, in a bowl, combine pear chutney and wild rice; set aside. When the squash is cooked, remove from the oven, scoop out and discard the seeds. Mound the chutney mixture into the squash halves, dividing it evenly among the 4 halves. Cover with foil. Return to the oven and bake until stuffing is heated through, about 15 minutes.

Mushrooms

MUSHROOMS ARE CALLED EUMYCOTA FUNGI, and they differ from both plants and animals. Fungi create spores, either in pores or in the gills on their caps, in order to reproduce. Wild mushrooms are gathered in late spring through fall, but a wide range of edible mushrooms are available in supermarkets and specialty food stores throughout the year because many varieties are now farmed. Mushrooms are included in the winter chapter because fresh vegetables are so abundant at other times of the year that they tend to overpower these earthy and delicious fruiting bodies, but feel free to use these recipes all year round.

Essential: Eating raw mushrooms (even farmed or edible wild varieties) may make you ill. Always cook mushrooms.

Good Preserving Varieties

Cremini, aka. brown: Rich and earthy in flavour; firm and excellent for spreads and preserves. Use them in the Mushroom Tapenade, page 512.

Cremini

Shiitake: Important for helping to prevent cancer, which makes them good for all kinds of preserves and other recipes; look for firm, puffy caps that have not caved in, which is a sign of deterioration.

Pink Oyster: Their beautiful pink colour makes them interesting in preserves.

Shiitake

Pink Oyster

King Trumpet: Firm and dense with a thick stem; buttery sweet; excellent in spreads and tapenade.

Portobello: Firm and dense; earthy and fairly rich in taste; their meaty texture helps them hold their shape in preserves.

King Trumpet

Purchasing/Storing

Select firm, dry mushrooms with no signs of softness or bruising. Best to use immediately, but keep dry and store in a paper container in the refrigerator for no longer than a day before preserving.

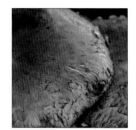

Portobello

Good With

- Spicy herbs such as rosemary, basil, bay, thyme, chervil, tarragon.
- Vegetables such as onions, garlic, tomatoes.
- Fruit such as apples, pears.
- Toasted almonds, pecans, walnuts.
- Chicken, beef, fish.

Preparation

Clean mushrooms by trimming the stems and rubbing the top side of the caps gently with a moistened paper towel.

mushroom risotto

I have served this delicious and easy "risotto" to family and guests several times, and not one person has detected that it wasn't prepared using the laborious, slow-cook-with-broth method. Be sure to cook the rice in chicken broth because that, along with the Mushroom Tapenade, is what gives the rice the rich and complex flavour of a traditional risotto. Grate Parmesan cheese over top or stir in 1 tbsp (15 mL) sour cream if you like. It's also delicious just as it comes out of the pot.

MAKES 4 SERVINGS

2 cups (500 mL) chicken broth or water
1 cup (250 mL) basmati rice
1 tbsp (15 mL) butter
1/2 cup (125 mL) Mushroom Tapenade
(see page 512)

In a saucepan, bring the chicken broth to a boil over high heat. Stir in the rice and bring back to a boil. Cover, reduce heat to low and cook (don't peek!) for 25 minutes. Remove the lid and fluff with a fork. Add butter, stirring until it melts and is evenly distributed. Stir in the Mushroom Tapenade.

mushroom tapenade

I promise you that six jars of this chunky blend of earthy, nutty and naturally salty spread will not last long once you realize all of the ways you can use it. Because of its richly dark and complex flavour, one jar of this is all you need for meat, grain and vegetable dishes—no long cooking methods or other flavour ingredients are required. It makes your life so easy! Each time I find a new use for Mushroom Tapenade, that dish immediately becomes my personal favourite. I started with Mushroom Risotto (page 511) and then mixed it with bread crumbs, patted it on salmon fillets and baked them into a crispy coating. Next came that same coating on chicken breasts, and now I am combining this absolutely brilliant blend with torn bread pieces and stuffing it into the cavities of eggplant and peppers and zucchini. No one will believe that these exceptional dishes consist of two or three ingredients and are ready in just the time it takes to bake them. A small food processor makes quick work of chopping mushrooms and olives.

MAKES 6 CUPS (1.5 L)

3 tbsp (45 mL) olive oil
2 cups (500 mL) chopped onions
4 cloves garlic, finely chopped
2 lb (1 kg) mushrooms, finely chopped
1 cup (250 mL) chicken broth

2 cups (500 mL) chopped pitted kalamata olives (see above)
2 tbsp (25 mL) freshly squeezed lemon juice
3/4 cup (175 mL) chopped sunflower seeds
3 tbsp (45 mL) chopped fresh oregano

1. In a saucepan, heat olive oil over medium heat. Add onion and cook, stirring occasionally, for 8 to 10 minutes or until soft. Add garlic, mushrooms and chicken broth. Bring the mixture to a light boil and simmer for 25 minutes, or until mushrroms are soft and liquid is reduced.

2. Meanwhile, heat six 1-cup (250 mL) jars in boiling water, and scald the lids, lifter, funnel and tongs (see page 18).

3. Add olives, lemon juice, sunflower seeds and oregano to the mushroom mixture. Boil for 2 minutes.

4. Fill hot jars, leaving a 1/4-inch (5 mm) headspace. Run a thin, non-metallic utensil around the inside of the jar to allow air to escape, and add more hot tapenade, if necessary, to leave a 1/4-inch (5 mm) headspace. Wipe rims, top with flat lids and screw on metal rings. Return jars to the hot water bath, topping up with hot water if necessary. Bring to a full rolling boil and process jars for 10 minutes (see page 19).

5. Remove canner lid and wait five minutes before removing jars to a towel rack to cool completely. Check seals, label and store in a cool place for up to 1 year.

Use: You will find dozens of uses for this flavourful spread/sauce. Open the jar, heat and toss with cooked rice (see Mushroom Risotto, page 511) or noodles for a homemade bistro-style dinner. Mix it with soy sauce or orange juice for stir-fried dishes. Use it as an open-face sandwich or canapé spread. Combine equal parts Mushroom Tapenade and bread crumbs and use as a coating for baked fish and chicken.

mushroom rice cakes

Rice and mushrooms come together in this flavourful vegetarian main course or side dish. Serve these cakes as starters, or build the meal around them as a main course. Having the right tools for the job makes life in the kitchen easier. For perfectly round and compact rice cake shapes, I use 3-1/2-inch (9 cm) round stainless steel rings. If you pick up the rice mixture in your hands and form it into a ball before stuffing it into the rings, it compacts enough for you to flip and remove the rings without having the cakes fall apart. Alternatively, you can use two dessert-size spoons and press the mixture into compact ovals (quenelles) before grilling.

If you can get it, Koshihikari rice, or "Koshi" rice—a premium, firm short-grain rice with a sweet taste and nutty aroma—is the best for forming rice cakes. When cooking the rice, don't let it get too dry because you want it to be slightly wet and very sticky in order to hold its shape in the cakes.

MAKES 6 CAKES, EACH 3-1/2 INCHES (9 CM)

2 cups (500 mL) chicken broth or water
1 cup (250 mL) Koshihikari rice or other sushi rice, sticky rice or red rice

1/2 cup (125 mL) Mushroom Tapenade (page 512)
2 tbsp (25 mL) black sesame seeds, optional

1. In a saucepan, bring the chicken broth to a boil over high heat. Stir in the rice and bring back to a boil. Cover, reduce heat to low and cook (don't peek!) for 25 minutes. Remove the lid and fluff with a fork. Re-cover and let stand on the burner for 5 minutes.

2. In a bowl, combine cooked rice with Mushroom Tapenade. Shape into 3-1/2-inch (9 cm) diameter cakes that are 3/4 to 1 inch (2 to 2.5 cm) high. In a lightly oiled skillet or grill, toast the rice cakes on each side for about 2 minutes or until browned. Sprinkle 2 tsp (10 mL) black sesame seeds, if using, on one side after flipping.

Winter Herbs

BY WINTERTIME, THE HERB GARDEN is dormant in the northern regions of North America, and the only fresh herbs we have come from window pots and greenhouse growers. Even so, there is usually a good supply of fresh parsley, cilantro and perhaps rosemary, thyme and sage available at supermarkets. This is the time to savour the preserves that have been so steadily moving from the preserving pan to the pantry shelf. Warming and tonic-dried herbs in teas are enjoyed now, and the hectic pace of preserving foods slows and shifts to gift making. Dried herbs can be used to decorate the outside of preserve jars and packaging. Aromatic and long-simmering herbs (oregano, rosemary, sage, thyme, hyssop and savory) lend their warming spiciness to heartier winter dishes.

Bay

With its sweet, slightly pungent, balsamic aroma and hints of nutmeg and camphor, the beauty of cooking with bay (*Laurus nobilis*) is that it releases its flavour slowly—an essential herb for slow, long cooking techniques. Pickles, chutneys, jams, stocks, soups, stews, sauces, marinades and stuffings benefit from the addition of fresh or dried bay leaves. Whole leaves are used in jars as both a flavour spike and decoration.

Ground bay may be hard to find, and it is difficult to grind your own (I've tried!). It is, however, one of the herbs found in Old Bay Seasoning, a crab and seafood seasoning that originated in Baltimore, Maryland, in 1939, so if you can get it, substitute Old Bay for ground bay in the Salsa Verde (see page 521), or omit the bay altogether.

Bouquet garni is the French name for a bundle of cooking herbs tied together with string and used to flavour slow-cooked dishes. Whole fresh sprigs and leaves are preferred, but dried herbs are a practical option. The traditional bouquet garni combination is thyme, parsley and bay. Often the sprigs of thyme and parsley are wrapped in a large fresh bay leaf, tied and hung to dry and stored in a cool, dark place for using throughout the winter months.

Horehound

Old-fashioned humbugs, those striped pillows of hard candy that taste piney and camphorish, were traditionally made with white horehound (*Marrubium vulgare*, right). With their square stems and pointed leaves growing as they do, it is not hard to see that horehound is a member of the Lamiaciae, or mint, family. The two parts of this plant's common name are thought to be from the following: hoar, meaning "old" or "grey," which is the colour of the leaves, and hound because it was used as a treatment for dog bites in ancient times. It acts as a cough and throat soother and expectorant, making it a valuable herb for the Soothing Winter Cough Syrup (page 522).

Hyssop

Even though it is not a particularly common herb, hyssop (*Hyssopus officinalis*) is still thought of by many as a staunch winter herb for chest and cough ailments. Hyssop is used in making liqueurs, Chartreuse being perhaps the most well known of the hyssop-flavoured ones. If you plan to make your own liqueur, Blackberry Cordial (page 105) or the Pomegranate Molasses (page 489), they would benefit from a few tablespoons of chopped fresh or dried hyssop. Fresh hyssop is particularly suited to strawberries, raspberries, apricots, peaches and cherries, so add a sprig or two to the sugar syrup (and even each jar) when canning these fruits.

Lavender

Tucker's Early lavender (right) is named after Art Tucker, co-author, with Thomas DeBaggio, of *The Big Book of Herbs* (see bibliography, page 526). Lavender (*Lavandula* spp.) is a fairly strong flavouring, not unlike saffron; floral and perfumy, it's definitely an acquired taste. My advice is to try a small amount in recipes before using the full amount called for. A sprig can be added to apple jelly and fruit jams, either in the mixture or in each jar. Fresh or dried lavender (available in specialty food stores) is also used to flavour vinegars and oils.

Lavender and santolina grow in the dry micro-climate of the Olympic Mountains in Washington. In North America, some of the top commercial lavender-growing areas are in California, Oregon, and a narrow strip of land between the mountains in Washington State, as well as the Juan de Fuca Strait centred around Sequim.

Lavender Garlic Paste: For a paste that adds the essence of summertime in the Mediterranean to winter dishes, try this easy flavour spike. In a mortar and pestle, or in a blender, mash together 3 tbsp (45 mL) dried organic lavender buds, 3 fresh garlic cloves, 1 piece of candied ginger and 1 cinnamon stick (2 inches/5 cm). Freeze in ice cube trays. Use as a flavour hit for stir-fried vegetables, mashed or puréed vegetables and rice, pasta or whole grain dishes.

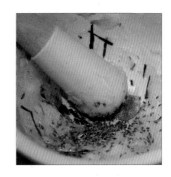

Savory

There are two types of savory: the annual summer savory (*Satureja hortensis*) and the woody perennial winter savory (*Satureja Montana*). Summer savory is milder and sweeter in flavour, while winter savory is hearty and most often used in preserves and dried for use all winter.

Essential: Always use organically grown, untreated herbs and flowers for preserving and cooking.

apricot compote with lavender and citrus

Bright and tangy, with just a hint of flowery lavender, this compote is unusual and beautiful on winter tables. I use it with pork dishes, but it really shines as a fruit sauce for all sorts of desserts. Leave the chunky texture and process in jars after cooking in step 1, or purée the mixture in a food processor for a smooth, thick spreadable sauce. If using fresh lavender buds, remember to increase the amount slightly.

MAKES 3 CUPS (750 ML)

20 dried apricot halves, coarsely chopped
1 cup (250 mL) orange juice
3 navel oranges, sectioned
1 lemon, peeled and chopped
1-1/2 cups (375 mL) granulated sugar

1 piece vanilla bean (4 inches/10 cm), split
2 tbsp (25 mL) dried organic lavender buds
1/2 tsp (2 mL) ground coriander seeds
1/2 tsp (2 mL) ground cinnamon

1. In a large saucepan, combine apricots, orange juice, orange sections, lemon, sugar, vanilla bean, lavender, coriander and cinnamon. Bring to a boil over medium-high heat. Reduce heat and gently simmer for about 60 minutes, adding more orange juice if necessary to keep the mixture from scorching. The fruit should be soft and the mixture thick.

2. Meanwhile, heat three 1-cup (250 mL) jars in boiling water, and scald the lids, lifter, funnel and tongs (see page 18).

3. Skim off and discard any foam. Fill hot jars, leaving a 1/4-inch (5 mm) headspace. Run a thin non-metallic utensil around the inside of the jar to allow air to escape. Add more hot compote, if necessary, to leave a 1/4-inch (5 mm) headspace. Wipe rims, top with flat lids and screw on metal rings. Return jars to the hot water bath, topping up with hot water if necessary. Bring to a full rolling boil and process jars for 10 minutes (see page 19).

4. Remove canner lid and wait 5 minutes before removing jars to a towel or rack to cool completely. Check seals, label and store in a cool place for up to 1 year.

salsa verde

Salsa verde ("green sauce") is an old dish, dating at least as far back as the Middle Ages. It's a sauce for any season, especially summer, when fresh green herbs are abundant, but I tend to make it in the winter. It finishes cooked vegetables, acts as a pasta sauce and lends a good flavour to baked fish and chicken. In the winter, use fresh parsley and spinach, and tip in a cube of Mediterranean Herb Paste (page 440) if you froze some in the fall. The hit of fresh greens is somehow appreciated a bit more when the temperature is at or below freezing and everything outside is white.

MAKES 3 CUPS (750 ML)

4 cloves garlic

1/4 cup (50 mL) almonds

1-1/2 cups (375 mL) lightly packed fresh flat-leaf parsley leaves

2 cups (500 mL) lightly packed fresh spinach leaves

2 tbsp (25 mL) dried savory or hyssop

1 tsp (5 mL) ground bay leaf, optional

2 slices country bread, crusts removed and cubed

1/4 cup (50 mL) sweet pickled onions or cucumber cubes, drained, brine reserved

1/2 cup (125 mL) olive oil

2 tbsp (25 mL) reserved sweet pickle brine

sea salt and freshly ground pepper

1. In a food processor or using a mortar and pestle, chop or crush the garlic and the almonds. Add parsley, spinach, hyssop and bay, if using, to the bowl and coarsely chop or grind. Add bread and onions to the bowl and coarsely chop or grind.

2. With the motor running, drizzle some olive oil into the mixture through the opening in the lid and keep pouring until the sauce reaches a soft consistency. If using a mortar, drizzle some olive oil over and work into the mixture with the pestle. Keep adding oil and working it in until the sauce reaches a soft and blended consistency. Add brine and process for a few seconds just to mix. Season to taste with salt and pepper.

soothing winter cough syrup

We hear about "active ingredients," and we know that many drugs contain plant-based healing constituents, but many of us have lost the knowledge of how to use herbs for simple remedies. This cough syrup relies on the warming qualities from herbs in the Labiatae family (hyssop, oregano, rosemary, sage, savory and thyme), as well as the restorative and tonic benefits from horehound. Use all of these herbs, or a combination of the herbs you have dried, in this simple syrup. Having a bottle of this effective throat soother in the medicine cabinet is comforting.

MAKES 1 CUP (250 ML)

2 cups (500 mL) water
1/4 cup (50 mL) crushed mixed dried winter herbs (see above)
1 cup (250 mL) granulated sugar

1. Bring the water to a boil. In a teapot, combine dried herbs and the water. Cover the pot and block the spout to trap evaporating medicinal oils. Let the tea steep for 30 minutes. Strain off herbs, pressing on them to release as much infused liquid as possible.

2. In a saucepan, bring the infused water to a boil over high heat. Add sugar and bring back to a boil, stirring constantly. Gently boil for about 5 minutes or until the syrup is thickened. Pour into a sterilized or clean jar; cap with the lid. Store in the refrigerator for 4 to 6 months.

acknowledgements

From my first meeting with my editor, Kirsten Hanson, I knew we were going to do great work together. Kirsten knows how to quell the fear—in my case, a white-knuckled fear of food photography—and bring out the best in a writer. Thanks to her and everyone at HarperCollins for enabling this gem of a book.

A great copy editor is like a great chef: gently tweaking, always letting the essence of the food shimmer, and never using a heavy hand. My sincere thanks to Julia Armstrong, a wordsmith whose gentle touch was perfectly in tune with the nature of my work.

This book takes a fresh look at a timeless subject, thanks in part to Laurie Dearie-Bruce, my "target group" representative, sounding board and positive thinker. Thank you, Laurie, for listening to my questions and helping me focus on what a "30-something" wants in a cookbook.

At many points in this odyssey, I discovered that there are some pretty serious preservers out there. Basia Halik, owner of The Harvest Room in Neustadt, Ontario, is one of them. The crisp February day I visited Basia, she was making Blood Orange Marmalade and simmering apples in order to render her own pectin—a two-day process. There, in her century stone house, surrounded by her collection of ironstone and pine, and the wreaths she makes from her garden's bounty, I spent an enchanted day photographing as she took me through the rituals of "putting food by." Thank you, Basia, for sharing a piece of your Eden with the many people who will pick up this book.

The people at Bernardin Canada are, in my view, the preserving experts. After all, they have been in the business of canning for over 100 years and, through their toll-free telephone number, offer genuine and safe advice to home canners. Thanks to them for answering my technical questions and supporting the testing of the recipes in this book by providing equipment.

Lee Valley Tools has carved a niche in the home artisan market with its excellent-quality woodworking, gardening, home craft, and kitchen tools and equipment. Its Maslin pan was used to test almost every single recipe in this book. Not once did I have a problem with scorching, because the pan is designed for preserving: heavy-bottomed and wider at the top for maximum evaporation. This is an essential piece of equipment if you plan to make preserves part of your seasonal kitchen rituals.

KitchenAid really did come to my aid during recipe testing. Its stand mixer, with the Rotor Slicer/ Shredder attachment, makes short work of slicing or shredding fresh cabbage, onions, beets and other vegetables for preserves. I particularly like it because the shredding is continuous—I can shred mountains of cabbage for coleslaw or sauerkraut without stopping to empty a bowl. For chopping functions, the KitchenAid dual-bowl food processor provided, in one machine, a small-quantity chopping bowl for spices and herbs, while the large, 12-cup (3 L) bowl handled the large amounts of fruit or vegetables I was chopping for most recipes. These machines are what make preserving for our generation less of a task and more of a joy.

Sincere thanks go to all my local land stewards: Simon de Boer, for garlic scapes, sunchokes and other organic herbs and vegetables; Andrew Barry, who grows asparagus, as did his father before him, and whose asparagus and strawberries were used in the tests; my friends Pie and Basia for their rhubarb; Filsinger's Organic Foods & Orchards for organic gooseberries, currants and cider vinegar, and for providing the setting for my photographs of several apple varieties, all from their orchards in Ayton, Ontario. Thanks as well to the people at Stokes Seeds Inc. for the day I spent wandering around their trial gardens—the largest in North America—photographing vegetables. Many of the shots of vegetables in this book were taken in that exciting garden, where both new and old varieties make their debut or return to centre stage.

For a very small village, Neustadt, Ontario, where I live and work, has its share of highly creative people. Richard Mund of Richard Mund Pottery has been working at his craft in the village for over 10 years, and his beautiful hand-painted pottery was the perfect vessel for showcasing my French Beans in Tomato Sauce (page 196). Neustadt Springs Brewery, winner of numerous awards, makes mighty fine beer using spring water from deep in the caverns of the 19th-century stone structure. Neustadt Lager went down beautifully on hot summer days after the Maslin pan had been cleaned for the final time.

Of course, my family always figures into my books, and this book is no exception. Thanks to Gary and Shannon McLaughlin, my partners in life.

Friends seem to become more precious to me with every passing year. I am blessed with bonds of mutual affection from all of the strands that are woven into the tapestry of my life: herbies, foodies, book club buddies, publishers and editors, and long-time friends from university days. The list is long—too long for me to mention individuals. But if you've ever received a jar of my preserves, I count you as a cherished friend.

sources/resources

General

http://growingtaste.com/vegetables.shtml
Desirable Vegetable Varieties: A very good site listing vegetable varieties and their quality according to taste. This is good reading, especially for home gardeners, and for home preservers to discuss with local growers.

http://www.seeds.ca/en.php
Seeds of Diversity: Canada's heritage seed program for gardeners, with a database of plant species, seed catalogue inventory, seed availability and historic seed catalogues. Consider supporting this valuable resource, even if you don't garden.

http://www.seedsavers.org/
Seed Savers Exchange: A non-profit, non-governmental, member-supported organization in the United States that saves and shares heirloom seeds.

http://www.sustainabletable.org/issues/buylocal/
Sustainable Table: A well-presented site with information on food choice issues, from additives to food safety to organic certification.

http://www.cog.ca
Canadian Organic Growers: Canada's national information network for organic farmers, gardeners and consumers.

http://www.ota.com
Organic Trade Association: A membership-based business association that promotes awareness and understanding of organic production, and provides a unified voice for the industry.

Preserving Equipment & Supplies

http://www.homecanning.com/can/
The Bernardin website offers solid, dependable home canning information and illustrated step-by-step guides for canning both high- and low-acid foods, as well as recipes. There is an online order service for home preserving products, and FAQs for instant help with preserving questions.

http://www.leevalley.com/
Lee Valley Tools is a catalogue business (with retail outlets in major Canadian cities) that offers high-quality canning equipment, including the Maslin pan I recommend for most of the preserves in this book. Online and free catalogue available.

http://www.kitchenaid.com
We all know what a stand mixer or food processor does, but the KitchenAid website has video clips of how to use the attachments, which helped me understand why I needed them for preserving.

http://www.richters.com
Richters Herb Specialists is a nursery and mail-order business dedicated to growing and selling herb plants, seeds, dried herbs, books and herb-related products. Online and free catalogue available; worldwide shipping of plants and seeds.

http://www.gilbertiesherbs.com
Gilbertie's Herb Gardens is the largest herb plant grower in the United States, supplying more than 400 varieties to nurseries and garden centres.

bibliography

Bernardin Guide to Home Canning. Canada: Bernardin Ltd., 2006.

Burrow, Jackie. *Home Preserves.* London: Treasure Press, 1985.

Carey, Nora. *Perfect Preserves.* New York: Stewart, Tabori & Chang, 1990.

Crocker, Pat. *Oregano.* Neustadt, ON: Riversong Studios Ltd., 2005.

DeBaggio, Thomas, and Arthur O. Tucker. *The Big Book of Herbs.* Loveland, CO: Interweave Press Inc., 2000.

Hazelton, Nika. *The Unabridged Vegetable Cookbook.* New York: M. Evans & Company Inc., 1976.

Johns, Leslie, and Violet Stevenson. *The Complete Book of Fruit.* London: Angus & Robertson Publishers, 1979.

Lupi, Simonetta, and Angelo Sorzio. *The Illustrated Book of Preserves.* Garden City, NY: Doubleday & Company Inc., 1986.

Norman, Jill. *Herbs & Spices.* New York: DK Publishing Inc., 2002.

Plagemann, Catherine. *Fine Preserving: M.F.K. Fisher's Annotated Edition.* Berkeley, CA: Aris Books, 1986.

Reich, Lee. *Uncommon Fruits Worthy of Attention.* Reading, MA: Addison-Wesley Publishing Company Ltd., 1991.

Wilson, C. Anne. *The Book of Marmalade.* New York: St. Martin's/Marek, 1985.

Woodward, Sarah. *Oranges and Lemons.* London: Conran Octopus Ltd., 2001.

index